DILBERT™

WORDS YOU DON'T WANT TO HEAR DURING YOUR ANNUAL PERFORMANCE REVIEW

A DILBERT™ BOOK
BY SCOTT ADAMS

B🌱XTREE

First published 2003 by Andrews McMeel Publishing, an Andrews McMeel Universal company, Kansas City, USA

First published in Great Britain 2003 by Boxtree
an imprint of Pan Macmillan Ltd
Pan Macmillan, 20 New Wharf Road, London N1 9RR
Basingstoke and Oxford
Associated companies throughout the world
www.panmacmillan.com

ISBN 0 7522 2422 0

3 5 7 9 8 6 4

A CIP catalogue record for this book is available from
the British Library.

Printed by The Bath Press Ltd, Bath

WORDS YOU DON'T WANT TO HEAR DURING YOUR ANNUAL PERFORMANCE REVIEW

Other DILBERT Books from BOXTREE

TREASURIES

Fugitive From the Cubicle Police
ISBN: 0-7522-2431-X

Seven Years of Highly Defective People
ISBN: 0-7522-2407-7

What Do You Call a Sociopath In a Cubicle? Answer: A Coworker
ISBN: 0-7522-2417-4

Dilbert Gives You the Business
ISBN: 0-7522-2394-1

Dilbert – A Treasury of Sunday Strips: Version 00
ISBN: 0-7522-7232-2

It's Obvious You Won't Survive by Your Wits Alone
ISBN: 0-7522-0201-4

COLLECTIONS

Excuse Me While I Wag
ISBN: 0-7522-2399-2

When Did Ignorance Become a Point of View?
ISBN: 0-7522-2412-3

Journey to Cubeville
ISBN: 0-7522-2384-4

Build a Better Life by Stealing Office Supplies
ISBN: 0-7522-0716-4

Shave the Wales
ISBN: 0-7522-0849-7

Bring Me the Head of Willy the Mailboy!
ISBN: 0-7522-0136-0

Dogbert's Clues for the Clueless
ISBN: 0-7522-0711-3

Another Day In Cubicle Paradise
ISBN: 0-7522-2486-7

Random Acts of Management
ISBN: 0-7522-7174-1

Don't Step in the Leadership
ISBN: 0-7522-2389-5

I'm Not Anti-Business, I'm Anti-Idiot
ISBN: 0-7522-2379-8

Casual Day Has Gone Too Far
ISBN: 0-7522-1119-6

Still Pumped from Using the Mouse
ISBN: 0-7522-2265-1

Always Postpone Meetings with Time-Wasting Morons
ISBN: 0-7522-0854-3

When Body Language Goes Bad
ISBN: 0-7522-2491-3

BEST OF DILBERT

The Best of Dilbert Volume 1
ISBN: 0-7522-6541-5

Best of Dilbert Volume 2
ISBN: 0-7522-1500-0

For ordering information, call 01625 677237

For the Queen of Imaginary Quilts

INTRODUCTION

If you are an "employee," sooner or later you will be subjected to a horrible humiliation that forensic scientists refer to as your "performance review." You will need a strategy for coping, and I can help.

I recommend working for a timid boss who likes to avoid confrontation. You can test whether your boss fits that description by bringing a huge bag of fertilizer to work and shoving his head into it, then sewing it to his shirt collar and laughing as he goes running around like a man with a bag-o-fertilizer head.

After that, if he says something about how humor helps morale and how you're like a member of the family, then you have a timid boss, and your performance review will be just fine. He'll give you "exceptional" ratings on every category just to lessen the chance you will cry, complain, glare, or sew his head into another bag.

The next best kind of boss is a lazy boss. If he asks you to write your own performance review, you're home free. Try to weave into your evaluation words like *Einsteinian, overlord, magnificent,* and *deeeee-licious.* Even if he crosses out a few of your descriptors, whatever slips through the cracks will still serve you well.

If your boss is neither timid nor lazy, you'll have to do things the hard way. Sacrifice your health and your personal life by working extra hard to earn that highest performance review rating. Bankers will tell you that the 1 percent higher raise you earn for being a star performer will add up over time, thanks to the miracle of compounding. But later, when they're alone, the bankers will laugh heartily at your working 50 percent harder for a 1 percent higher raise. And they'll mock you for not understanding that compounding doesn't apply to people who spend all their extra money on beer to forget their jobs. Bankers are funny.

Or you could ignore your performance review altogether, and wait until Dogbert conquers the planet and makes all non-*Dilbert*-readers our personal domestic servants. To become a member of Dogbert's New Ruling Class (DNRC), and get the free *Dilbert Newsletter* that is published approximately whenever I feel like it, go to www.dilbert.com and follow the subscription instructions. If that doesn't work for some reason, send an e-mail to newsletter@unitedmedia.com.

S. Adams

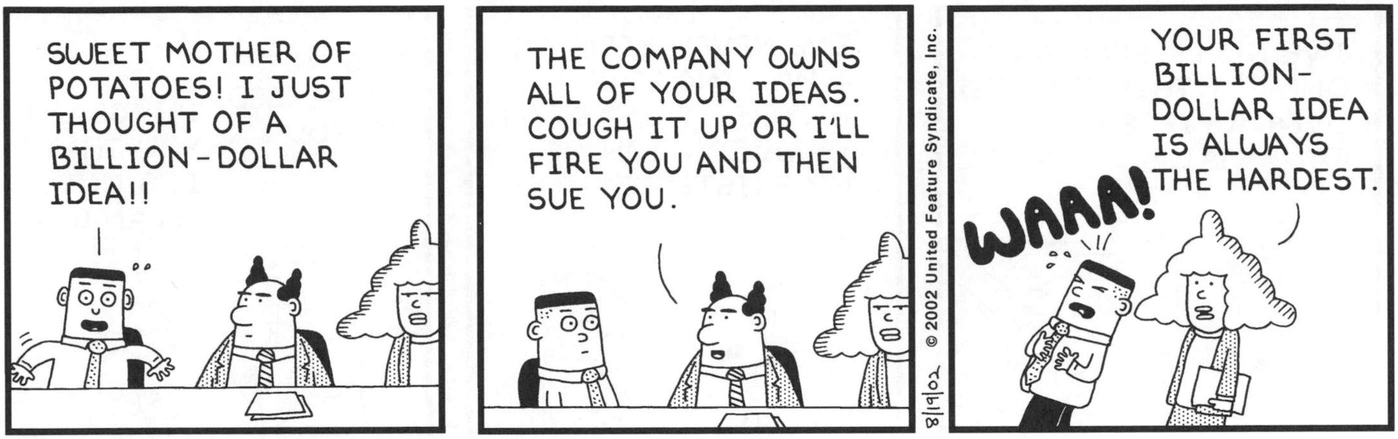
SWEET MOTHER OF POTATOES! I JUST THOUGHT OF A BILLION-DOLLAR IDEA!!
THE COMPANY OWNS ALL OF YOUR IDEAS. COUGH IT UP OR I'LL FIRE YOU AND THEN SUE YOU.
8/19/02 © 2002 United Feature Syndicate, Inc.
YOUR FIRST BILLION-DOLLAR IDEA IS ALWAYS THE HARDEST.
WAAA!

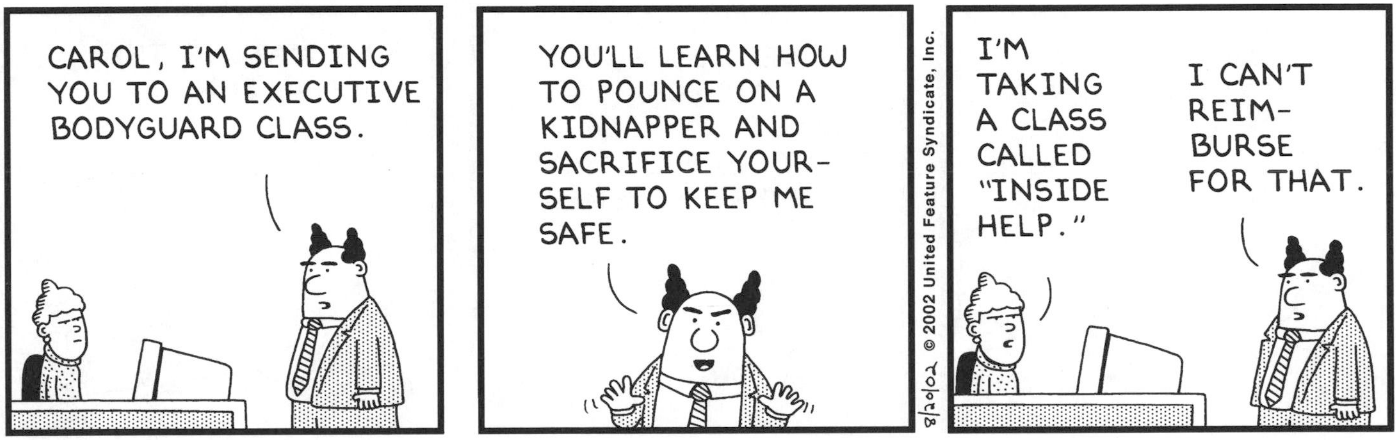
CAROL, I'M SENDING YOU TO AN EXECUTIVE BODYGUARD CLASS.
YOU'LL LEARN HOW TO POUNCE ON A KIDNAPPER AND SACRIFICE YOURSELF TO KEEP ME SAFE.
8/20/02 © 2002 United Feature Syndicate, Inc.
I'M TAKING A CLASS CALLED "INSIDE HELP."
I CAN'T REIMBURSE FOR THAT.

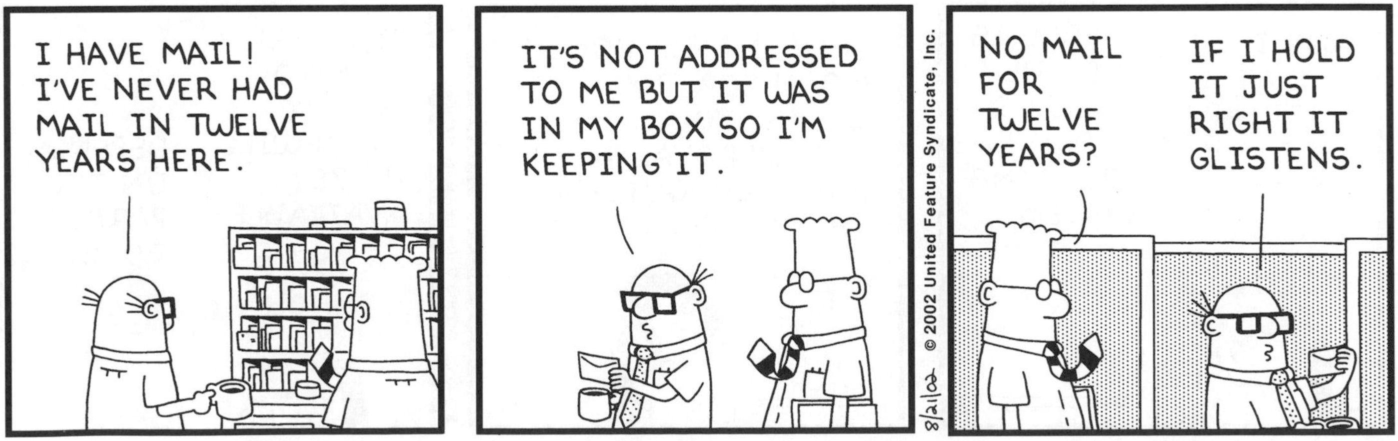
I HAVE MAIL! I'VE NEVER HAD MAIL IN TWELVE YEARS HERE.
IT'S NOT ADDRESSED TO ME BUT IT WAS IN MY BOX SO I'M KEEPING IT.
8/21/02 © 2002 United Feature Syndicate, Inc.
NO MAIL FOR TWELVE YEARS?
IF I HOLD IT JUST RIGHT IT GLISTENS.

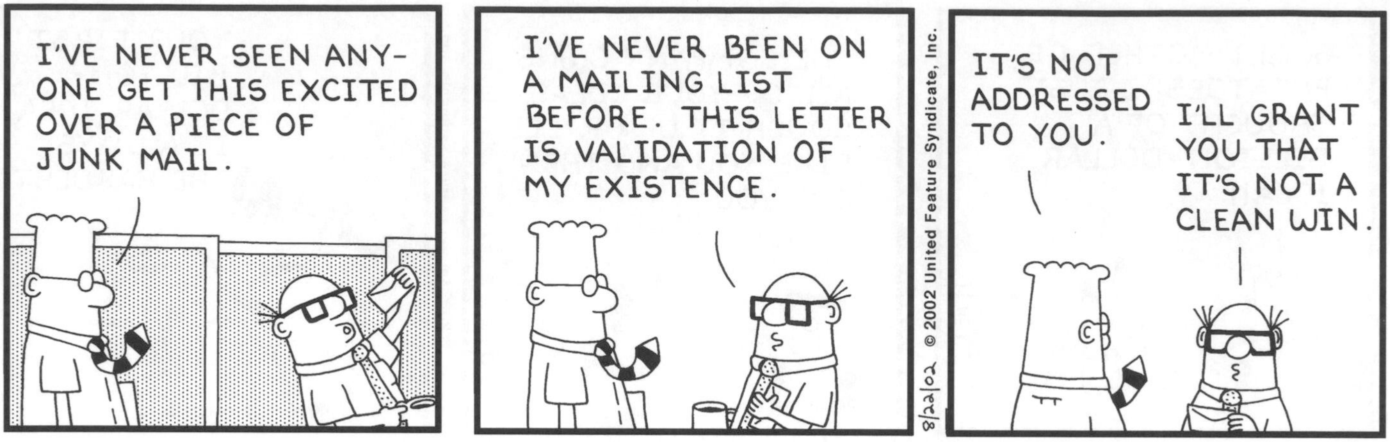
I'VE NEVER SEEN ANYONE GET THIS EXCITED OVER A PIECE OF JUNK MAIL.
I'VE NEVER BEEN ON A MAILING LIST BEFORE. THIS LETTER IS VALIDATION OF MY EXISTENCE.
8/22/02 © 2002 United Feature Syndicate, Inc.
IT'S NOT ADDRESSED TO YOU.
I'LL GRANT YOU THAT IT'S NOT A CLEAN WIN.

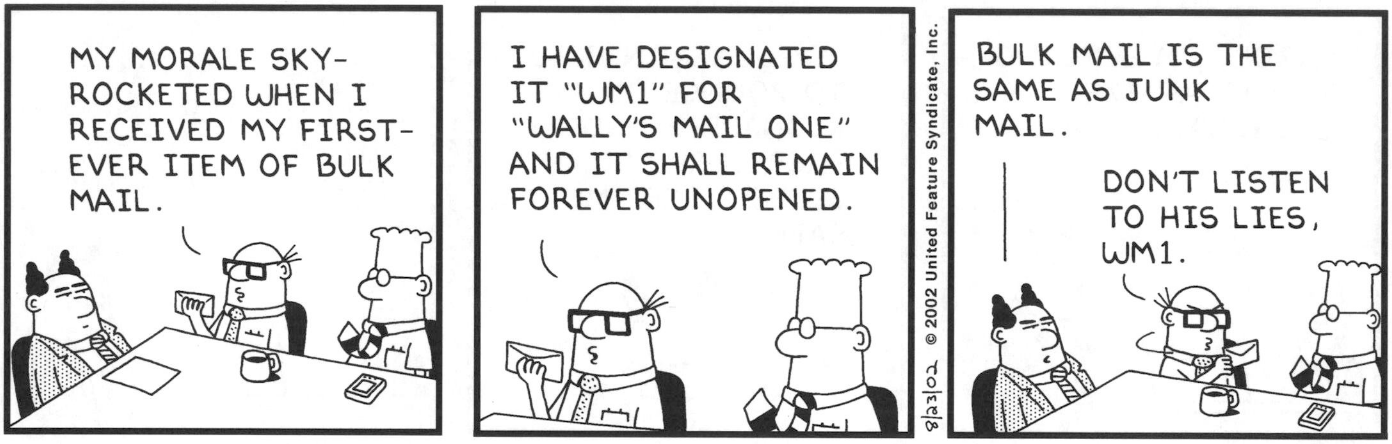
MY MORALE SKYROCKETED WHEN I RECEIVED MY FIRST-EVER ITEM OF BULK MAIL.
I HAVE DESIGNATED IT "WM1" FOR "WALLY'S MAIL ONE" AND IT SHALL REMAIN FOREVER UNOPENED.
8/23/02 © 2002 United Feature Syndicate, Inc.
BULK MAIL IS THE SAME AS JUNK MAIL.
DON'T LISTEN TO HIS LIES, WM1.

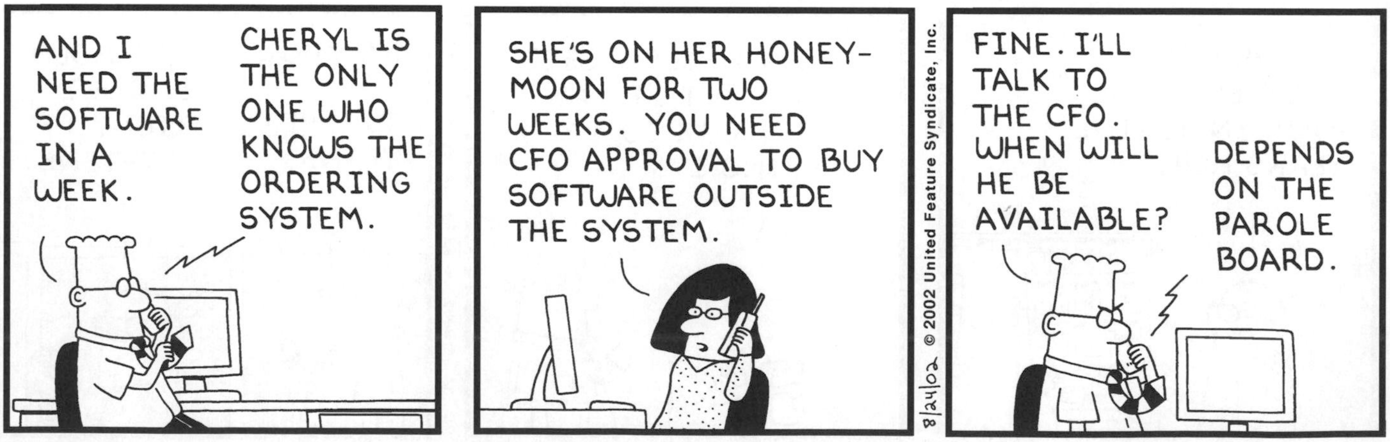
AND I NEED THE SOFTWARE IN A WEEK.
CHERYL IS THE ONLY ONE WHO KNOWS THE ORDERING SYSTEM.
SHE'S ON HER HONEYMOON FOR TWO WEEKS. YOU NEED CFO APPROVAL TO BUY SOFTWARE OUTSIDE THE SYSTEM.
8/24/02 © 2002 United Feature Syndicate, Inc.
FINE. I'LL TALK TO THE CFO. WHEN WILL HE BE AVAILABLE?
DEPENDS ON THE PAROLE BOARD.

MAKE THE BOX BLUER.
A LITTLE MORE... A LITTLE MORE... A LITTLE MORE...
THAT'S IT!!
WHEN YOU GET TIRED OF MICROMANAGING ME...
PUT THIS SAMPLE OF MY BLOOD UNDER A MICROSCOPE SO YOU CAN MANAGE ME ON A CELLULAR LEVEL.
AND HERE'S A BOOK BY ERWIN SCHRÖDINGER IN CASE YOU'D LIKE TO MANAGE ME ON A QUANTUM LEVEL!
DO YOU UNDERSTAND WHAT I'M SAYING?
FREE GIFTS.
NOW I WANT ALL OF YOU WHITE BLOOD CELLS TO SPELL "HI."
8/25/02

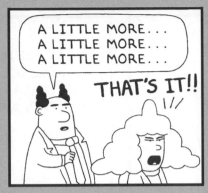

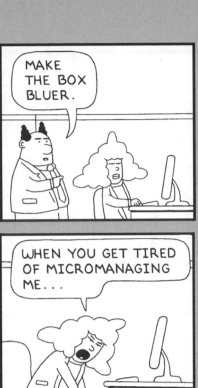

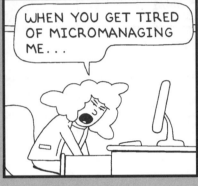

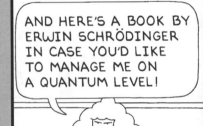

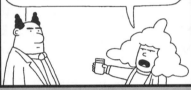

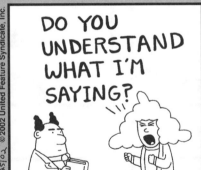

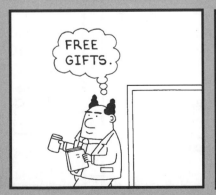

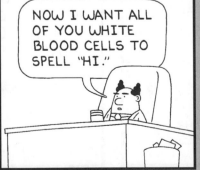

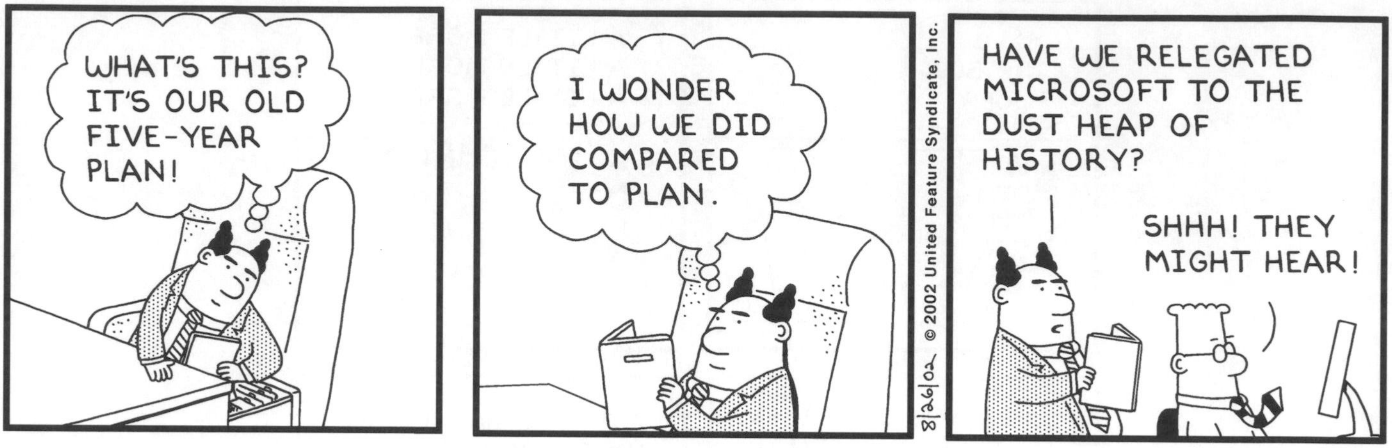
WHAT'S THIS? IT'S OUR OLD FIVE-YEAR PLAN!
I WONDER HOW WE DID COMPARED TO PLAN.
8/26/02 © 2002 United Feature Syndicate, Inc.
HAVE WE RELEGATED MICROSOFT TO THE DUST HEAP OF HISTORY?
SHHH! THEY MIGHT HEAR!

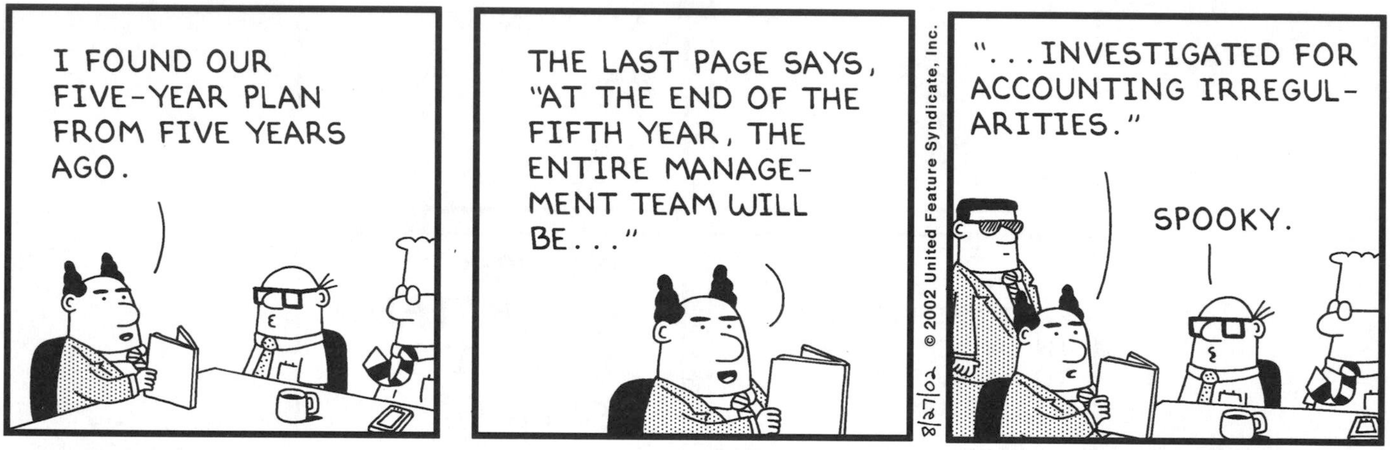
I FOUND OUR FIVE-YEAR PLAN FROM FIVE YEARS AGO.
THE LAST PAGE SAYS, "AT THE END OF THE FIFTH YEAR, THE ENTIRE MANAGE-MENT TEAM WILL BE..."
8/27/02 © 2002 United Feature Syndicate, Inc.
"...INVESTIGATED FOR ACCOUNTING IRREGUL-ARITIES."
SPOOKY.

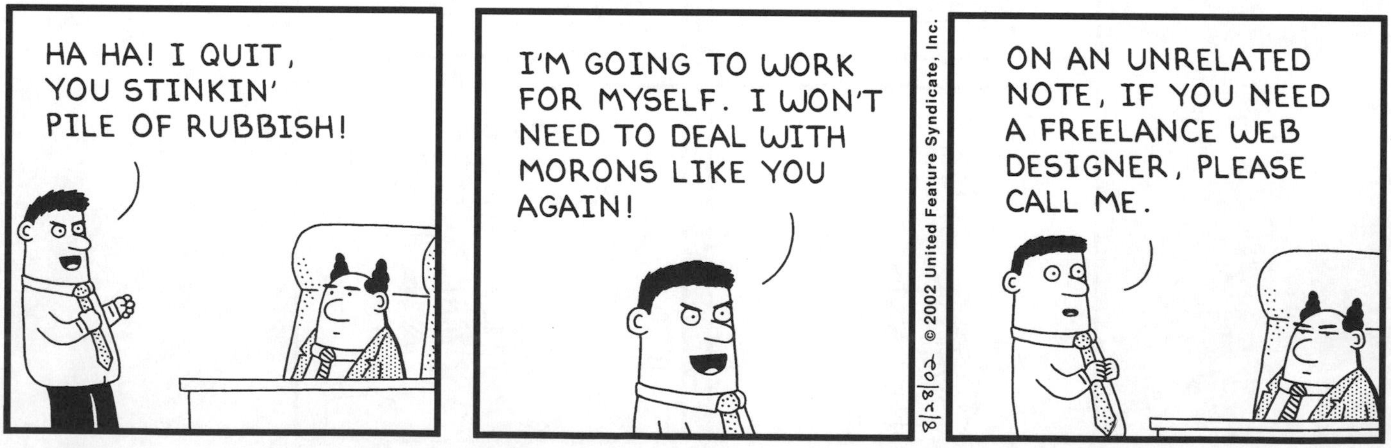
HA HA! I QUIT, YOU STINKIN' PILE OF RUBBISH!
I'M GOING TO WORK FOR MYSELF. I WON'T NEED TO DEAL WITH MORONS LIKE YOU AGAIN!
8/28/02 © 2002 United Feature Syndicate, Inc.
ON AN UNRELATED NOTE, IF YOU NEED A FREELANCE WEB DESIGNER, PLEASE CALL ME.

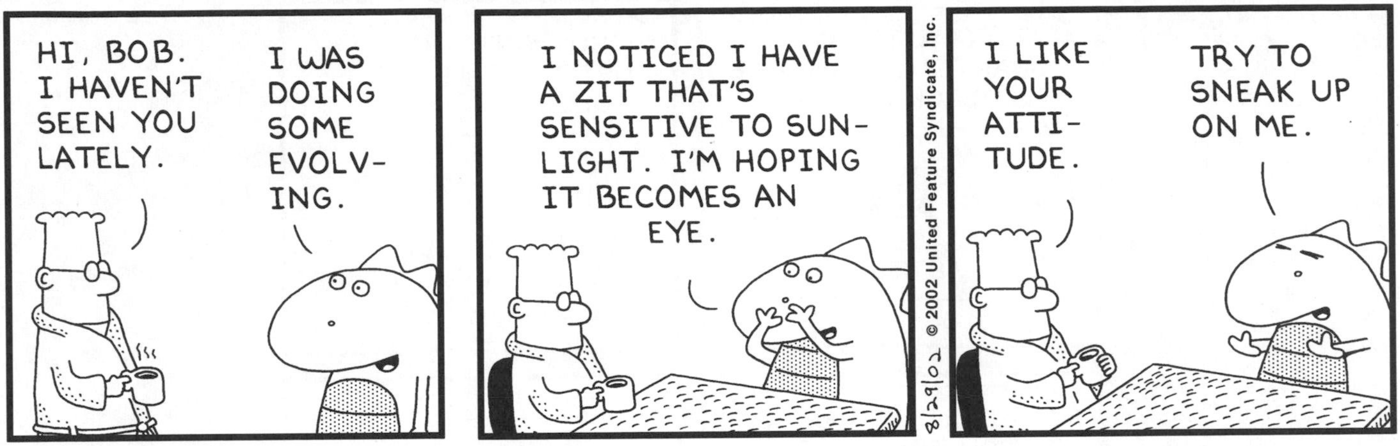
HI, BOB. I HAVEN'T SEEN YOU LATELY.
I WAS DOING SOME EVOLVING.
I NOTICED I HAVE A ZIT THAT'S SENSITIVE TO SUNLIGHT. I'M HOPING IT BECOMES AN EYE.
8/29/02 © 2002 United Feature Syndicate, Inc.
I LIKE YOUR ATTITUDE.
TRY TO SNEAK UP ON ME.

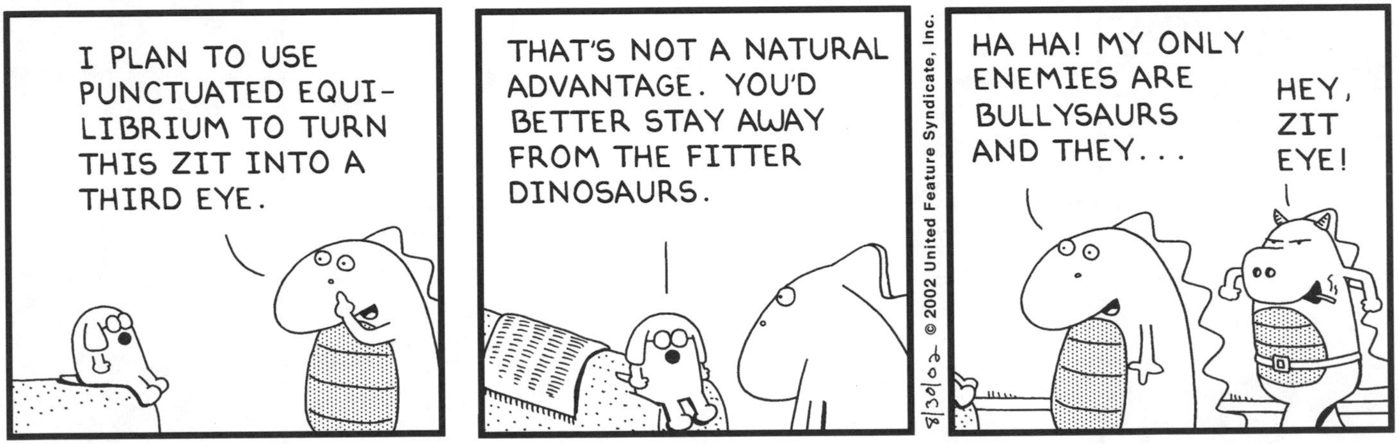
I PLAN TO USE PUNCTUATED EQUILIBRIUM TO TURN THIS ZIT INTO A THIRD EYE.
THAT'S NOT A NATURAL ADVANTAGE. YOU'D BETTER STAY AWAY FROM THE FITTER DINOSAURS.
8/30/02 © 2002 United Feature Syndicate, Inc.
HA HA! MY ONLY ENEMIES ARE BULLYSAURS AND THEY...
HEY, ZIT EYE!

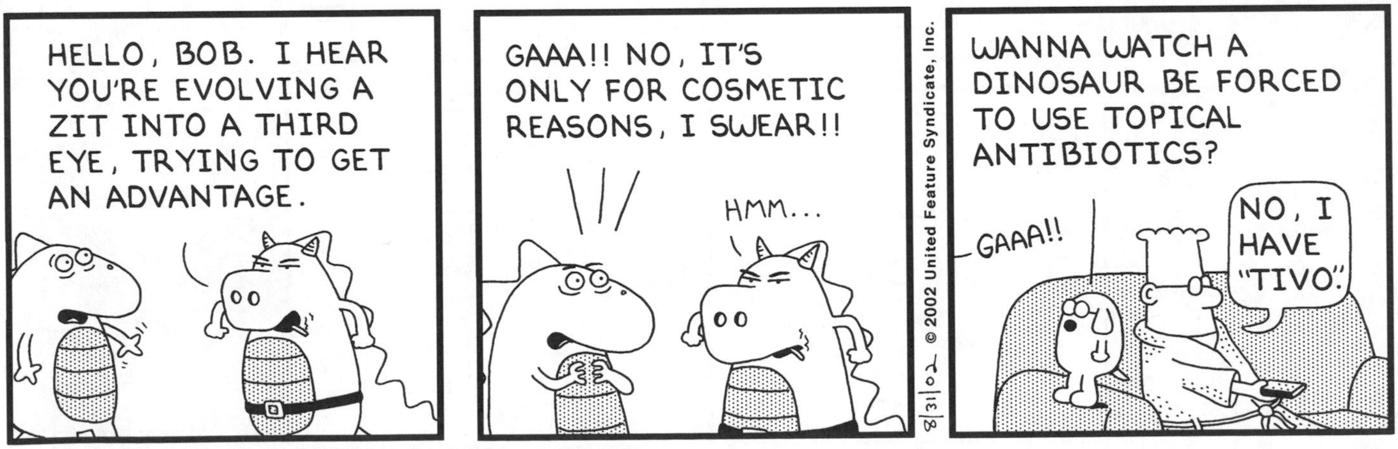
HELLO, BOB. I HEAR YOU'RE EVOLVING A ZIT INTO A THIRD EYE, TRYING TO GET AN ADVANTAGE.
GAAA!! NO, IT'S ONLY FOR COSMETIC REASONS, I SWEAR!!
HMM...
8/31/02 © 2002 United Feature Syndicate, Inc.
WANNA WATCH A DINOSAUR BE FORCED TO USE TOPICAL ANTIBIOTICS?
GAAA!!
NO, I HAVE "TIVO".

WELCOME TO MY QUARTERLY EMPLOYEE FEEDBACK MEETING.
WHO WANTS TO GET THE BALL ROLLING?
IT WOULD BE HELPFUL IF YOU TOLD US OUR COMPANY'S LONG TERM STRATEGY.
OH, WOULD IT?
WHY? SO YOU CAN LEAK IT TO OUR COMPETITORS?
©2002 United Feature Syndicate, Inc.
9/1/02
HERE'S YOUR STUPID SUGGESTION IN MY HAND! I'M CRUSHING IT! CRUSH, CRUSH, CRUSH!!!
NOW I'LL CHEW IT UP SO I CAN SPIT IT IN YOUR CUBICLE-DWELLING FACE!!!
YOU FELL IN THAT TRAP LAST QUARTER TOO.
AN OPTI-MIST'S LIFE IS NEVER EASY.

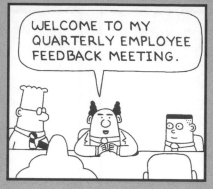

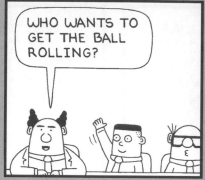

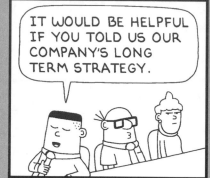

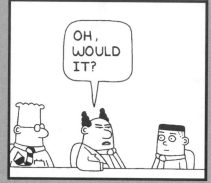

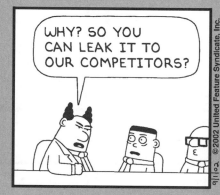

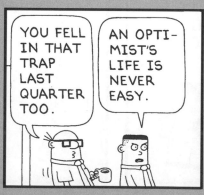

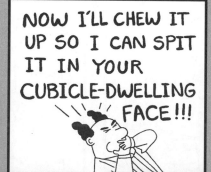

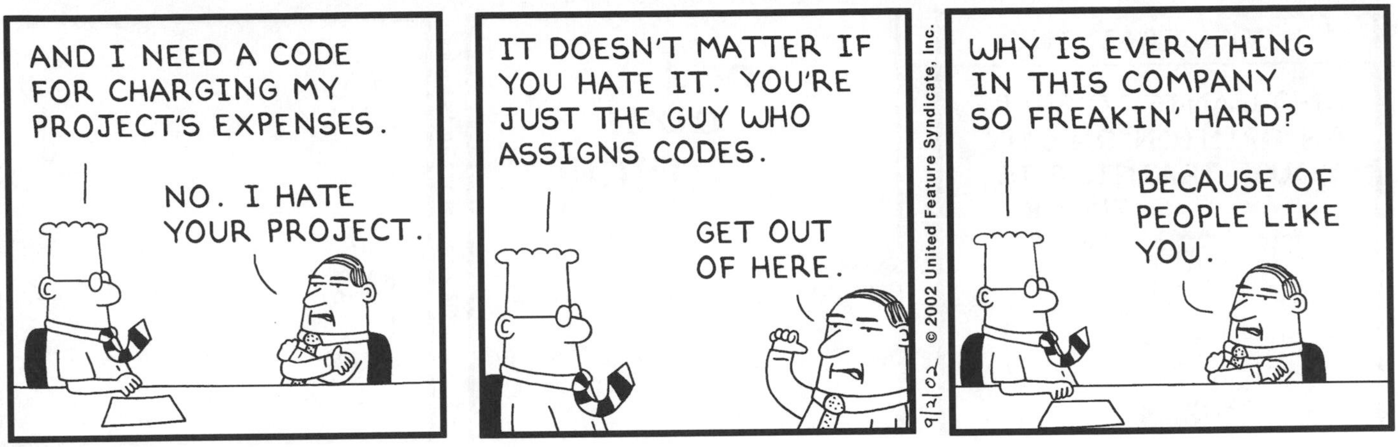
AND I NEED A CODE FOR CHARGING MY PROJECT'S EXPENSES.
NO. I HATE YOUR PROJECT.
IT DOESN'T MATTER IF YOU HATE IT. YOU'RE JUST THE GUY WHO ASSIGNS CODES.
GET OUT OF HERE.
9/2/02 © 2002 United Feature Syndicate, Inc.
WHY IS EVERYTHING IN THIS COMPANY SO FREAKIN' HARD?
BECAUSE OF PEOPLE LIKE YOU.

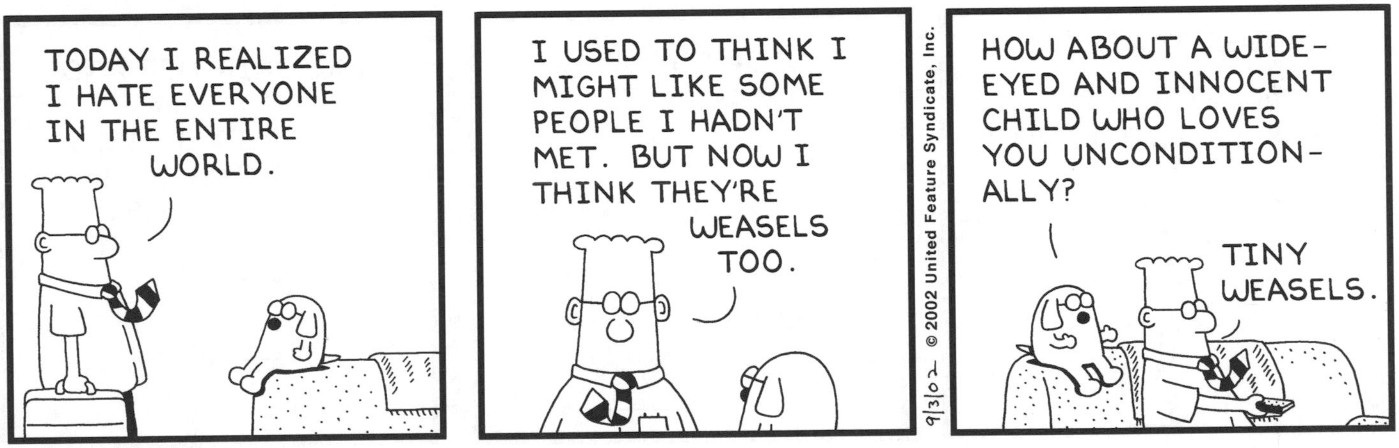
TODAY I REALIZED I HATE EVERYONE IN THE ENTIRE WORLD.
I USED TO THINK I MIGHT LIKE SOME PEOPLE I HADN'T MET. BUT NOW I THINK THEY'RE WEASELS TOO.
9/3/02 © 2002 United Feature Syndicate, Inc.
HOW ABOUT A WIDE-EYED AND INNOCENT CHILD WHO LOVES YOU UNCONDITION-ALLY?
TINY WEASELS.

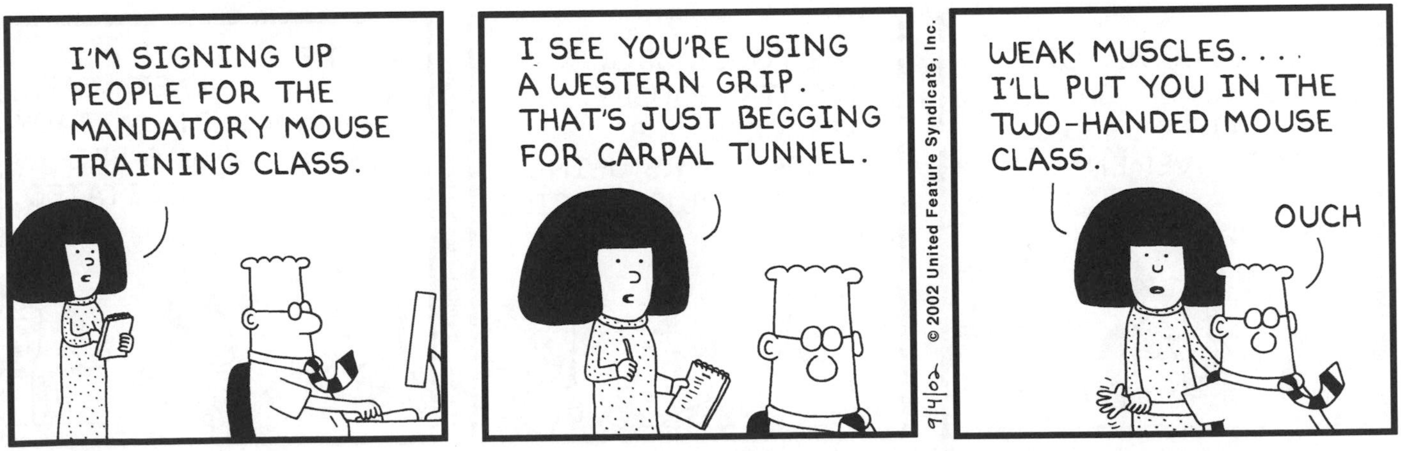
I'M SIGNING UP PEOPLE FOR THE MANDATORY MOUSE TRAINING CLASS.
I SEE YOU'RE USING A WESTERN GRIP. THAT'S JUST BEGGING FOR CARPAL TUNNEL.
9/4/02 © 2002 United Feature Syndicate, Inc.
WEAK MUSCLES.... I'LL PUT YOU IN THE TWO-HANDED MOUSE CLASS.
OUCH

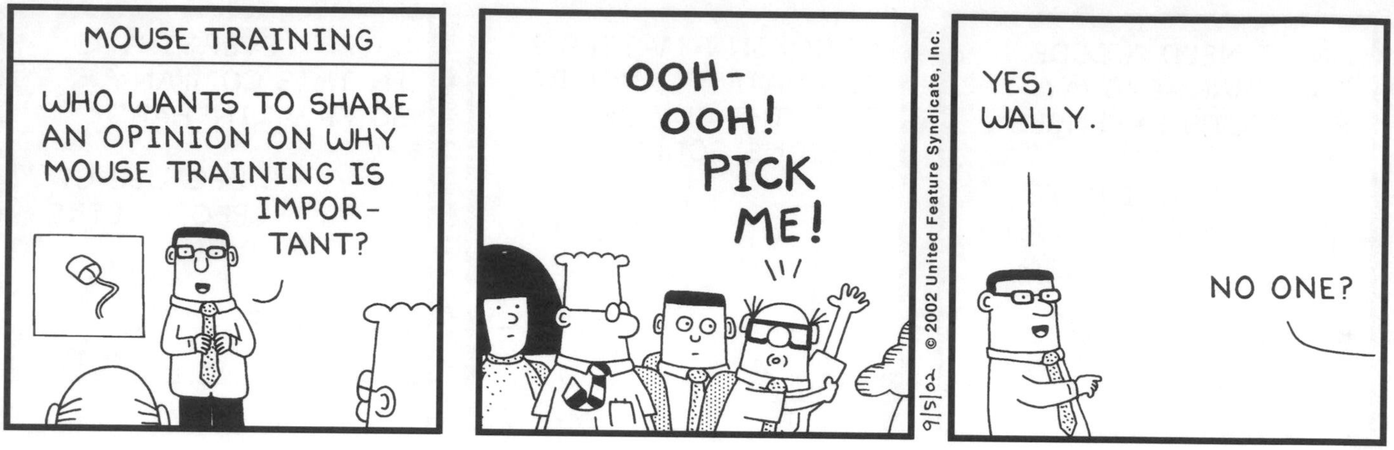
MOUSE TRAINING
WHO WANTS TO SHARE AN OPINION ON WHY MOUSE TRAINING IS IMPOR-TANT?
OOH-OOH! PICK ME!
YES, WALLY.
NO ONE?
9/5/02 © 2002 United Feature Syndicate, Inc.

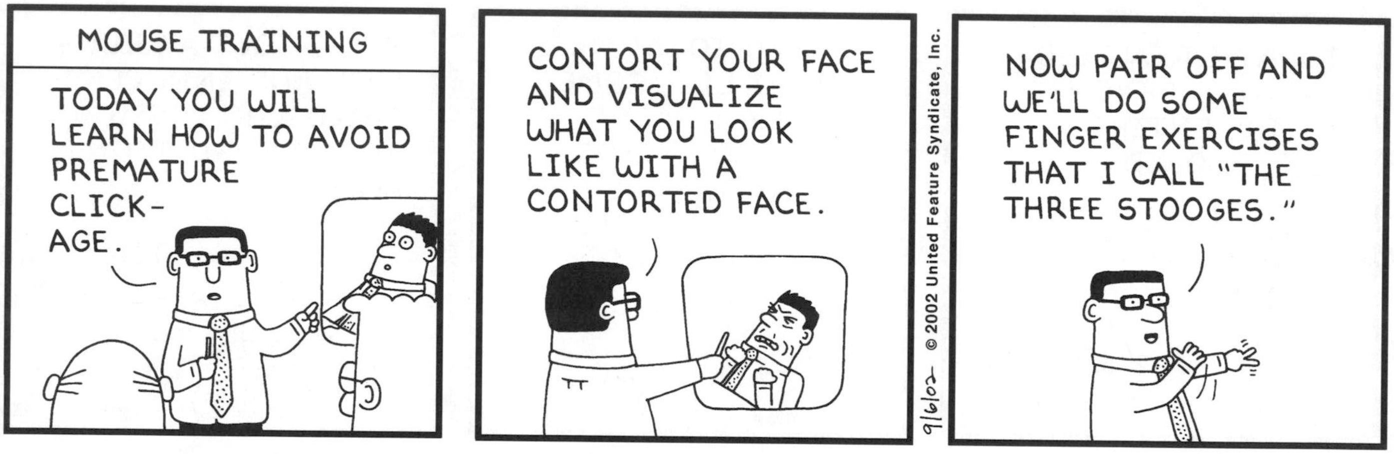
MOUSE TRAINING
TODAY YOU WILL LEARN HOW TO AVOID PREMATURE CLICK-AGE.
CONTORT YOUR FACE AND VISUALIZE WHAT YOU LOOK LIKE WITH A CONTORTED FACE.
NOW PAIR OFF AND WE'LL DO SOME FINGER EXERCISES THAT I CALL "THE THREE STOOGES."
9/6/02 © 2002 United Feature Syndicate, Inc.

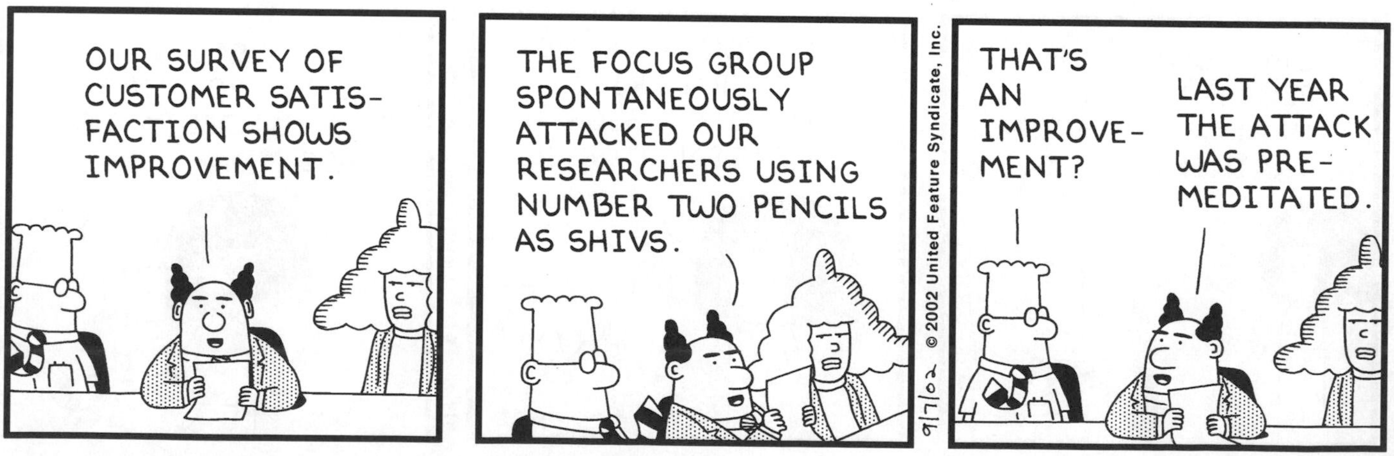
OUR SURVEY OF CUSTOMER SATIS-FACTION SHOWS IMPROVEMENT.
THE FOCUS GROUP SPONTANEOUSLY ATTACKED OUR RESEARCHERS USING NUMBER TWO PENCILS AS SHIVS.
THAT'S AN IMPROVE-MENT?
LAST YEAR THE ATTACK WAS PRE-MEDITATED.
9/7/02 © 2002 United Feature Syndicate, Inc.

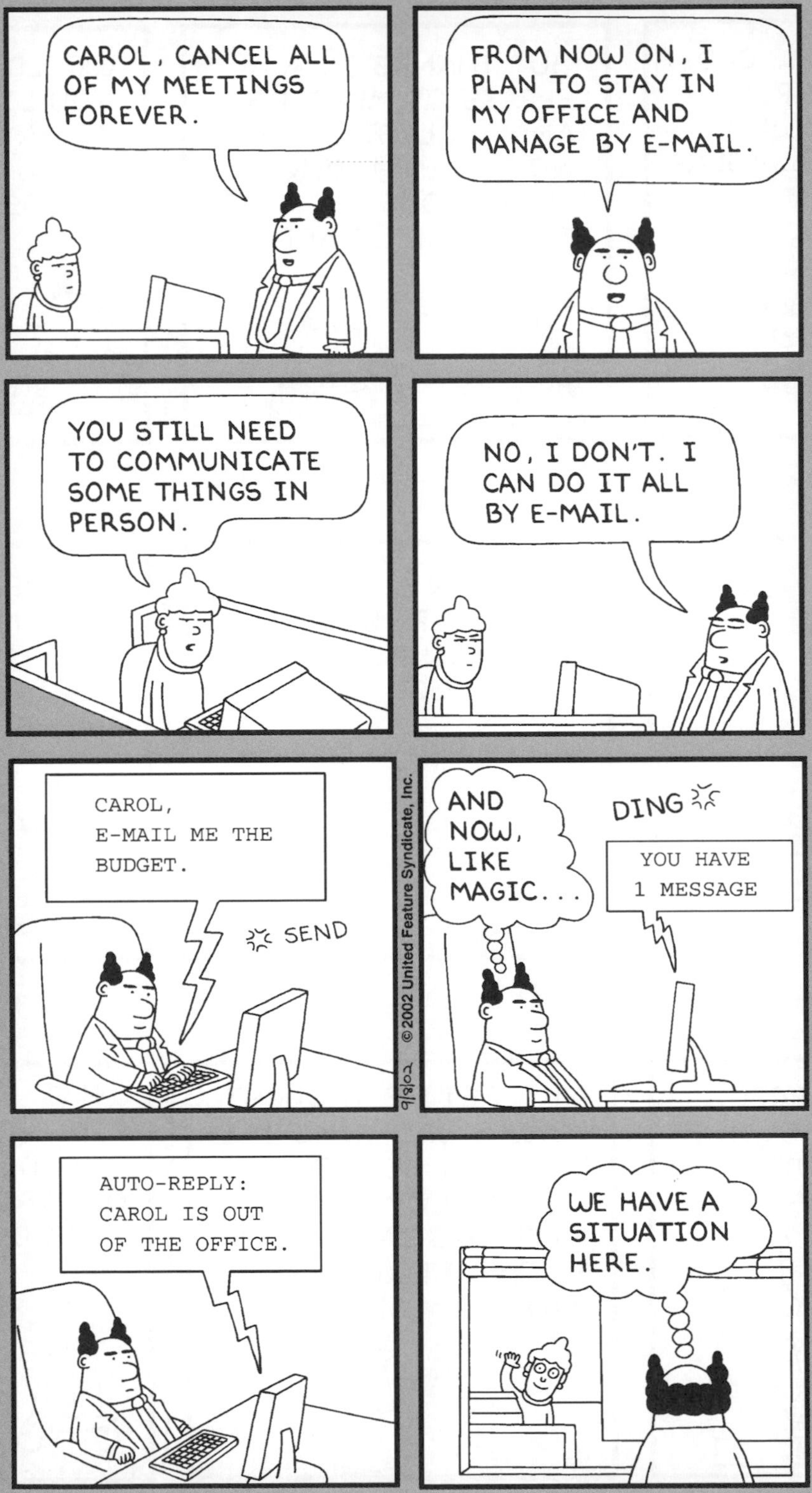
CAROL, CANCEL ALL OF MY MEETINGS FOREVER.
FROM NOW ON, I PLAN TO STAY IN MY OFFICE AND MANAGE BY E-MAIL.
YOU STILL NEED TO COMMUNICATE SOME THINGS IN PERSON.
NO, I DON'T. I CAN DO IT ALL BY E-MAIL.
CAROL, E-MAIL ME THE BUDGET.
SEND
©2002 United Feature Syndicate, Inc.
AND NOW, LIKE MAGIC...
DING
YOU HAVE 1 MESSAGE
AUTO-REPLY: CAROL IS OUT OF THE OFFICE.
WE HAVE A SITUATION HERE.

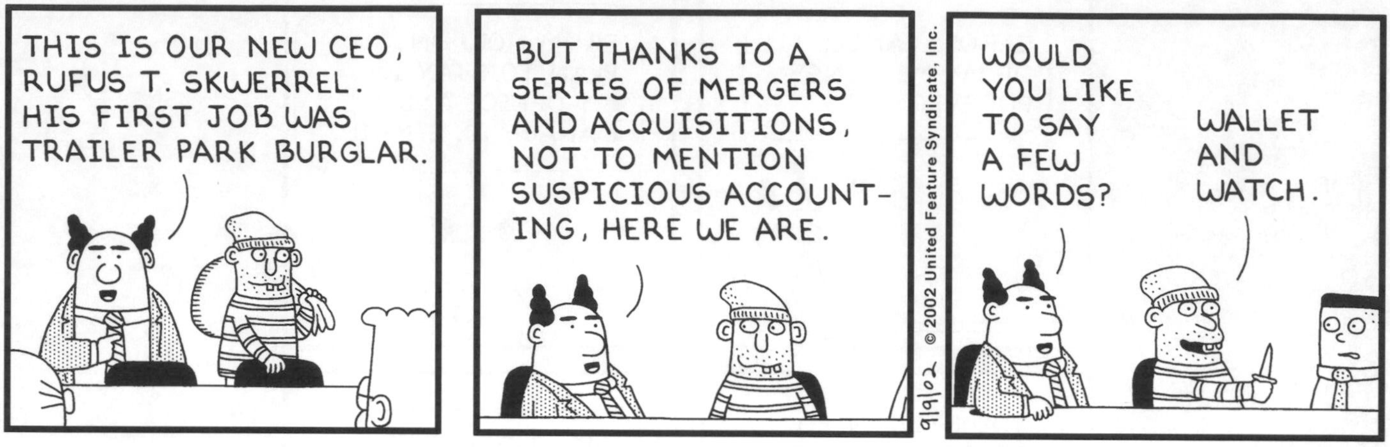
THIS IS OUR NEW CEO, RUFUS T. SKWERREL. HIS FIRST JOB WAS TRAILER PARK BURGLAR.
BUT THANKS TO A SERIES OF MERGERS AND ACQUISITIONS, NOT TO MENTION SUSPICIOUS ACCOUNT-ING, HERE WE ARE.
9/9/02 © 2002 United Feature Syndicate, Inc.
WOULD YOU LIKE TO SAY A FEW WORDS?
WALLET AND WATCH.

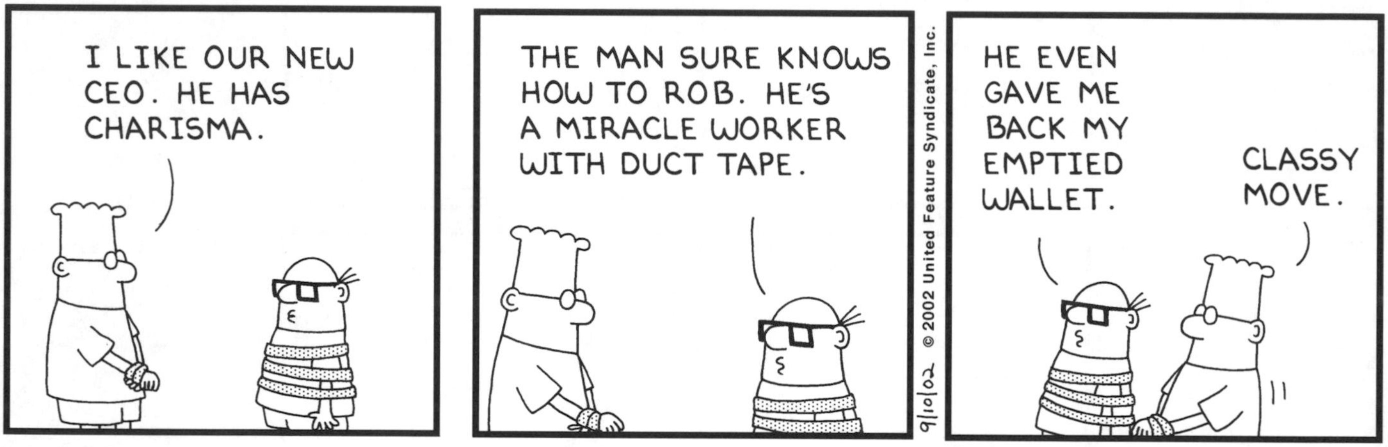
I LIKE OUR NEW CEO. HE HAS CHARISMA.
THE MAN SURE KNOWS HOW TO ROB. HE'S A MIRACLE WORKER WITH DUCT TAPE.
9/10/02 © 2002 United Feature Syndicate, Inc.
HE EVEN GAVE ME BACK MY EMPTIED WALLET.
CLASSY MOVE.

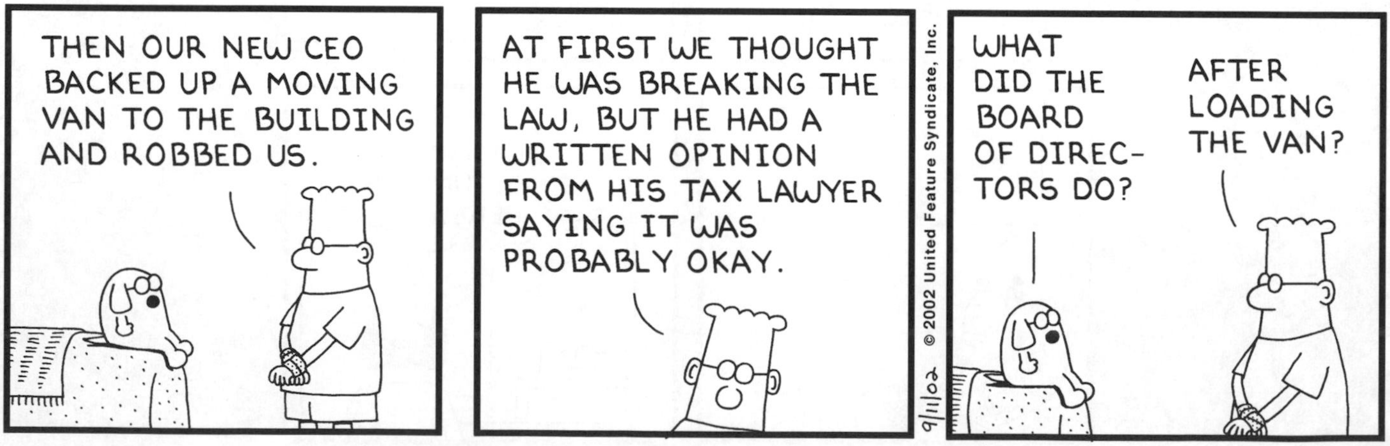
THEN OUR NEW CEO BACKED UP A MOVING VAN TO THE BUILDING AND ROBBED US.
AT FIRST WE THOUGHT HE WAS BREAKING THE LAW, BUT HE HAD A WRITTEN OPINION FROM HIS TAX LAWYER SAYING IT WAS PROBABLY OKAY.
9/11/02 © 2002 United Feature Syndicate, Inc.
WHAT DID THE BOARD OF DIREC-TORS DO?
AFTER LOADING THE VAN?

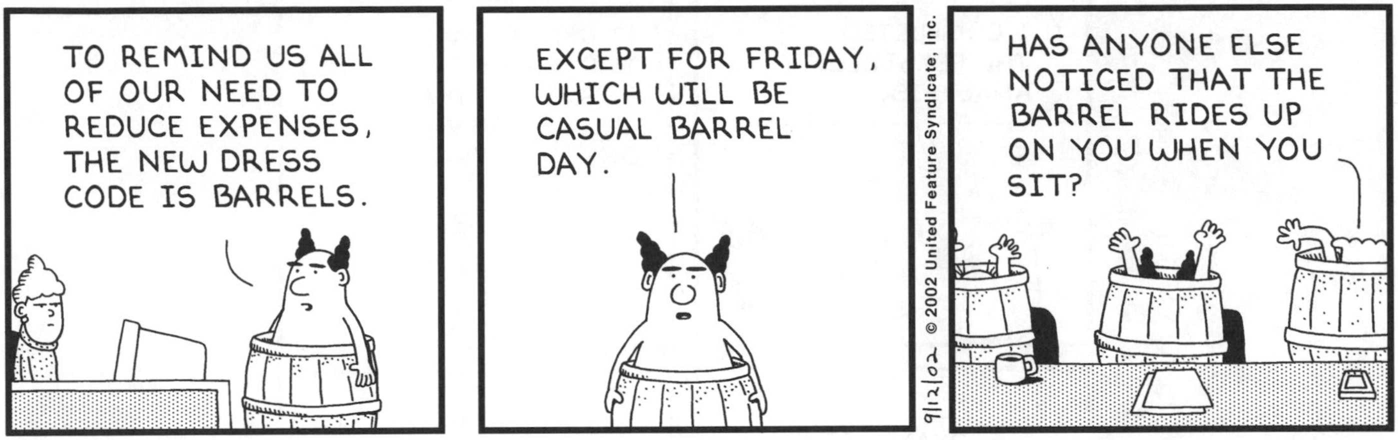
TO REMIND US ALL OF OUR NEED TO REDUCE EXPENSES, THE NEW DRESS CODE IS BARRELS.
EXCEPT FOR FRIDAY, WHICH WILL BE CASUAL BARREL DAY.
9/12/02 © 2002 United Feature Syndicate, Inc.
HAS ANYONE ELSE NOTICED THAT THE BARREL RIDES UP ON YOU WHEN YOU SIT?

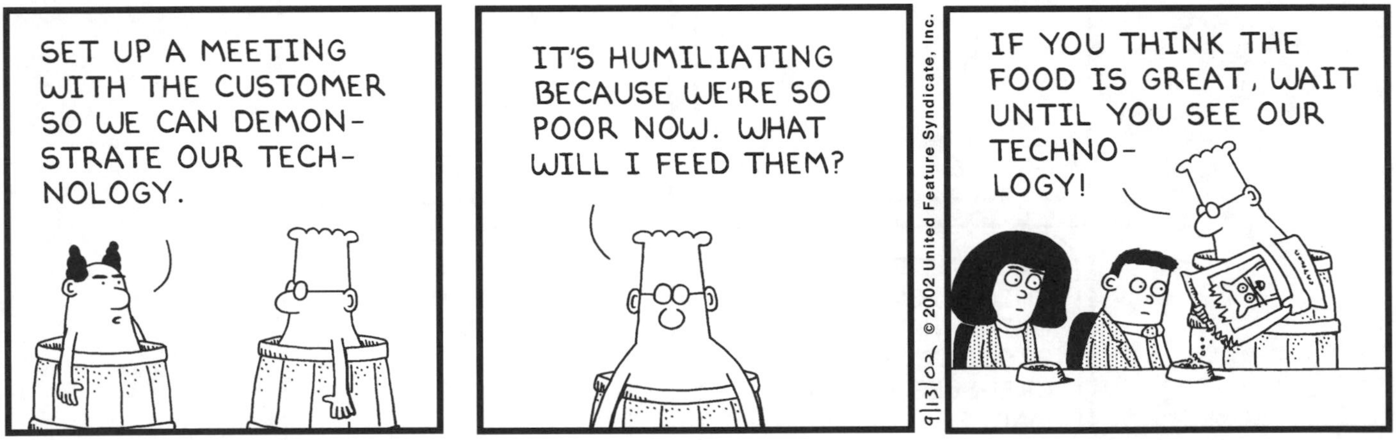
SET UP A MEETING WITH THE CUSTOMER SO WE CAN DEMON-STRATE OUR TECH-NOLOGY.
IT'S HUMILIATING BECAUSE WE'RE SO POOR NOW. WHAT WILL I FEED THEM?
9/13/02 © 2002 United Feature Syndicate, Inc.
IF YOU THINK THE FOOD IS GREAT, WAIT UNTIL YOU SEE OUR TECHNO-LOGY!

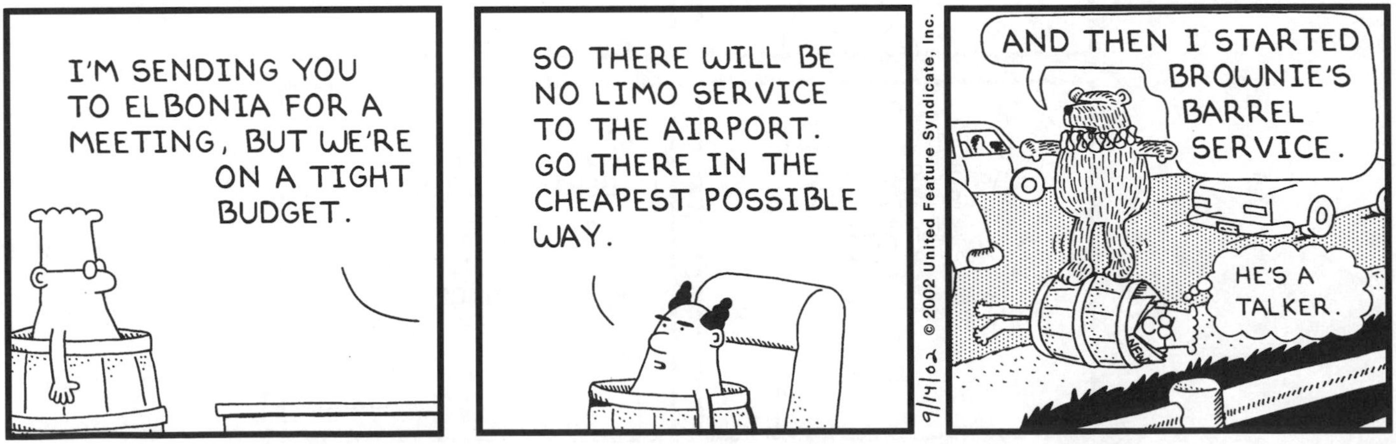
I'M SENDING YOU TO ELBONIA FOR A MEETING, BUT WE'RE ON A TIGHT BUDGET.
SO THERE WILL BE NO LIMO SERVICE TO THE AIRPORT. GO THERE IN THE CHEAPEST POSSIBLE WAY.
9/14/02 © 2002 United Feature Syndicate, Inc.
AND THEN I STARTED BROWNIE'S BARREL SERVICE.
HE'S A TALKER.

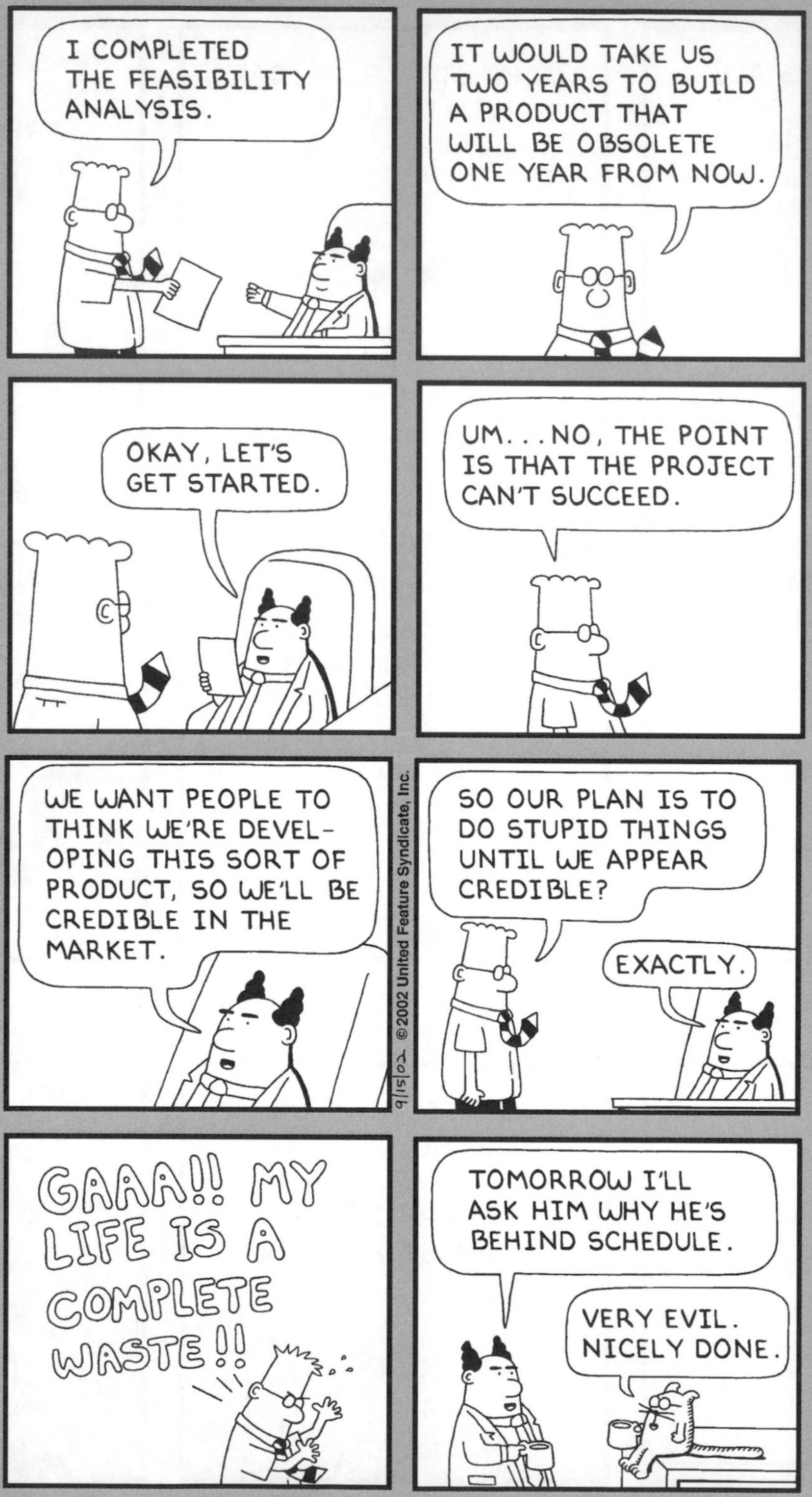
I COMPLETED THE FEASIBILITY ANALYSIS.
IT WOULD TAKE US TWO YEARS TO BUILD A PRODUCT THAT WILL BE OBSOLETE ONE YEAR FROM NOW.
OKAY, LET'S GET STARTED.
UM...NO, THE POINT IS THAT THE PROJECT CAN'T SUCCEED.
WE WANT PEOPLE TO THINK WE'RE DEVEL-OPING THIS SORT OF PRODUCT, SO WE'LL BE CREDIBLE IN THE MARKET.
9/15/02 ©2002 United Feature Syndicate, Inc.
SO OUR PLAN IS TO DO STUPID THINGS UNTIL WE APPEAR CREDIBLE?
EXACTLY.
GAAA!! MY LIFE IS A COMPLETE WASTE!!
TOMORROW I'LL ASK HIM WHY HE'S BEHIND SCHEDULE.
VERY EVIL. NICELY DONE.

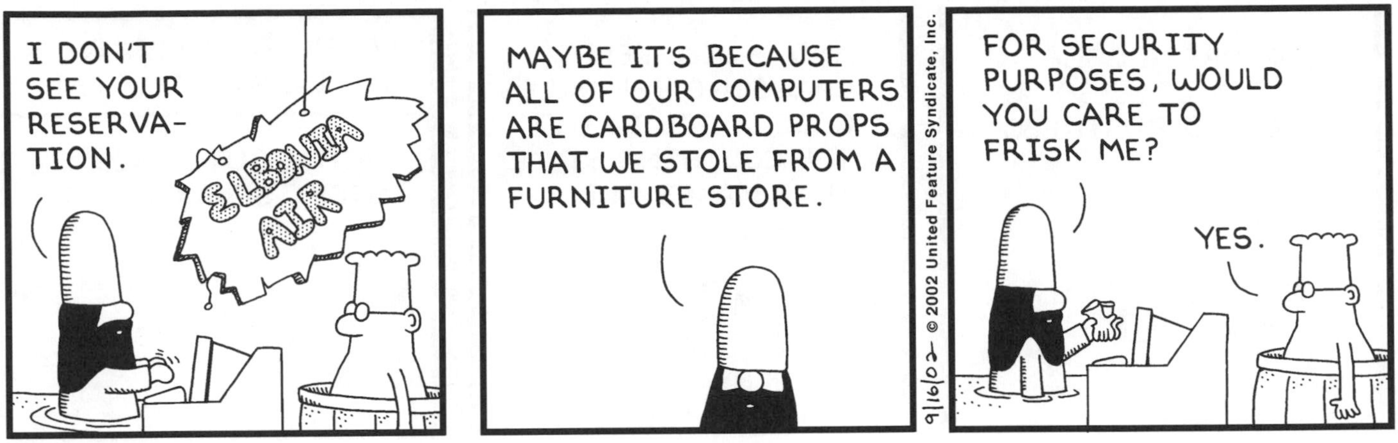
I DON'T SEE YOUR RESERVATION.
ELBONIA AIR
MAYBE IT'S BECAUSE ALL OF OUR COMPUTERS ARE CARDBOARD PROPS THAT WE STOLE FROM A FURNITURE STORE.
9/16/02 © 2002 United Feature Syndicate, Inc.
FOR SECURITY PURPOSES, WOULD YOU CARE TO FRISK ME?
YES.

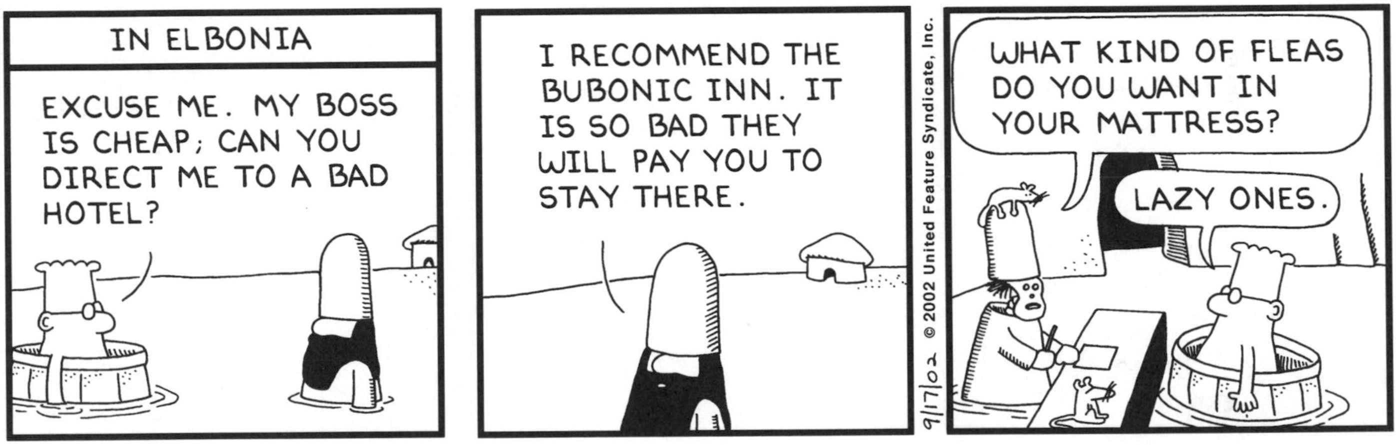
IN ELBONIA
EXCUSE ME. MY BOSS IS CHEAP; CAN YOU DIRECT ME TO A BAD HOTEL?
I RECOMMEND THE BUBONIC INN. IT IS SO BAD THEY WILL PAY YOU TO STAY THERE.
9/17/02 © 2002 United Feature Syndicate, Inc.
WHAT KIND OF FLEAS DO YOU WANT IN YOUR MATTRESS?
LAZY ONES.

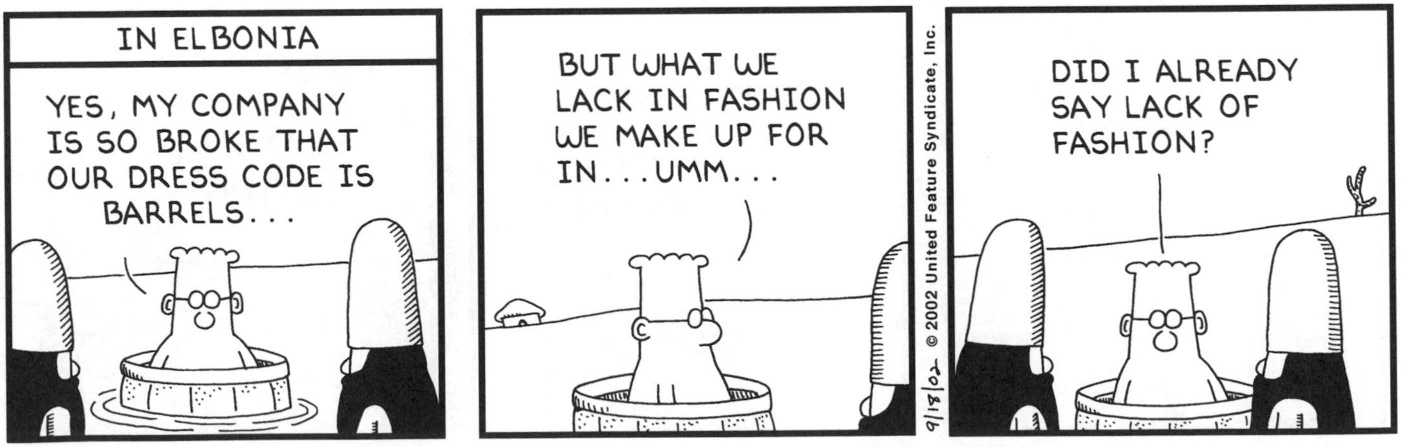
IN ELBONIA
YES, MY COMPANY IS SO BROKE THAT OUR DRESS CODE IS BARRELS...
BUT WHAT WE LACK IN FASHION WE MAKE UP FOR IN...UMM...
9/18/02 © 2002 United Feature Syndicate, Inc.
DID I ALREADY SAY LACK OF FASHION?

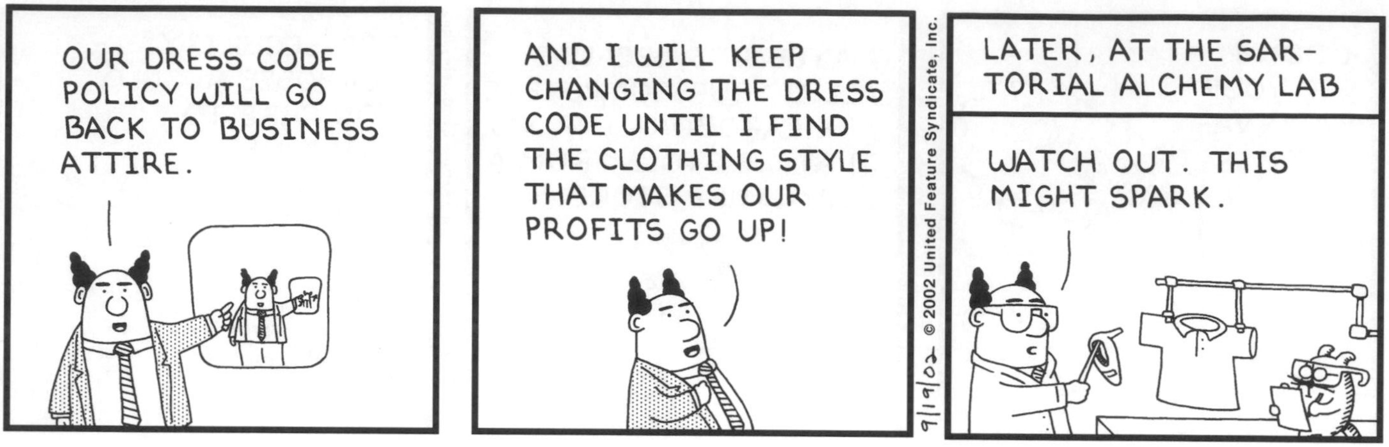
OUR DRESS CODE POLICY WILL GO BACK TO BUSINESS ATTIRE.
AND I WILL KEEP CHANGING THE DRESS CODE UNTIL I FIND THE CLOTHING STYLE THAT MAKES OUR PROFITS GO UP!
9/19/02 © 2002 United Feature Syndicate, Inc.
LATER, AT THE SARTORIAL ALCHEMY LAB
WATCH OUT. THIS MIGHT SPARK.

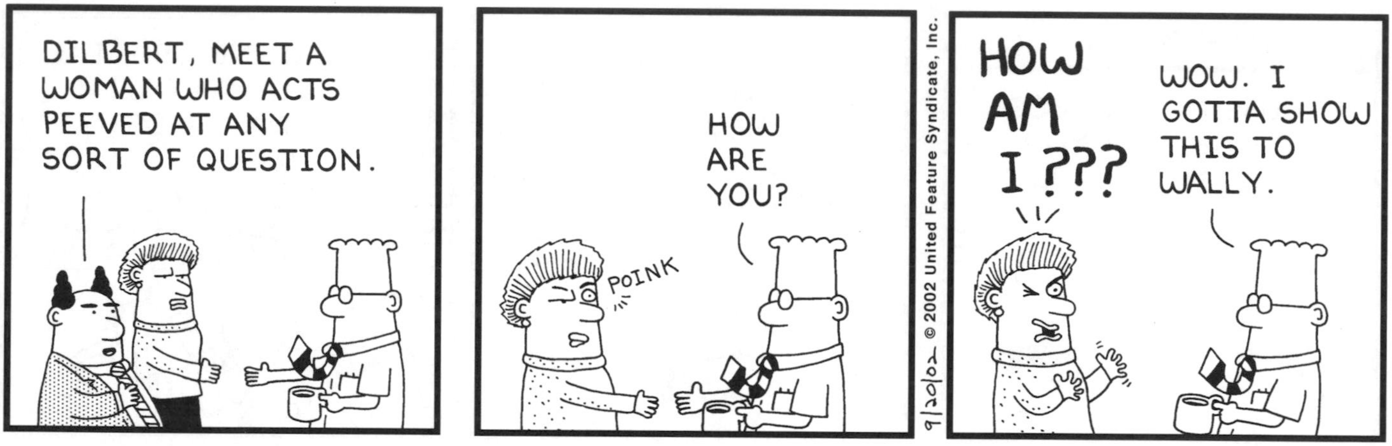
DILBERT, MEET A WOMAN WHO ACTS PEEVED AT ANY SORT OF QUESTION.
HOW ARE YOU?
POINK
9/20/02 © 2002 United Feature Syndicate, Inc.
HOW AM I ???
WOW. I GOTTA SHOW THIS TO WALLY.

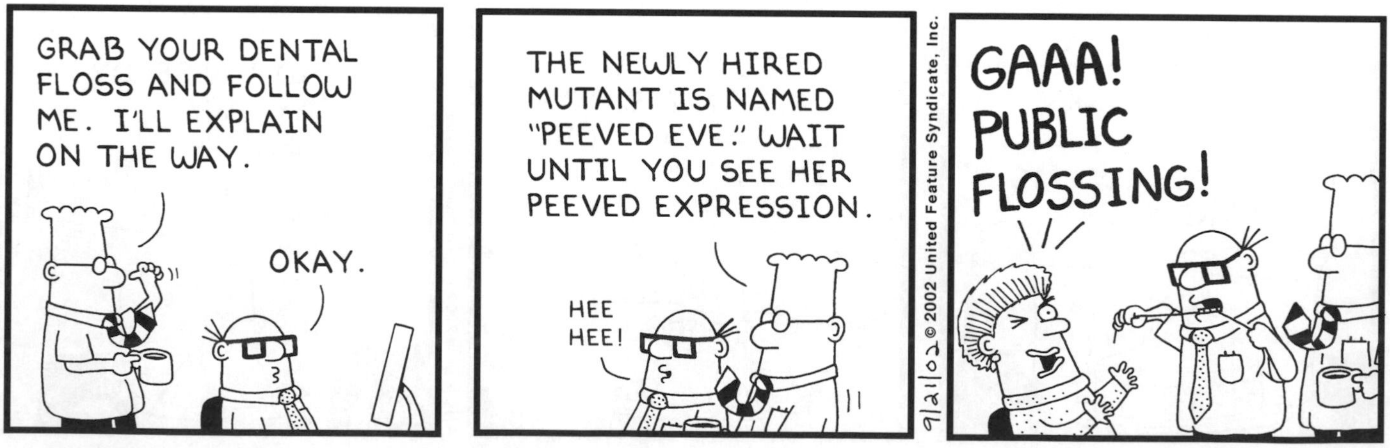
GRAB YOUR DENTAL FLOSS AND FOLLOW ME. I'LL EXPLAIN ON THE WAY.
OKAY.
THE NEWLY HIRED MUTANT IS NAMED "PEEVED EVE." WAIT UNTIL YOU SEE HER PEEVED EXPRESSION.
HEE HEE!
9/21/02 © 2002 United Feature Syndicate, Inc.
GAAA! PUBLIC FLOSSING!

FULL SERVICE BROKER
I'M BOB WEASELTON, YOUR FULL-SERVICE STOCKBROKER.
THERE ARE TWO WAYS WE CAN GO HERE.
OPTION ONE: I ACT AS IF BROKERS KNOW WHICH STOCKS ARE BETTER THAN OTHERS.
THEN I'LL EARN YOUR TRUST BY COMPARING YOUR PORTFOLIO TO MISLEADING BENCH-MARKS.
BUT I PREFER A MORE DIRECT APPROACH.
OPTION TWO: I SELL YOU WHATEVER GARBAGE EARNS ME THE BIGGEST COMMISSION.
WOULD YOU DO ME A FAVOR AND LIE TO ME?
NICE HAIRCUT.
9/22/02 ©2002 United Feature Syndicate, Inc.

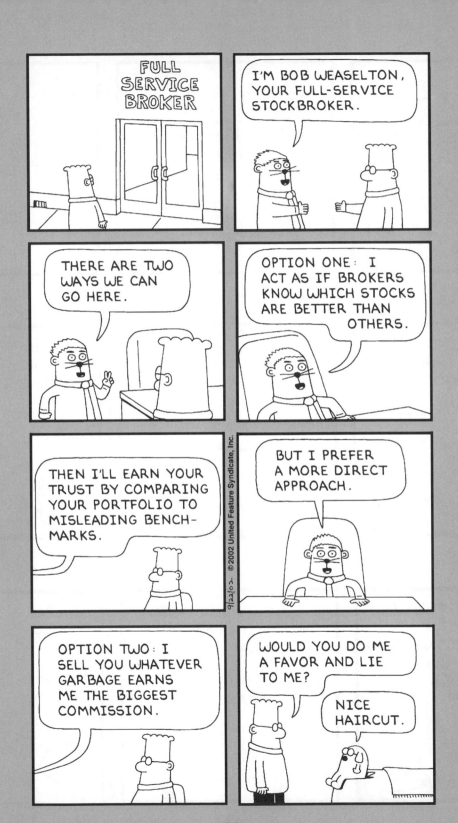

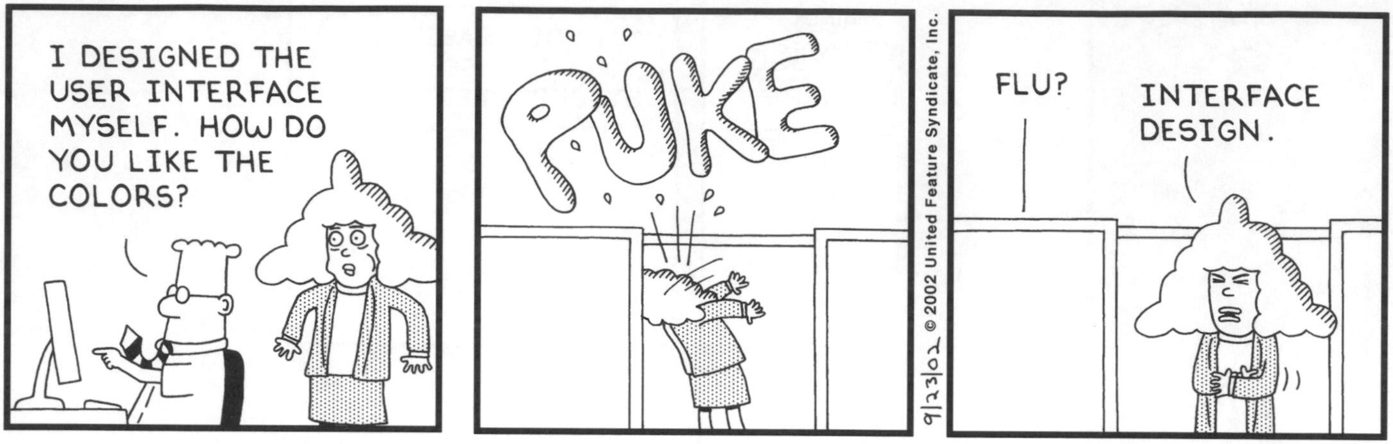
I DESIGNED THE USER INTERFACE MYSELF. HOW DO YOU LIKE THE COLORS?
PUKE
FLU?
INTERFACE DESIGN.
9/23/02 © 2002 United Feature Syndicate, Inc.

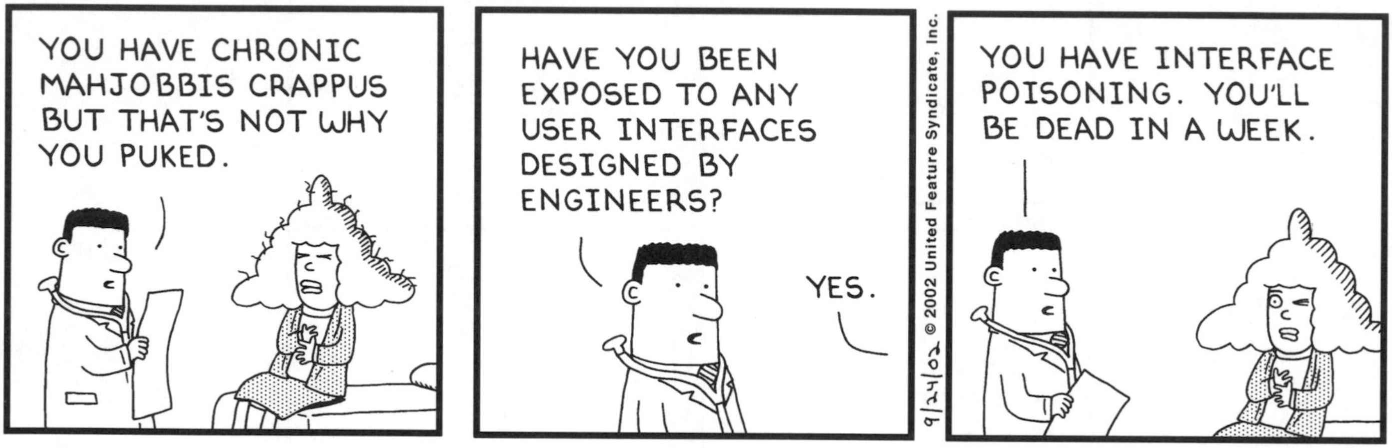
YOU HAVE CHRONIC MAHJOBBIS CRAPPUS BUT THAT'S NOT WHY YOU PUKED.
HAVE YOU BEEN EXPOSED TO ANY USER INTERFACES DESIGNED BY ENGINEERS?
YES.
YOU HAVE INTERFACE POISONING. YOU'LL BE DEAD IN A WEEK.
9/24/02 © 2002 United Feature Syndicate, Inc.

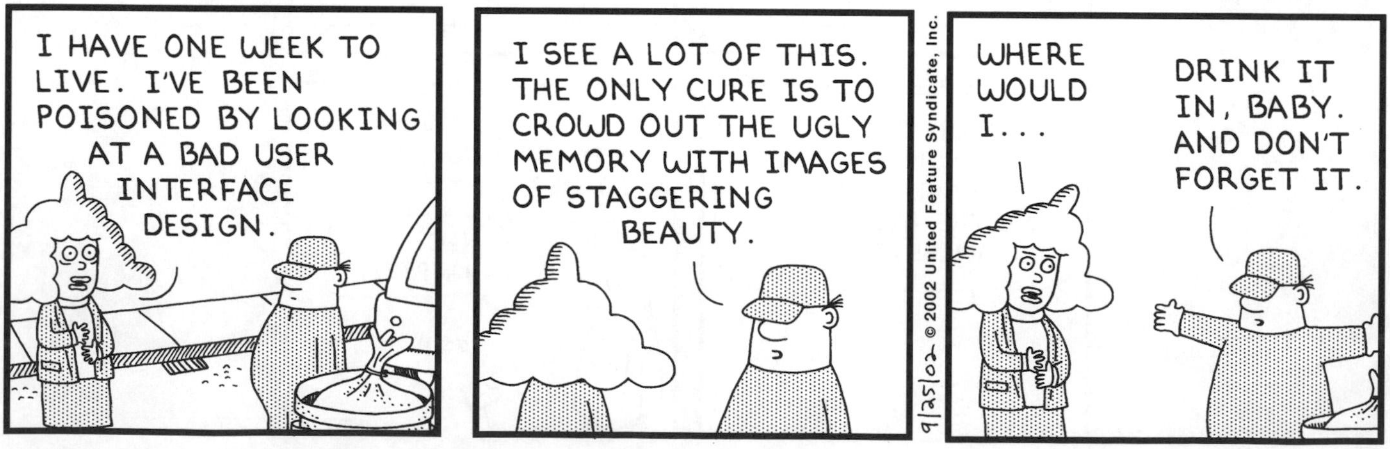
I HAVE ONE WEEK TO LIVE. I'VE BEEN POISONED BY LOOKING AT A BAD USER INTERFACE DESIGN.
I SEE A LOT OF THIS. THE ONLY CURE IS TO CROWD OUT THE UGLY MEMORY WITH IMAGES OF STAGGERING BEAUTY.
WHERE WOULD I . . .
DRINK IT IN, BABY. AND DON'T FORGET IT.
9/25/02 © 2002 United Feature Syndicate, Inc.

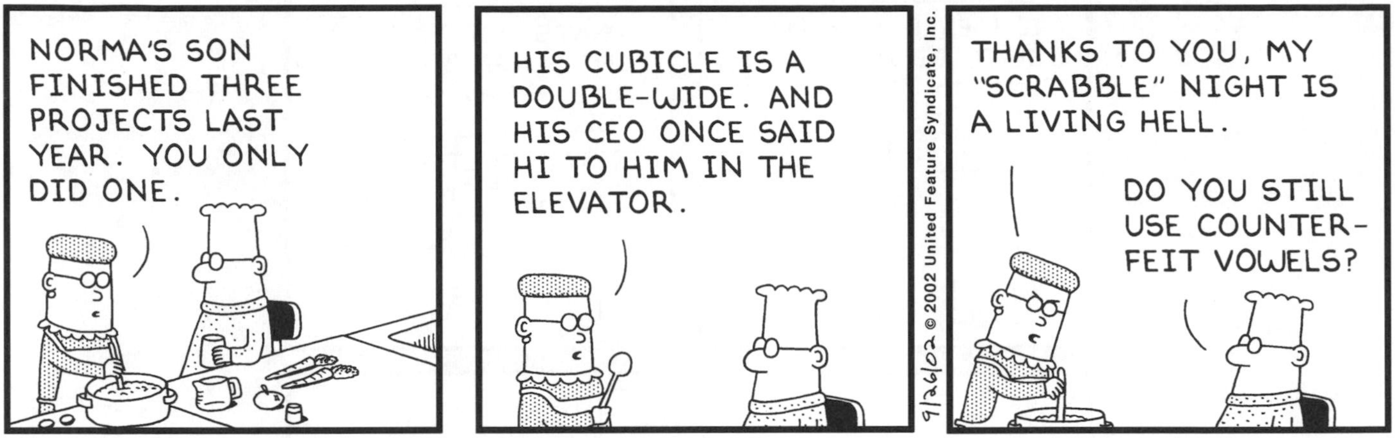
NORMA'S SON FINISHED THREE PROJECTS LAST YEAR. YOU ONLY DID ONE.
HIS CUBICLE IS A DOUBLE-WIDE. AND HIS CEO ONCE SAID HI TO HIM IN THE ELEVATOR.
9/26/02 © 2002 United Feature Syndicate, Inc.
THANKS TO YOU, MY "SCRABBLE" NIGHT IS A LIVING HELL.
DO YOU STILL USE COUNTER-FEIT VOWELS?

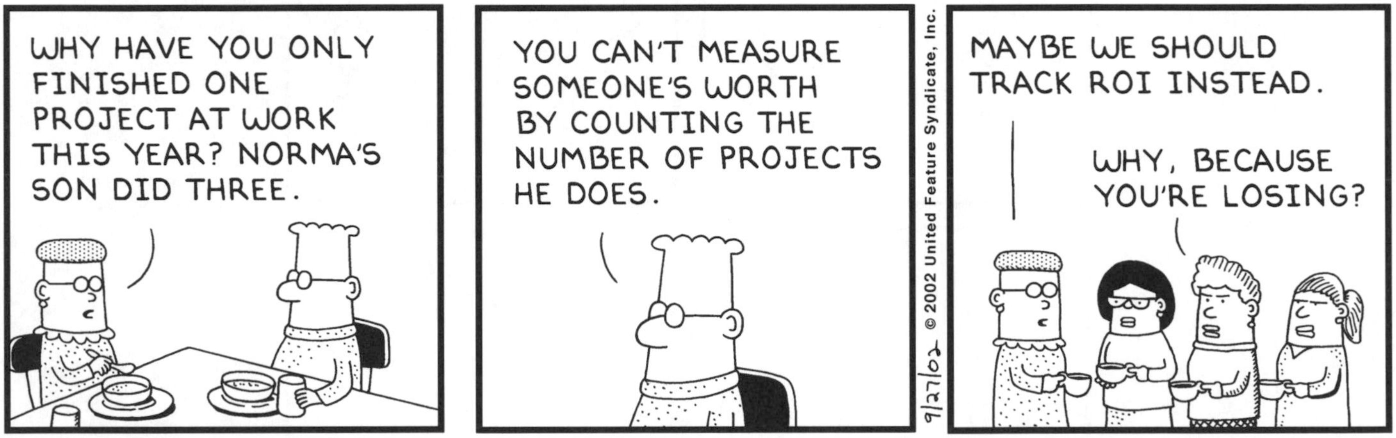
WHY HAVE YOU ONLY FINISHED ONE PROJECT AT WORK THIS YEAR? NORMA'S SON DID THREE.
YOU CAN'T MEASURE SOMEONE'S WORTH BY COUNTING THE NUMBER OF PROJECTS HE DOES.
9/27/02 © 2002 United Feature Syndicate, Inc.
MAYBE WE SHOULD TRACK ROI INSTEAD.
WHY, BECAUSE YOU'RE LOSING?

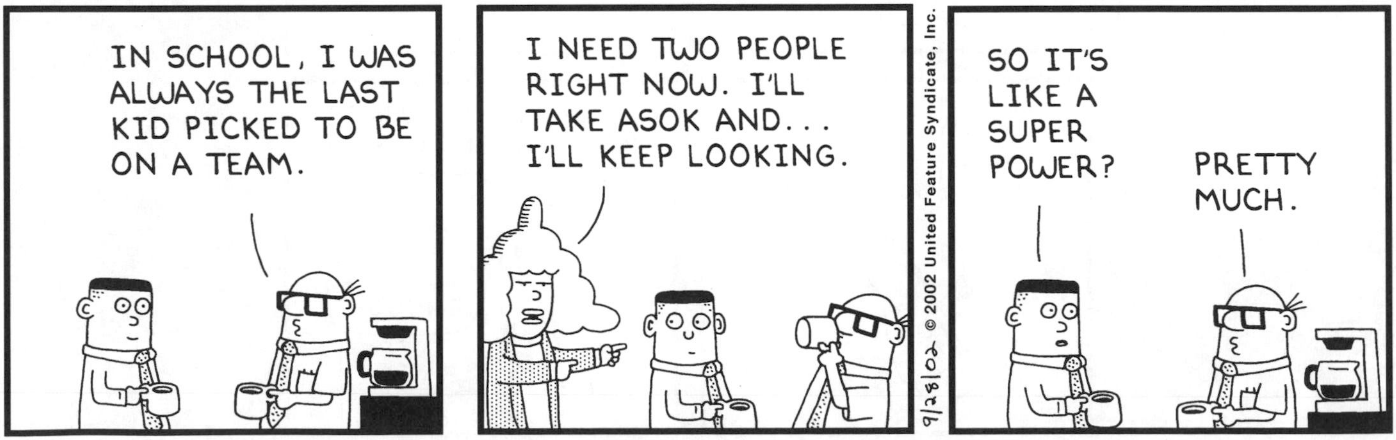
IN SCHOOL, I WAS ALWAYS THE LAST KID PICKED TO BE ON A TEAM.
I NEED TWO PEOPLE RIGHT NOW. I'LL TAKE ASOK AND... I'LL KEEP LOOKING.
9/28/02 © 2002 United Feature Syndicate, Inc.
SO IT'S LIKE A SUPER POWER?
PRETTY MUCH.

TELL EVERYONE I'LL BE THERE IN A MINUTE.
SNIFF
WHAT'S ALL THAT SNIFFING ABOUT? DO YOU HAVE A COLD?
LITTLE ONE.
MMPH
COUGH
GAAA!!! I TOOK A DIRECT HIT!
© 2002 United Feature Syndicate, Inc.
9/29/02
THE COOTIES ARE BURROWING INTO MY SKIN.
I'M UNCLEAN!!
I HOPE THAT'S WHAT MOTIVATION LOOKS LIKE.
CLOSE ENOUGH.

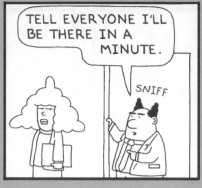

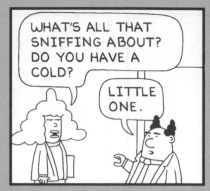

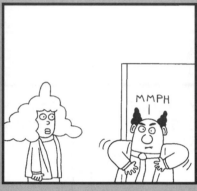

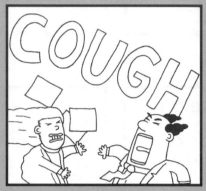

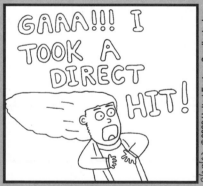

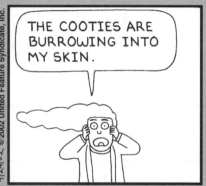

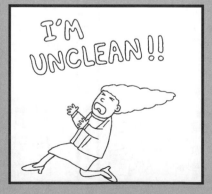

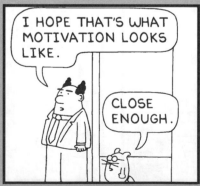

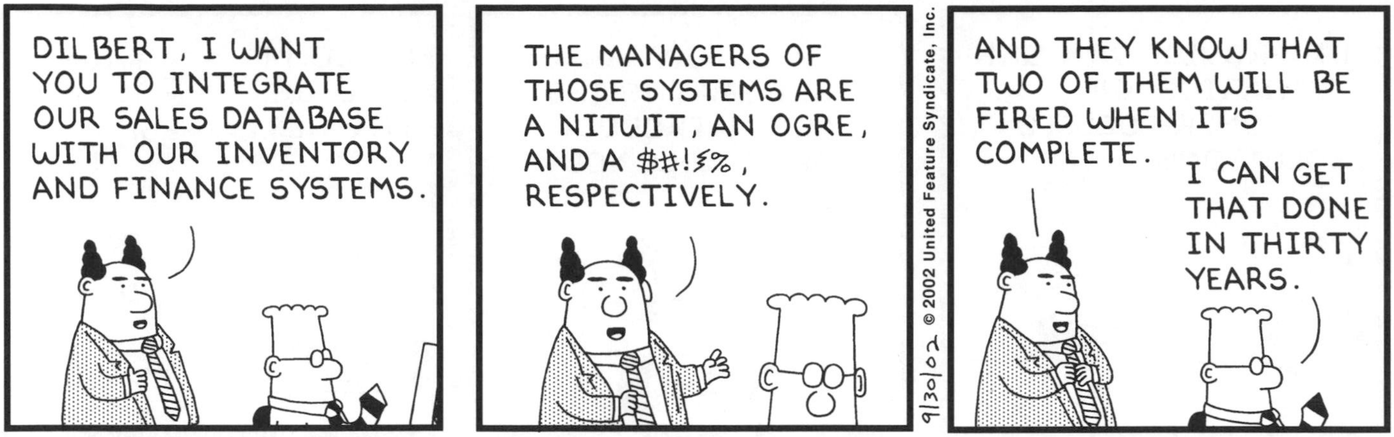
DILBERT, I WANT YOU TO INTEGRATE OUR SALES DATABASE WITH OUR INVENTORY AND FINANCE SYSTEMS.
THE MANAGERS OF THOSE SYSTEMS ARE A NITWIT, AN OGRE, AND A #$!$%, RESPECTIVELY.
9/30/02 © 2002 United Feature Syndicate, Inc.
AND THEY KNOW THAT TWO OF THEM WILL BE FIRED WHEN IT'S COMPLETE.
I CAN GET THAT DONE IN THIRTY YEARS.

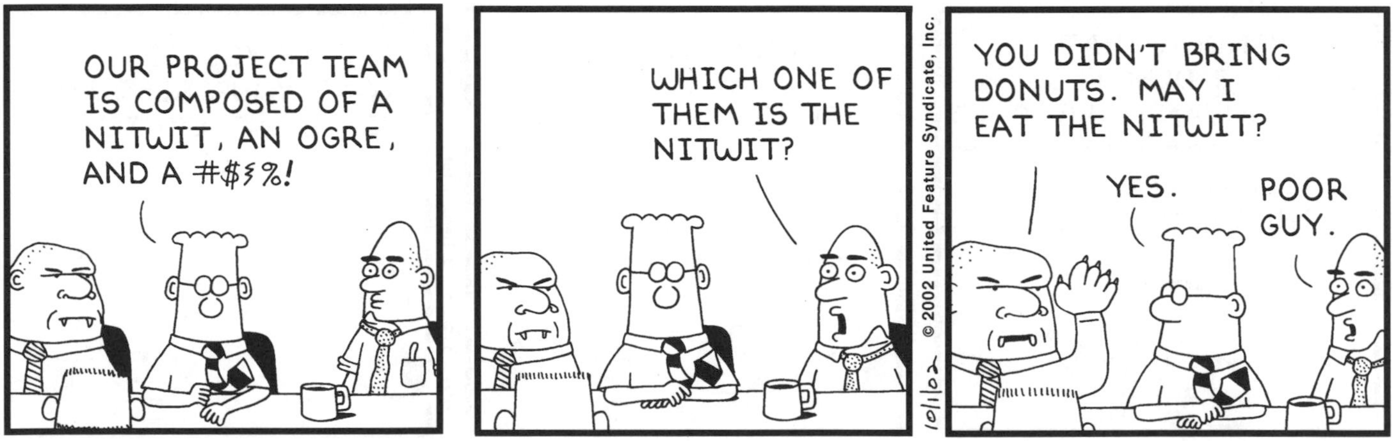
OUR PROJECT TEAM IS COMPOSED OF A NITWIT, AN OGRE, AND A #$$%!
WHICH ONE OF THEM IS THE NITWIT?
10/1/02 © 2002 United Feature Syndicate, Inc.
YOU DIDN'T BRING DONUTS. MAY I EAT THE NITWIT?
YES.
POOR GUY.

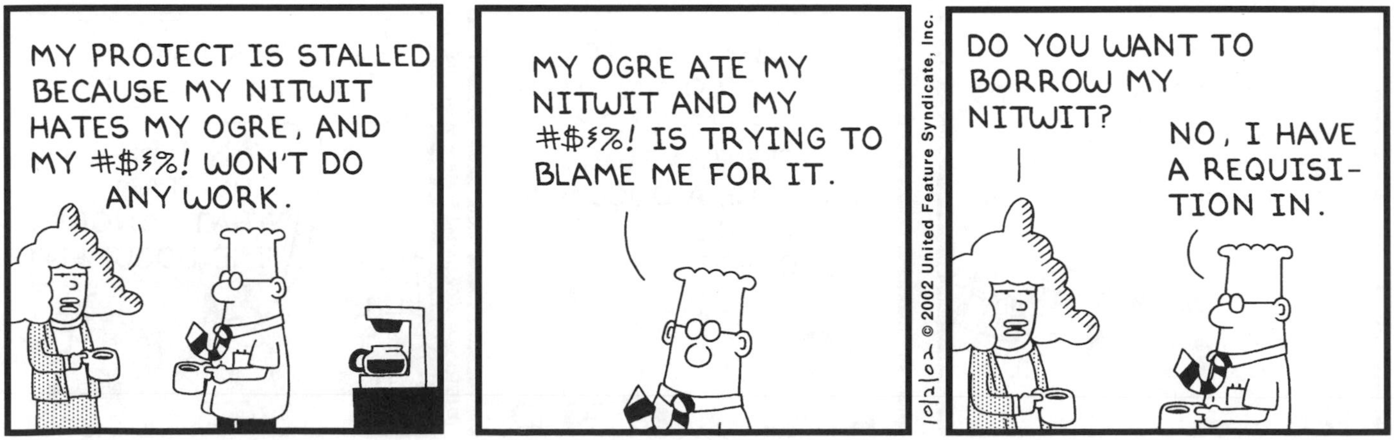
MY PROJECT IS STALLED BECAUSE MY NITWIT HATES MY OGRE, AND MY #$$%! WON'T DO ANY WORK.
MY OGRE ATE MY NITWIT AND MY #$$%! IS TRYING TO BLAME ME FOR IT.
10/2/02 © 2002 United Feature Syndicate, Inc.
DO YOU WANT TO BORROW MY NITWIT?
NO, I HAVE A REQUISITION IN.

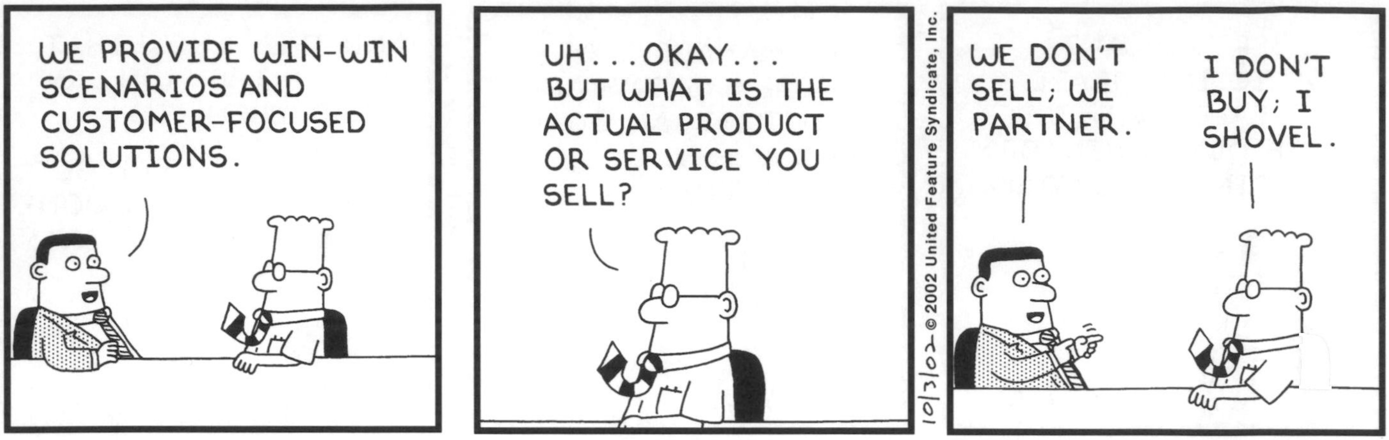
WE PROVIDE WIN-WIN SCENARIOS AND CUSTOMER-FOCUSED SOLUTIONS.
UH...OKAY... BUT WHAT IS THE ACTUAL PRODUCT OR SERVICE YOU SELL?
10/3/02 © 2002 United Feature Syndicate, Inc.
WE DON'T SELL; WE PARTNER.
I DON'T BUY; I SHOVEL.

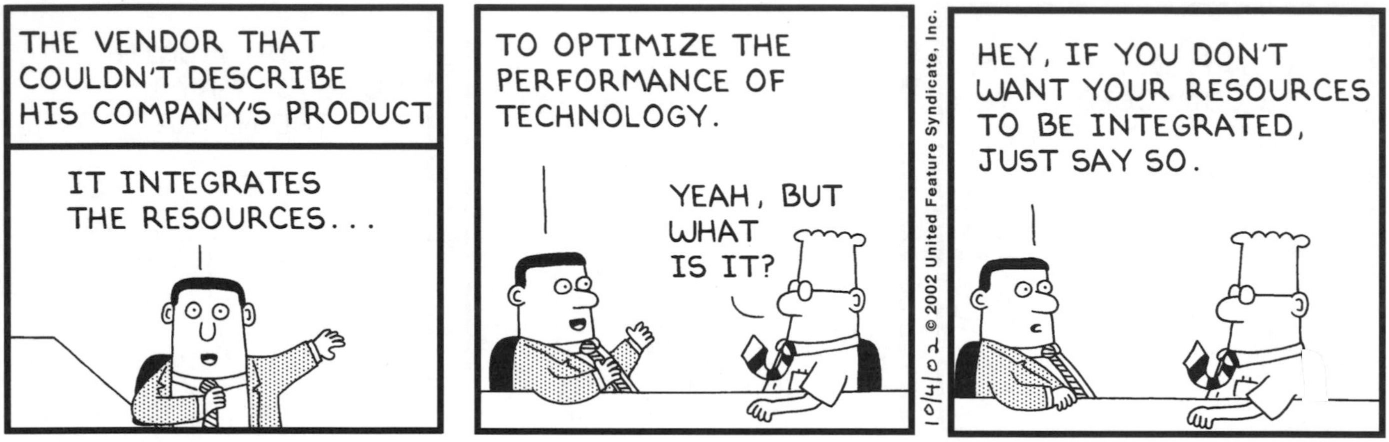
THE VENDOR THAT COULDN'T DESCRIBE HIS COMPANY'S PRODUCT
IT INTEGRATES THE RESOURCES...
TO OPTIMIZE THE PERFORMANCE OF TECHNOLOGY.
YEAH, BUT WHAT IS IT?
10/4/02 © 2002 United Feature Syndicate, Inc.
HEY, IF YOU DON'T WANT YOUR RESOURCES TO BE INTEGRATED, JUST SAY SO.

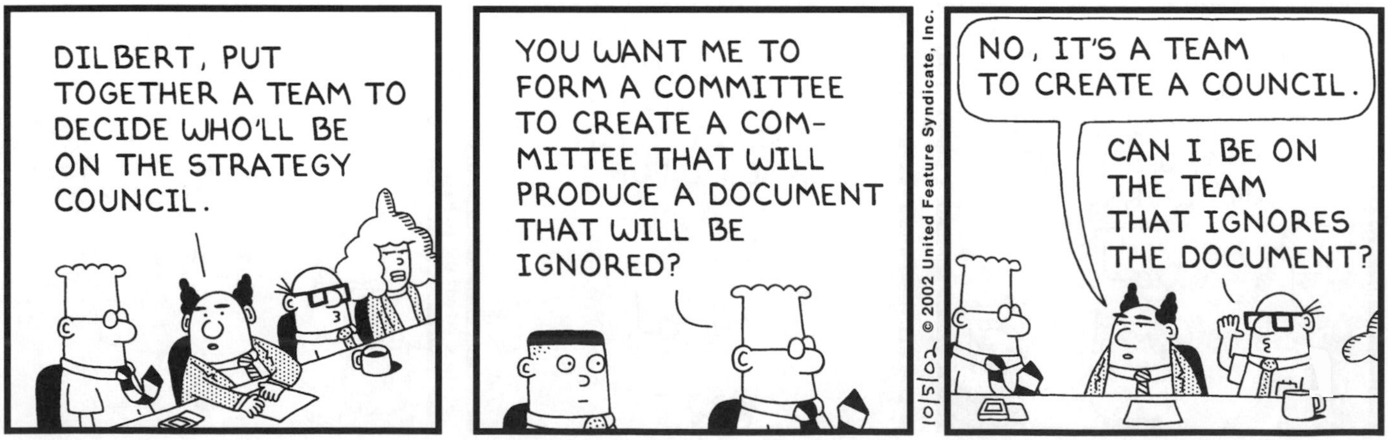
DILBERT, PUT TOGETHER A TEAM TO DECIDE WHO'LL BE ON THE STRATEGY COUNCIL.
YOU WANT ME TO FORM A COMMITTEE TO CREATE A COM-MITTEE THAT WILL PRODUCE A DOCUMENT THAT WILL BE IGNORED?
10/5/02 © 2002 United Feature Syndicate, Inc.
NO, IT'S A TEAM TO CREATE A COUNCIL.
CAN I BE ON THE TEAM THAT IGNORES THE DOCUMENT?

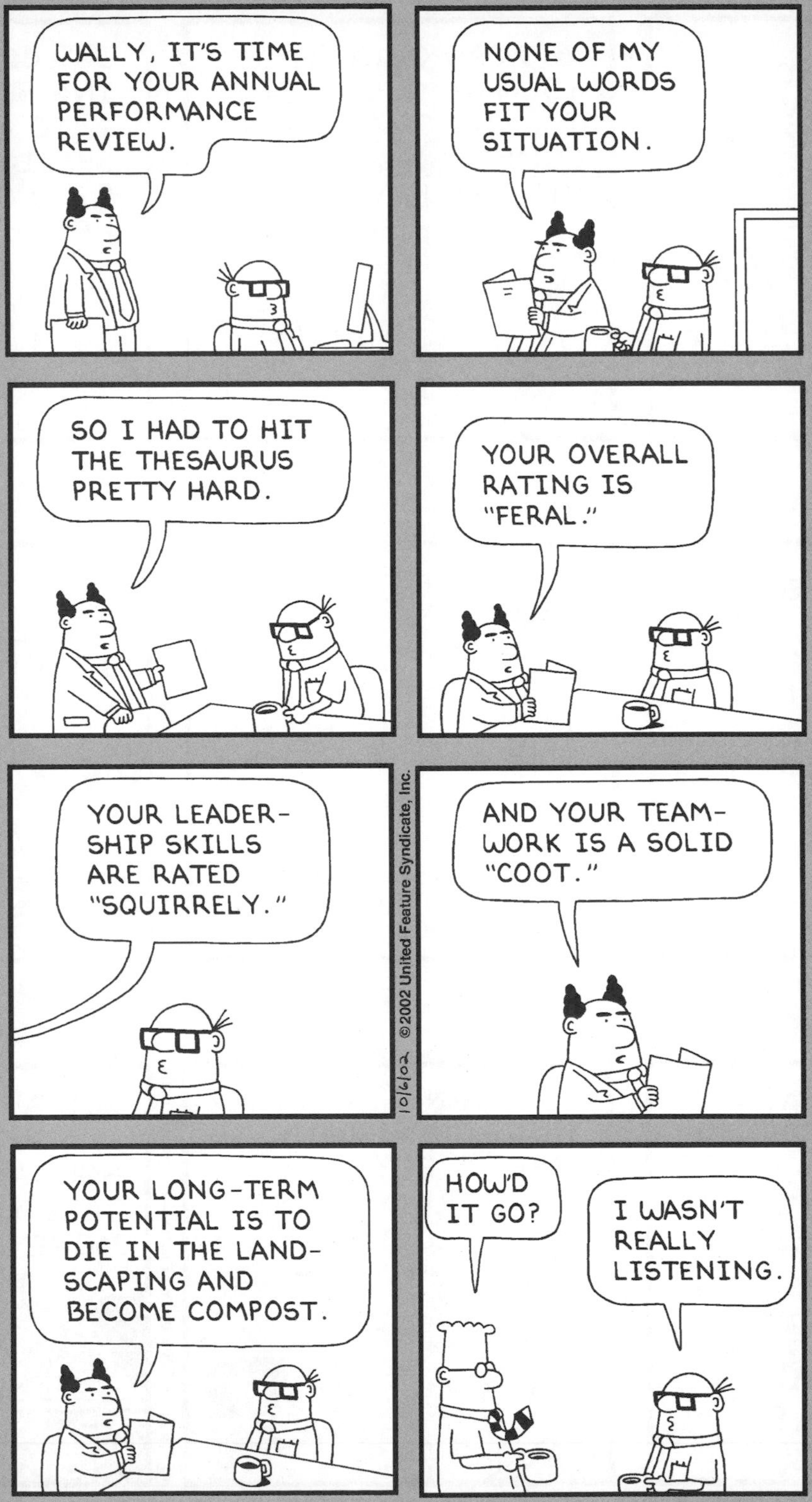
WALLY, IT'S TIME FOR YOUR ANNUAL PERFORMANCE REVIEW.
NONE OF MY USUAL WORDS FIT YOUR SITUATION.
SO I HAD TO HIT THE THESAURUS PRETTY HARD.
YOUR OVERALL RATING IS "FERAL."
YOUR LEADER-SHIP SKILLS ARE RATED "SQUIRRELY."
AND YOUR TEAM-WORK IS A SOLID "COOT."
YOUR LONG-TERM POTENTIAL IS TO DIE IN THE LAND-SCAPING AND BECOME COMPOST.
HOW'D IT GO?
I WASN'T REALLY LISTENING.
©2002 United Feature Syndicate, Inc.
10/6/02

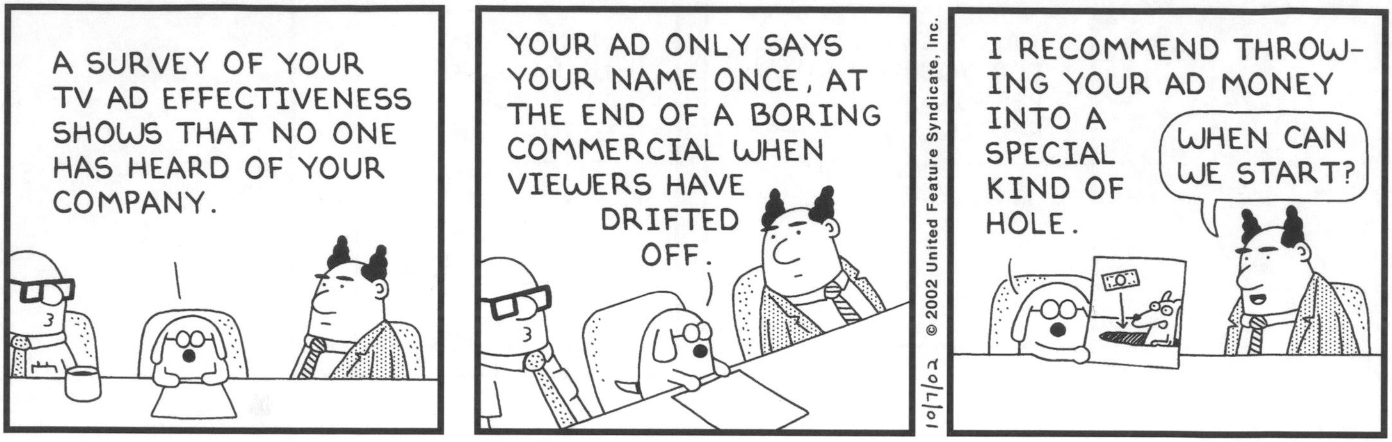
A SURVEY OF YOUR TV AD EFFECTIVENESS SHOWS THAT NO ONE HAS HEARD OF YOUR COMPANY.
YOUR AD ONLY SAYS YOUR NAME ONCE, AT THE END OF A BORING COMMERCIAL WHEN VIEWERS HAVE DRIFTED OFF.
10/7/02 © 2002 United Feature Syndicate, Inc.
I RECOMMEND THROWING YOUR AD MONEY INTO A SPECIAL KIND OF HOLE.
WHEN CAN WE START?

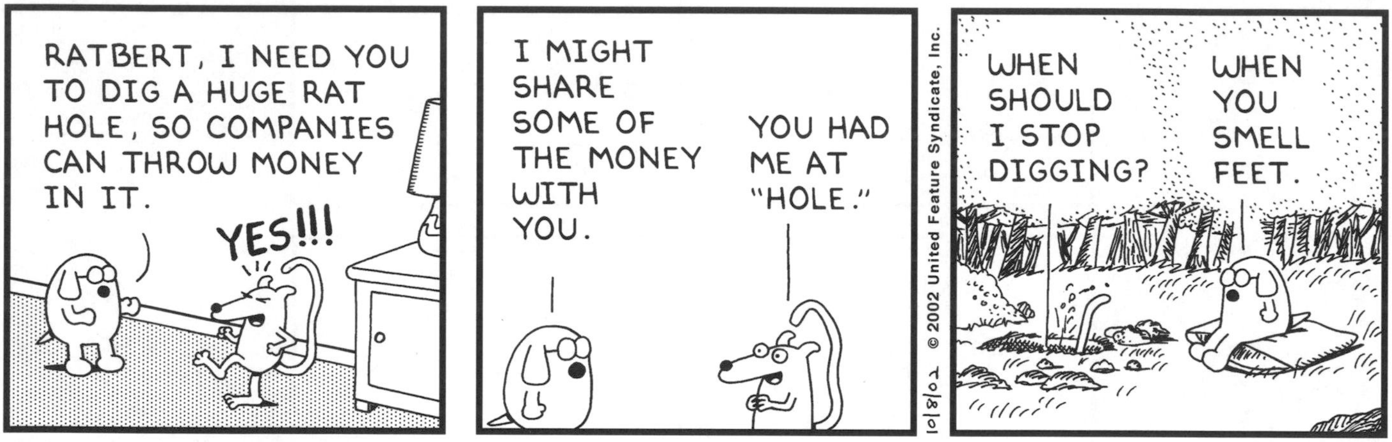
RATBERT, I NEED YOU TO DIG A HUGE RAT HOLE, SO COMPANIES CAN THROW MONEY IN IT.
YES!!!
I MIGHT SHARE SOME OF THE MONEY WITH YOU.
YOU HAD ME AT "HOLE."
10/8/02 © 2002 United Feature Syndicate, Inc.
WHEN SHOULD I STOP DIGGING?
WHEN YOU SMELL FEET.

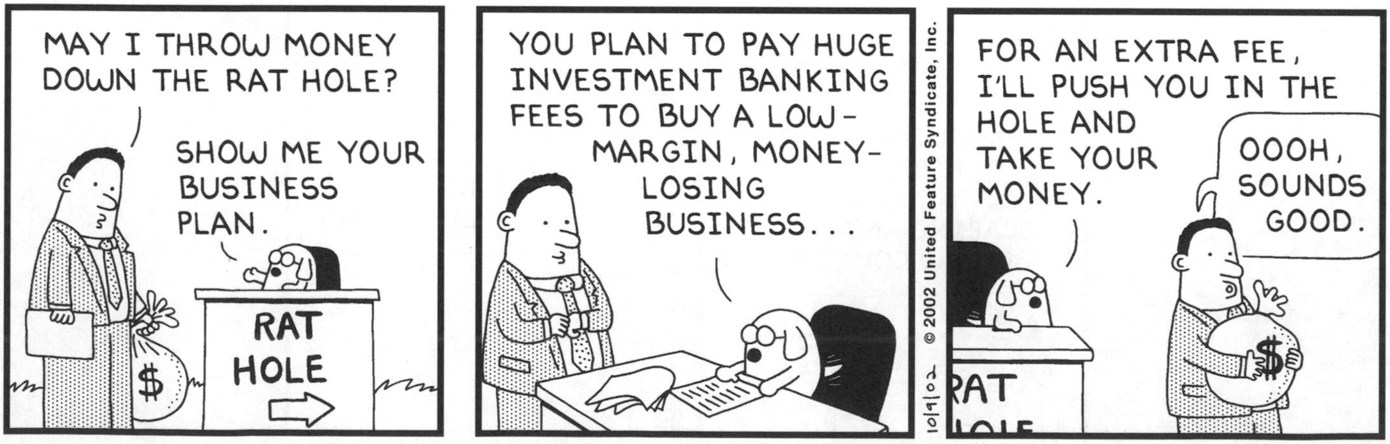
MAY I THROW MONEY DOWN THE RAT HOLE?
SHOW ME YOUR BUSINESS PLAN.
RAT HOLE
YOU PLAN TO PAY HUGE INVESTMENT BANKING FEES TO BUY A LOW-MARGIN, MONEY-LOSING BUSINESS...
10/9/02 © 2002 United Feature Syndicate, Inc.
FOR AN EXTRA FEE, I'LL PUSH YOU IN THE HOLE AND TAKE YOUR MONEY.
OOOH, SOUNDS GOOD.

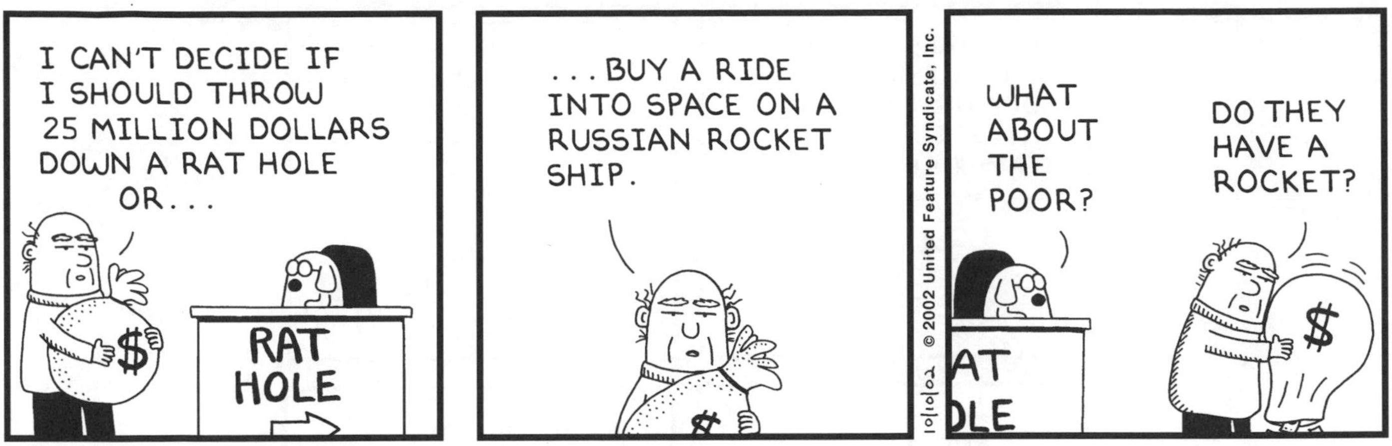
I CAN'T DECIDE IF I SHOULD THROW 25 MILLION DOLLARS DOWN A RAT HOLE OR...
RAT HOLE
...BUY A RIDE INTO SPACE ON A RUSSIAN ROCKET SHIP.
10/10/02 © 2002 United Feature Syndicate, Inc.
WHAT ABOUT THE POOR?
DO THEY HAVE A ROCKET?

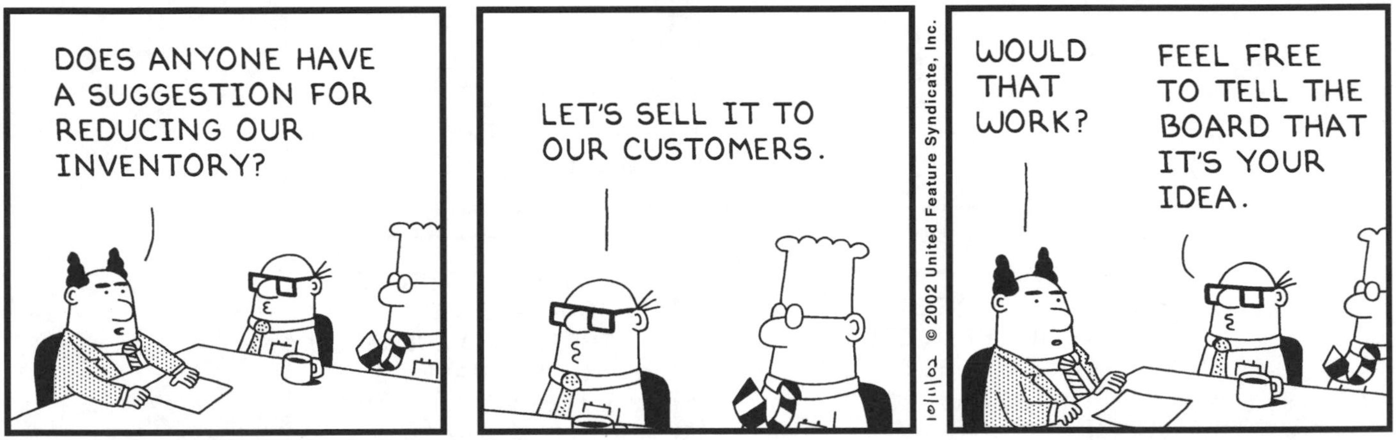
DOES ANYONE HAVE A SUGGESTION FOR REDUCING OUR INVENTORY?
LET'S SELL IT TO OUR CUSTOMERS.
10/11/02 © 2002 United Feature Syndicate, Inc.
WOULD THAT WORK?
FEEL FREE TO TELL THE BOARD THAT IT'S YOUR IDEA.

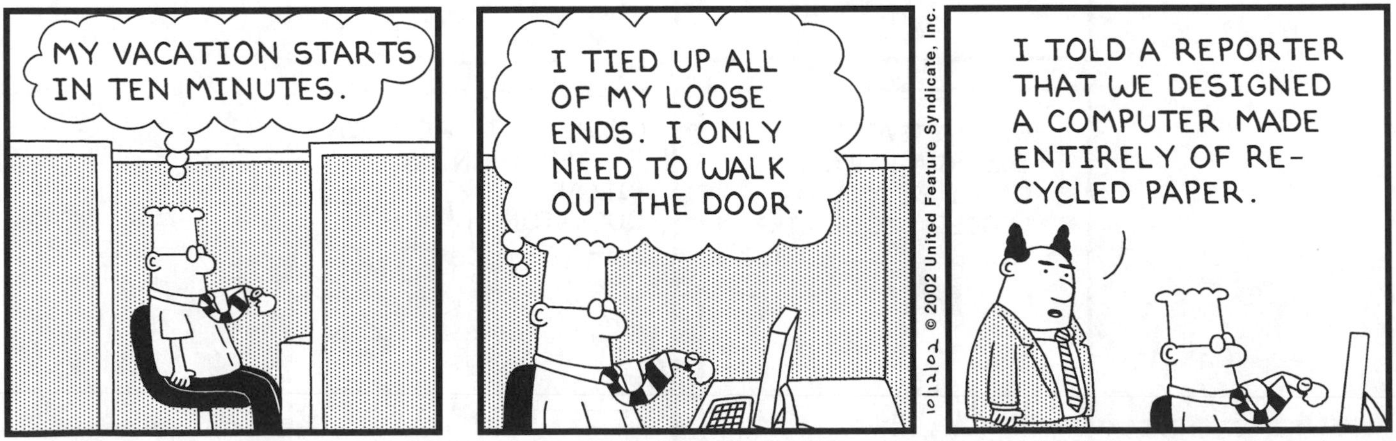
MY VACATION STARTS IN TEN MINUTES.
I TIED UP ALL OF MY LOOSE ENDS. I ONLY NEED TO WALK OUT THE DOOR.
10/12/02 © 2002 United Feature Syndicate, Inc.
I TOLD A REPORTER THAT WE DESIGNED A COMPUTER MADE ENTIRELY OF RE-CYCLED PAPER.

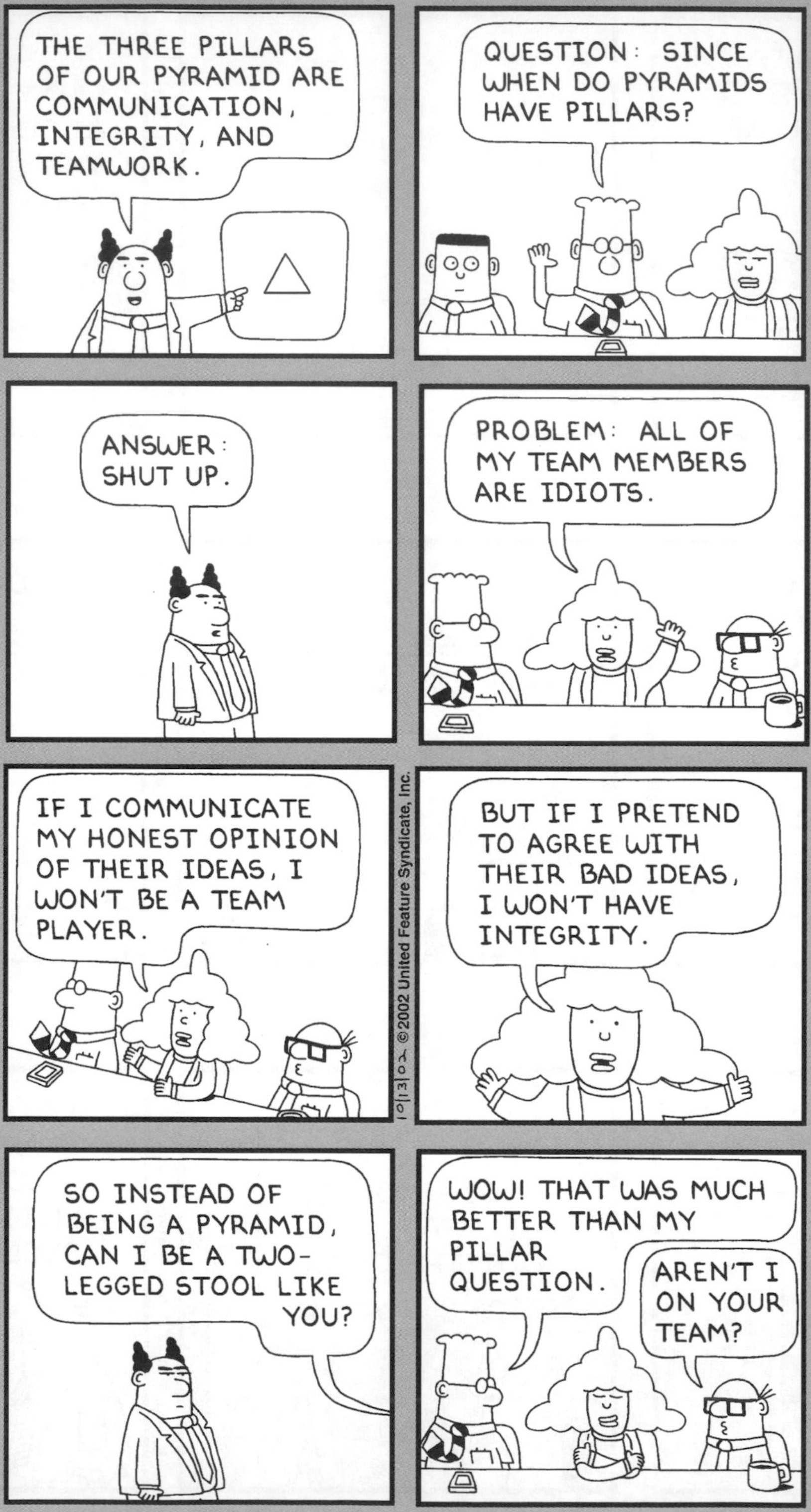
THE THREE PILLARS OF OUR PYRAMID ARE COMMUNICATION, INTEGRITY, AND TEAMWORK.
QUESTION: SINCE WHEN DO PYRAMIDS HAVE PILLARS?
ANSWER: SHUT UP.
PROBLEM: ALL OF MY TEAM MEMBERS ARE IDIOTS.
IF I COMMUNICATE MY HONEST OPINION OF THEIR IDEAS, I WON'T BE A TEAM PLAYER.
BUT IF I PRETEND TO AGREE WITH THEIR BAD IDEAS, I WON'T HAVE INTEGRITY.
SO INSTEAD OF BEING A PYRAMID, CAN I BE A TWO-LEGGED STOOL LIKE YOU?
WOW! THAT WAS MUCH BETTER THAN MY PILLAR QUESTION.
AREN'T I ON YOUR TEAM?
10/13/02 ©2002 United Feature Syndicate, Inc.

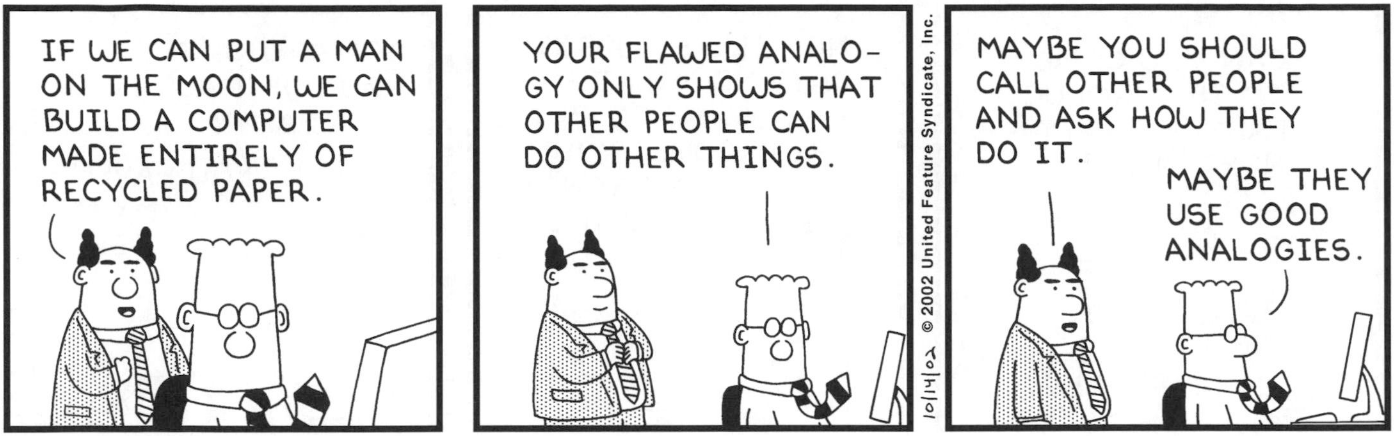
IF WE CAN PUT A MAN ON THE MOON, WE CAN BUILD A COMPUTER MADE ENTIRELY OF RECYCLED PAPER.
YOUR FLAWED ANALO-GY ONLY SHOWS THAT OTHER PEOPLE CAN DO OTHER THINGS.
10/14/02 © 2002 United Feature Syndicate, Inc.
MAYBE YOU SHOULD CALL OTHER PEOPLE AND ASK HOW THEY DO IT.
MAYBE THEY USE GOOD ANALOGIES.

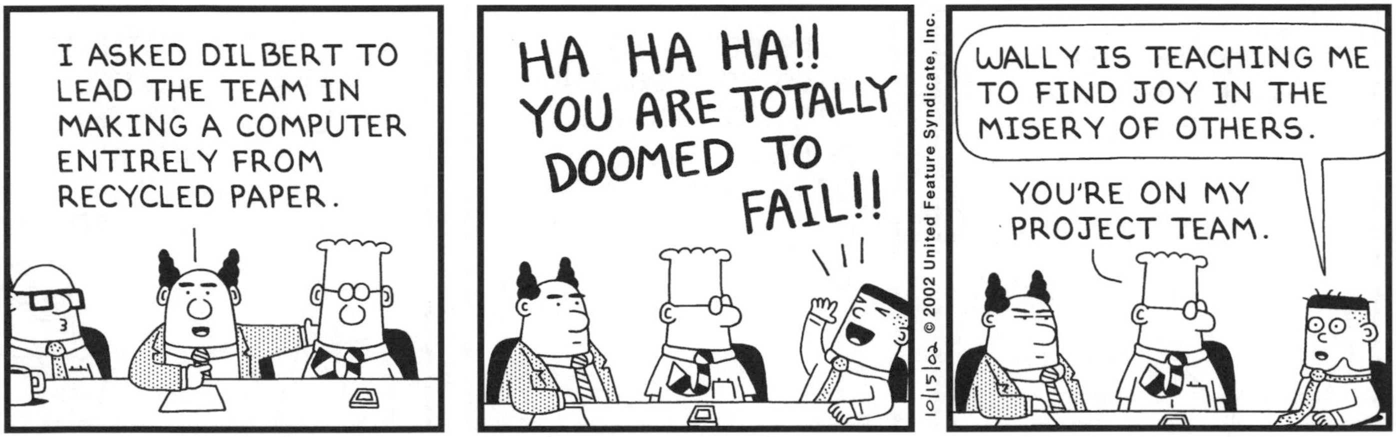
I ASKED DILBERT TO LEAD THE TEAM IN MAKING A COMPUTER ENTIRELY FROM RECYCLED PAPER.
HA HA HA!! YOU ARE TOTALLY DOOMED TO FAIL!!
10/15/02 © 2002 United Feature Syndicate, Inc.
WALLY IS TEACHING ME TO FIND JOY IN THE MISERY OF OTHERS.
YOU'RE ON MY PROJECT TEAM.

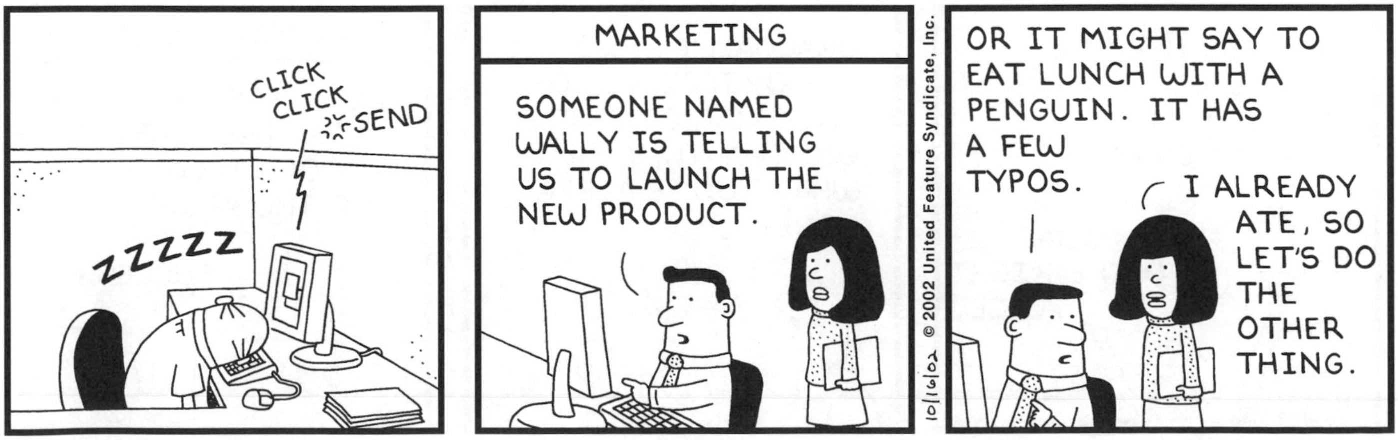
CLICK CLICK
SEND
ZZZZZ
MARKETING
SOMEONE NAMED WALLY IS TELLING US TO LAUNCH THE NEW PRODUCT.
10/16/02 © 2002 United Feature Syndicate, Inc.
OR IT MIGHT SAY TO EAT LUNCH WITH A PENGUIN. IT HAS A FEW TYPOS.
I ALREADY ATE, SO LET'S DO THE OTHER THING.

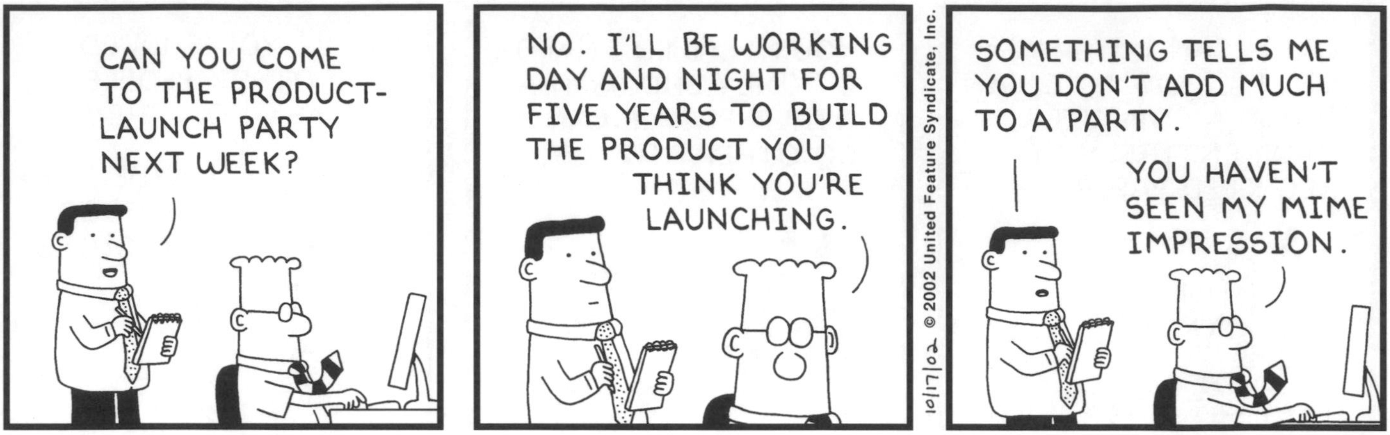
CAN YOU COME TO THE PRODUCT-LAUNCH PARTY NEXT WEEK?
NO. I'LL BE WORKING DAY AND NIGHT FOR FIVE YEARS TO BUILD THE PRODUCT YOU THINK YOU'RE LAUNCHING.
10/17/02 © 2002 United Feature Syndicate, Inc.
SOMETHING TELLS ME YOU DON'T ADD MUCH TO A PARTY.
YOU HAVEN'T SEEN MY MIME IMPRESSION.

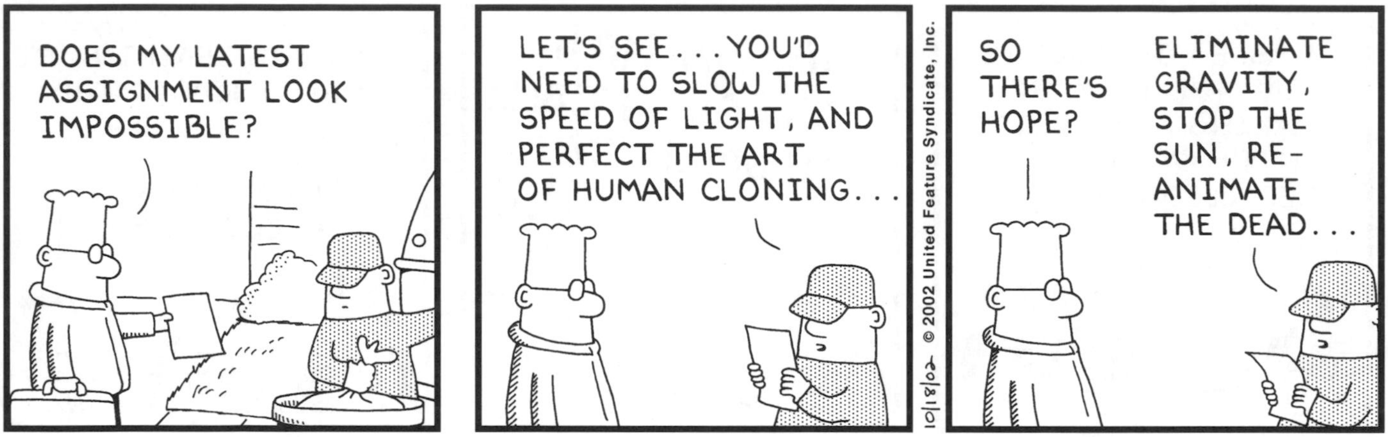
DOES MY LATEST ASSIGNMENT LOOK IMPOSSIBLE?
LET'S SEE... YOU'D NEED TO SLOW THE SPEED OF LIGHT, AND PERFECT THE ART OF HUMAN CLONING...
10/18/02 © 2002 United Feature Syndicate, Inc.
SO THERE'S HOPE?
ELIMINATE GRAVITY, STOP THE SUN, RE-ANIMATE THE DEAD...

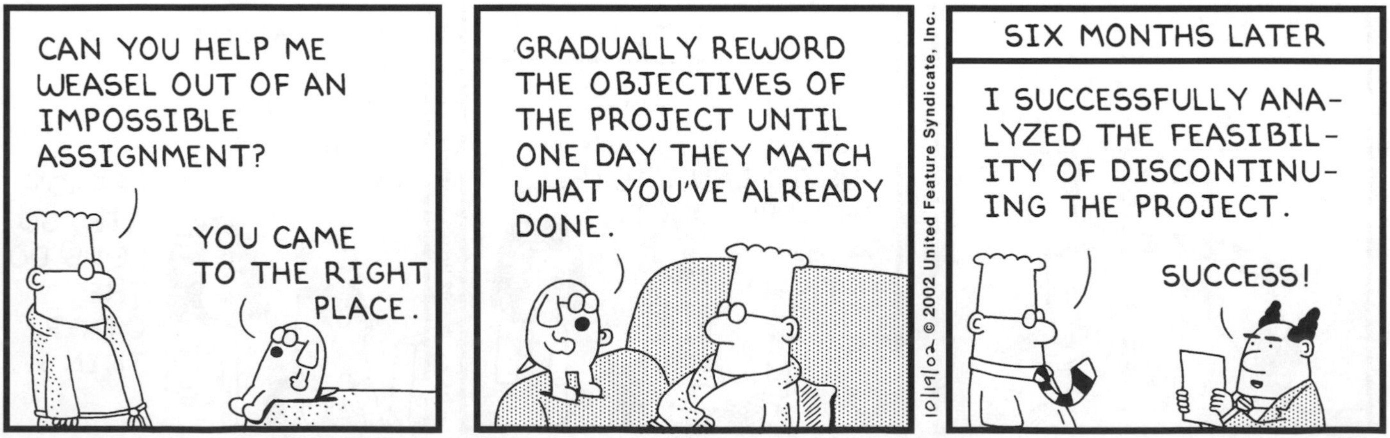
CAN YOU HELP ME WEASEL OUT OF AN IMPOSSIBLE ASSIGNMENT?
YOU CAME TO THE RIGHT PLACE.
GRADUALLY REWORD THE OBJECTIVES OF THE PROJECT UNTIL ONE DAY THEY MATCH WHAT YOU'VE ALREADY DONE.
10/19/02 © 2002 United Feature Syndicate, Inc.
SIX MONTHS LATER
I SUCCESSFULLY ANALYZED THE FEASIBILITY OF DISCONTINUING THE PROJECT.
SUCCESS!

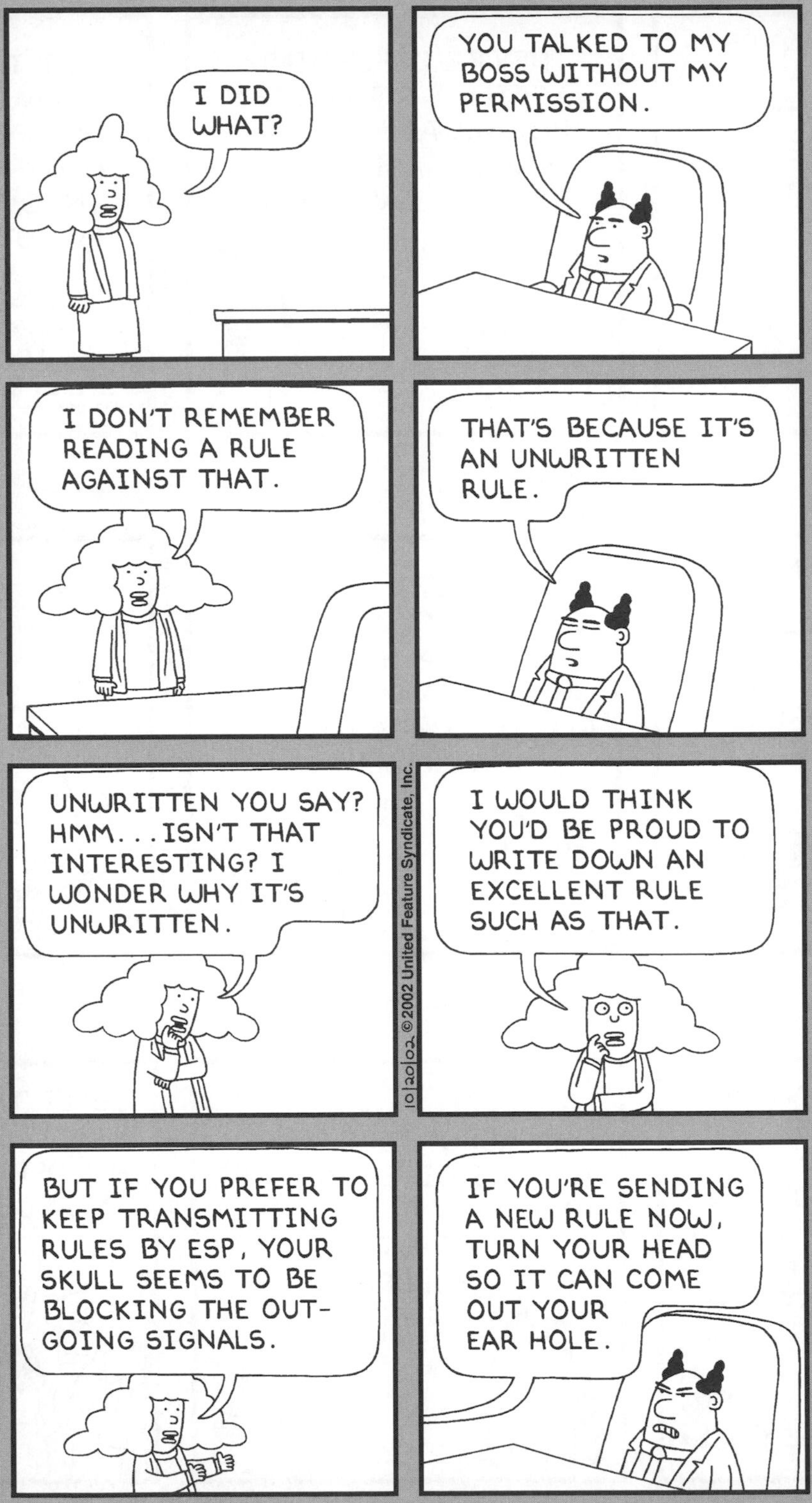
I DID WHAT?
YOU TALKED TO MY BOSS WITHOUT MY PERMISSION.
I DON'T REMEMBER READING A RULE AGAINST THAT.
THAT'S BECAUSE IT'S AN UNWRITTEN RULE.
UNWRITTEN YOU SAY? HMM. . . ISN'T THAT INTERESTING? I WONDER WHY IT'S UNWRITTEN.
I WOULD THINK YOU'D BE PROUD TO WRITE DOWN AN EXCELLENT RULE SUCH AS THAT.
BUT IF YOU PREFER TO KEEP TRANSMITTING RULES BY ESP, YOUR SKULL SEEMS TO BE BLOCKING THE OUT-GOING SIGNALS.
IF YOU'RE SENDING A NEW RULE NOW, TURN YOUR HEAD SO IT CAN COME OUT YOUR EAR HOLE.
10/20/02 ©2002 United Feature Syndicate, Inc.

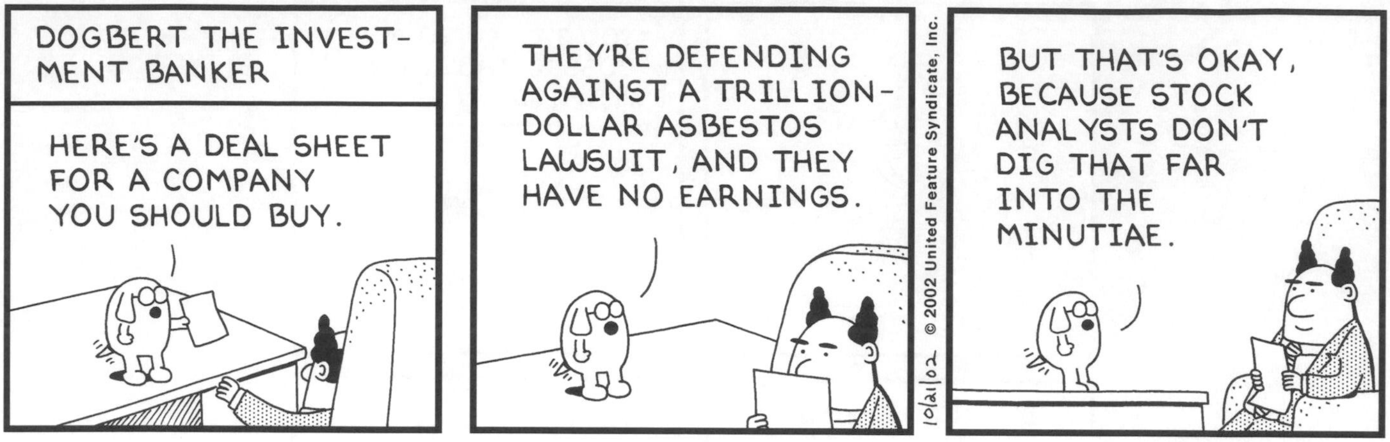
DOGBERT THE INVEST-MENT BANKER
HERE'S A DEAL SHEET FOR A COMPANY YOU SHOULD BUY.
THEY'RE DEFENDING AGAINST A TRILLION-DOLLAR ASBESTOS LAWSUIT, AND THEY HAVE NO EARNINGS.
10/21/02 © 2002 United Feature Syndicate, Inc.
BUT THAT'S OKAY, BECAUSE STOCK ANALYSTS DON'T DIG THAT FAR INTO THE MINUTIAE.

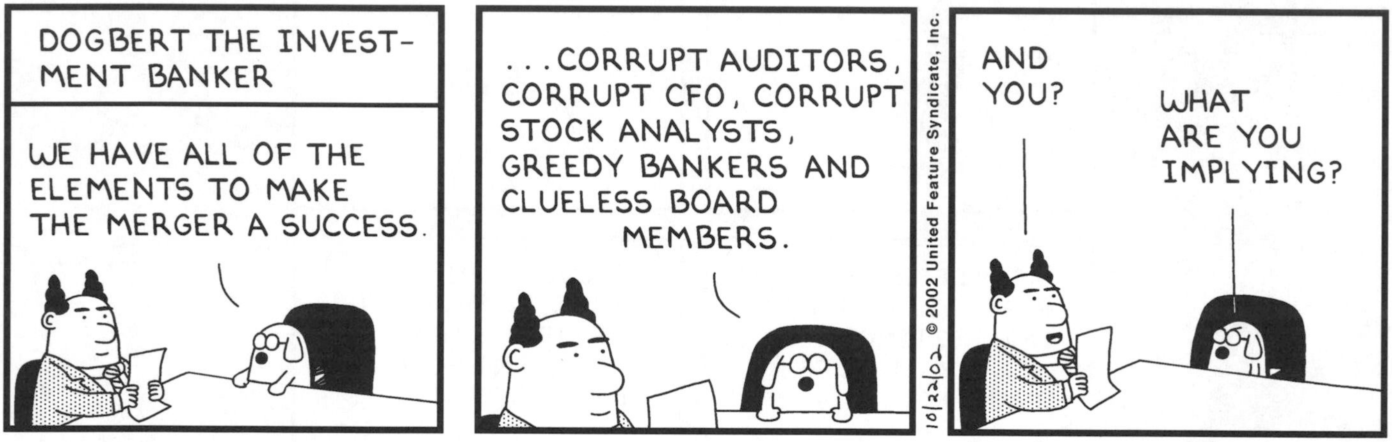
DOGBERT THE INVEST-MENT BANKER
WE HAVE ALL OF THE ELEMENTS TO MAKE THE MERGER A SUCCESS.
...CORRUPT AUDITORS, CORRUPT CFO, CORRUPT STOCK ANALYSTS, GREEDY BANKERS AND CLUELESS BOARD MEMBERS.
10/22/02 © 2002 United Feature Syndicate, Inc.
AND YOU?
WHAT ARE YOU IMPLYING?

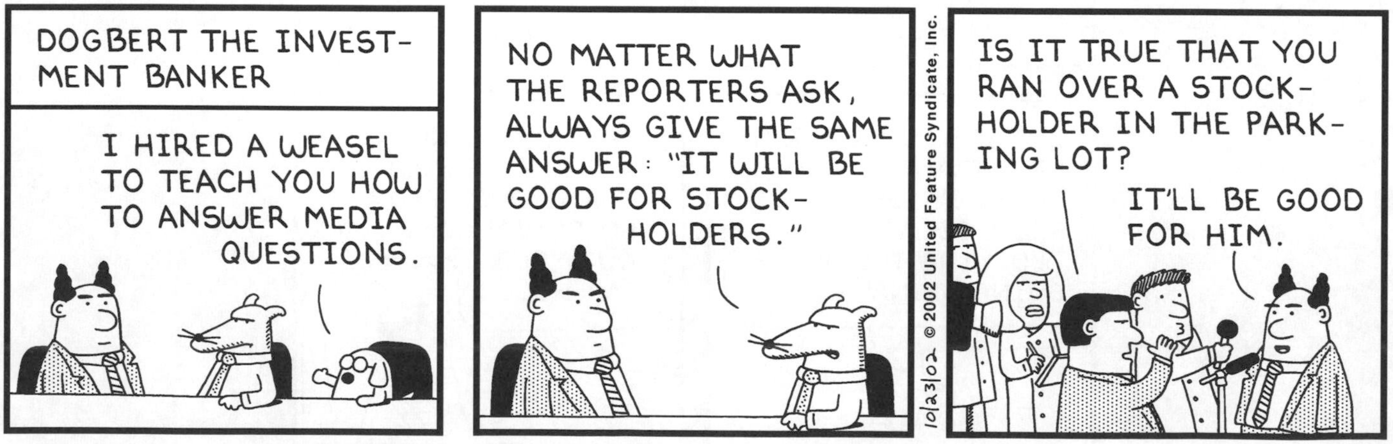
DOGBERT THE INVEST-MENT BANKER
I HIRED A WEASEL TO TEACH YOU HOW TO ANSWER MEDIA QUESTIONS.
NO MATTER WHAT THE REPORTERS ASK, ALWAYS GIVE THE SAME ANSWER: "IT WILL BE GOOD FOR STOCK-HOLDERS."
10/23/02 © 2002 United Feature Syndicate, Inc.
IS IT TRUE THAT YOU RAN OVER A STOCK-HOLDER IN THE PARK-ING LOT?
IT'LL BE GOOD FOR HIM.

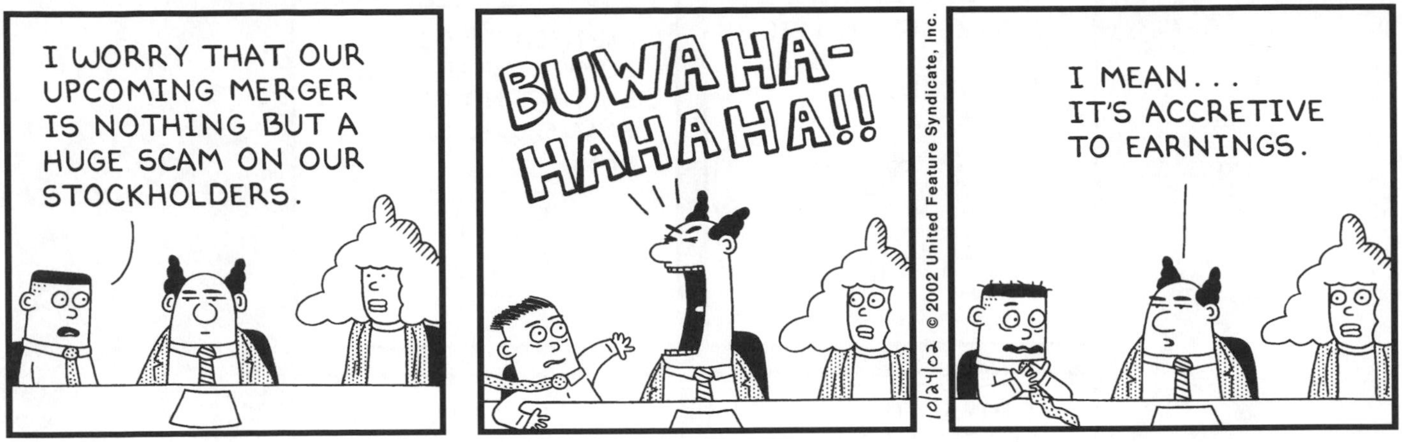
I WORRY THAT OUR UPCOMING MERGER IS NOTHING BUT A HUGE SCAM ON OUR STOCKHOLDERS.
BUWAHA-HAHAHA!!
10/24/02 © 2002 United Feature Syndicate, Inc.
I MEAN... IT'S ACCRETIVE TO EARNINGS.

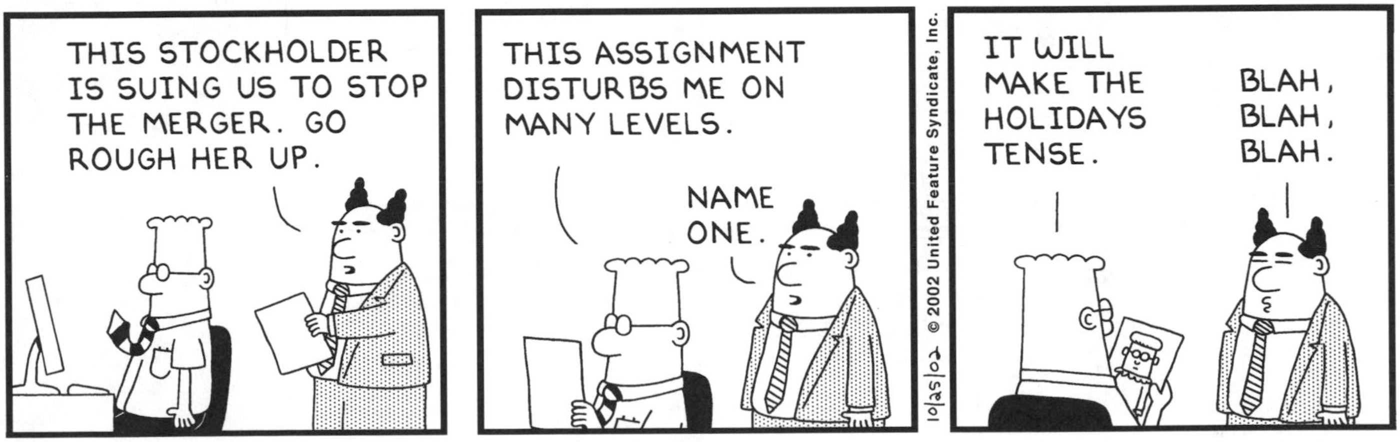
THIS STOCKHOLDER IS SUING US TO STOP THE MERGER. GO ROUGH HER UP.
THIS ASSIGNMENT DISTURBS ME ON MANY LEVELS.
NAME ONE.
10/25/02 © 2002 United Feature Syndicate, Inc.
IT WILL MAKE THE HOLIDAYS TENSE.
BLAH, BLAH, BLAH.

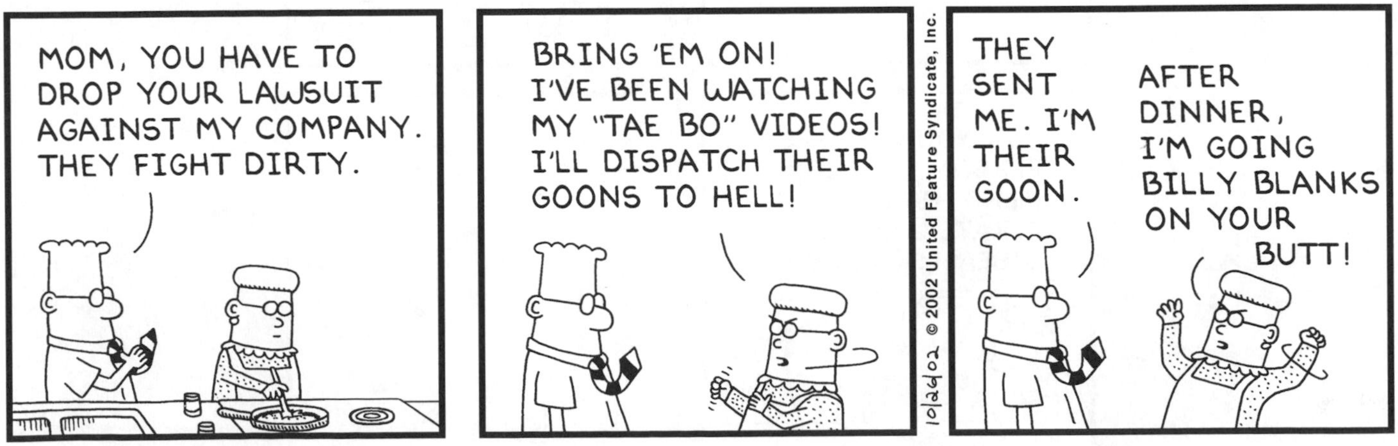
MOM, YOU HAVE TO DROP YOUR LAWSUIT AGAINST MY COMPANY. THEY FIGHT DIRTY.
BRING 'EM ON! I'VE BEEN WATCHING MY "TAE BO" VIDEOS! I'LL DISPATCH THEIR GOONS TO HELL!
10/26/02 © 2002 United Feature Syndicate, Inc.
THEY SENT ME. I'M THEIR GOON.
AFTER DINNER, I'M GOING BILLY BLANKS ON YOUR BUTT!

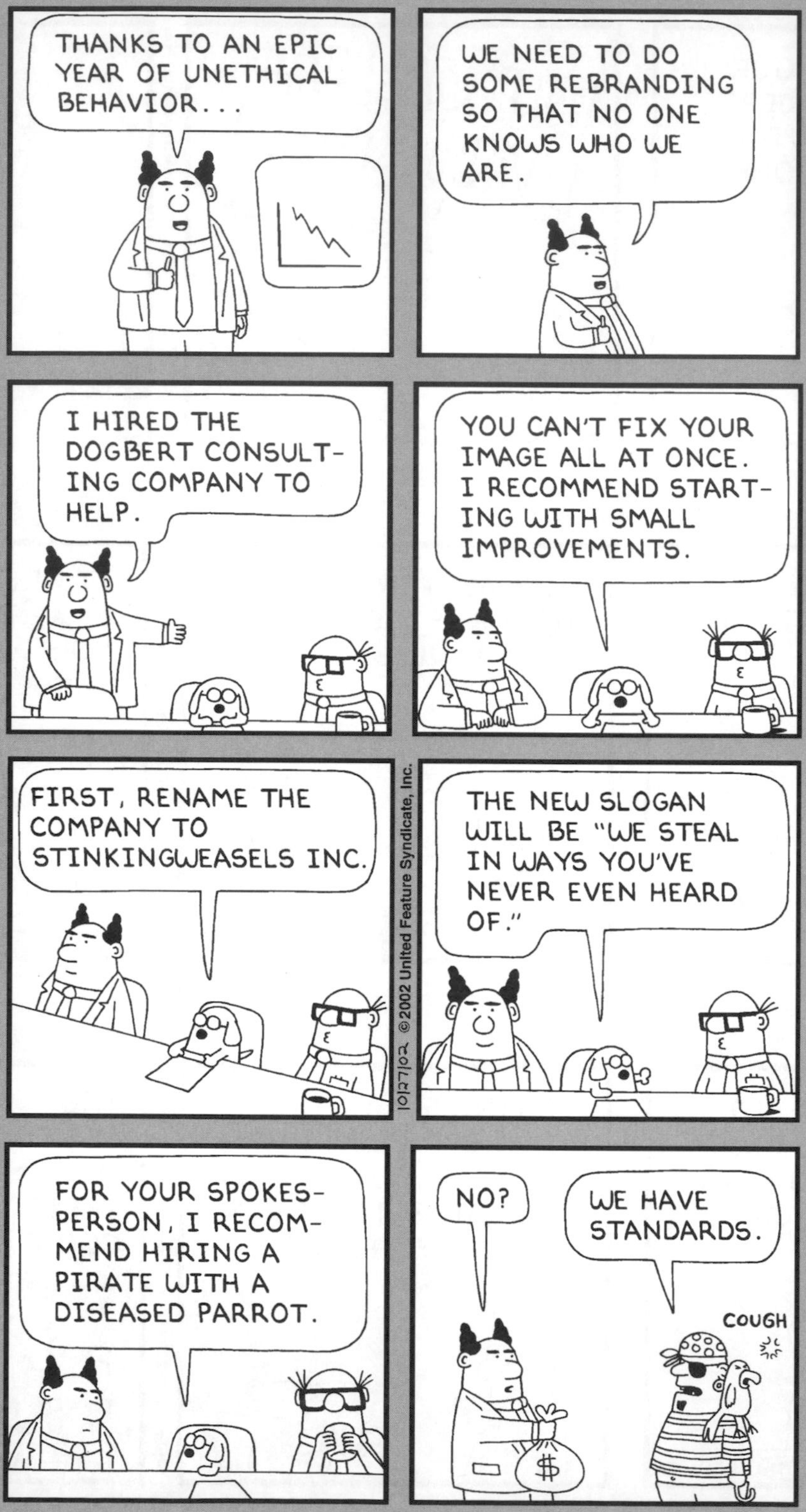
THANKS TO AN EPIC YEAR OF UNETHICAL BEHAVIOR...
WE NEED TO DO SOME REBRANDING SO THAT NO ONE KNOWS WHO WE ARE.
I HIRED THE DOGBERT CONSULTING COMPANY TO HELP.
YOU CAN'T FIX YOUR IMAGE ALL AT ONCE. I RECOMMEND STARTING WITH SMALL IMPROVEMENTS.
FIRST, RENAME THE COMPANY TO STINKINGWEASELS INC.
10/27/02 ©2002 United Feature Syndicate, Inc.
THE NEW SLOGAN WILL BE "WE STEAL IN WAYS YOU'VE NEVER EVEN HEARD OF."
FOR YOUR SPOKESPERSON, I RECOMMEND HIRING A PIRATE WITH A DISEASED PARROT.
NO?
WE HAVE STANDARDS.
COUGH
$

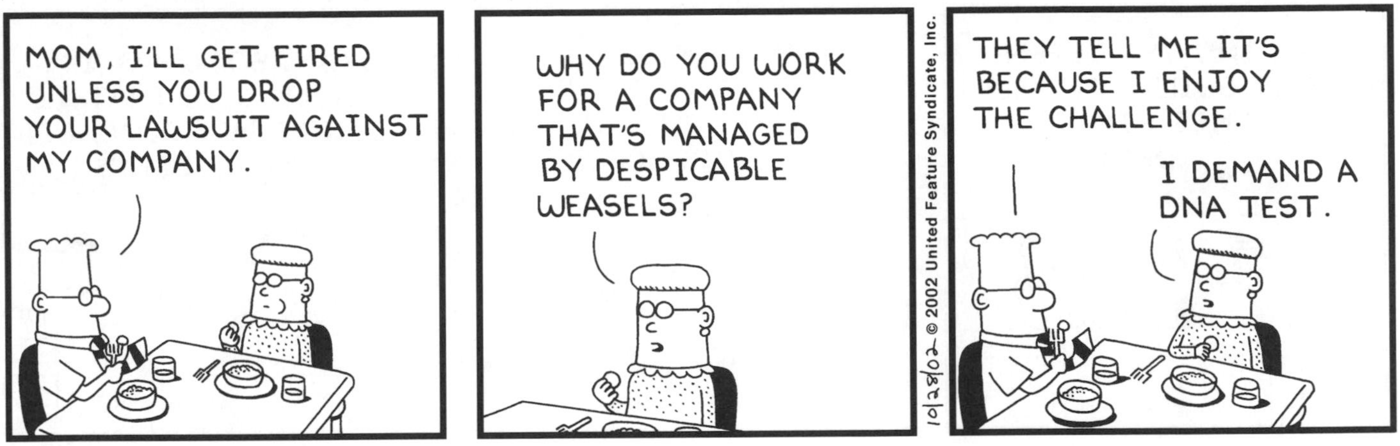
MOM, I'LL GET FIRED UNLESS YOU DROP YOUR LAWSUIT AGAINST MY COMPANY.
WHY DO YOU WORK FOR A COMPANY THAT'S MANAGED BY DESPICABLE WEASELS?
10/28/02 © 2002 United Feature Syndicate, Inc.
THEY TELL ME IT'S BECAUSE I ENJOY THE CHALLENGE.
I DEMAND A DNA TEST.

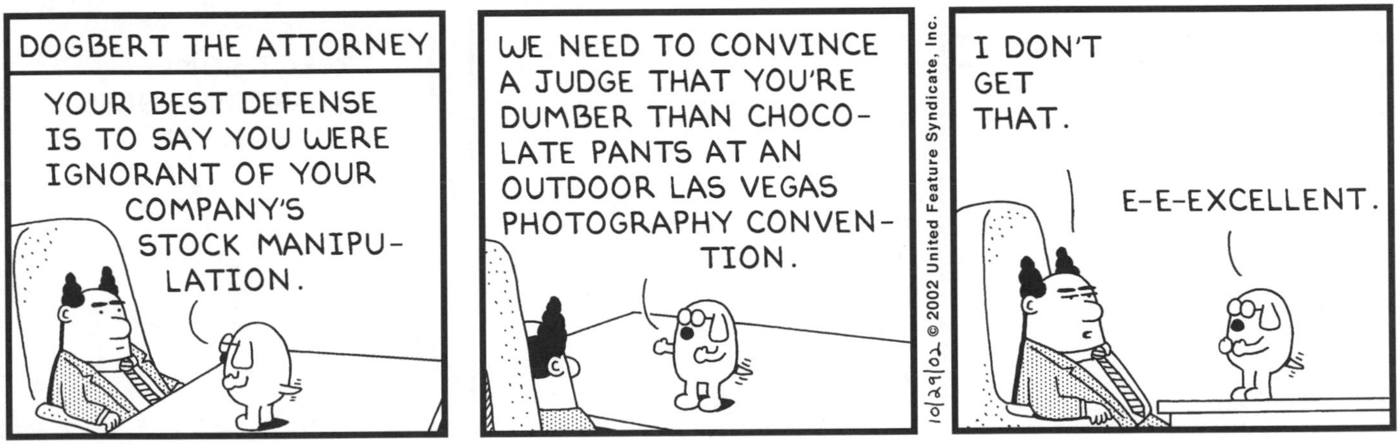
DOGBERT THE ATTORNEY
YOUR BEST DEFENSE IS TO SAY YOU WERE IGNORANT OF YOUR COMPANY'S STOCK MANIPU-LATION.
WE NEED TO CONVINCE A JUDGE THAT YOU'RE DUMBER THAN CHOCO-LATE PANTS AT AN OUTDOOR LAS VEGAS PHOTOGRAPHY CONVEN-TION.
10/29/02 © 2002 United Feature Syndicate, Inc.
I DON'T GET THAT.
E-E-EXCELLENT.

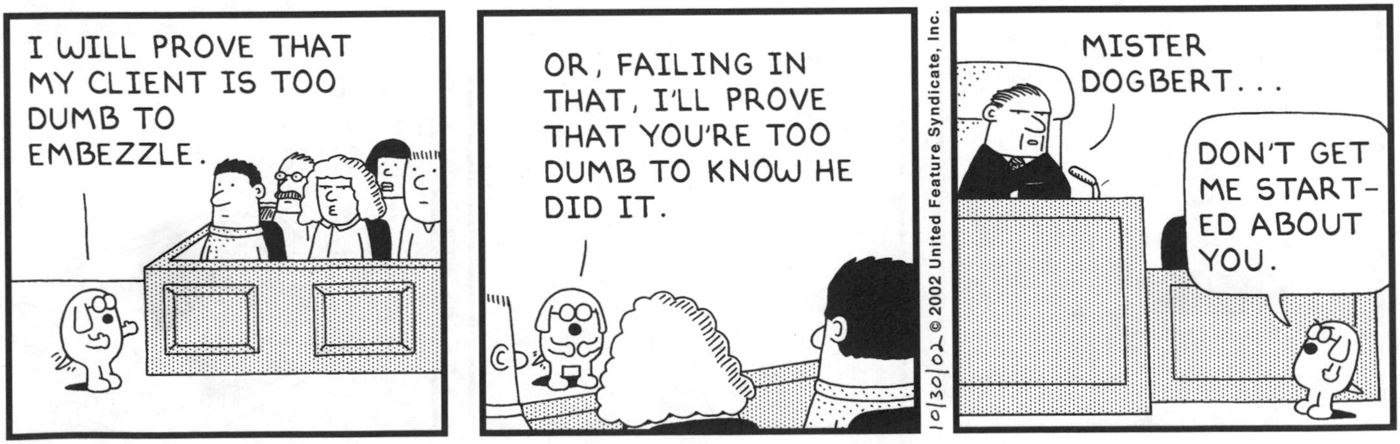
I WILL PROVE THAT MY CLIENT IS TOO DUMB TO EMBEZZLE.
OR, FAILING IN THAT, I'LL PROVE THAT YOU'RE TOO DUMB TO KNOW HE DID IT.
10/30/02 © 2002 United Feature Syndicate, Inc.
MISTER DOGBERT...
DON'T GET ME START-ED ABOUT YOU.

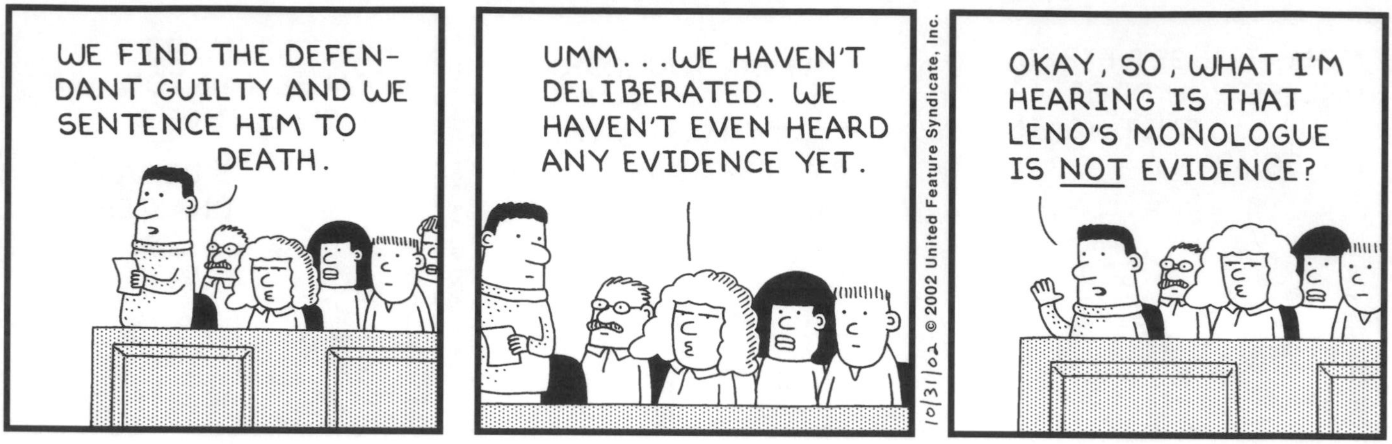
WE FIND THE DEFEN-
DANT GUILTY AND WE
SENTENCE HIM TO
DEATH.
UMM...WE HAVEN'T
DELIBERATED. WE
HAVEN'T EVEN HEARD
ANY EVIDENCE YET.
10/31/02 © 2002 United Feature Syndicate, Inc.
OKAY, SO, WHAT I'M
HEARING IS THAT
LENO'S MONOLOGUE
IS NOT EVIDENCE?

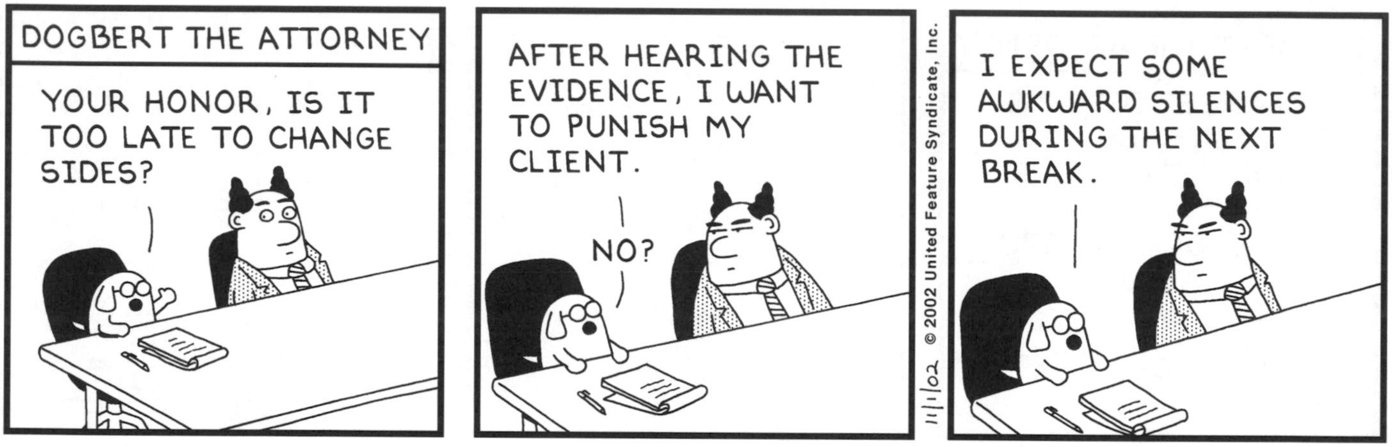
DOGBERT THE ATTORNEY
YOUR HONOR, IS IT
TOO LATE TO CHANGE
SIDES?
AFTER HEARING THE
EVIDENCE, I WANT
TO PUNISH MY
CLIENT.
NO?
11/1/02 © 2002 United Feature Syndicate, Inc.
I EXPECT SOME
AWKWARD SILENCES
DURING THE NEXT
BREAK.

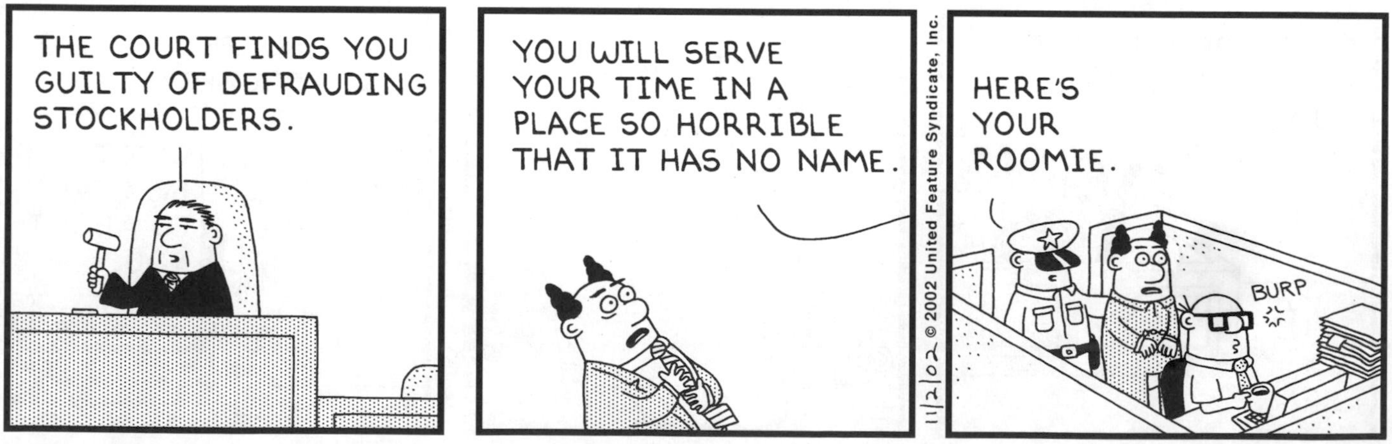
THE COURT FINDS YOU
GUILTY OF DEFRAUDING
STOCKHOLDERS.
YOU WILL SERVE
YOUR TIME IN A
PLACE SO HORRIBLE
THAT IT HAS NO NAME.
11/2/02 © 2002 United Feature Syndicate, Inc.
HERE'S
YOUR
ROOMIE.
BURP

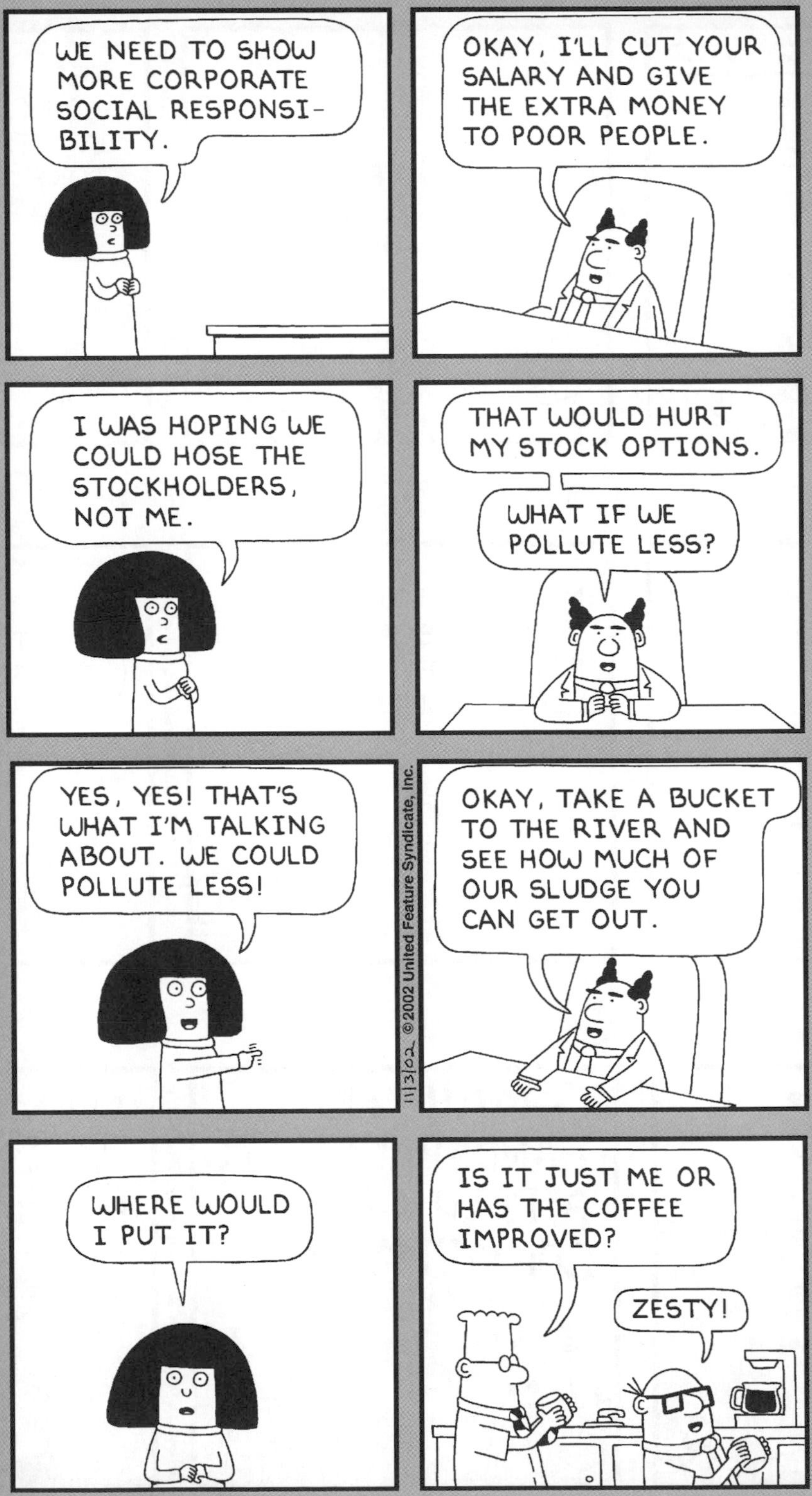
WE NEED TO SHOW MORE CORPORATE SOCIAL RESPONSI- BILITY.
OKAY, I'LL CUT YOUR SALARY AND GIVE THE EXTRA MONEY TO POOR PEOPLE.
I WAS HOPING WE COULD HOSE THE STOCKHOLDERS, NOT ME.
THAT WOULD HURT MY STOCK OPTIONS.
WHAT IF WE POLLUTE LESS?
YES, YES! THAT'S WHAT I'M TALKING ABOUT. WE COULD POLLUTE LESS!
OKAY, TAKE A BUCKET TO THE RIVER AND SEE HOW MUCH OF OUR SLUDGE YOU CAN GET OUT.
WHERE WOULD I PUT IT?
IS IT JUST ME OR HAS THE COFFEE IMPROVED?
ZESTY!
11/3/02 ©2002 United Feature Syndicate, Inc.

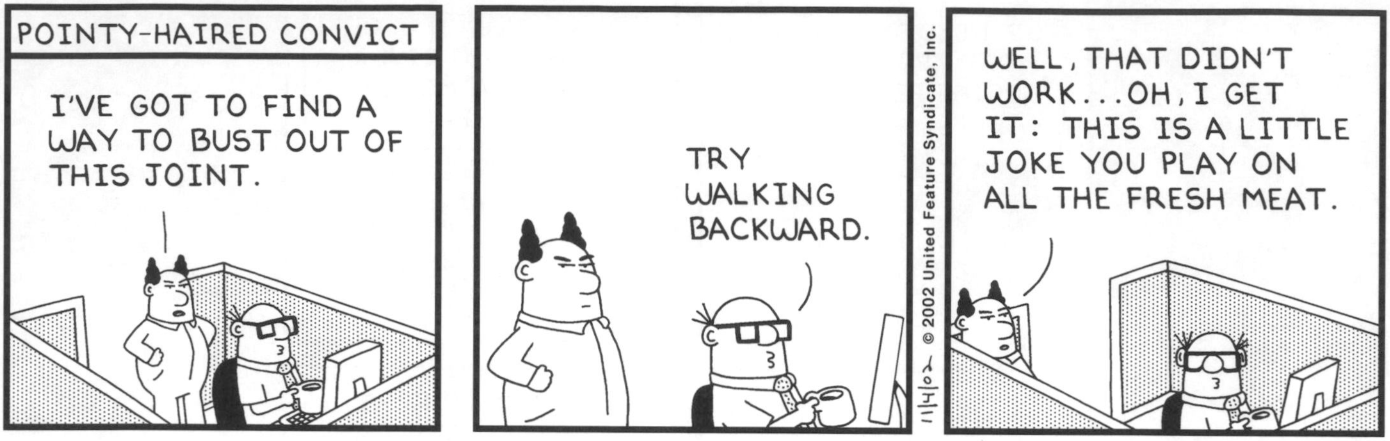
POINTY-HAIRED CONVICT
I'VE GOT TO FIND A WAY TO BUST OUT OF THIS JOINT.
TRY WALKING BACKWARD.
11/4/02 © 2002 United Feature Syndicate, Inc.
WELL, THAT DIDN'T WORK...OH, I GET IT: THIS IS A LITTLE JOKE YOU PLAY ON ALL THE FRESH MEAT.

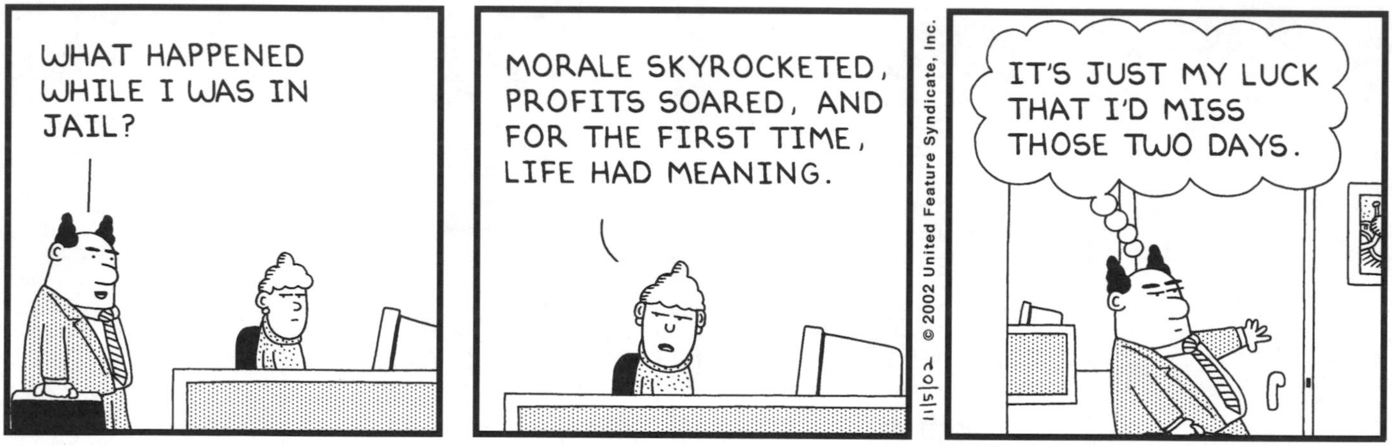
WHAT HAPPENED WHILE I WAS IN JAIL?
MORALE SKYROCKETED, PROFITS SOARED, AND FOR THE FIRST TIME, LIFE HAD MEANING.
11/5/02 © 2002 United Feature Syndicate, Inc.
IT'S JUST MY LUCK THAT I'D MISS THOSE TWO DAYS.

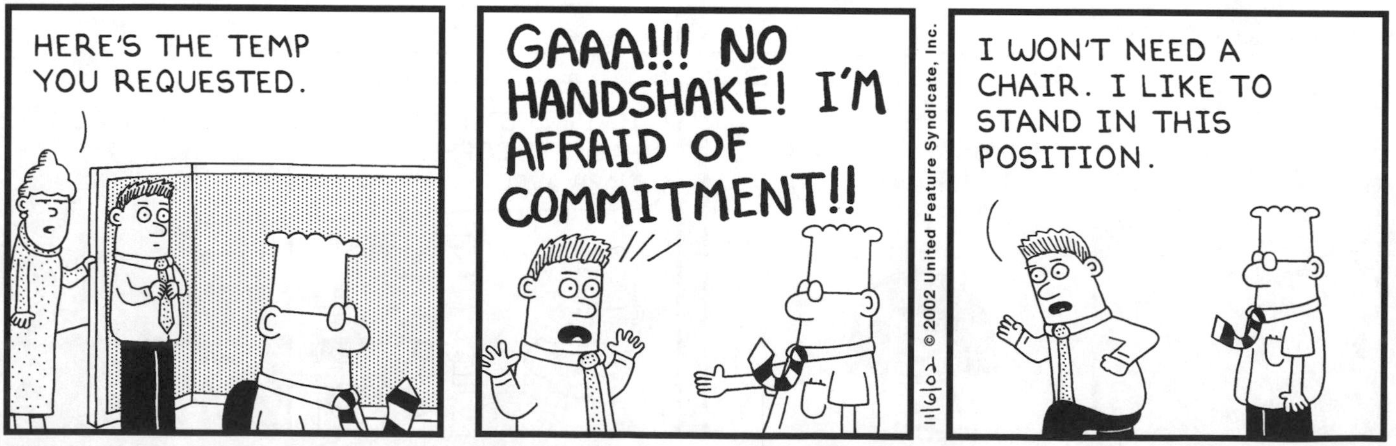
HERE'S THE TEMP YOU REQUESTED.
GAAA!!! NO HANDSHAKE! I'M AFRAID OF COMMITMENT!!
11/6/02 © 2002 United Feature Syndicate, Inc.
I WON'T NEED A CHAIR. I LIKE TO STAND IN THIS POSITION.

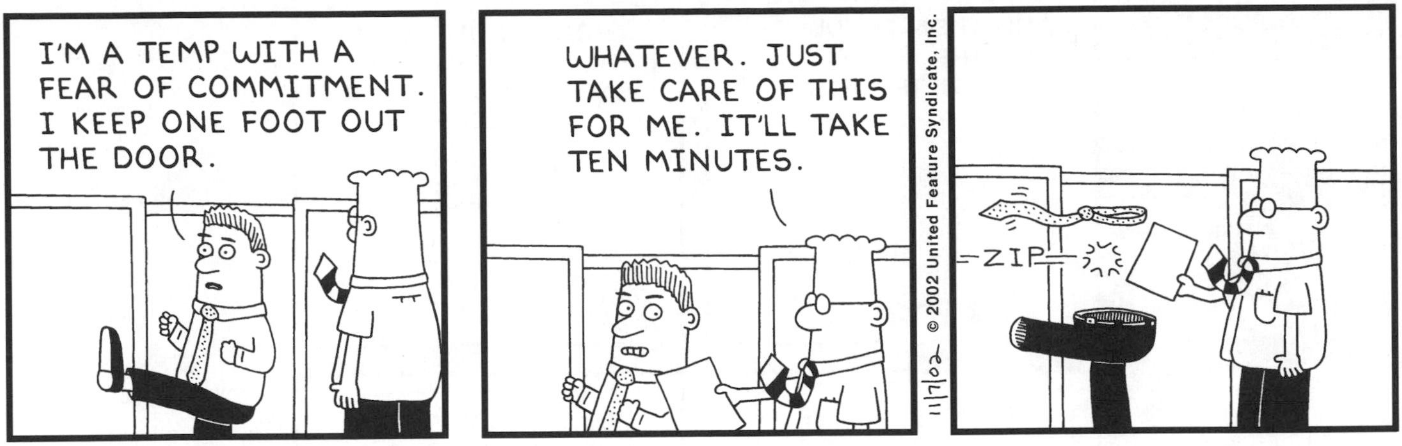
I'M A TEMP WITH A FEAR OF COMMITMENT. I KEEP ONE FOOT OUT THE DOOR.
WHATEVER. JUST TAKE CARE OF THIS FOR ME. IT'LL TAKE TEN MINUTES.
11/7/02 © 2002 United Feature Syndicate, Inc.
ZIP

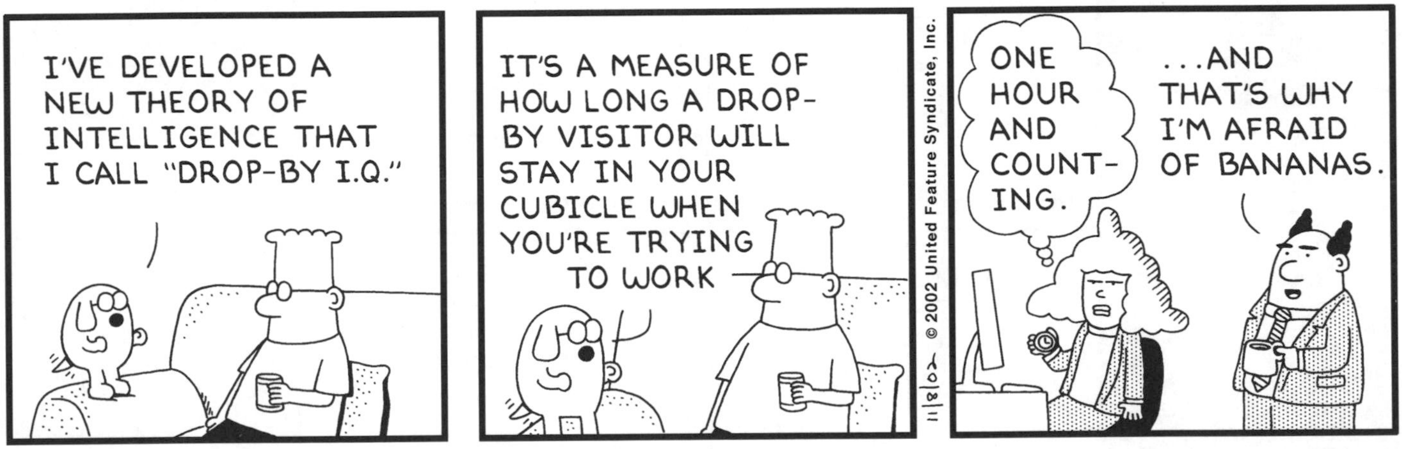
I'VE DEVELOPED A NEW THEORY OF INTELLIGENCE THAT I CALL "DROP-BY I.Q."
IT'S A MEASURE OF HOW LONG A DROP-BY VISITOR WILL STAY IN YOUR CUBICLE WHEN YOU'RE TRYING TO WORK
11/8/02 © 2002 United Feature Syndicate, Inc.
ONE HOUR AND COUNT-ING.
...AND THAT'S WHY I'M AFRAID OF BANANAS.

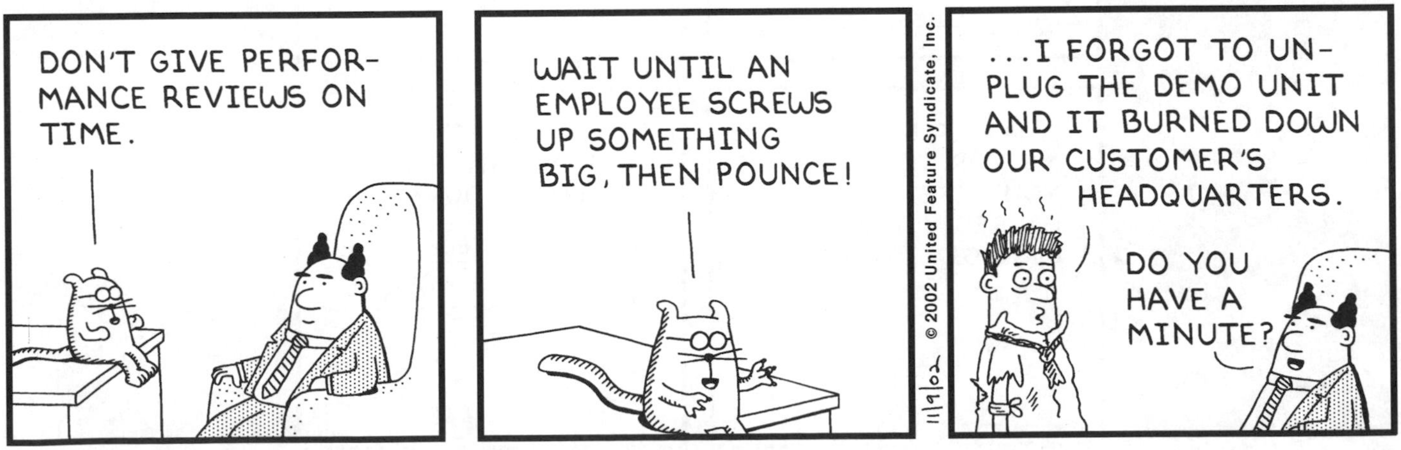
DON'T GIVE PERFOR-MANCE REVIEWS ON TIME.
WAIT UNTIL AN EMPLOYEE SCREWS UP SOMETHING BIG, THEN POUNCE!
11/9/02 © 2002 United Feature Syndicate, Inc.
...I FORGOT TO UN-PLUG THE DEMO UNIT AND IT BURNED DOWN OUR CUSTOMER'S HEADQUARTERS.
DO YOU HAVE A MINUTE?

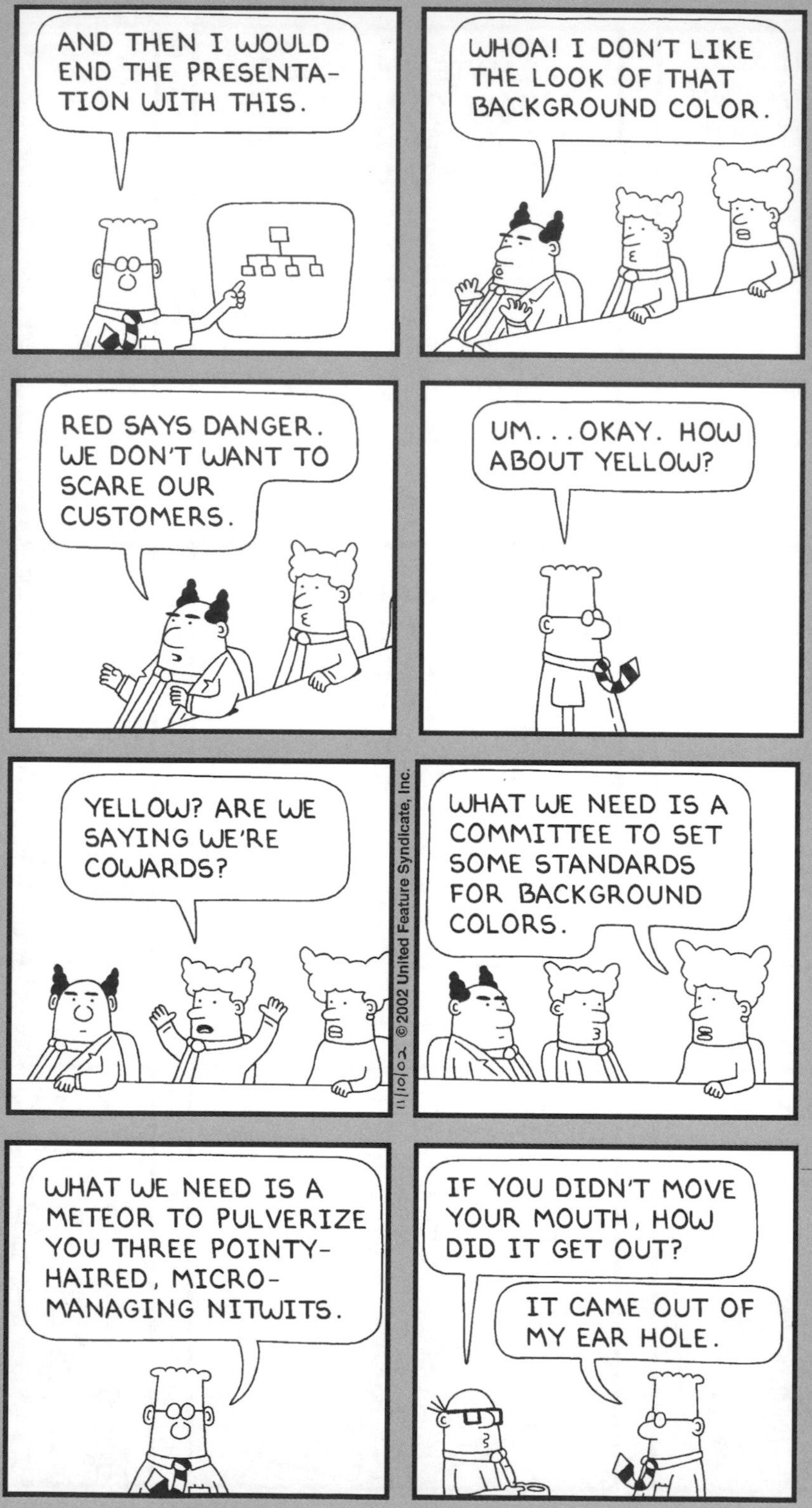
AND THEN I WOULD END THE PRESENTATION WITH THIS.
WHOA! I DON'T LIKE THE LOOK OF THAT BACKGROUND COLOR.
RED SAYS DANGER. WE DON'T WANT TO SCARE OUR CUSTOMERS.
UM...OKAY. HOW ABOUT YELLOW?
YELLOW? ARE WE SAYING WE'RE COWARDS?
WHAT WE NEED IS A COMMITTEE TO SET SOME STANDARDS FOR BACKGROUND COLORS.
WHAT WE NEED IS A METEOR TO PULVERIZE YOU THREE POINTY-HAIRED, MICRO-MANAGING NITWITS.
IF YOU DIDN'T MOVE YOUR MOUTH, HOW DID IT GET OUT?
IT CAME OUT OF MY EAR HOLE.

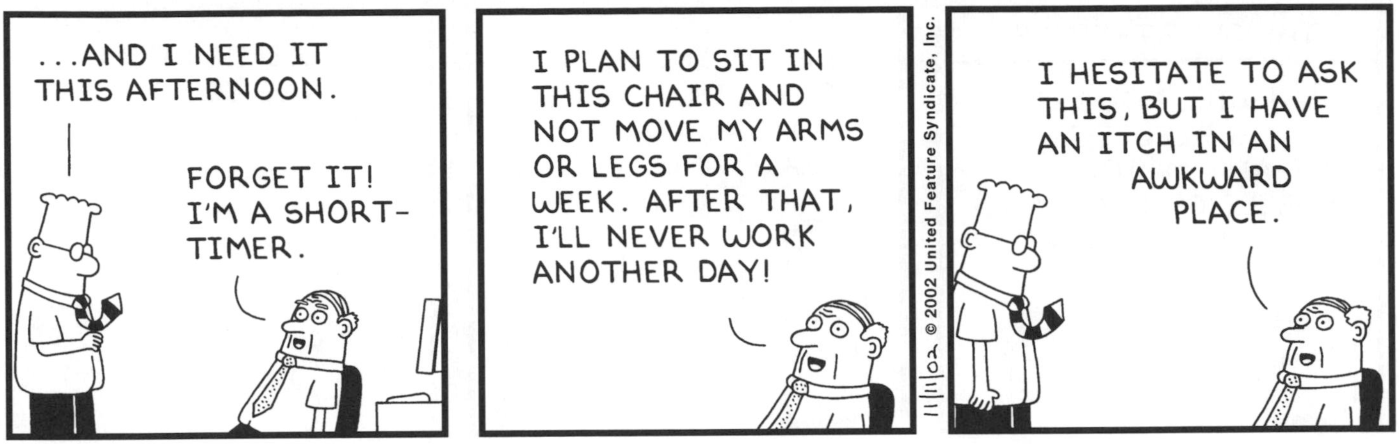
...AND I NEED IT THIS AFTERNOON.
FORGET IT! I'M A SHORT-TIMER.
I PLAN TO SIT IN THIS CHAIR AND NOT MOVE MY ARMS OR LEGS FOR A WEEK. AFTER THAT, I'LL NEVER WORK ANOTHER DAY!
11/11/02 © 2002 United Feature Syndicate, Inc.
I HESITATE TO ASK THIS, BUT I HAVE AN ITCH IN AN AWKWARD PLACE.

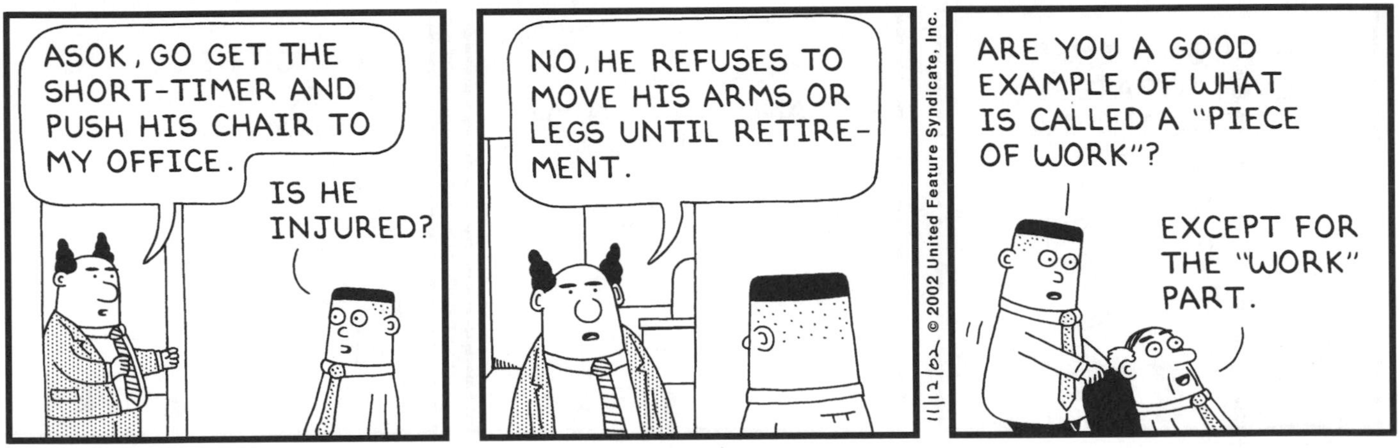
ASOK, GO GET THE SHORT-TIMER AND PUSH HIS CHAIR TO MY OFFICE.
IS HE INJURED?
NO, HE REFUSES TO MOVE HIS ARMS OR LEGS UNTIL RETIREMENT.
11/12/02 © 2002 United Feature Syndicate, Inc.
ARE YOU A GOOD EXAMPLE OF WHAT IS CALLED A "PIECE OF WORK"?
EXCEPT FOR THE "WORK" PART.

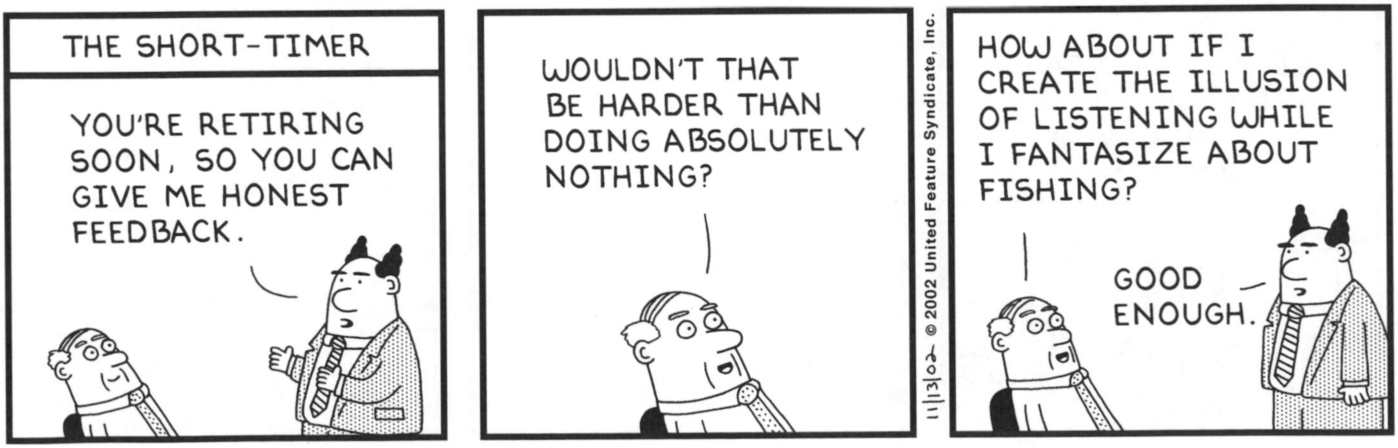
THE SHORT-TIMER
YOU'RE RETIRING SOON, SO YOU CAN GIVE ME HONEST FEEDBACK.
WOULDN'T THAT BE HARDER THAN DOING ABSOLUTELY NOTHING?
11/13/02 © 2002 United Feature Syndicate, Inc.
HOW ABOUT IF I CREATE THE ILLUSION OF LISTENING WHILE I FANTASIZE ABOUT FISHING?
GOOD ENOUGH.

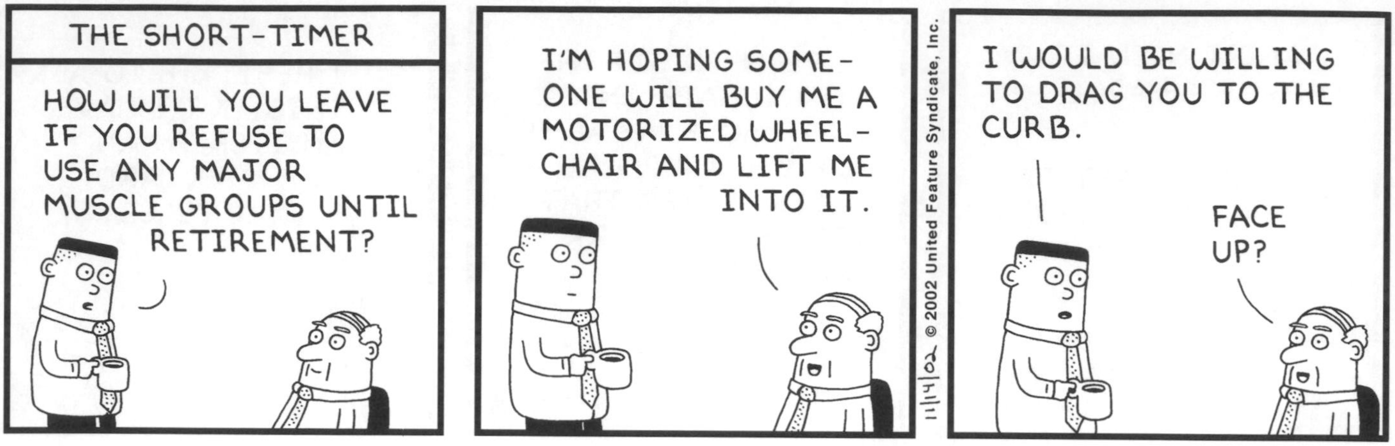
THE SHORT-TIMER
HOW WILL YOU LEAVE IF YOU REFUSE TO USE ANY MAJOR MUSCLE GROUPS UNTIL RETIREMENT?
I'M HOPING SOME-ONE WILL BUY ME A MOTORIZED WHEEL-CHAIR AND LIFT ME INTO IT.
11/14/02 © 2002 United Feature Syndicate, Inc.
I WOULD BE WILLING TO DRAG YOU TO THE CURB.
FACE UP?

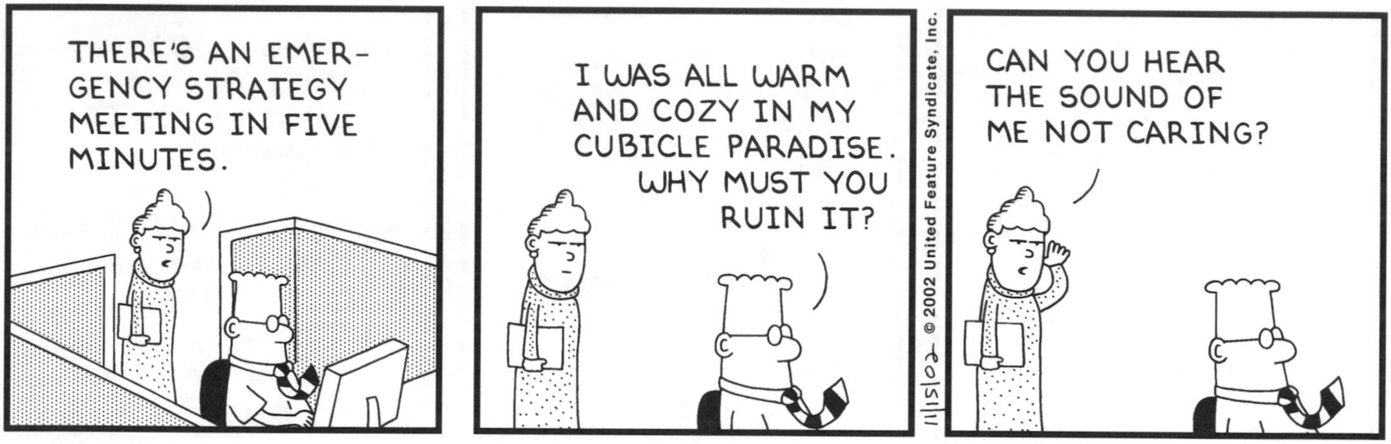
THERE'S AN EMER-GENCY STRATEGY MEETING IN FIVE MINUTES.
I WAS ALL WARM AND COZY IN MY CUBICLE PARADISE. WHY MUST YOU RUIN IT?
11/15/02 © 2002 United Feature Syndicate, Inc.
CAN YOU HEAR THE SOUND OF ME NOT CARING?

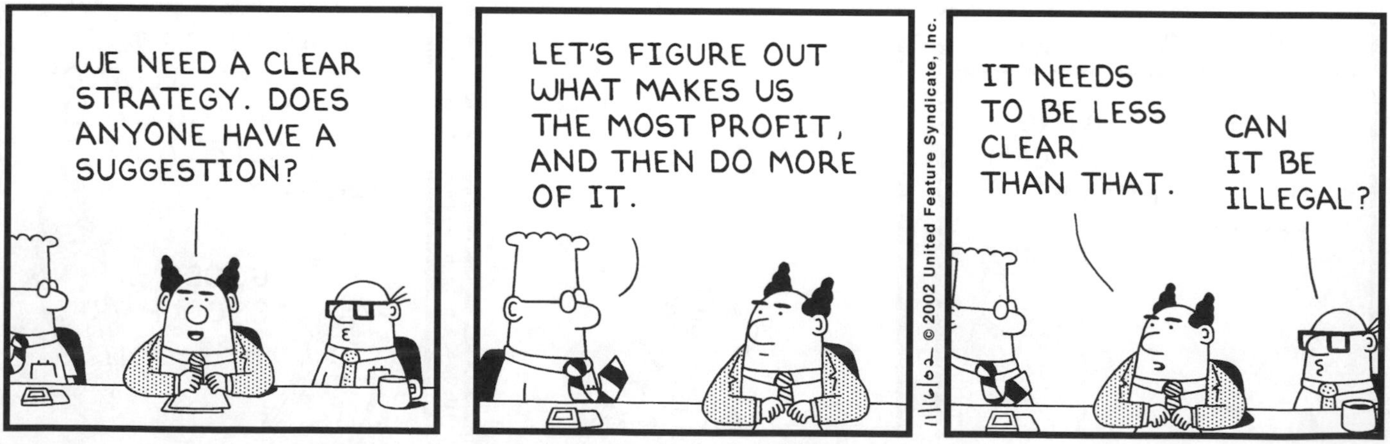
WE NEED A CLEAR STRATEGY. DOES ANYONE HAVE A SUGGESTION?
LET'S FIGURE OUT WHAT MAKES US THE MOST PROFIT, AND THEN DO MORE OF IT.
11/16/02 © 2002 United Feature Syndicate, Inc.
IT NEEDS TO BE LESS CLEAR THAN THAT.
CAN IT BE ILLEGAL?

THE ORIGINAL SCHEDULE LOOKED LIKE THIS...
ONE MONTH FOR A MANAGEMENT DECISION AND ONE YEAR TO DO THE PROJECT.
DECIDE
DO
THE REVISED SCHEDULE IS THIS...
ONE YEAR OF INDECISION FOLLOWED BY INTENSE PRESSURE TO DO THE IMPOSSIBLE BEFORE THE DEADLINE.
INDECISION
NO WAY
NOW IF YOU'LL EACH TAKE A PAIR OF 3-D GLASSES...
©2002 United Feature Syndicate, Inc.
11/17/02
YOU CAN SEE THE LAYERS OF MANAGEMENT INCOMPETENCE PRACTICALLY JUMP OUT AT YOU.
NOW SCRATCH ONE OF THESE SCENTED CARDS TO SNIFF THE UNMISTAKABLE ODOR OF DOOM.
I DON'T SMELL ANYTHING. IS MINE BROKEN?

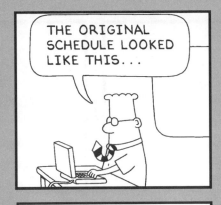

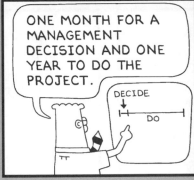

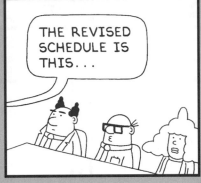

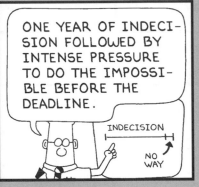

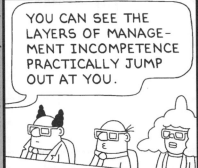

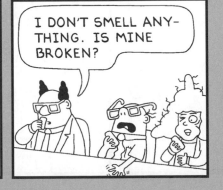

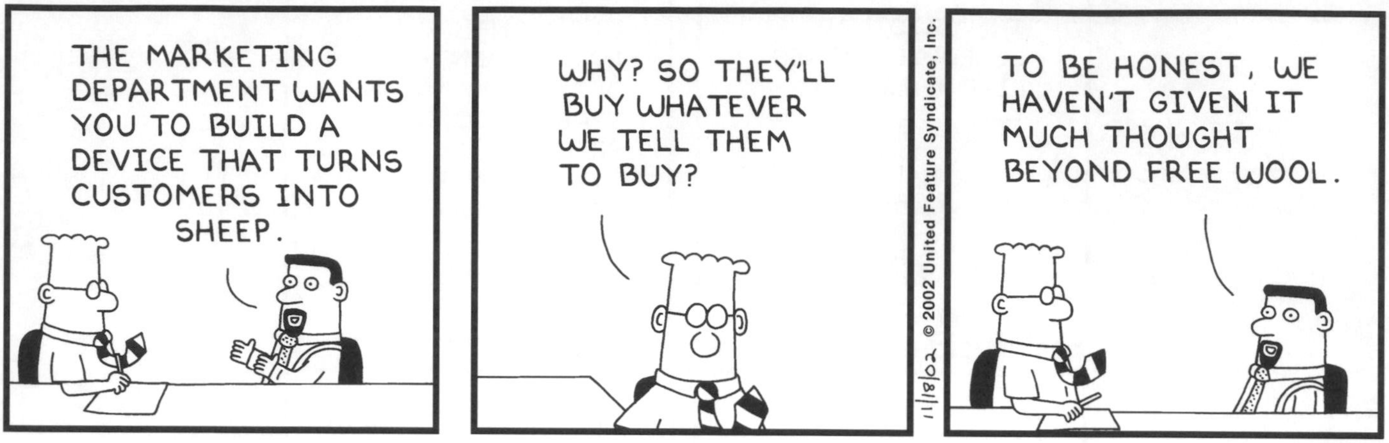
THE MARKETING DEPARTMENT WANTS YOU TO BUILD A DEVICE THAT TURNS CUSTOMERS INTO SHEEP.
WHY? SO THEY'LL BUY WHATEVER WE TELL THEM TO BUY?
11/18/02 © 2002 United Feature Syndicate, Inc.
TO BE HONEST, WE HAVEN'T GIVEN IT MUCH THOUGHT BEYOND FREE WOOL.

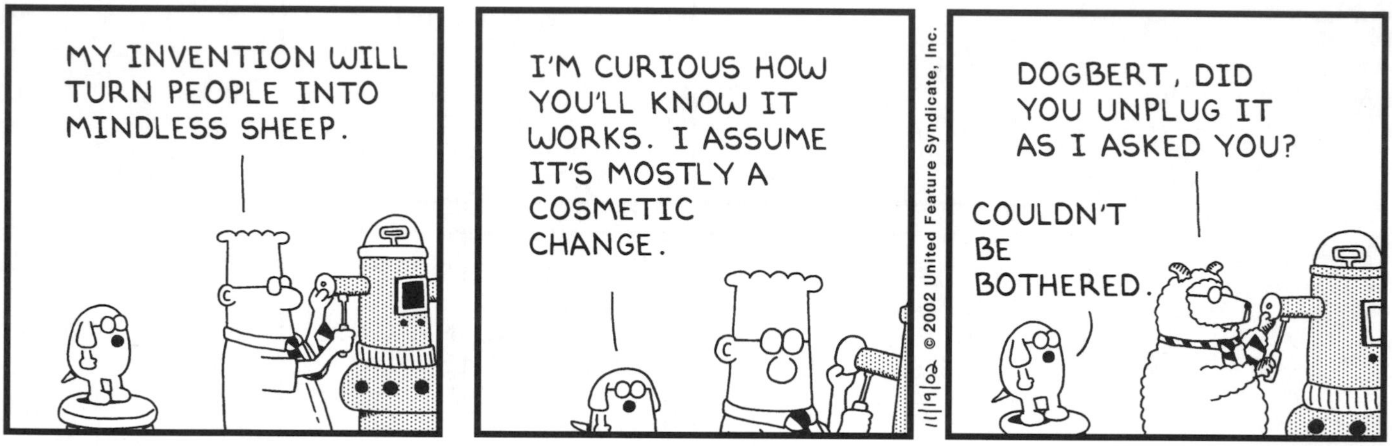
MY INVENTION WILL TURN PEOPLE INTO MINDLESS SHEEP.
I'M CURIOUS HOW YOU'LL KNOW IT WORKS. I ASSUME IT'S MOSTLY A COSMETIC CHANGE.
11/19/02 © 2002 United Feature Syndicate, Inc.
DOGBERT, DID YOU UNPLUG IT AS I ASKED YOU?
COULDN'T BE BOTHERED.

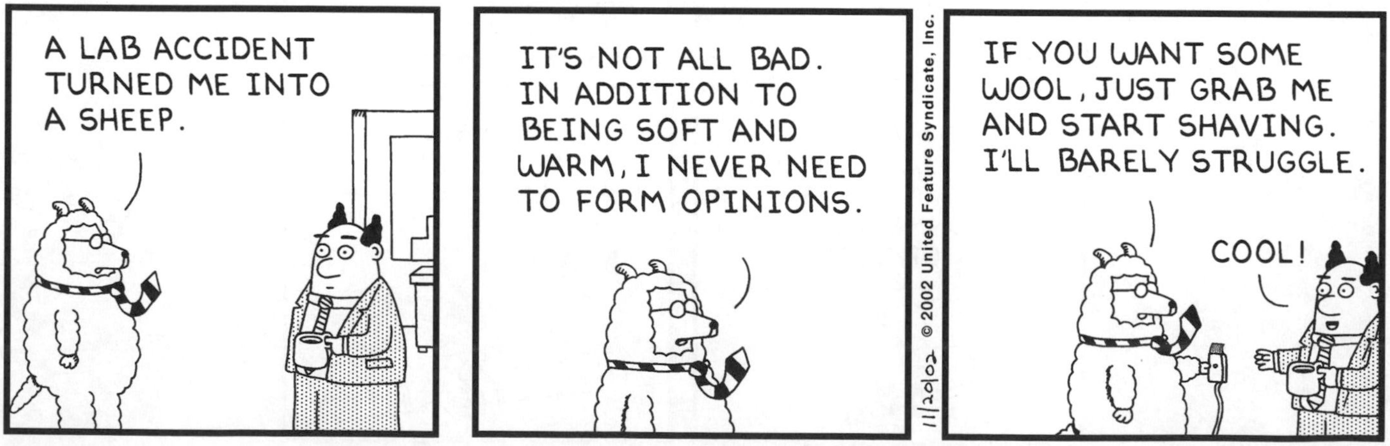
A LAB ACCIDENT TURNED ME INTO A SHEEP.
IT'S NOT ALL BAD. IN ADDITION TO BEING SOFT AND WARM, I NEVER NEED TO FORM OPINIONS.
11/20/02 © 2002 United Feature Syndicate, Inc.
IF YOU WANT SOME WOOL, JUST GRAB ME AND START SHAVING. I'LL BARELY STRUGGLE.
COOL!

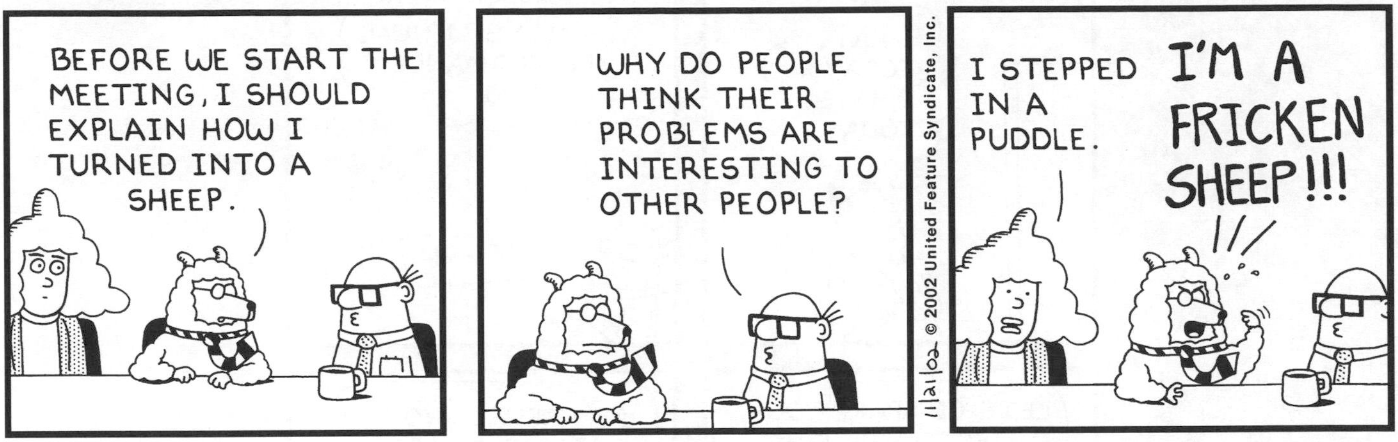
BEFORE WE START THE MEETING, I SHOULD EXPLAIN HOW I TURNED INTO A SHEEP.
WHY DO PEOPLE THINK THEIR PROBLEMS ARE INTERESTING TO OTHER PEOPLE?
11/21/02 © 2002 United Feature Syndicate, Inc.
I STEPPED IN A PUDDLE.
I'M A FRICKEN SHEEP!!!

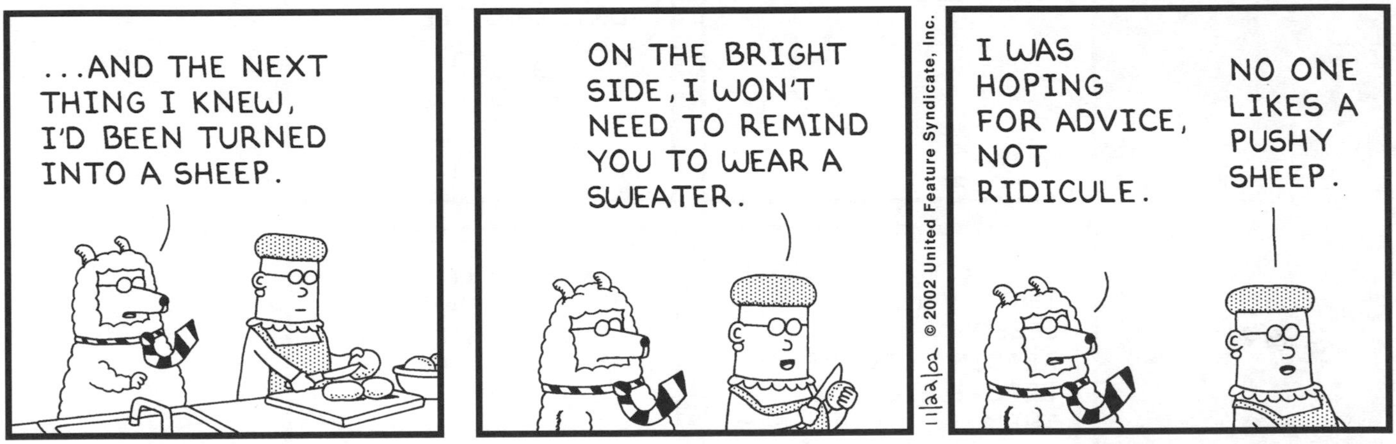
...AND THE NEXT THING I KNEW, I'D BEEN TURNED INTO A SHEEP.
ON THE BRIGHT SIDE, I WON'T NEED TO REMIND YOU TO WEAR A SWEATER.
11/22/02 © 2002 United Feature Syndicate, Inc.
I WAS HOPING FOR ADVICE, NOT RIDICULE.
NO ONE LIKES A PUSHY SHEEP.

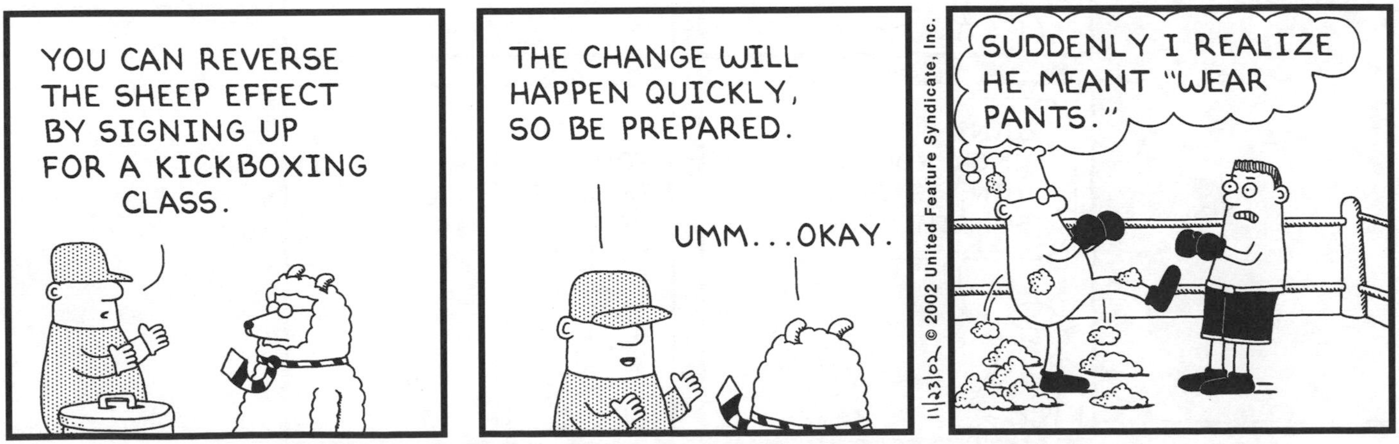
YOU CAN REVERSE THE SHEEP EFFECT BY SIGNING UP FOR A KICKBOXING CLASS.
THE CHANGE WILL HAPPEN QUICKLY, SO BE PREPARED.
UMM...OKAY.
11/23/02 © 2002 United Feature Syndicate, Inc.
SUDDENLY I REALIZE HE MEANT "WEAR PANTS."

I HATE TODAY... I HATE TODAY.
WALLY'S ANNUAL PERFORMANCE REVIEW.
LET'S COMPARE YOUR OBJECTIVES WITH...
WHAT THE...?
APPARENTLY YOUR OBJECTIVES ARE "PLAY COMPUTER SOLITAIRE AND DRINK COFFEE."
I HOPE YOU'RE LEARNING A VALUABLE LESSON ABOUT READING DOCUMENTS BEFORE SIGNING THEM.
OKAY, WE'LL USE WHAT WE HAVE. HOW MANY GAMES OF SOLITAIRE DID YOU WIN?
WIN? I DIDN'T KNOW YOU COULD WIN. IS THAT SOMETHING NEW?
HE MADE YOU THE EMPLOYEE OF THE MONTH?
HE THINKS HE SIGNED A WARNING FOR MY FILE.
11/24/02 © 2002 United Feature Syndicate, Inc.

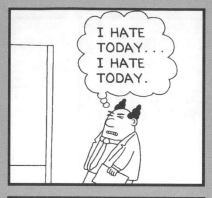

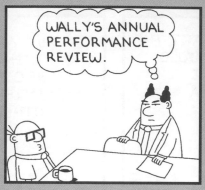

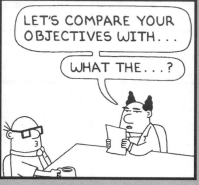

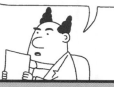

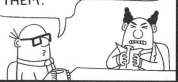

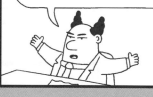

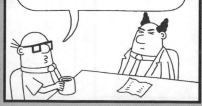

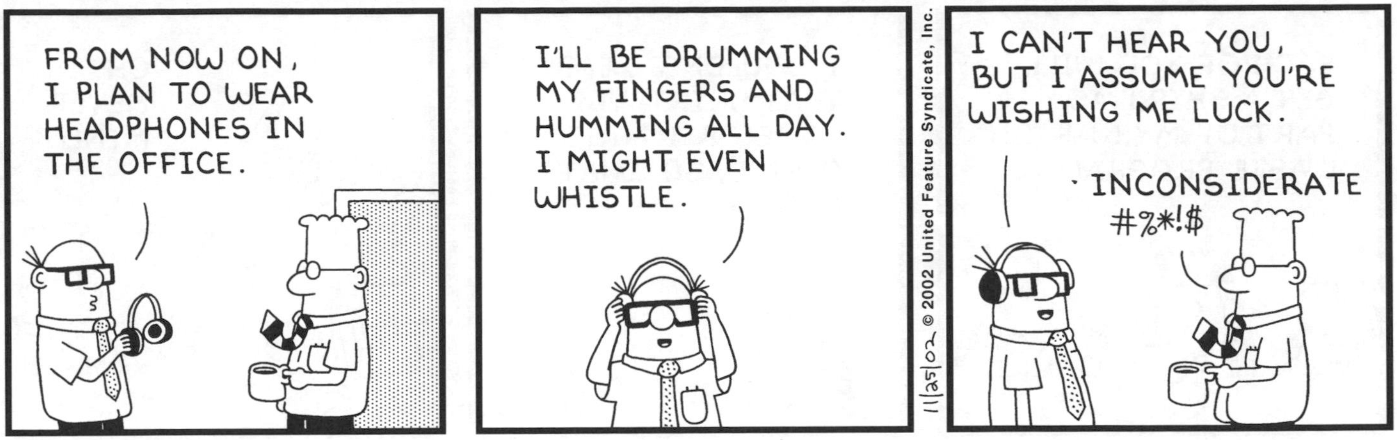
FROM NOW ON, I PLAN TO WEAR HEADPHONES IN THE OFFICE.
I'LL BE DRUMMING MY FINGERS AND HUMMING ALL DAY. I MIGHT EVEN WHISTLE.
11/25/02 © 2002 United Feature Syndicate, Inc.
I CAN'T HEAR YOU, BUT I ASSUME YOU'RE WISHING ME LUCK.
INCONSIDERATE #%*!$

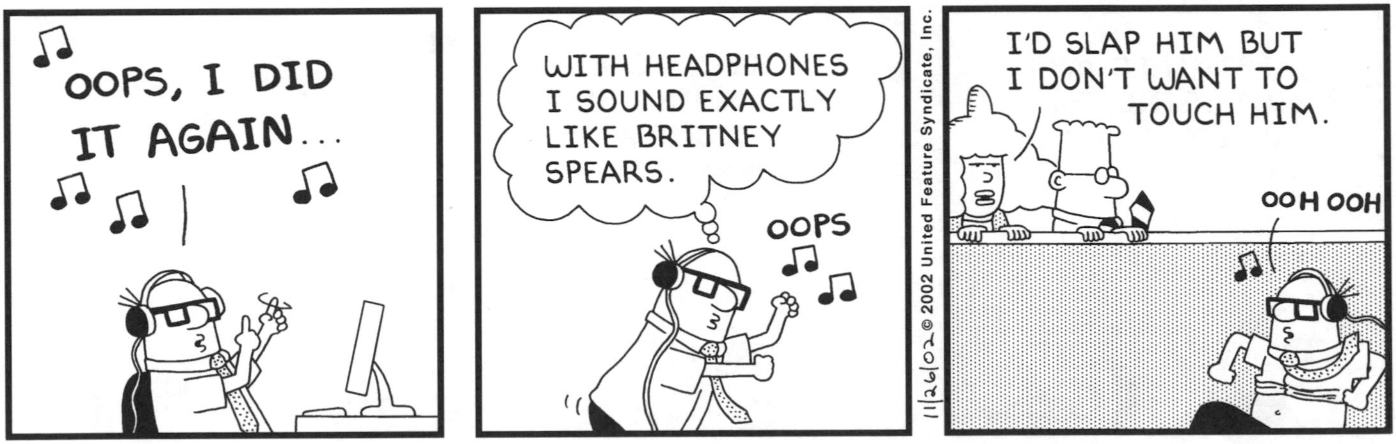
OOPS, I DID IT AGAIN...
WITH HEADPHONES I SOUND EXACTLY LIKE BRITNEY SPEARS.
OOPS
11/26/02 © 2002 United Feature Syndicate, Inc.
I'D SLAP HIM BUT I DON'T WANT TO TOUCH HIM.
OOH OOH

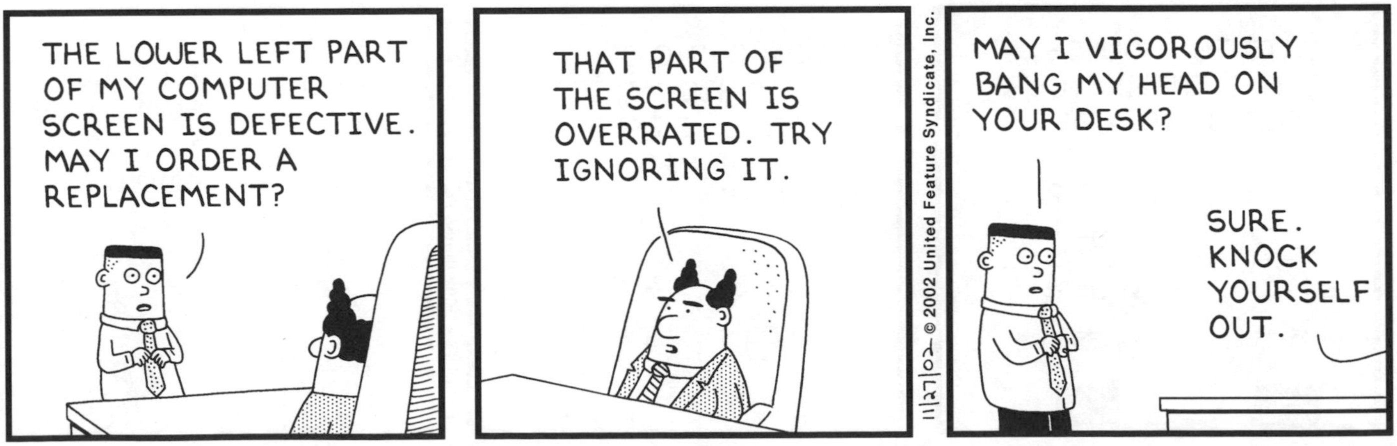
THE LOWER LEFT PART OF MY COMPUTER SCREEN IS DEFECTIVE. MAY I ORDER A REPLACEMENT?
THAT PART OF THE SCREEN IS OVERRATED. TRY IGNORING IT.
11/27/02 © 2002 United Feature Syndicate, Inc.
MAY I VIGOROUSLY BANG MY HEAD ON YOUR DESK?
SURE. KNOCK YOURSELF OUT.

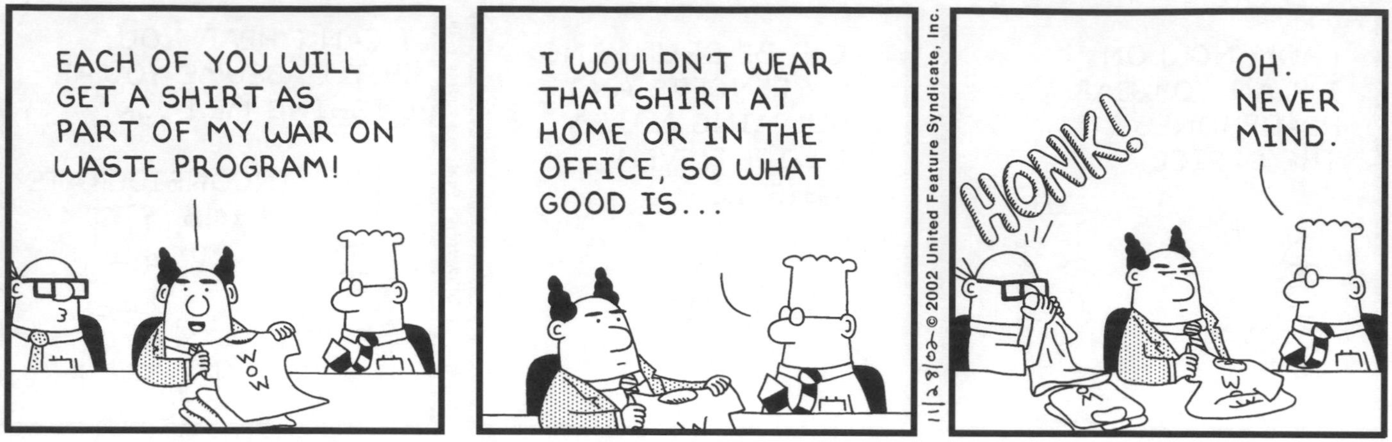
EACH OF YOU WILL GET A SHIRT AS PART OF MY WAR ON WASTE PROGRAM!
WOW
I WOULDN'T WEAR THAT SHIRT AT HOME OR IN THE OFFICE, SO WHAT GOOD IS...
11/28/02 © 2002 United Feature Syndicate, Inc.
HONK!
OH. NEVER MIND.

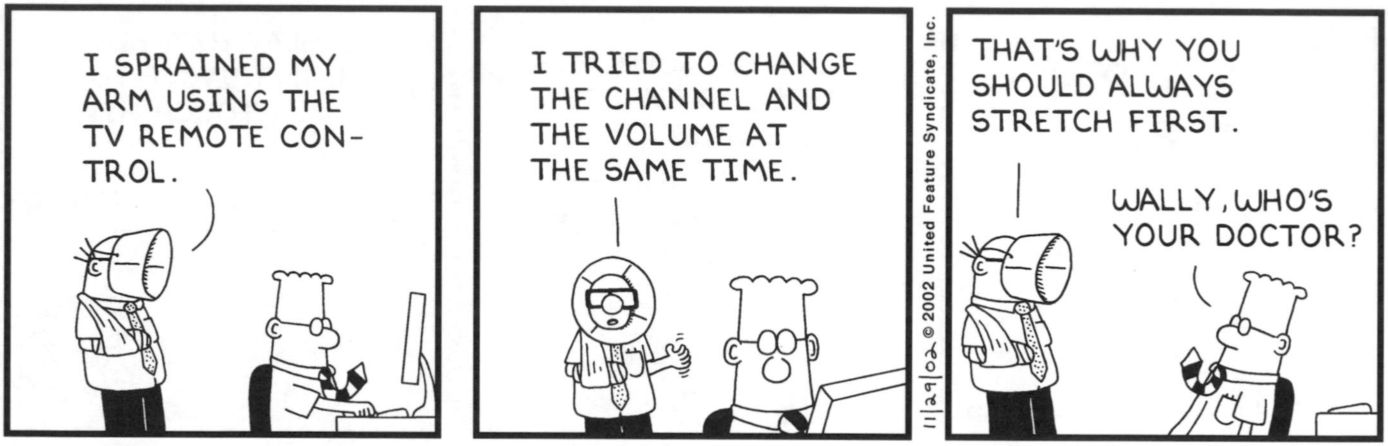
I SPRAINED MY ARM USING THE TV REMOTE CON-TROL.
I TRIED TO CHANGE THE CHANNEL AND THE VOLUME AT THE SAME TIME.
11/29/02 © 2002 United Feature Syndicate, Inc.
THAT'S WHY YOU SHOULD ALWAYS STRETCH FIRST.
WALLY, WHO'S YOUR DOCTOR?

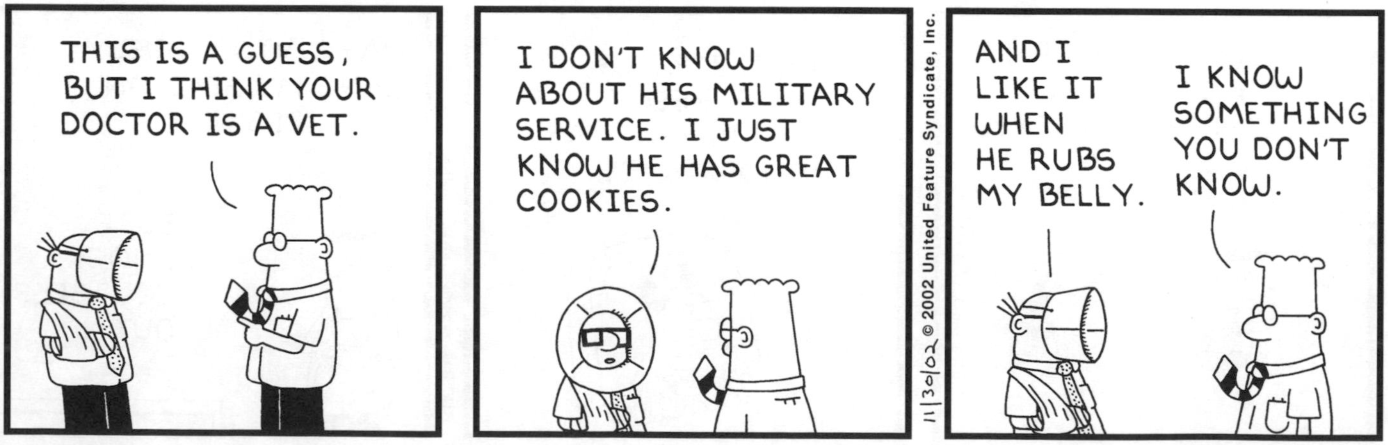
THIS IS A GUESS, BUT I THINK YOUR DOCTOR IS A VET.
I DON'T KNOW ABOUT HIS MILITARY SERVICE. I JUST KNOW HE HAS GREAT COOKIES.
11/30/02 © 2002 United Feature Syndicate, Inc.
AND I LIKE IT WHEN HE RUBS MY BELLY.
I KNOW SOMETHING YOU DON'T KNOW.

DILBERT, RESEARCH THIS EXPENSE AND FIND OUT WHAT IT'S FOR.
IT'S ONLY $2.37.
IT COULD TAKE ALL DAY TO TRACK IT DOWN!
I'M A HIGHLY TRAINED ENGINEER, NOT A CLERK.
HOW CAN YOU JUSTIFY WASTING A VALUABLE EMPLOYEE LIKE ME ON A TRIVIAL TASK LIKE THIS?!!
THAT REMINDS ME: YOUR PROJECT GOT CANCELED. THIS IS YOUR ONLY ASSIGN- MENT.
WOO-HOO!
IN YOUR FACE!!!
I WONDER IF HE'LL FIND OUT I SPENT $2.37 ON HIS "KUDOS" AWARD.
©2002 United Feature Syndicate, Inc.
12/1/02

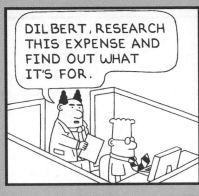

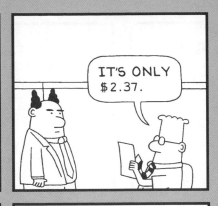

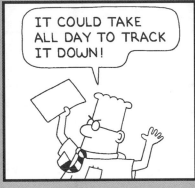

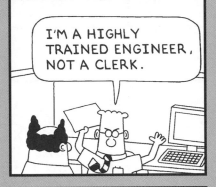

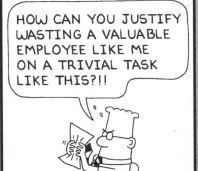

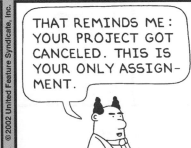

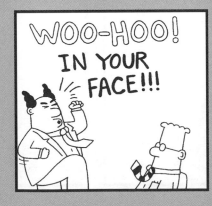

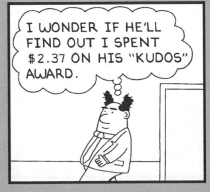

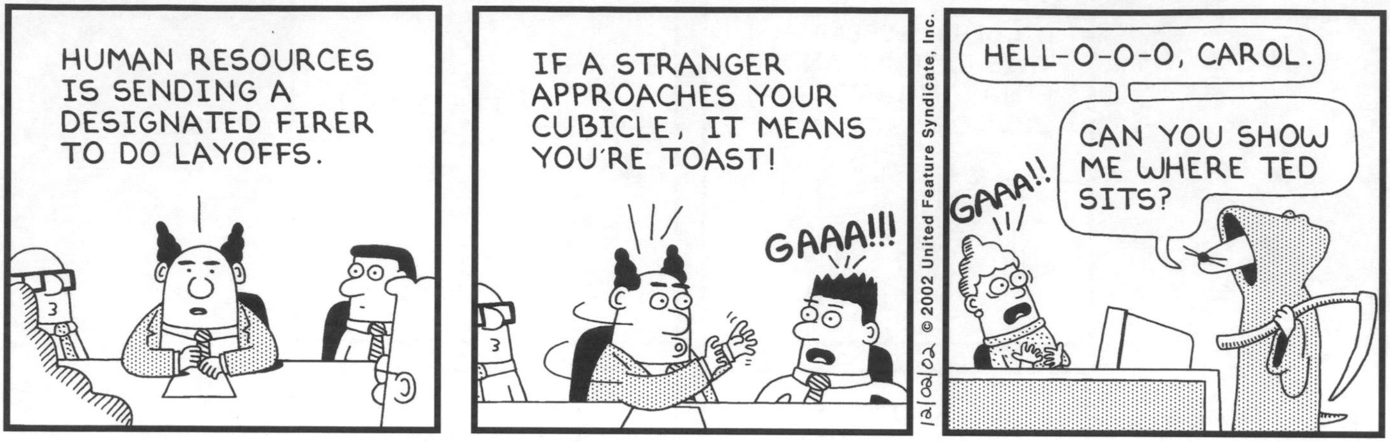
HUMAN RESOURCES IS SENDING A DESIGNATED FIRER TO DO LAYOFFS.
IF A STRANGER APPROACHES YOUR CUBICLE, IT MEANS YOU'RE TOAST!
GAAA!!!
12/02/02 © 2002 United Feature Syndicate, Inc.
HELL-O-O-O, CAROL.
CAN YOU SHOW ME WHERE TED SITS?
GAAA!!

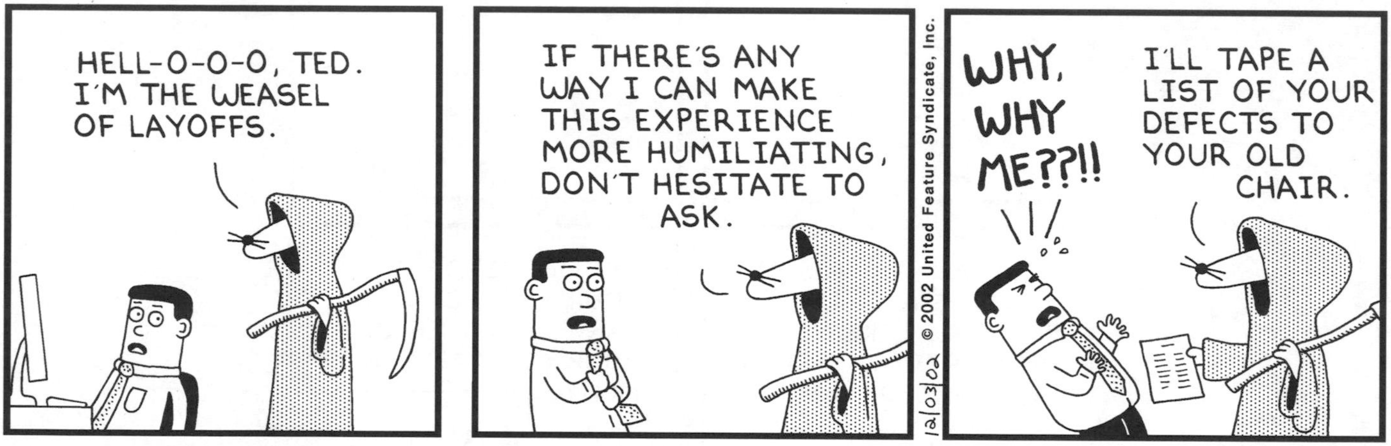
HELL-O-O-O, TED. I'M THE WEASEL OF LAYOFFS.
IF THERE'S ANY WAY I CAN MAKE THIS EXPERIENCE MORE HUMILIATING, DON'T HESITATE TO ASK.
12/03/02 © 2002 United Feature Syndicate, Inc.
WHY, WHY ME??!!
I'LL TAPE A LIST OF YOUR DEFECTS TO YOUR OLD CHAIR.

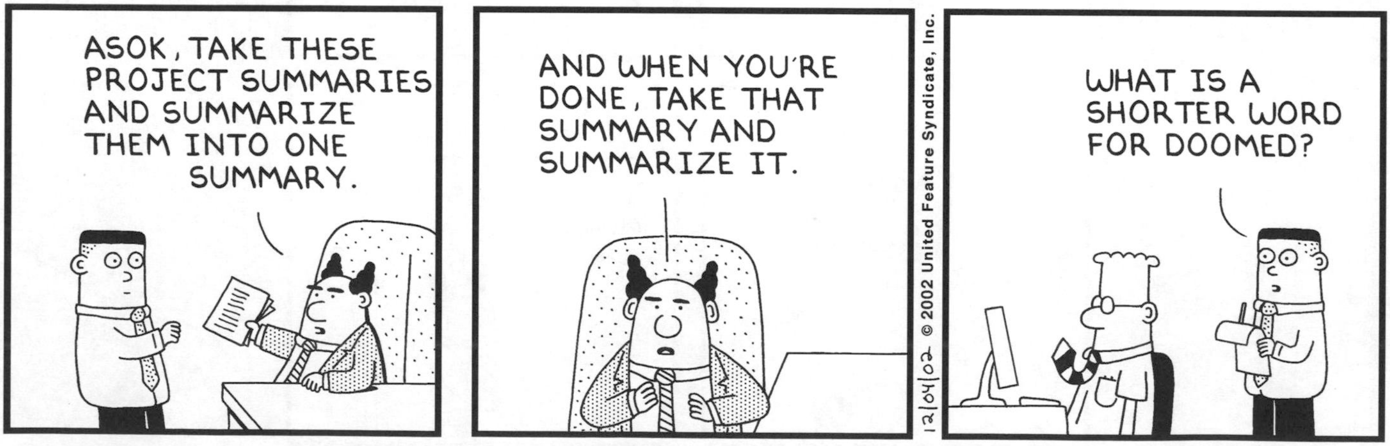
ASOK, TAKE THESE PROJECT SUMMARIES AND SUMMARIZE THEM INTO ONE SUMMARY.
AND WHEN YOU'RE DONE, TAKE THAT SUMMARY AND SUMMARIZE IT.
12/04/02 © 2002 United Feature Syndicate, Inc.
WHAT IS A SHORTER WORD FOR DOOMED?

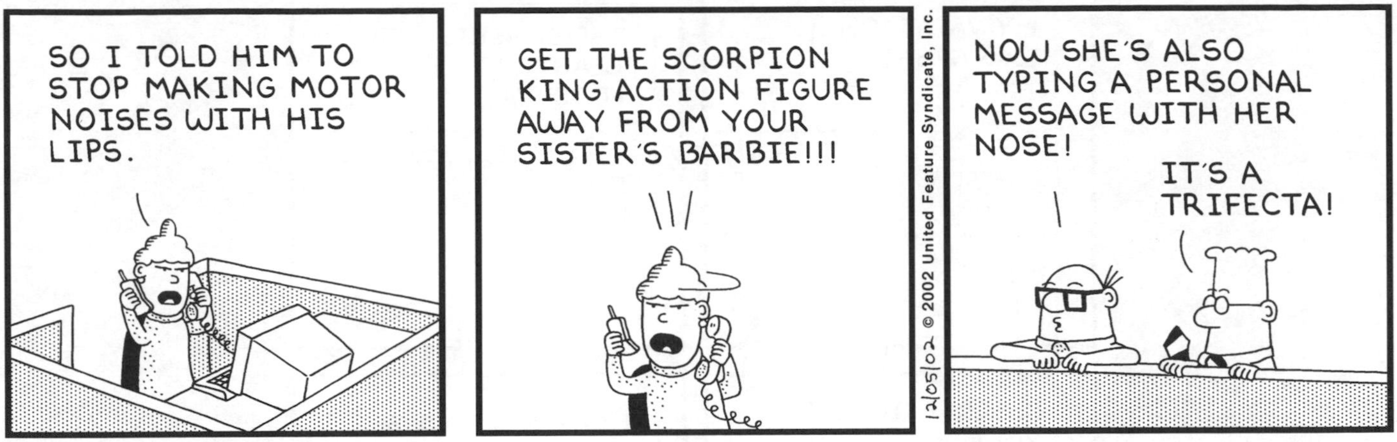
SO I TOLD HIM TO STOP MAKING MOTOR NOISES WITH HIS LIPS.
GET THE SCORPION KING ACTION FIGURE AWAY FROM YOUR SISTER'S BARBIE!!!
12/05/02 © 2002 United Feature Syndicate, Inc.
NOW SHE'S ALSO TYPING A PERSONAL MESSAGE WITH HER NOSE!
IT'S A TRIFECTA!

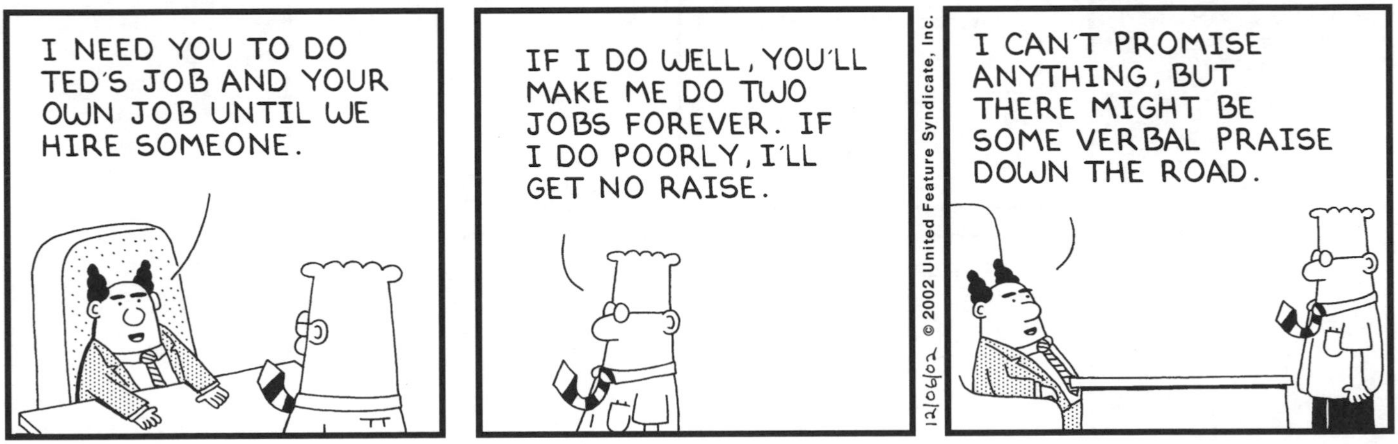
I NEED YOU TO DO TED'S JOB AND YOUR OWN JOB UNTIL WE HIRE SOMEONE.
IF I DO WELL, YOU'LL MAKE ME DO TWO JOBS FOREVER. IF I DO POORLY, I'LL GET NO RAISE.
12/06/02 © 2002 United Feature Syndicate, Inc.
I CAN'T PROMISE ANYTHING, BUT THERE MIGHT BE SOME VERBAL PRAISE DOWN THE ROAD.

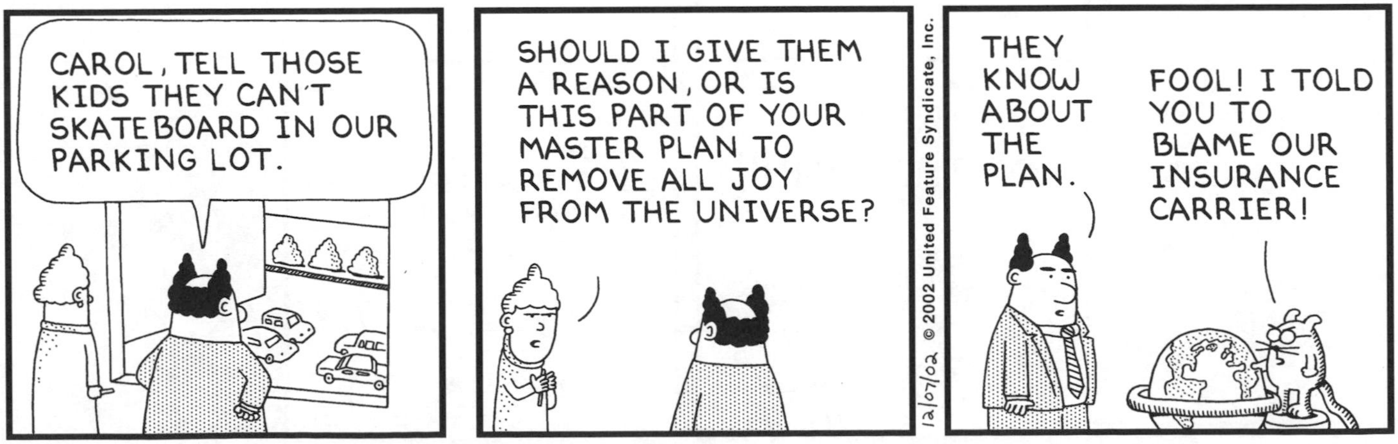
CAROL, TELL THOSE KIDS THEY CAN'T SKATEBOARD IN OUR PARKING LOT.
SHOULD I GIVE THEM A REASON, OR IS THIS PART OF YOUR MASTER PLAN TO REMOVE ALL JOY FROM THE UNIVERSE?
12/07/02 © 2002 United Feature Syndicate, Inc.
THEY KNOW ABOUT THE PLAN.
FOOL! I TOLD YOU TO BLAME OUR INSURANCE CARRIER!

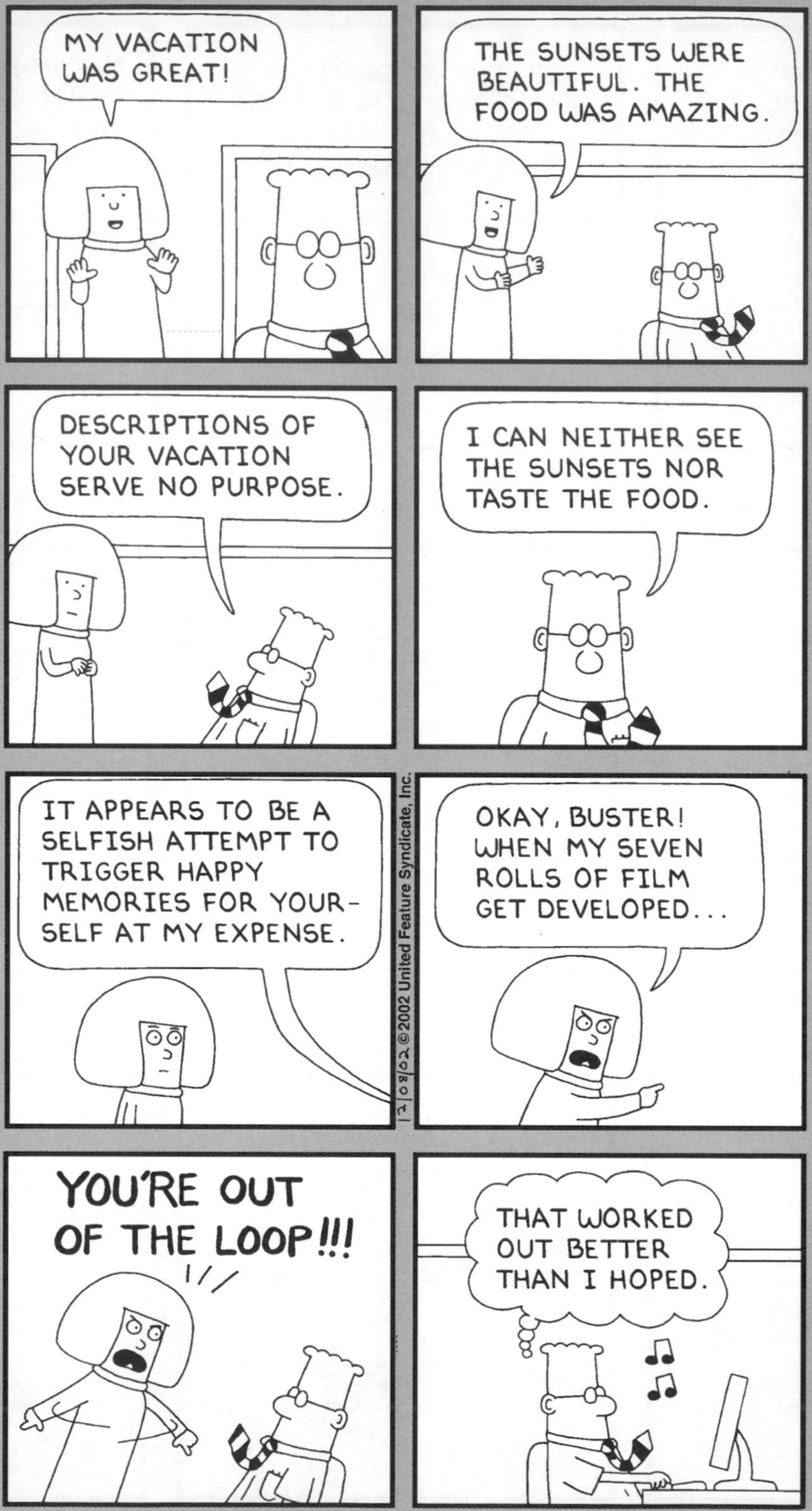
MY VACATION WAS GREAT!
THE SUNSETS WERE BEAUTIFUL. THE FOOD WAS AMAZING.
DESCRIPTIONS OF YOUR VACATION SERVE NO PURPOSE.
I CAN NEITHER SEE THE SUNSETS NOR TASTE THE FOOD.
IT APPEARS TO BE A SELFISH ATTEMPT TO TRIGGER HAPPY MEMORIES FOR YOURSELF AT MY EXPENSE.
OKAY, BUSTER! WHEN MY SEVEN ROLLS OF FILM GET DEVELOPED...
YOU'RE OUT OF THE LOOP!!!
THAT WORKED OUT BETTER THAN I HOPED.
12/08/02 © 2002 United Feature Syndicate, Inc.

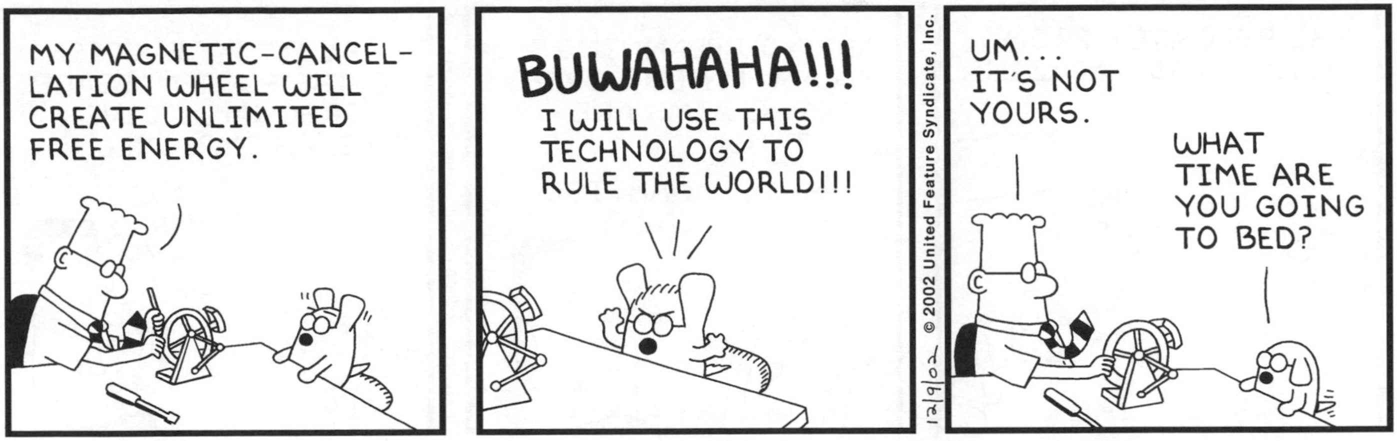
MY MAGNETIC-CANCEL-LATION WHEEL WILL CREATE UNLIMITED FREE ENERGY.
BUWAHAHA!!!
I WILL USE THIS TECHNOLOGY TO RULE THE WORLD!!!
UM... IT'S NOT YOURS.
WHAT TIME ARE YOU GOING TO BED?
12/9/02 © 2002 United Feature Syndicate, Inc.

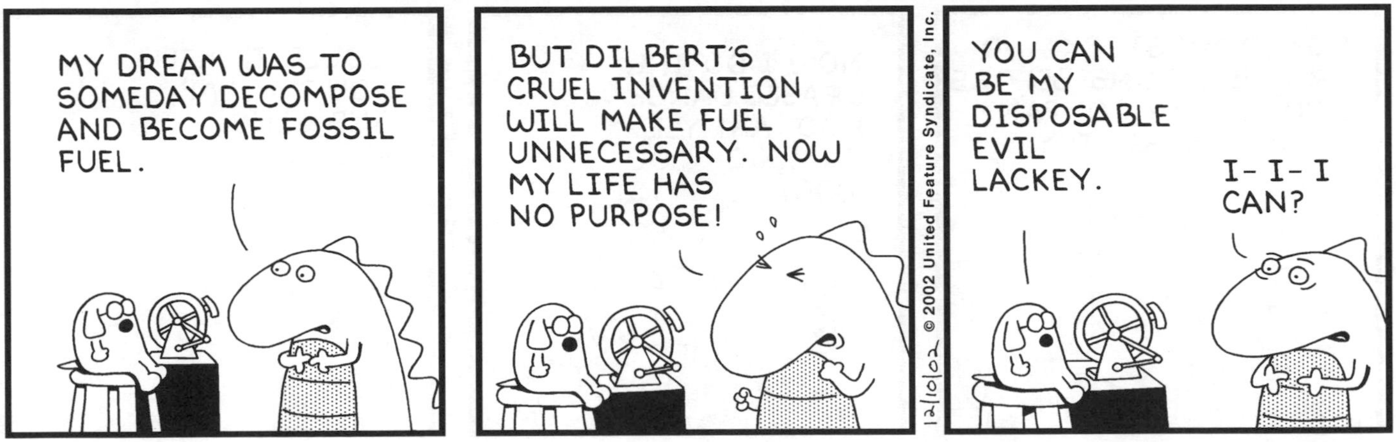
MY DREAM WAS TO SOMEDAY DECOMPOSE AND BECOME FOSSIL FUEL.
BUT DILBERT'S CRUEL INVENTION WILL MAKE FUEL UNNECESSARY. NOW MY LIFE HAS NO PURPOSE!
YOU CAN BE MY DISPOSABLE EVIL LACKEY.
I- I- I CAN?
12/10/02 © 2002 United Feature Syndicate, Inc.

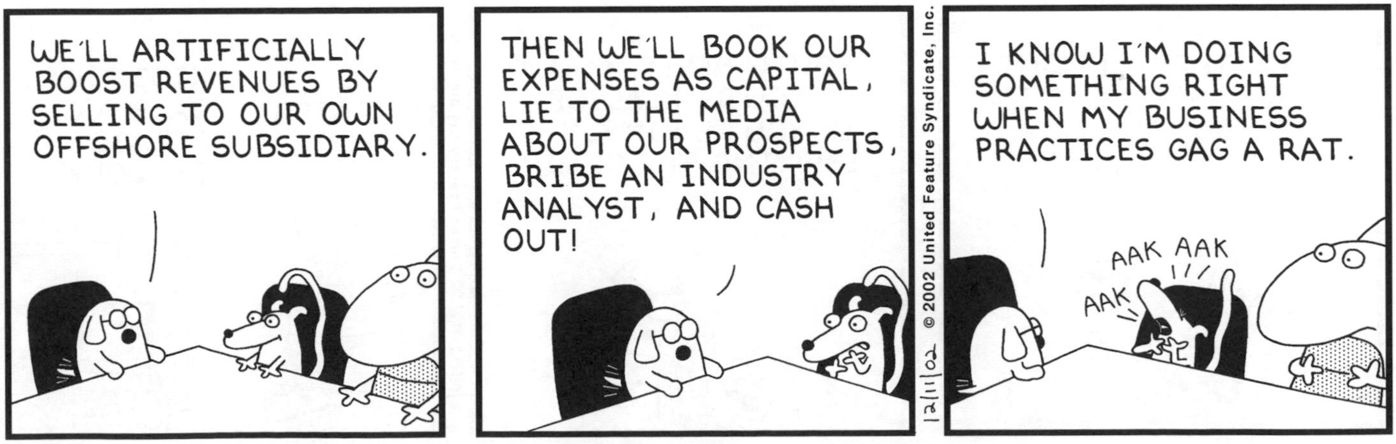
WE'LL ARTIFICIALLY BOOST REVENUES BY SELLING TO OUR OWN OFFSHORE SUBSIDIARY.
THEN WE'LL BOOK OUR EXPENSES AS CAPITAL, LIE TO THE MEDIA ABOUT OUR PROSPECTS, BRIBE AN INDUSTRY ANALYST, AND CASH OUT!
I KNOW I'M DOING SOMETHING RIGHT WHEN MY BUSINESS PRACTICES GAG A RAT.
AAK AAK
AAK
12/11/02 © 2002 United Feature Syndicate, Inc.

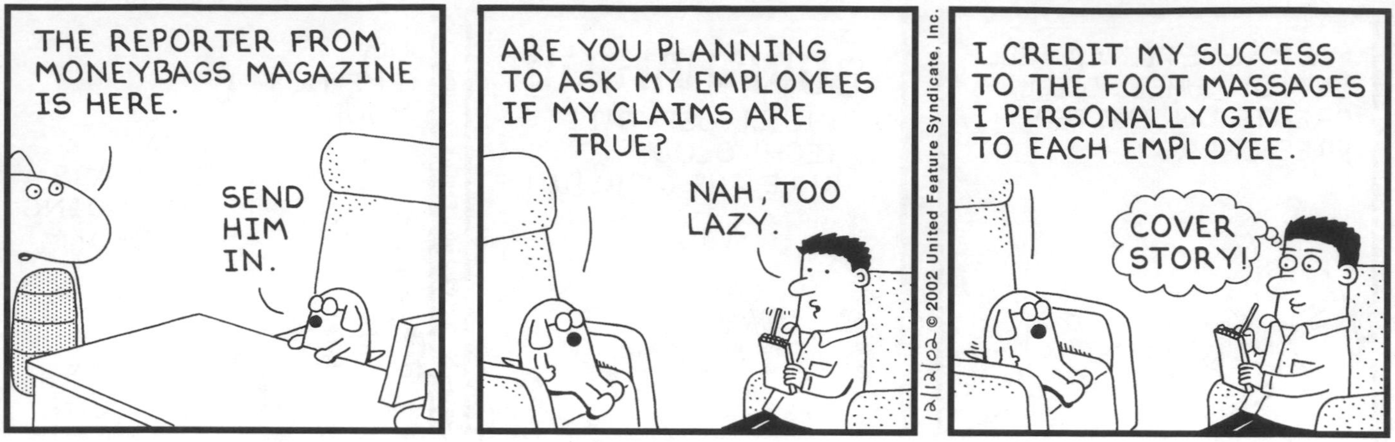
THE REPORTER FROM MONEYBAGS MAGAZINE IS HERE.
SEND HIM IN.
ARE YOU PLANNING TO ASK MY EMPLOYEES IF MY CLAIMS ARE TRUE?
NAH, TOO LAZY.
12/12/02 © 2002 United Feature Syndicate, Inc.
I CREDIT MY SUCCESS TO THE FOOT MASSAGES I PERSONALLY GIVE TO EACH EMPLOYEE.
COVER STORY!

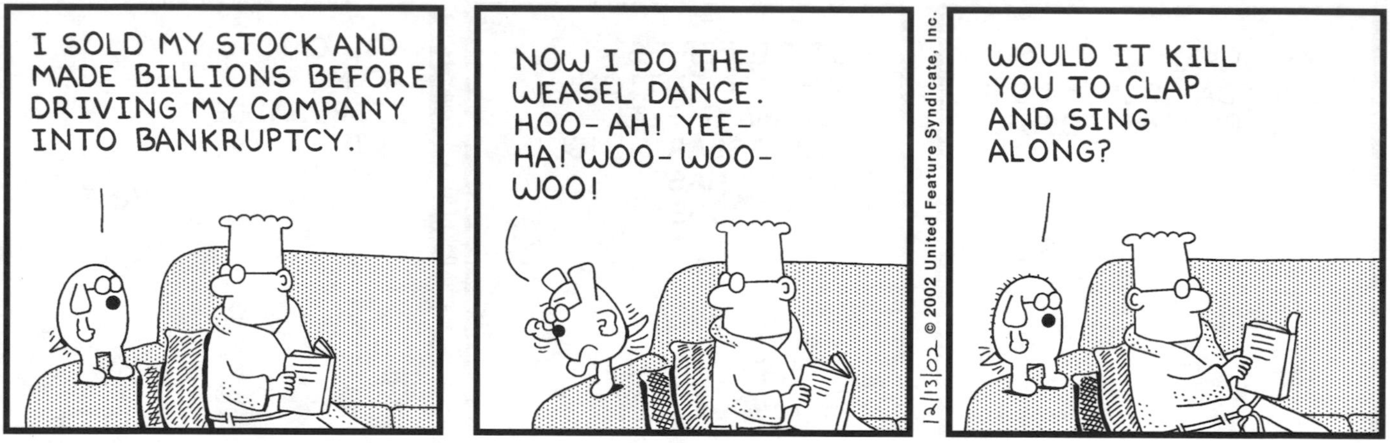
I SOLD MY STOCK AND MADE BILLIONS BEFORE DRIVING MY COMPANY INTO BANKRUPTCY.
NOW I DO THE WEASEL DANCE. HOO-AH! YEE-HA! WOO-WOO-WOO!
12/13/02 © 2002 United Feature Syndicate, Inc.
WOULD IT KILL YOU TO CLAP AND SING ALONG?

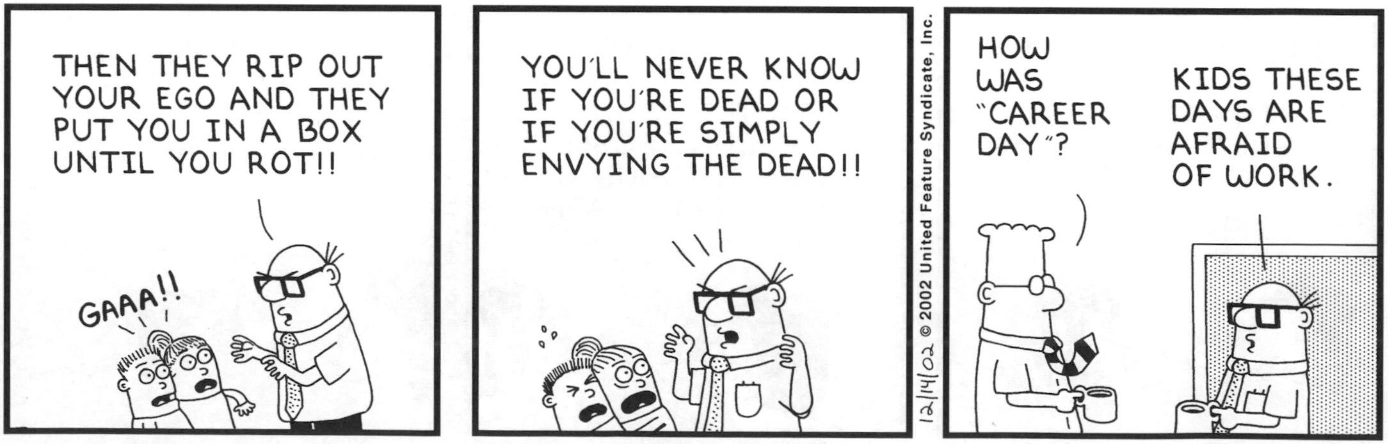
THEN THEY RIP OUT YOUR EGO AND THEY PUT YOU IN A BOX UNTIL YOU ROT!!
GAAA!!
YOU'LL NEVER KNOW IF YOU'RE DEAD OR IF YOU'RE SIMPLY ENVYING THE DEAD!!
12/14/02 © 2002 United Feature Syndicate, Inc.
HOW WAS "CAREER DAY"?
KIDS THESE DAYS ARE AFRAID OF WORK.

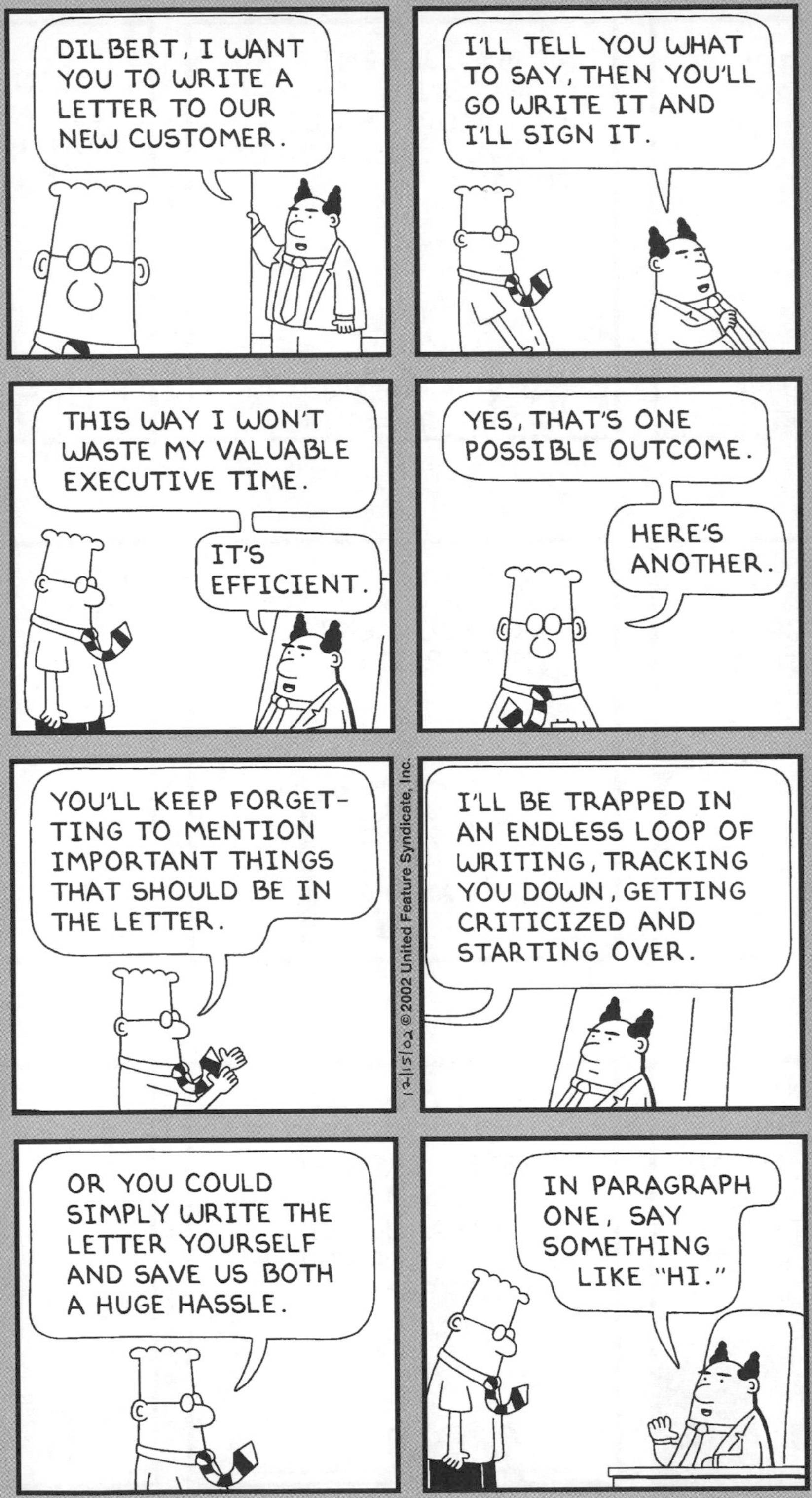
DILBERT, I WANT YOU TO WRITE A LETTER TO OUR NEW CUSTOMER.
I'LL TELL YOU WHAT TO SAY, THEN YOU'LL GO WRITE IT AND I'LL SIGN IT.
THIS WAY I WON'T WASTE MY VALUABLE EXECUTIVE TIME.
IT'S EFFICIENT.
YES, THAT'S ONE POSSIBLE OUTCOME.
HERE'S ANOTHER.
YOU'LL KEEP FORGET-TING TO MENTION IMPORTANT THINGS THAT SHOULD BE IN THE LETTER.
I'LL BE TRAPPED IN AN ENDLESS LOOP OF WRITING, TRACKING YOU DOWN, GETTING CRITICIZED AND STARTING OVER.
12/15/02 © 2002 United Feature Syndicate, Inc.
OR YOU COULD SIMPLY WRITE THE LETTER YOURSELF AND SAVE US BOTH A HUGE HASSLE.
IN PARAGRAPH ONE, SAY SOMETHING LIKE "HI."

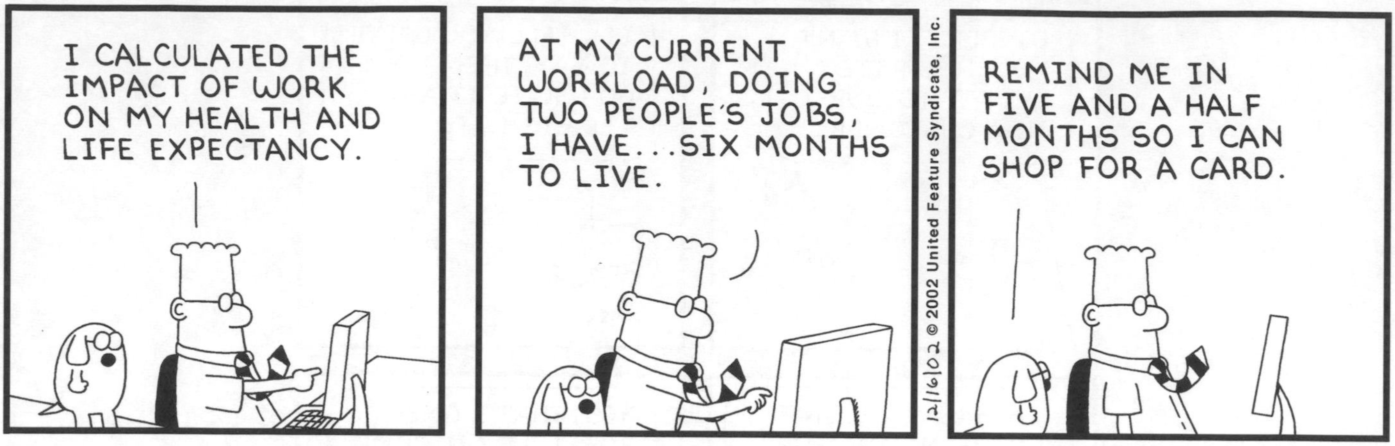
I CALCULATED THE IMPACT OF WORK ON MY HEALTH AND LIFE EXPECTANCY.
AT MY CURRENT WORKLOAD, DOING TWO PEOPLE'S JOBS, I HAVE...SIX MONTHS TO LIVE.
12/16/02 © 2002 United Feature Syndicate, Inc.
REMIND ME IN FIVE AND A HALF MONTHS SO I CAN SHOP FOR A CARD.

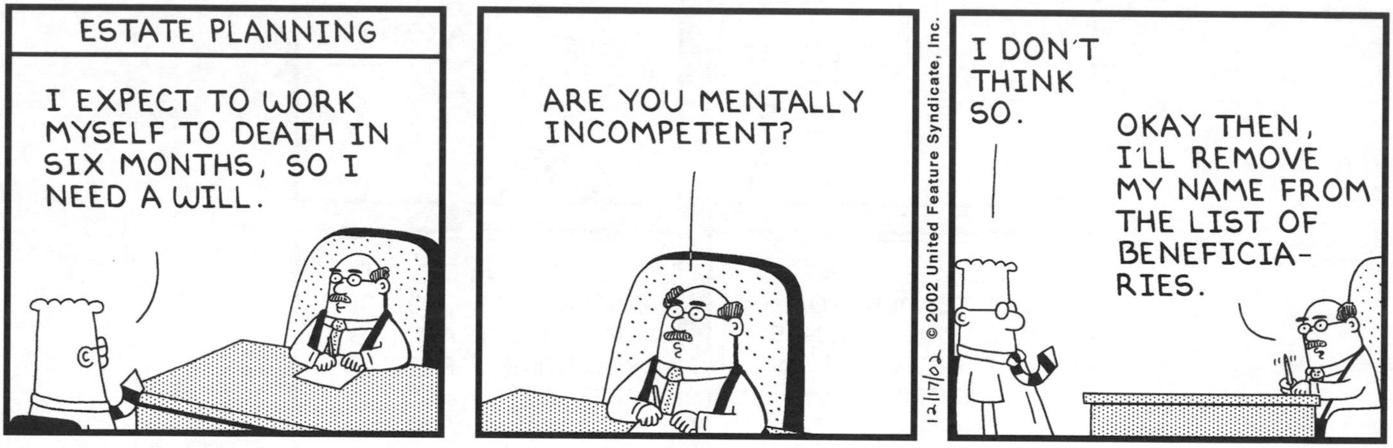
ESTATE PLANNING
I EXPECT TO WORK MYSELF TO DEATH IN SIX MONTHS, SO I NEED A WILL.
ARE YOU MENTALLY INCOMPETENT?
12/17/02 © 2002 United Feature Syndicate, Inc.
I DON'T THINK SO.
OKAY THEN, I'LL REMOVE MY NAME FROM THE LIST OF BENEFICIA-RIES.

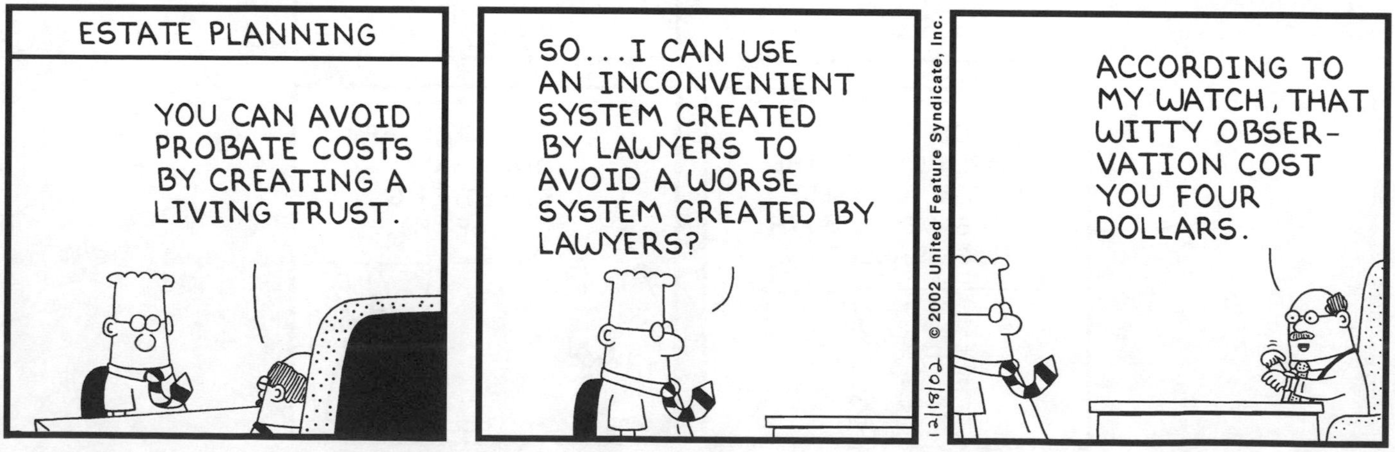
ESTATE PLANNING
YOU CAN AVOID PROBATE COSTS BY CREATING A LIVING TRUST.
SO...I CAN USE AN INCONVENIENT SYSTEM CREATED BY LAWYERS TO AVOID A WORSE SYSTEM CREATED BY LAWYERS?
12/18/02 © 2002 United Feature Syndicate, Inc.
ACCORDING TO MY WATCH, THAT WITTY OBSER-VATION COST YOU FOUR DOLLARS.

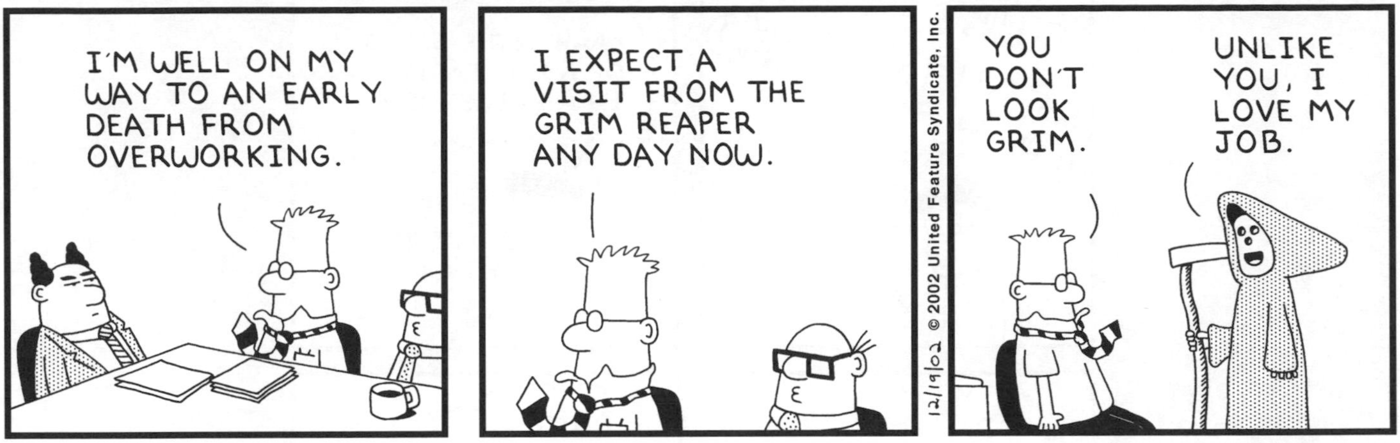
I'M WELL ON MY WAY TO AN EARLY DEATH FROM OVERWORKING.
I EXPECT A VISIT FROM THE GRIM REAPER ANY DAY NOW.
12/19/02 © 2002 United Feature Syndicate, Inc.
YOU DON'T LOOK GRIM.
UNLIKE YOU, I LOVE MY JOB.

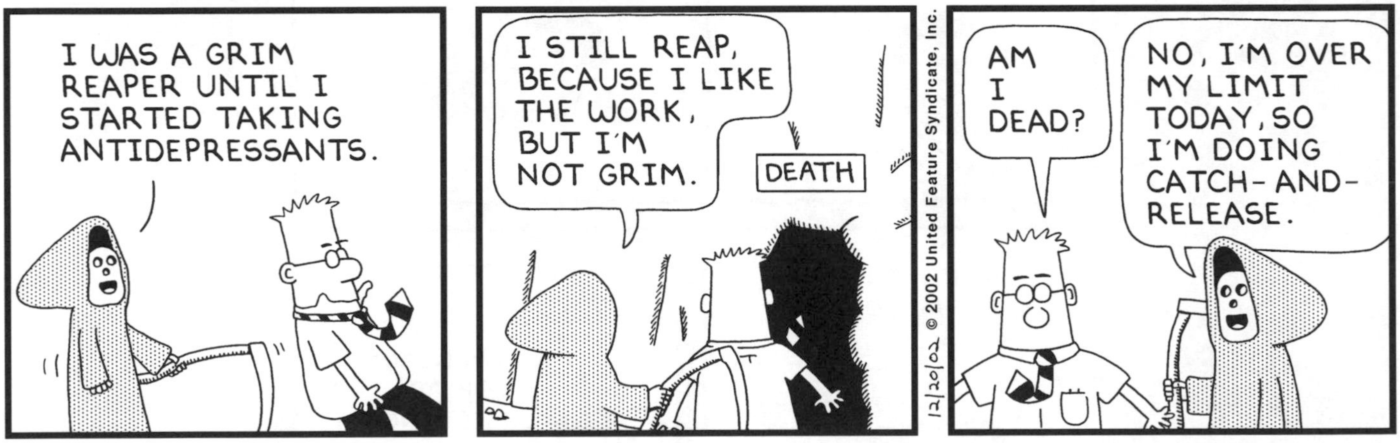
I WAS A GRIM REAPER UNTIL I STARTED TAKING ANTIDEPRESSANTS.
I STILL REAP, BECAUSE I LIKE THE WORK, BUT I'M NOT GRIM.
DEATH
12/20/02 © 2002 United Feature Syndicate, Inc.
AM I DEAD?
NO, I'M OVER MY LIMIT TODAY, SO I'M DOING CATCH-AND-RELEASE.

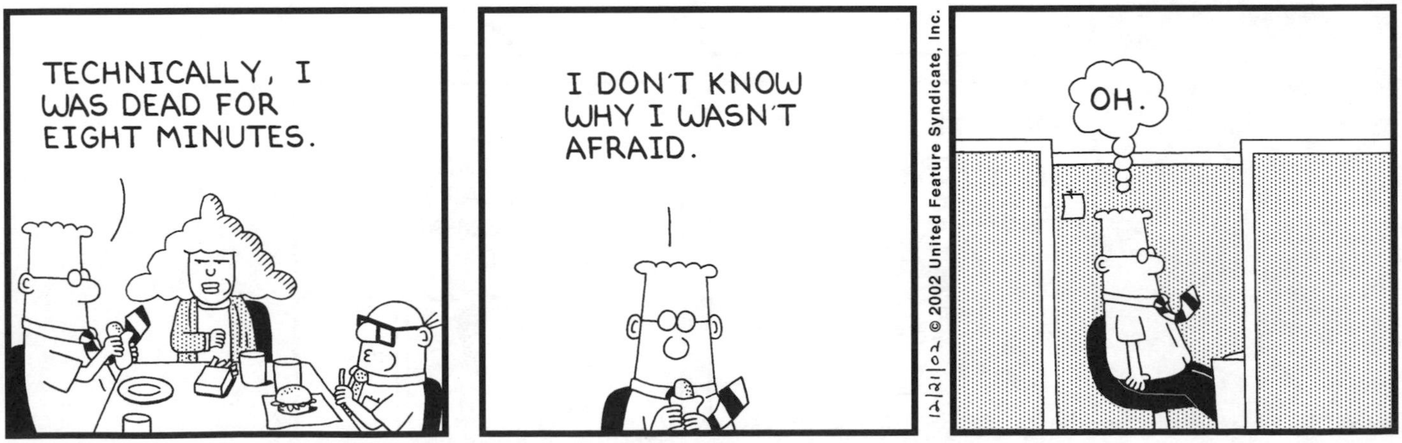
TECHNICALLY, I WAS DEAD FOR EIGHT MINUTES.
I DON'T KNOW WHY I WASN'T AFRAID.
12/21/02 © 2002 United Feature Syndicate, Inc.
OH.

THE ADVENTURES OF PAUL OOSHEN*
(*SAY IT FAST)
AAAH... THE SCENT OF A HOG FARM IN A RAINSTORM.
OIL FOR FINGERS.
ONION SANDWICH.
ANNOYING NASAL SOUNDS.
SNIFF SNORT
LEAKY COFFEE MUG.
I'M READY FOR MY MEETING.
YES! YES! I AGREE TO EVERYTHING! PLEASE LEAVE!!
I DIDN'T EVEN NEED TO LEAN OVER HER KEYBOARD WITH MY SUGAR DOUGHNUT.
12/22/02 © 2002 United Feature Syndicate, Inc.

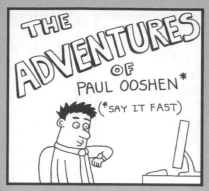

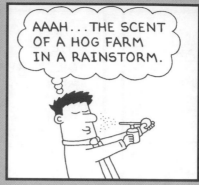

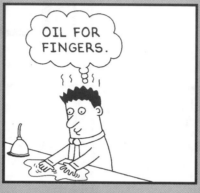

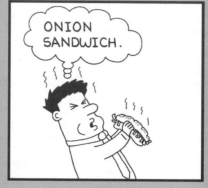

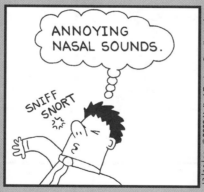

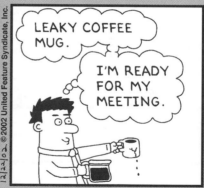

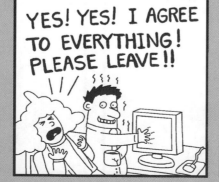

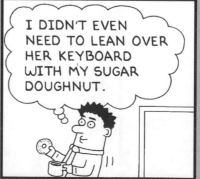

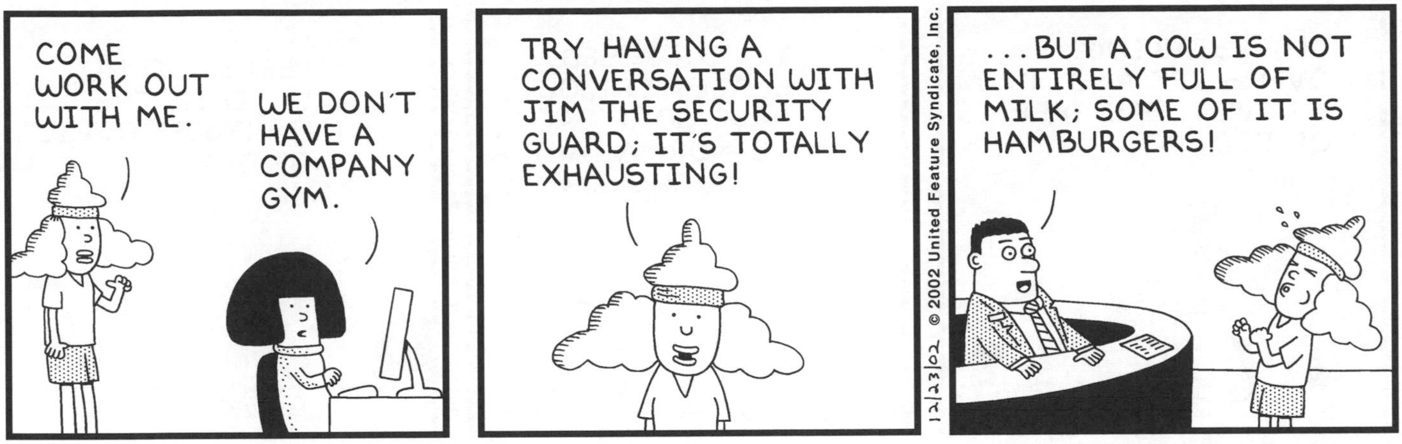
COME WORK OUT WITH ME.
WE DON'T HAVE A COMPANY GYM.
TRY HAVING A CONVERSATION WITH JIM THE SECURITY GUARD; IT'S TOTALLY EXHAUSTING!
12/23/02 © 2002 United Feature Syndicate, Inc.
...BUT A COW IS NOT ENTIRELY FULL OF MILK; SOME OF IT IS HAMBURGERS!

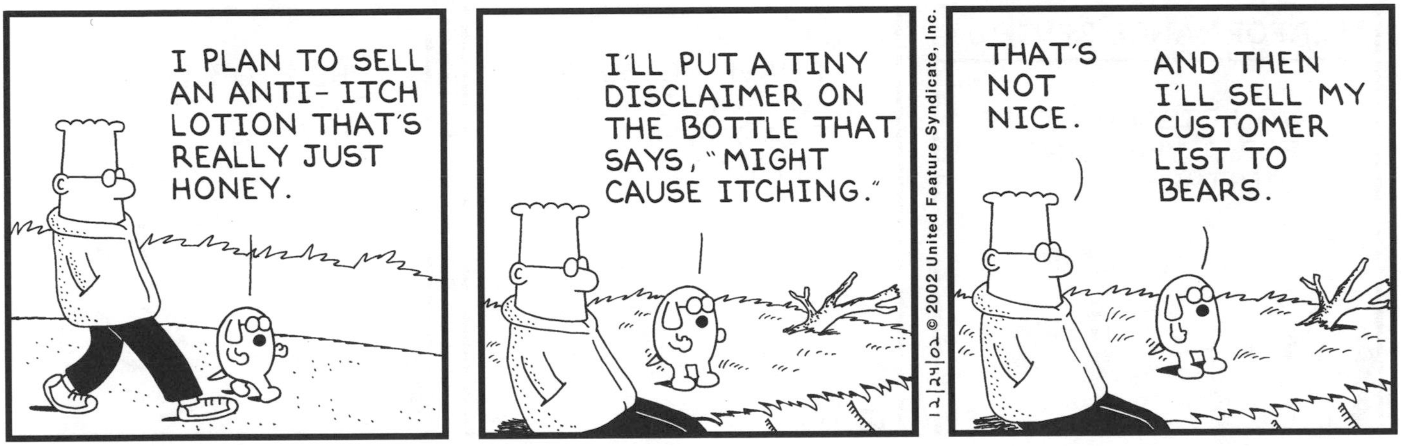
I PLAN TO SELL AN ANTI-ITCH LOTION THAT'S REALLY JUST HONEY.
I'LL PUT A TINY DISCLAIMER ON THE BOTTLE THAT SAYS, "MIGHT CAUSE ITCHING."
12/24/02 © 2002 United Feature Syndicate, Inc.
THAT'S NOT NICE.
AND THEN I'LL SELL MY CUSTOMER LIST TO BEARS.

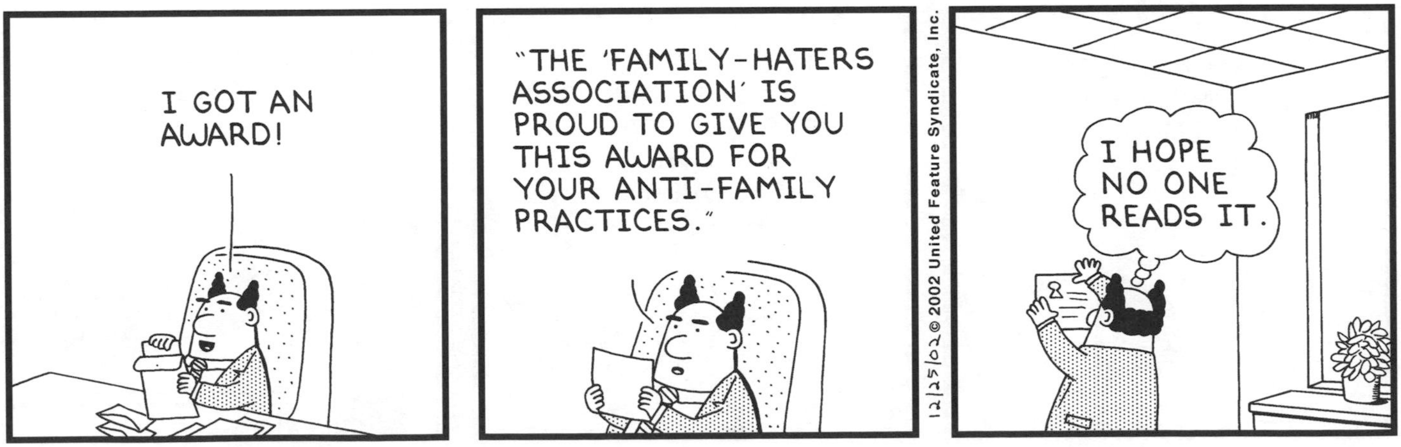
I GOT AN AWARD!
"THE 'FAMILY-HATERS ASSOCIATION' IS PROUD TO GIVE YOU THIS AWARD FOR YOUR ANTI-FAMILY PRACTICES."
12/25/02 © 2002 United Feature Syndicate, Inc.
I HOPE NO ONE READS IT.

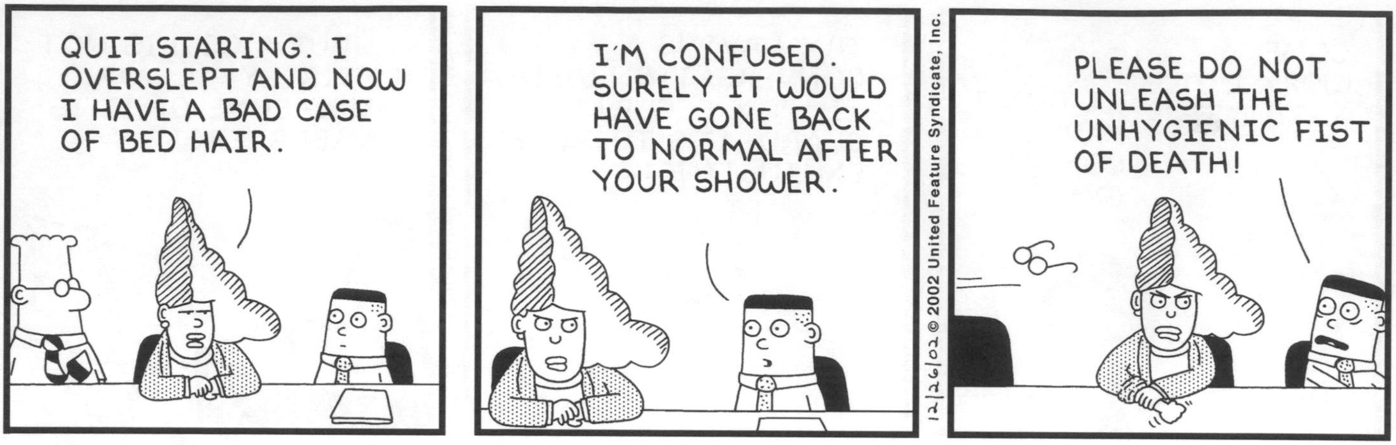
QUIT STARING. I OVERSLEPT AND NOW I HAVE A BAD CASE OF BED HAIR.
I'M CONFUSED. SURELY IT WOULD HAVE GONE BACK TO NORMAL AFTER YOUR SHOWER.
12/26/02 © 2002 United Feature Syndicate, Inc.
PLEASE DO NOT UNLEASH THE UNHYGIENIC FIST OF DEATH!

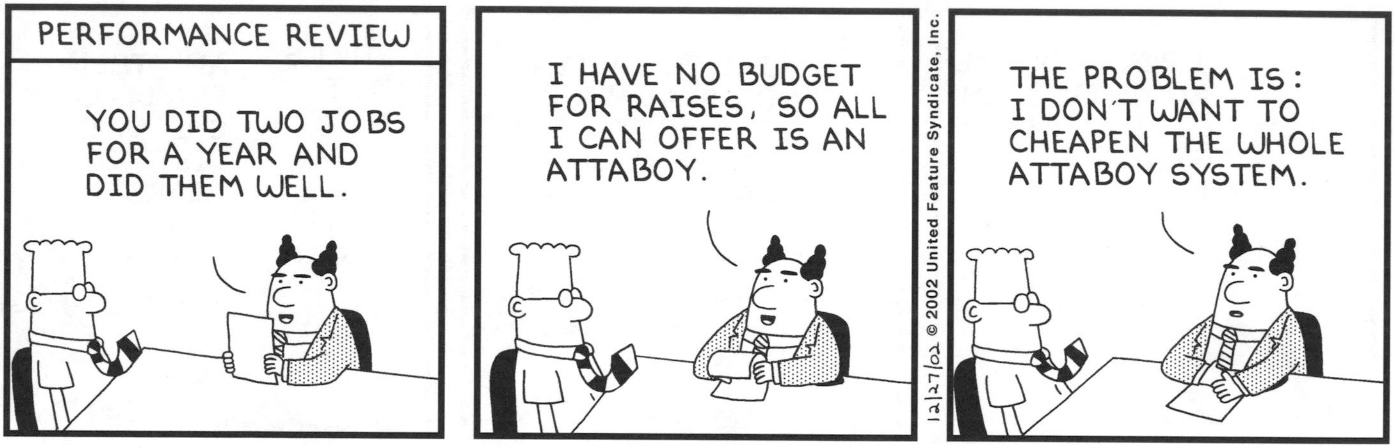
PERFORMANCE REVIEW
YOU DID TWO JOBS FOR A YEAR AND DID THEM WELL.
I HAVE NO BUDGET FOR RAISES, SO ALL I CAN OFFER IS AN ATTABOY.
12/27/02 © 2002 United Feature Syndicate, Inc.
THE PROBLEM IS: I DON'T WANT TO CHEAPEN THE WHOLE ATTABOY SYSTEM.

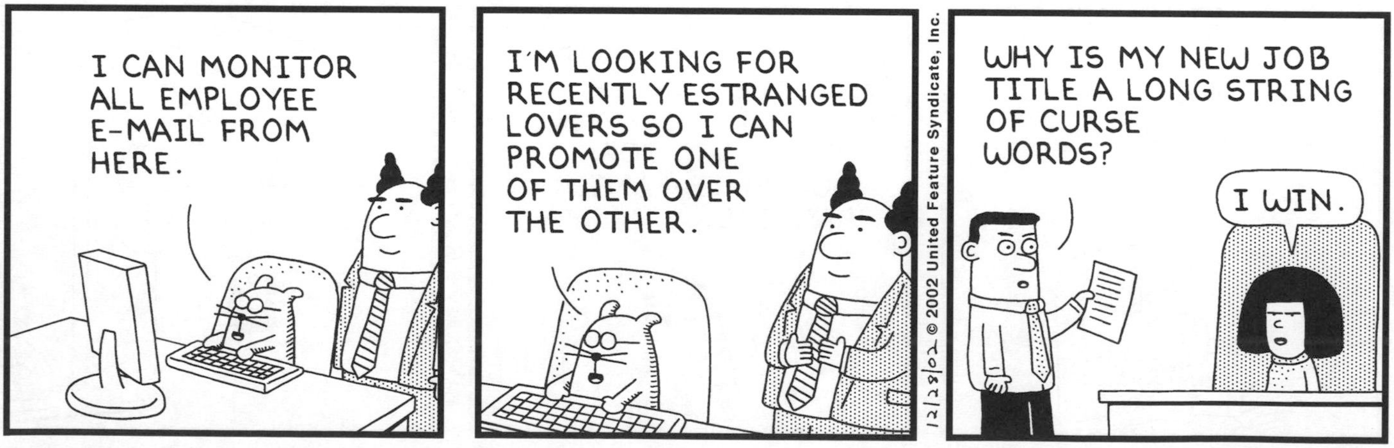
I CAN MONITOR ALL EMPLOYEE E-MAIL FROM HERE.
I'M LOOKING FOR RECENTLY ESTRANGED LOVERS SO I CAN PROMOTE ONE OF THEM OVER THE OTHER.
12/28/02 © 2002 United Feature Syndicate, Inc.
WHY IS MY NEW JOB TITLE A LONG STRING OF CURSE WORDS?
I WIN.

CAROL, CALL THE POLICE. MY CAR HAS BEEN STOLEN.
IS IT LIKE THE LAST THREE TIMES THAT YOU THOUGHT IT HAD BEEN STOLEN?
AND LATER YOU REALIZED THAT YOU JUST FORGOT WHERE YOU PARKED IT?
NO. THIS TIME IS DIFFERENT. MY CAR IS TOTALLY GONE.
WATCH ME USE MY MAGIC POWERS TO MAKE YOUR CAR REAPPEAR IN THE PARKING LOT.
PRESTO AUTO REAPPEARO!!!
AFTER ALL THE OTHER CARS LEAVE THE PARKING LOT, YOUR CAR WILL APPEAR.
FREAKY.
12/29/02 © 2002 United Feature Syndicate, Inc.

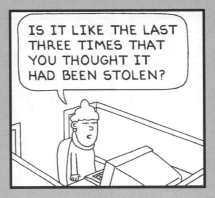

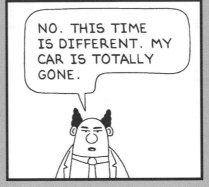

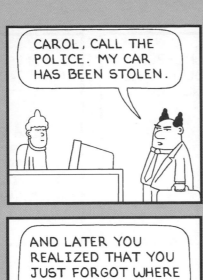

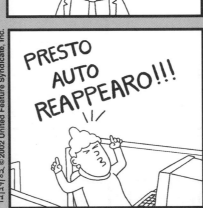

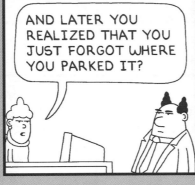

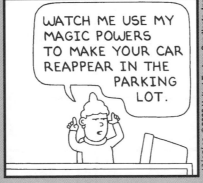

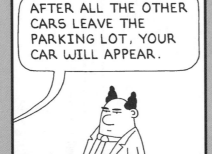

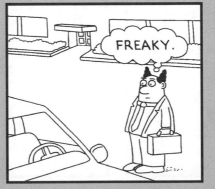

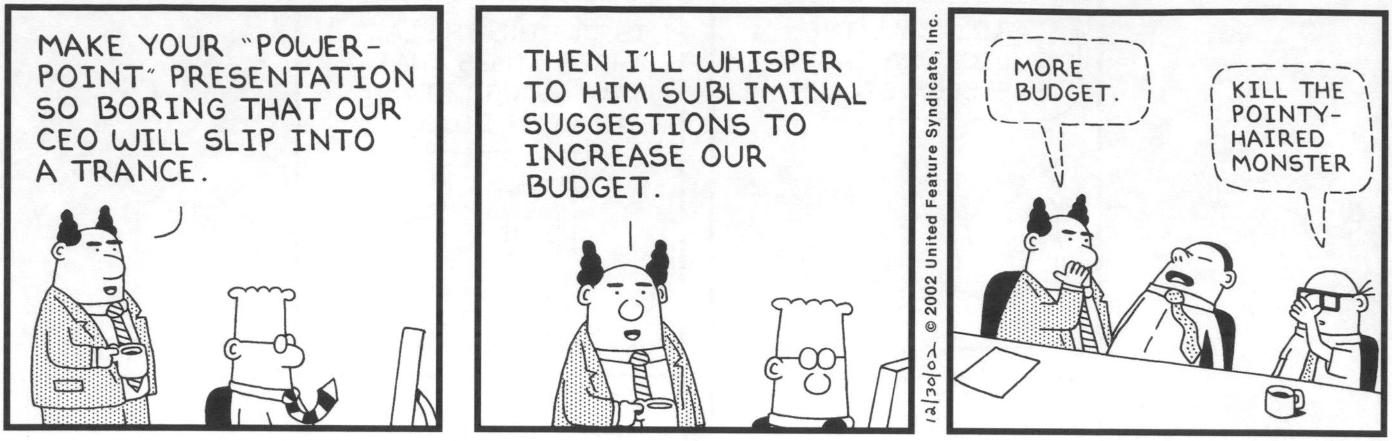
MAKE YOUR "POWER-POINT" PRESENTATION SO BORING THAT OUR CEO WILL SLIP INTO A TRANCE.
THEN I'LL WHISPER TO HIM SUBLIMINAL SUGGESTIONS TO INCREASE OUR BUDGET.
MORE BUDGET.
KILL THE POINTY-HAIRED MONSTER
12/30/02 © 2002 United Feature Syndicate, Inc.

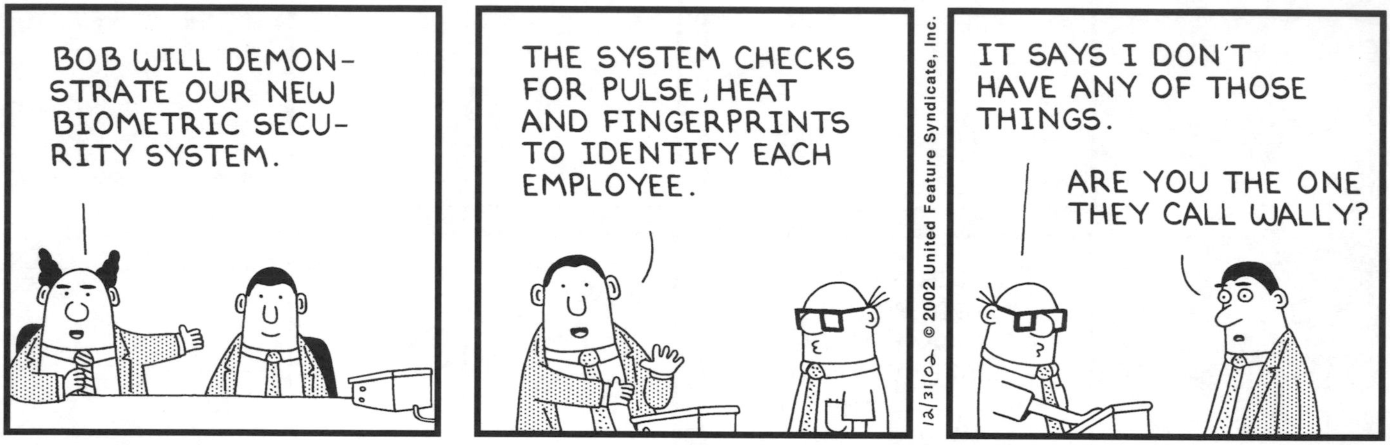
BOB WILL DEMON-STRATE OUR NEW BIOMETRIC SECU-RITY SYSTEM.
THE SYSTEM CHECKS FOR PULSE, HEAT AND FINGERPRINTS TO IDENTIFY EACH EMPLOYEE.
IT SAYS I DON'T HAVE ANY OF THOSE THINGS.
ARE YOU THE ONE THEY CALL WALLY?
12/31/02 © 2002 United Feature Syndicate, Inc.

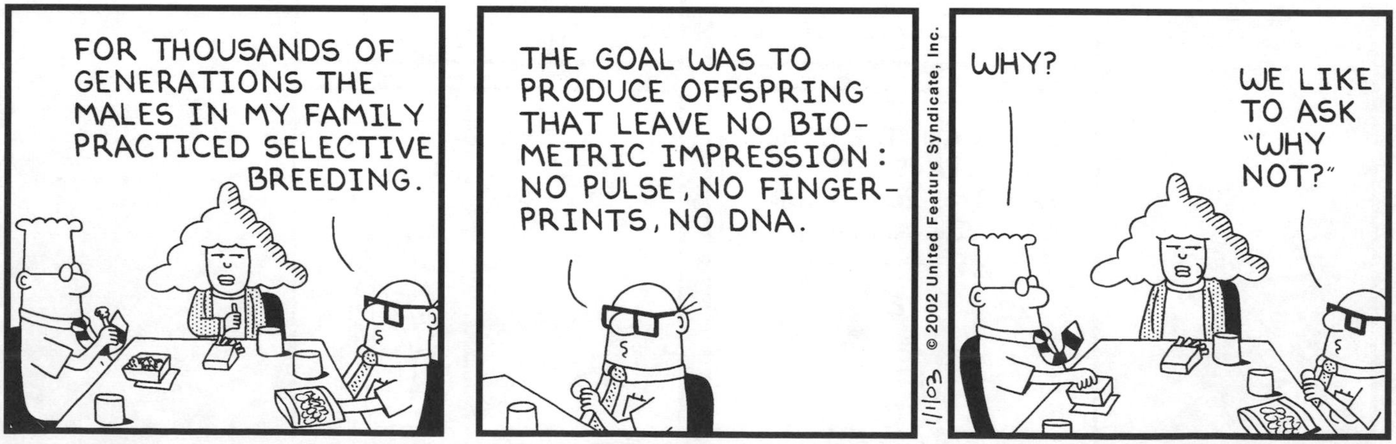
FOR THOUSANDS OF GENERATIONS THE MALES IN MY FAMILY PRACTICED SELECTIVE BREEDING.
THE GOAL WAS TO PRODUCE OFFSPRING THAT LEAVE NO BIO-METRIC IMPRESSION: NO PULSE, NO FINGER-PRINTS, NO DNA.
WHY?
WE LIKE TO ASK "WHY NOT?"
1/1/03 © 2002 United Feature Syndicate, Inc.

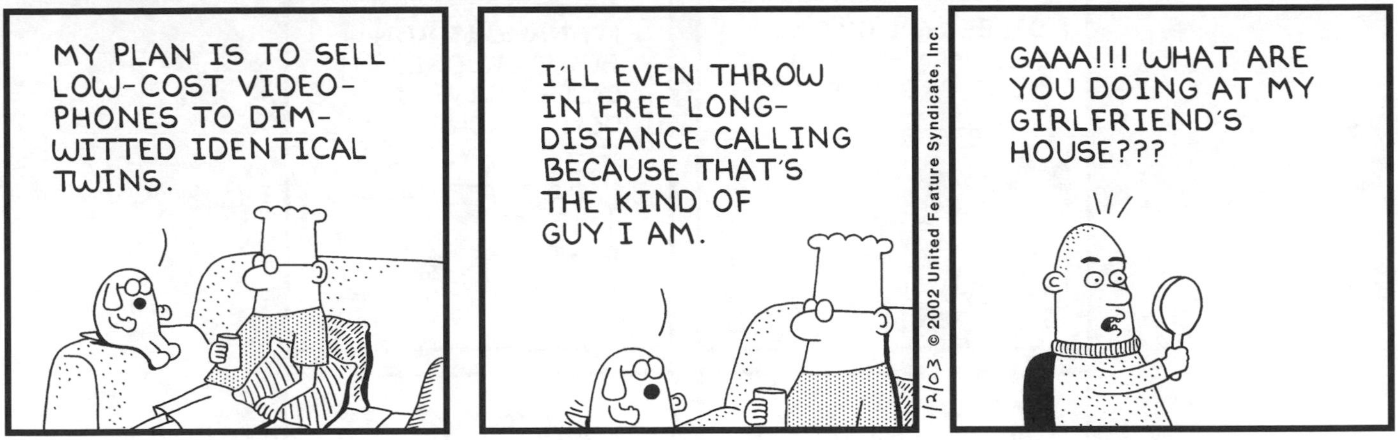
MY PLAN IS TO SELL LOW-COST VIDEO-PHONES TO DIM-WITTED IDENTICAL TWINS.
I'LL EVEN THROW IN FREE LONG-DISTANCE CALLING BECAUSE THAT'S THE KIND OF GUY I AM.
1/2/03 © 2002 United Feature Syndicate, Inc.
GAAA!!! WHAT ARE YOU DOING AT MY GIRLFRIEND'S HOUSE???

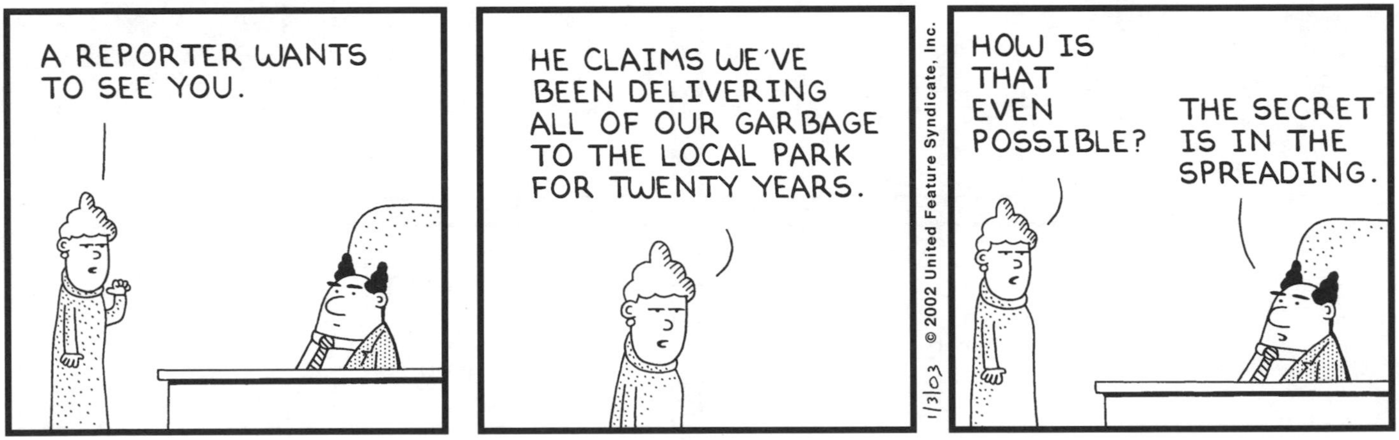
A REPORTER WANTS TO SEE YOU.
HE CLAIMS WE'VE BEEN DELIVERING ALL OF OUR GARBAGE TO THE LOCAL PARK FOR TWENTY YEARS.
1/3/03 © 2002 United Feature Syndicate, Inc.
HOW IS THAT EVEN POSSIBLE?
THE SECRET IS IN THE SPREADING.

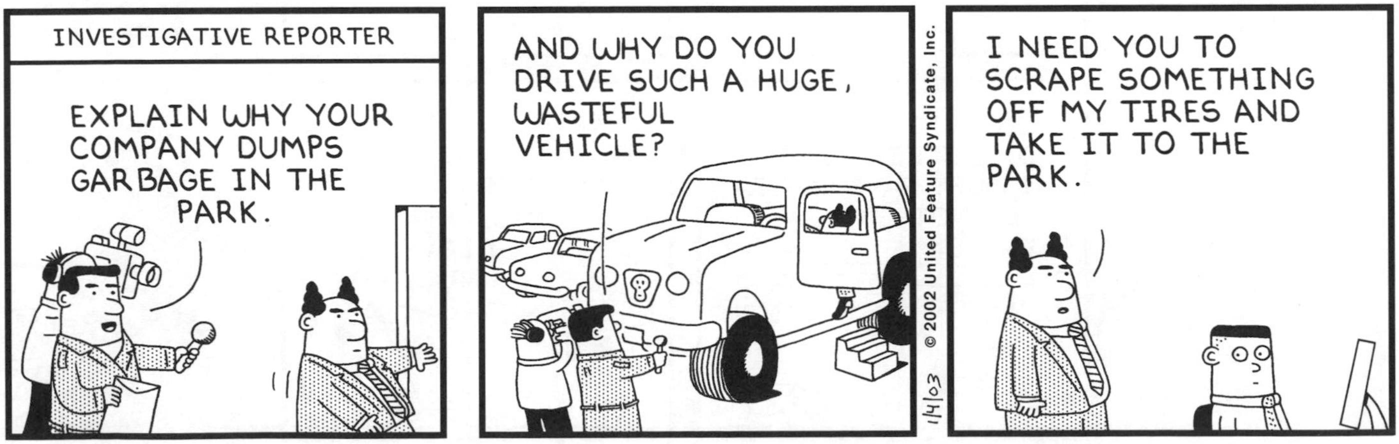
INVESTIGATIVE REPORTER
EXPLAIN WHY YOUR COMPANY DUMPS GARBAGE IN THE PARK.
AND WHY DO YOU DRIVE SUCH A HUGE, WASTEFUL VEHICLE?
1/4/03 © 2002 United Feature Syndicate, Inc.
I NEED YOU TO SCRAPE SOMETHING OFF MY TIRES AND TAKE IT TO THE PARK.

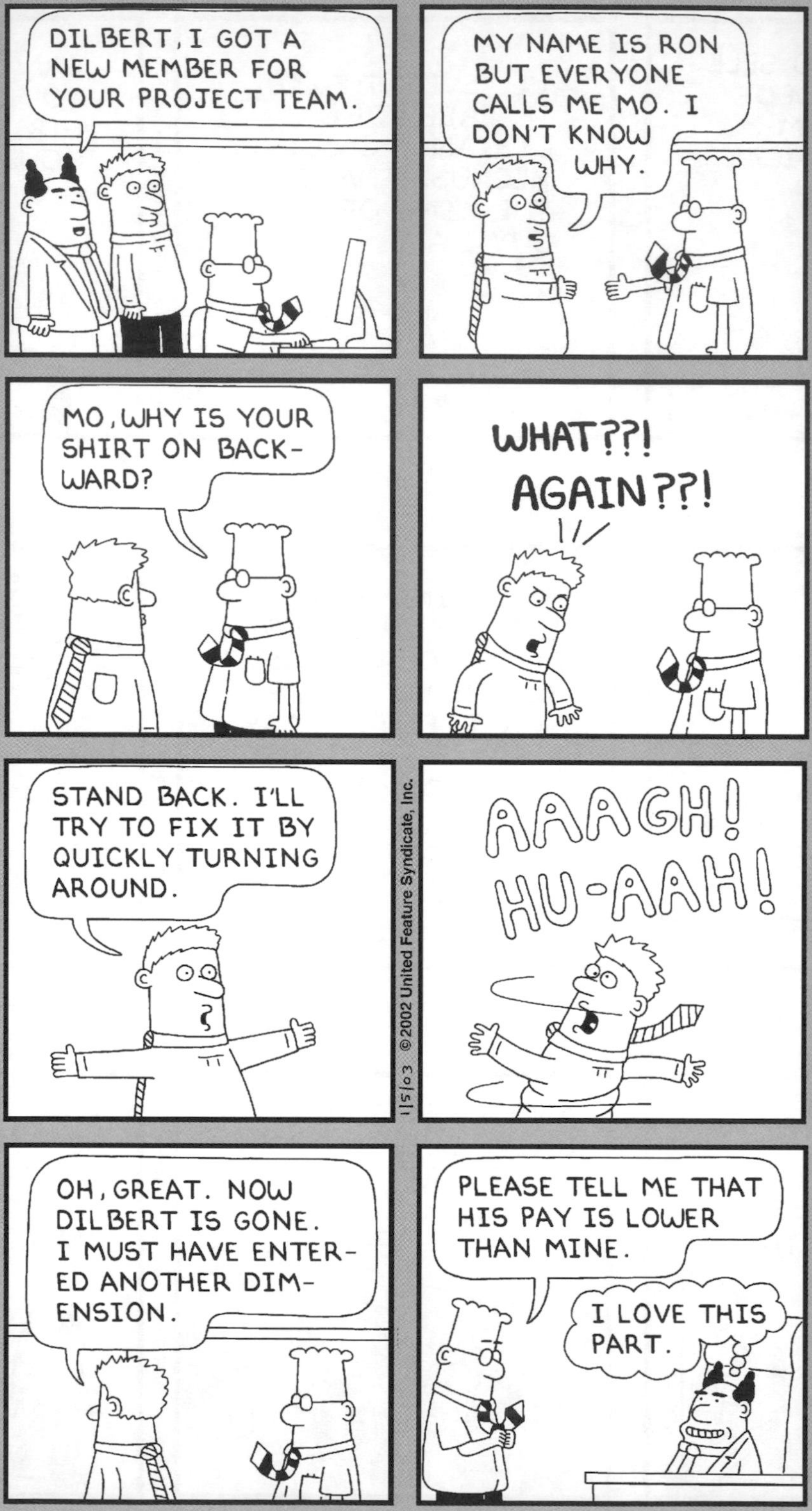
DILBERT, I GOT A NEW MEMBER FOR YOUR PROJECT TEAM.
MY NAME IS RON BUT EVERYONE CALLS ME MO. I DON'T KNOW WHY.
MO, WHY IS YOUR SHIRT ON BACK-WARD?
WHAT??!
AGAIN??!
STAND BACK. I'LL TRY TO FIX IT BY QUICKLY TURNING AROUND.
AAAGH!
HU-AAH!
OH, GREAT. NOW DILBERT IS GONE. I MUST HAVE ENTER-ED ANOTHER DIM-ENSION.
PLEASE TELL ME THAT HIS PAY IS LOWER THAN MINE.
I LOVE THIS PART.
1/5/03 ©2002 United Feature Syndicate, Inc.

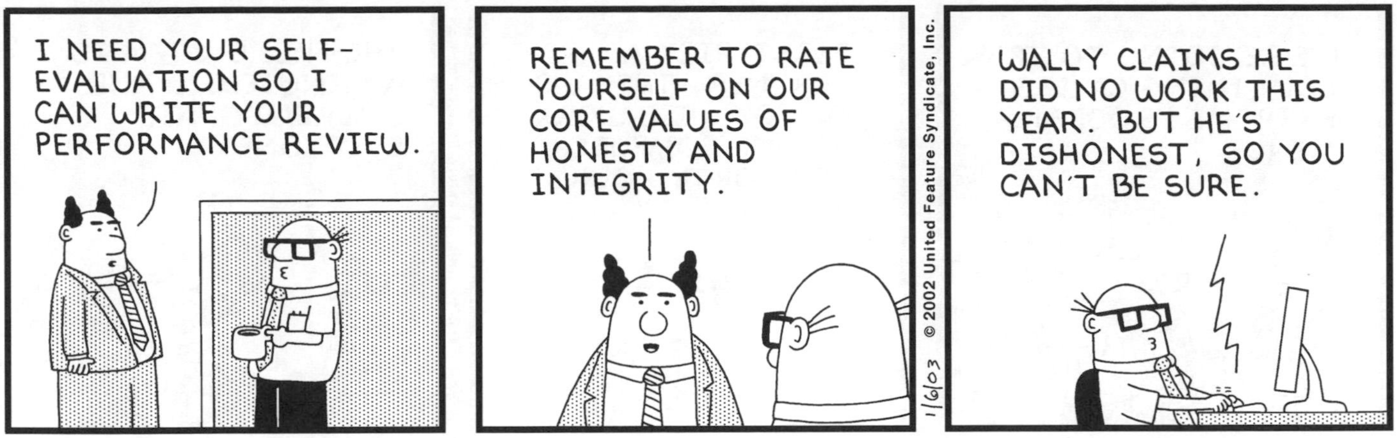
I NEED YOUR SELF-EVALUATION SO I CAN WRITE YOUR PERFORMANCE REVIEW.
REMEMBER TO RATE YOURSELF ON OUR CORE VALUES OF HONESTY AND INTEGRITY.
1/6/03 © 2002 United Feature Syndicate, Inc.
WALLY CLAIMS HE DID NO WORK THIS YEAR. BUT HE'S DISHONEST, SO YOU CAN'T BE SURE.

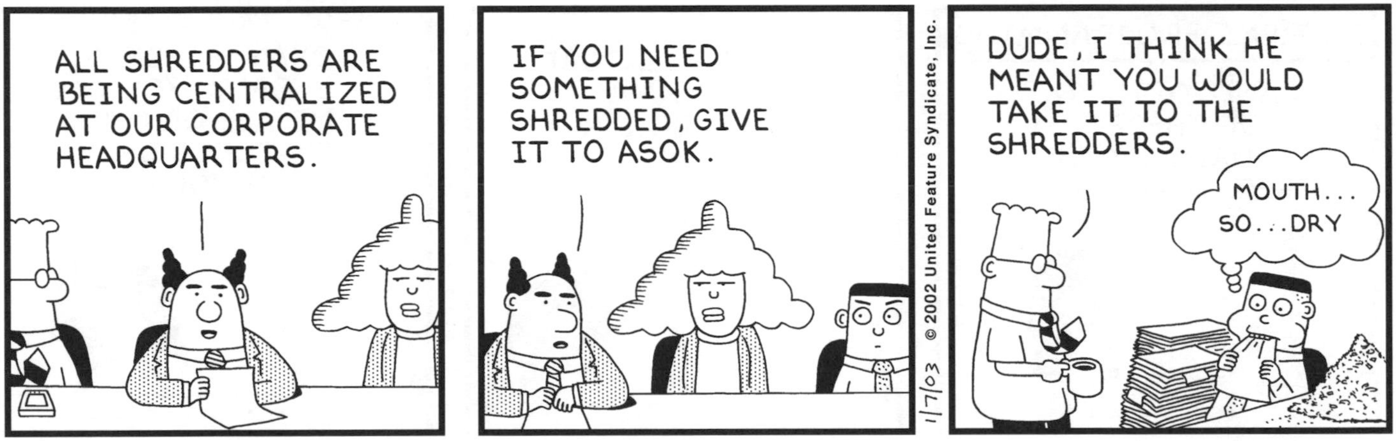
ALL SHREDDERS ARE BEING CENTRALIZED AT OUR CORPORATE HEADQUARTERS.
IF YOU NEED SOMETHING SHREDDED, GIVE IT TO ASOK.
1/7/03 © 2002 United Feature Syndicate, Inc.
DUDE, I THINK HE MEANT YOU WOULD TAKE IT TO THE SHREDDERS.
MOUTH... SO... DRY

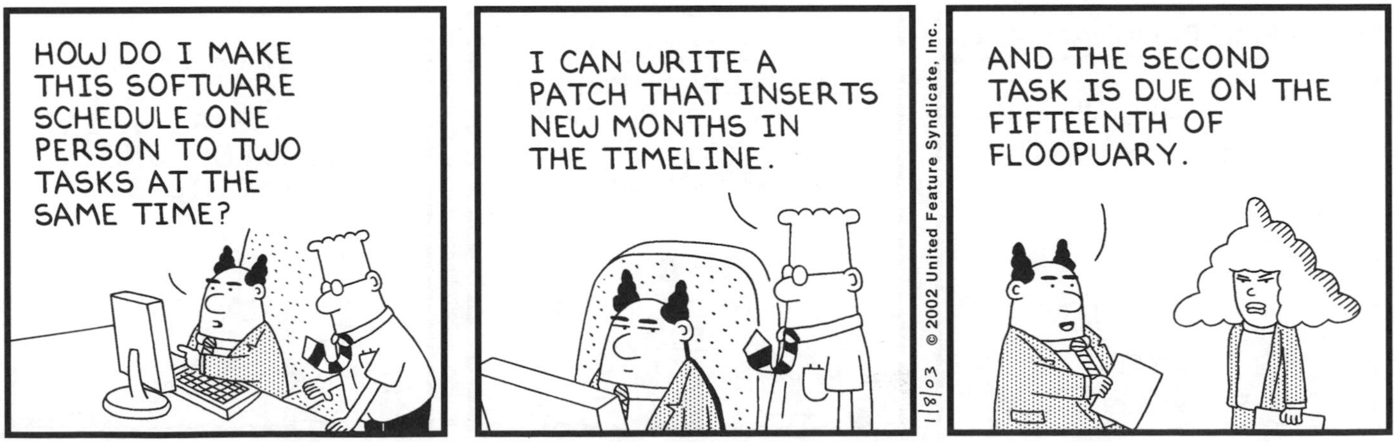
HOW DO I MAKE THIS SOFTWARE SCHEDULE ONE PERSON TO TWO TASKS AT THE SAME TIME?
I CAN WRITE A PATCH THAT INSERTS NEW MONTHS IN THE TIMELINE.
1/8/03 © 2002 United Feature Syndicate, Inc.
AND THE SECOND TASK IS DUE ON THE FIFTEENTH OF FLOOPUARY.

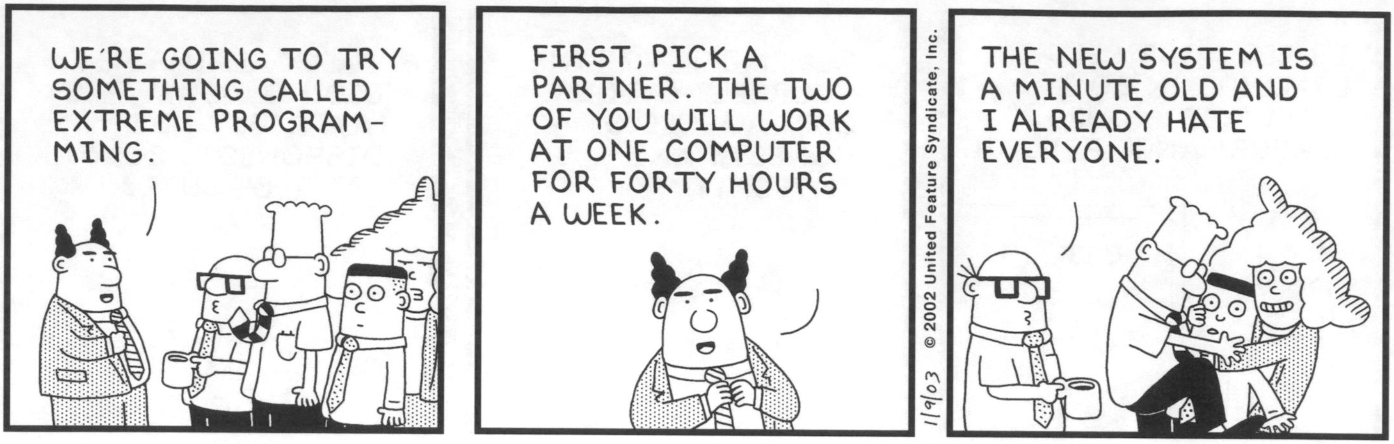
WE'RE GOING TO TRY SOMETHING CALLED EXTREME PROGRAMMING.
FIRST, PICK A PARTNER. THE TWO OF YOU WILL WORK AT ONE COMPUTER FOR FORTY HOURS A WEEK.
1/9/03 © 2002 United Feature Syndicate, Inc.
THE NEW SYSTEM IS A MINUTE OLD AND I ALREADY HATE EVERYONE.

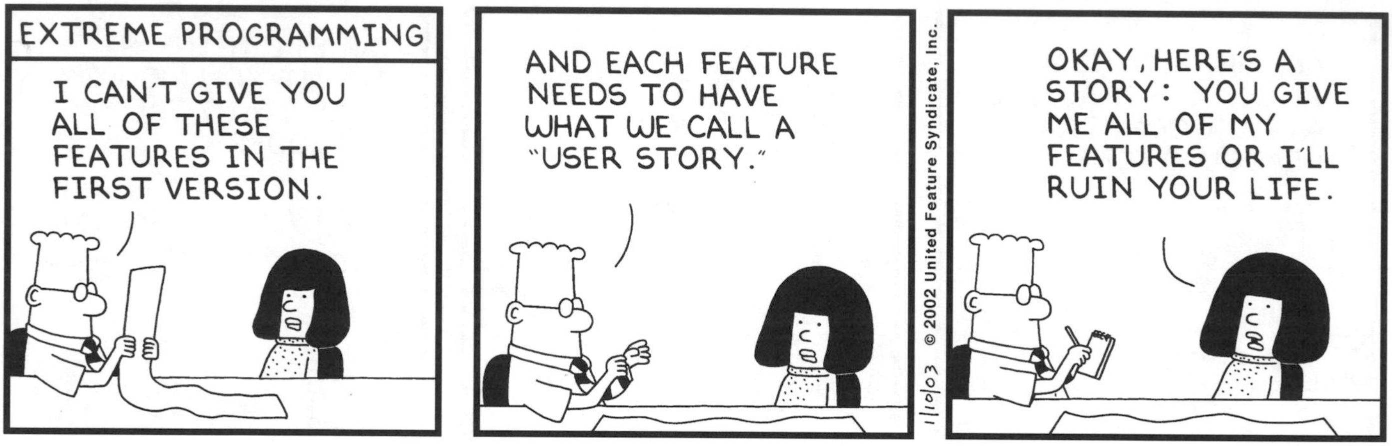
EXTREME PROGRAMMING
I CAN'T GIVE YOU ALL OF THESE FEATURES IN THE FIRST VERSION.
AND EACH FEATURE NEEDS TO HAVE WHAT WE CALL A "USER STORY."
1/10/03 © 2002 United Feature Syndicate, Inc.
OKAY, HERE'S A STORY: YOU GIVE ME ALL OF MY FEATURES OR I'LL RUIN YOUR LIFE.

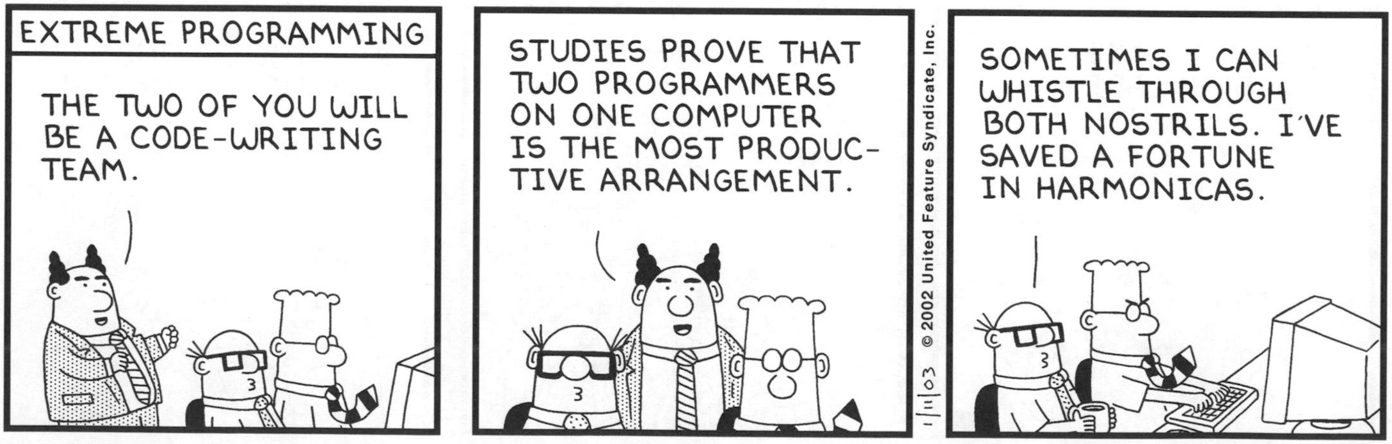
EXTREME PROGRAMMING
THE TWO OF YOU WILL BE A CODE-WRITING TEAM.
STUDIES PROVE THAT TWO PROGRAMMERS ON ONE COMPUTER IS THE MOST PRODUCTIVE ARRANGEMENT.
1/11/03 © 2002 United Feature Syndicate, Inc.
SOMETIMES I CAN WHISTLE THROUGH BOTH NOSTRILS. I'VE SAVED A FORTUNE IN HARMONICAS.

I THOUGHT OF A GREAT IDEA.
YOU COULD LET THE PROJECT MANAGERS MANAGE THEIR OWN BUDGETS...WHAT?
YOU'RE GIVING ME A LOOK. I MUST TRY TO GUESS WHAT IT MEANS.
WE DON'T DO THINGS THAT WAY? IF IT WERE A GOOD IDEA YOU'D ALREADY BE DOING IT?
MY IDEAS ARE POORLY CONCEIVED?! I CAN'T SEE THE BIG PICTURE?!
1/12/03 © 2003 United Feature Syndicate, Inc.
GAAA!!! I AM IGNORANT AND WORTHLESS!!
I MUST PUMMEL MYSELF WITH MY OWN TINY FISTS!!
OW! OW!
THEY'RE KINDA SELF-MANAGED NOW.
VERY EVIL; I PURR IN YOUR GENERAL DIRECTION.

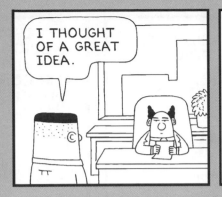

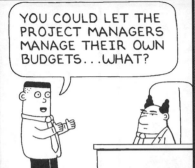

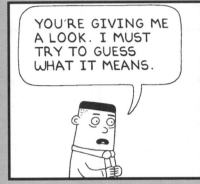

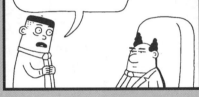

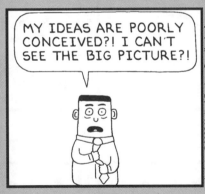

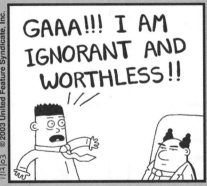

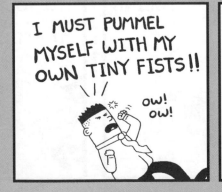

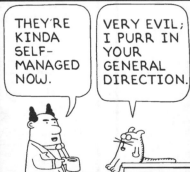

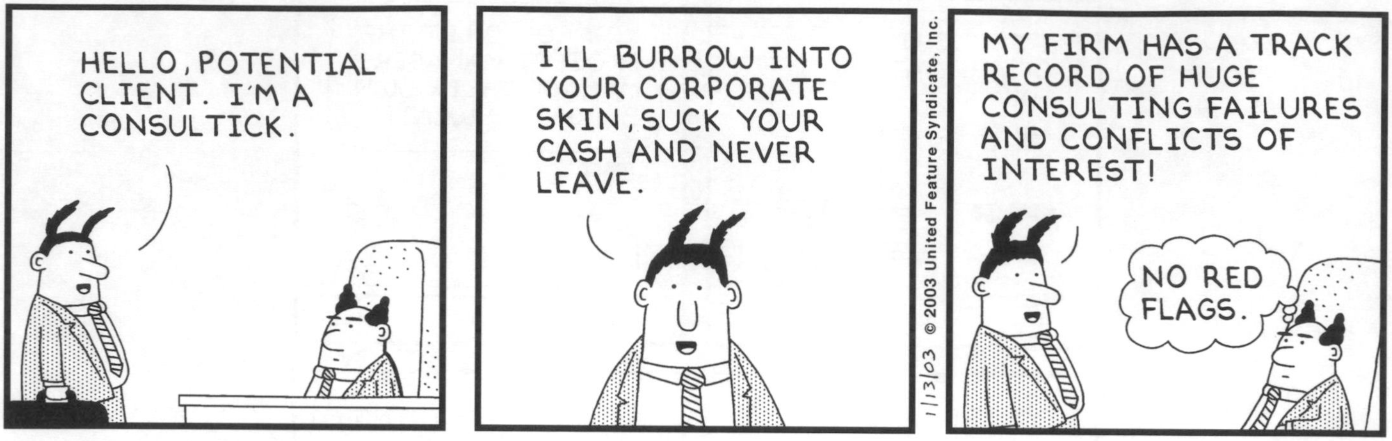
HELLO, POTENTIAL CLIENT. I'M A CONSULTICK.
I'LL BURROW INTO YOUR CORPORATE SKIN, SUCK YOUR CASH AND NEVER LEAVE.
1/13/03 © 2003 United Feature Syndicate, Inc.
MY FIRM HAS A TRACK RECORD OF HUGE CONSULTING FAILURES AND CONFLICTS OF INTEREST!
NO RED FLAGS.

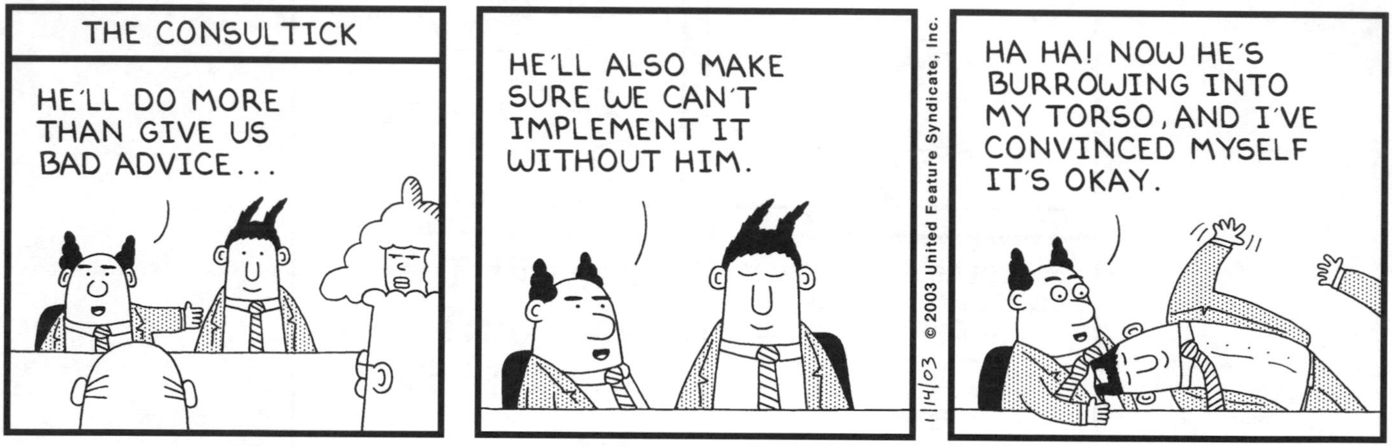
THE CONSULTICK
HE'LL DO MORE THAN GIVE US BAD ADVICE...
HE'LL ALSO MAKE SURE WE CAN'T IMPLEMENT IT WITHOUT HIM.
1/14/03 © 2003 United Feature Syndicate, Inc.
HA HA! NOW HE'S BURROWING INTO MY TORSO, AND I'VE CONVINCED MYSELF IT'S OKAY.

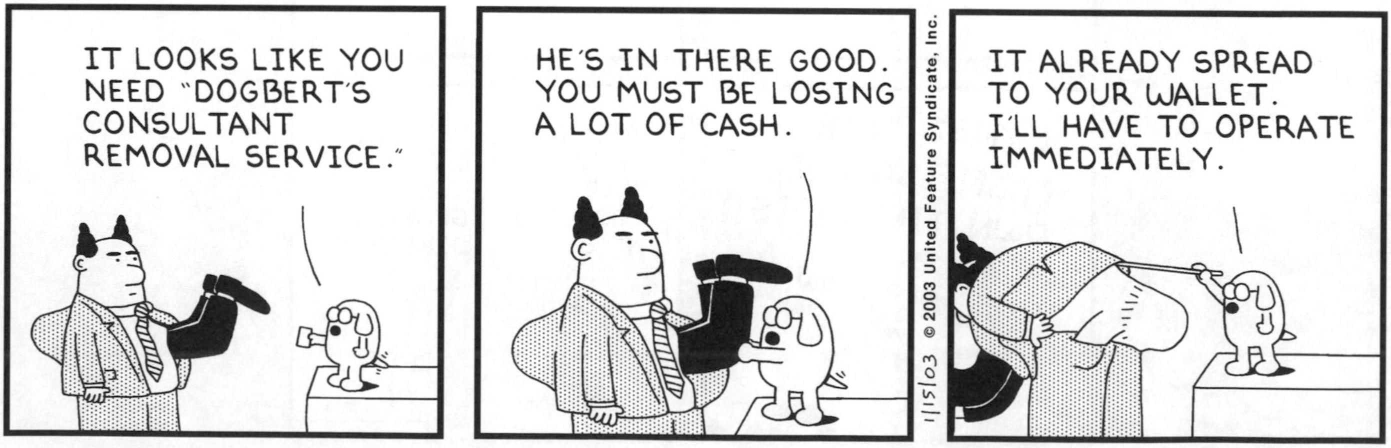
IT LOOKS LIKE YOU NEED "DOGBERT'S CONSULTANT REMOVAL SERVICE."
HE'S IN THERE GOOD. YOU MUST BE LOSING A LOT OF CASH.
1/15/03 © 2003 United Feature Syndicate, Inc.
IT ALREADY SPREAD TO YOUR WALLET. I'LL HAVE TO OPERATE IMMEDIATELY.

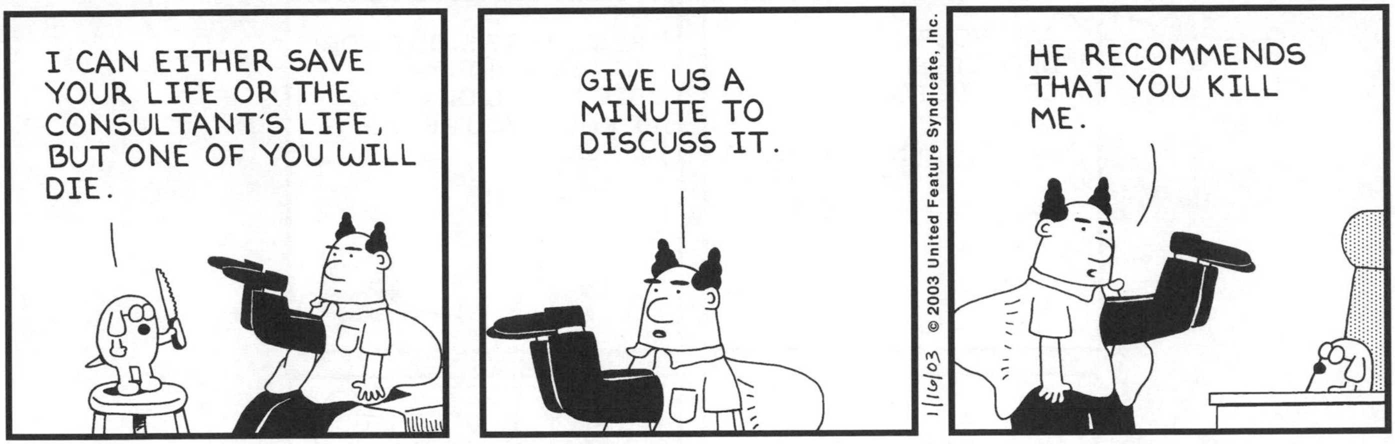
I CAN EITHER SAVE YOUR LIFE OR THE CONSULTANT'S LIFE, BUT ONE OF YOU WILL DIE.
GIVE US A MINUTE TO DISCUSS IT.
1/16/03 © 2003 United Feature Syndicate, Inc.
HE RECOMMENDS THAT YOU KILL ME.

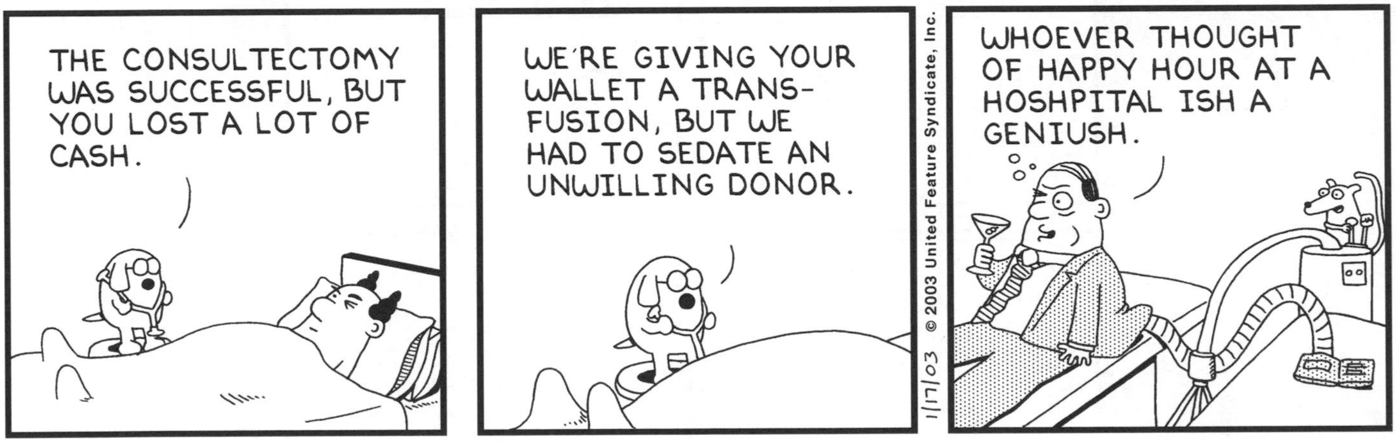
THE CONSULTECTOMY WAS SUCCESSFUL, BUT YOU LOST A LOT OF CASH.
WE'RE GIVING YOUR WALLET A TRANS-FUSION, BUT WE HAD TO SEDATE AN UNWILLING DONOR.
1/17/03 © 2003 United Feature Syndicate, Inc.
WHOEVER THOUGHT OF HAPPY HOUR AT A HOSHPITAL ISH A GENIUSH.

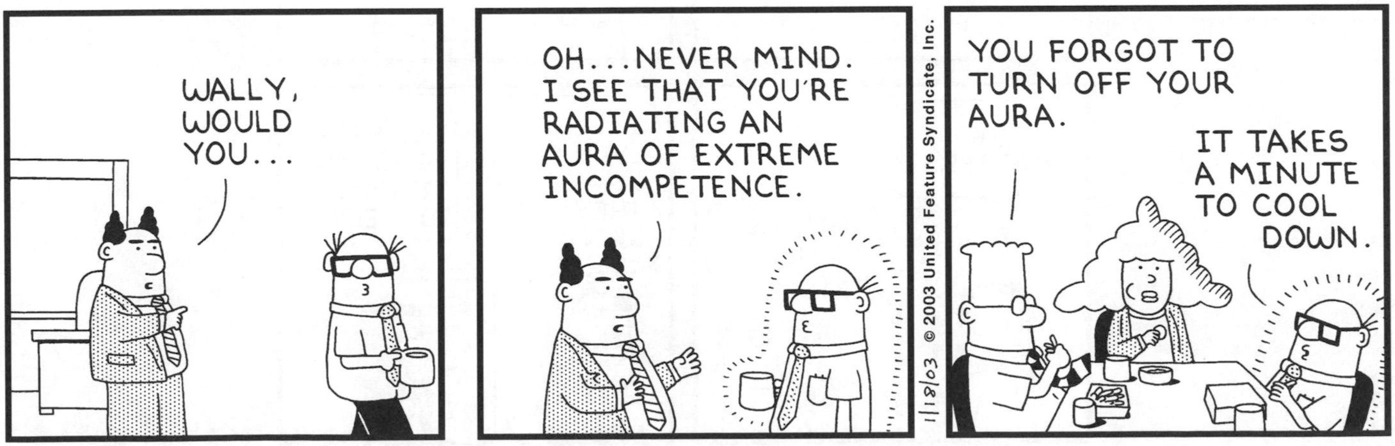
WALLY, WOULD YOU...
OH...NEVER MIND. I SEE THAT YOU'RE RADIATING AN AURA OF EXTREME INCOMPETENCE.
1/18/03 © 2003 United Feature Syndicate, Inc.
YOU FORGOT TO TURN OFF YOUR AURA.
IT TAKES A MINUTE TO COOL DOWN.

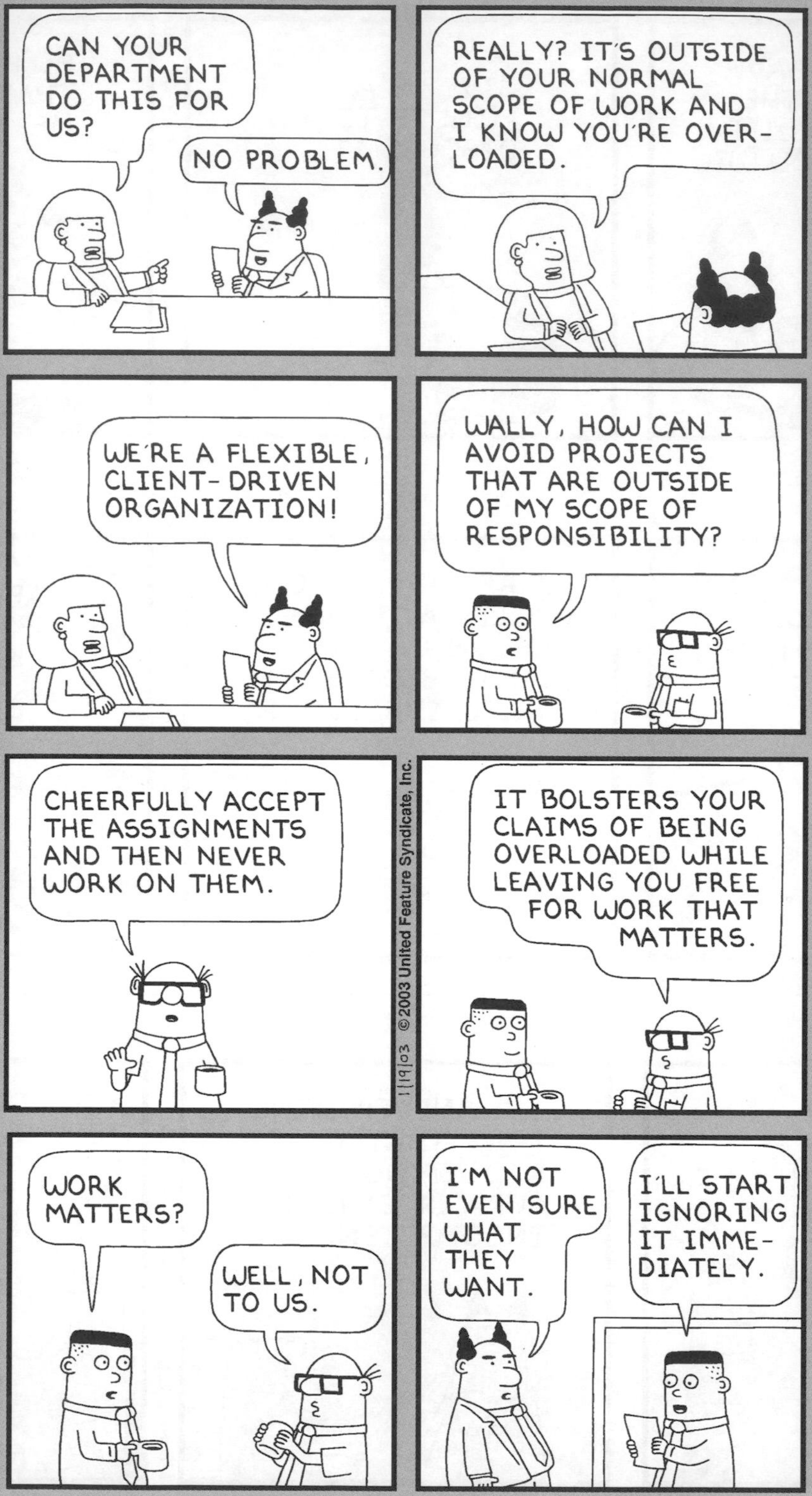
CAN YOUR DEPARTMENT DO THIS FOR US?
NO PROBLEM.
REALLY? IT'S OUTSIDE OF YOUR NORMAL SCOPE OF WORK AND I KNOW YOU'RE OVER-LOADED.
WE'RE A FLEXIBLE, CLIENT-DRIVEN ORGANIZATION!
WALLY, HOW CAN I AVOID PROJECTS THAT ARE OUTSIDE OF MY SCOPE OF RESPONSIBILITY?
CHEERFULLY ACCEPT THE ASSIGNMENTS AND THEN NEVER WORK ON THEM.
1/19/03 ©2003 United Feature Syndicate, Inc.
IT BOLSTERS YOUR CLAIMS OF BEING OVERLOADED WHILE LEAVING YOU FREE FOR WORK THAT MATTERS.
WORK MATTERS?
WELL, NOT TO US.
I'M NOT EVEN SURE WHAT THEY WANT.
I'LL START IGNORING IT IMME-DIATELY.

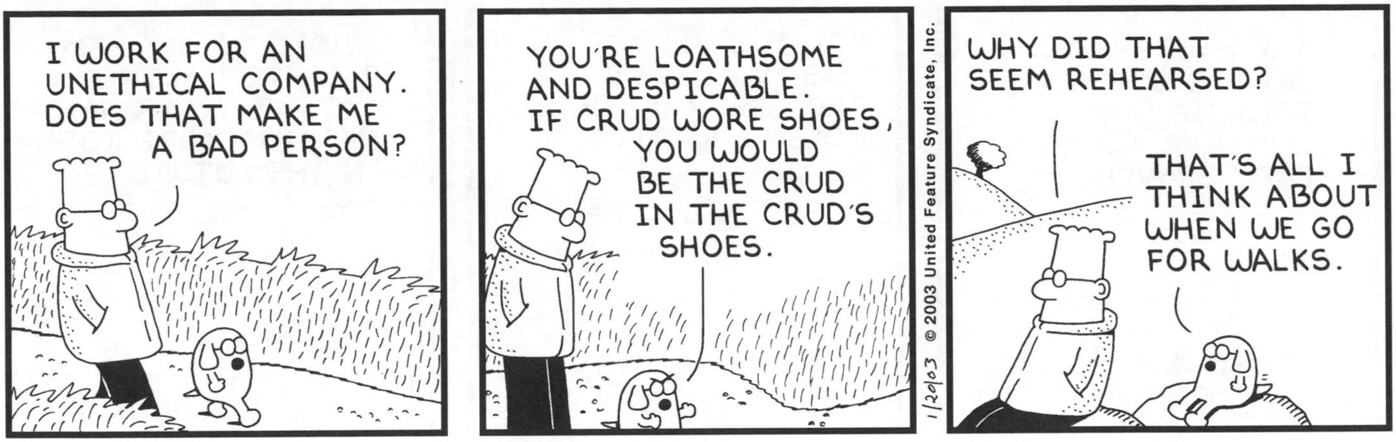
I WORK FOR AN UNETHICAL COMPANY. DOES THAT MAKE ME A BAD PERSON?
YOU'RE LOATHSOME AND DESPICABLE. IF CRUD WORE SHOES, YOU WOULD BE THE CRUD IN THE CRUD'S SHOES.
1/20/03 © 2003 United Feature Syndicate, Inc.
WHY DID THAT SEEM REHEARSED?
THAT'S ALL I THINK ABOUT WHEN WE GO FOR WALKS.

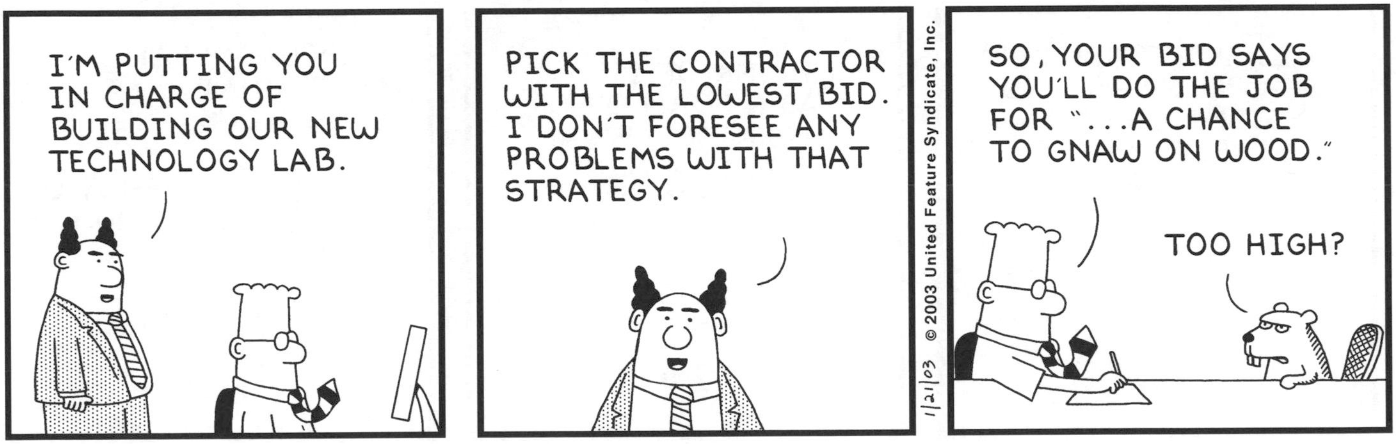
I'M PUTTING YOU IN CHARGE OF BUILDING OUR NEW TECHNOLOGY LAB.
PICK THE CONTRACTOR WITH THE LOWEST BID. I DON'T FORESEE ANY PROBLEMS WITH THAT STRATEGY.
1/21/03 © 2003 United Feature Syndicate, Inc.
SO, YOUR BID SAYS YOU'LL DO THE JOB FOR "...A CHANCE TO GNAW ON WOOD."
TOO HIGH?

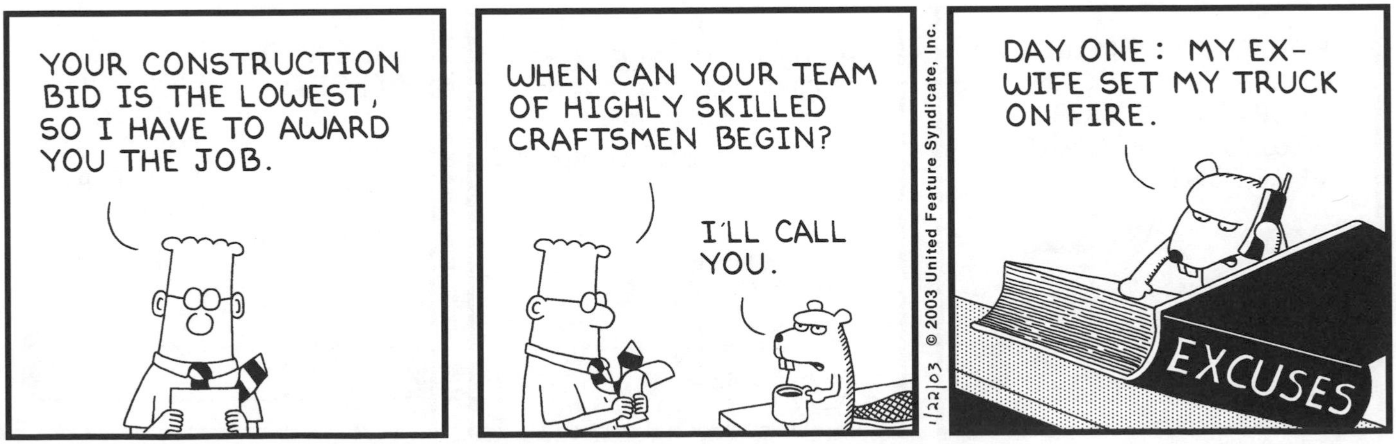
YOUR CONSTRUCTION BID IS THE LOWEST, SO I HAVE TO AWARD YOU THE JOB.
WHEN CAN YOUR TEAM OF HIGHLY SKILLED CRAFTSMEN BEGIN?
I'LL CALL YOU.
1/22/03 © 2003 United Feature Syndicate, Inc.
DAY ONE: MY EX-WIFE SET MY TRUCK ON FIRE.
EXCUSES

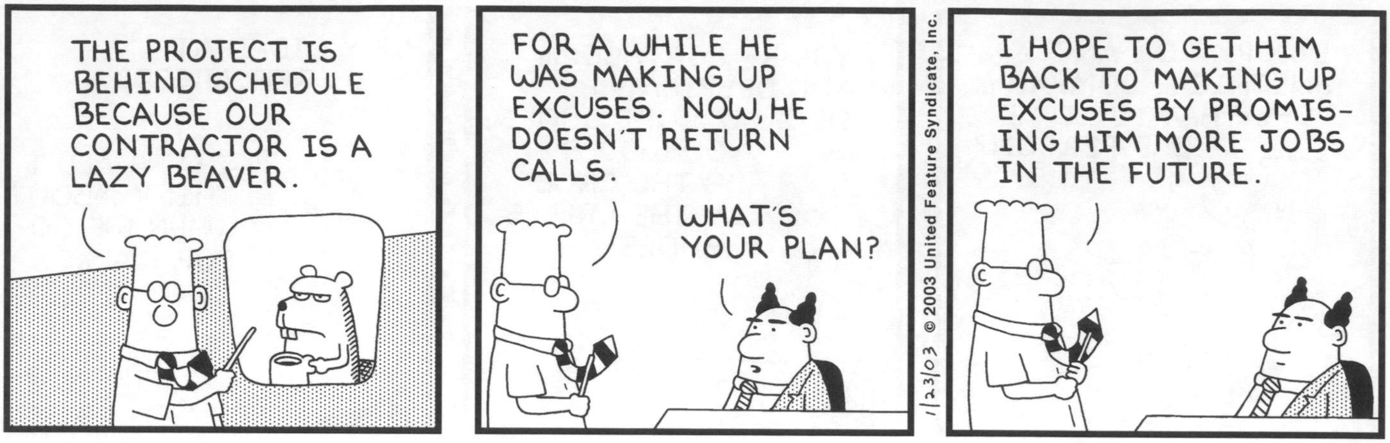
THE PROJECT IS BEHIND SCHEDULE BECAUSE OUR CONTRACTOR IS A LAZY BEAVER.
FOR A WHILE HE WAS MAKING UP EXCUSES. NOW, HE DOESN'T RETURN CALLS.
WHAT'S YOUR PLAN?
1/23/03 © 2003 United Feature Syndicate, Inc.
I HOPE TO GET HIM BACK TO MAKING UP EXCUSES BY PROMIS-ING HIM MORE JOBS IN THE FUTURE.

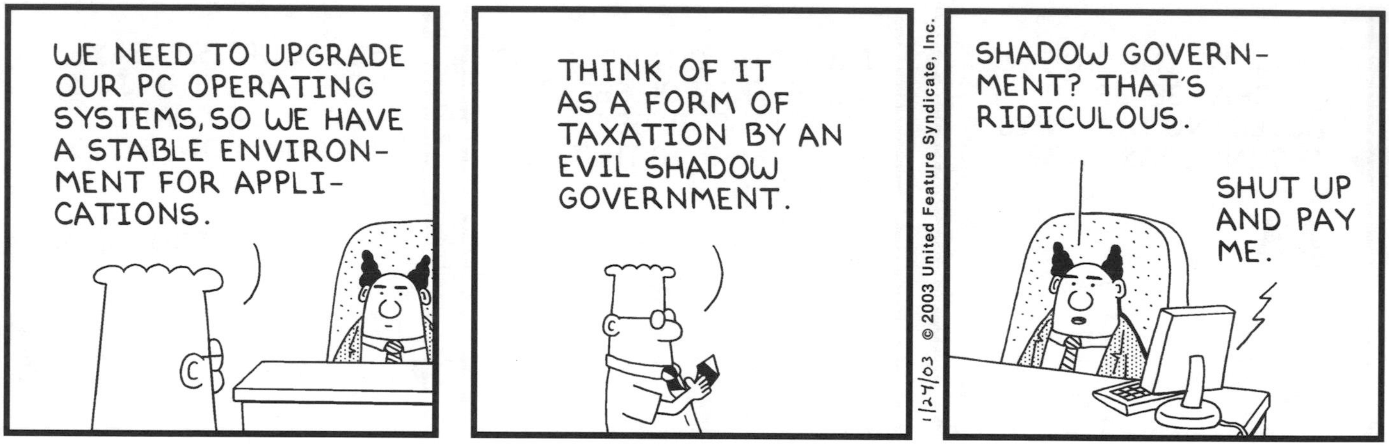
WE NEED TO UPGRADE OUR PC OPERATING SYSTEMS, SO WE HAVE A STABLE ENVIRON-MENT FOR APPLI-CATIONS.
THINK OF IT AS A FORM OF TAXATION BY AN EVIL SHADOW GOVERNMENT.
1/24/03 © 2003 United Feature Syndicate, Inc.
SHADOW GOVERN-MENT? THAT'S RIDICULOUS.
SHUT UP AND PAY ME.

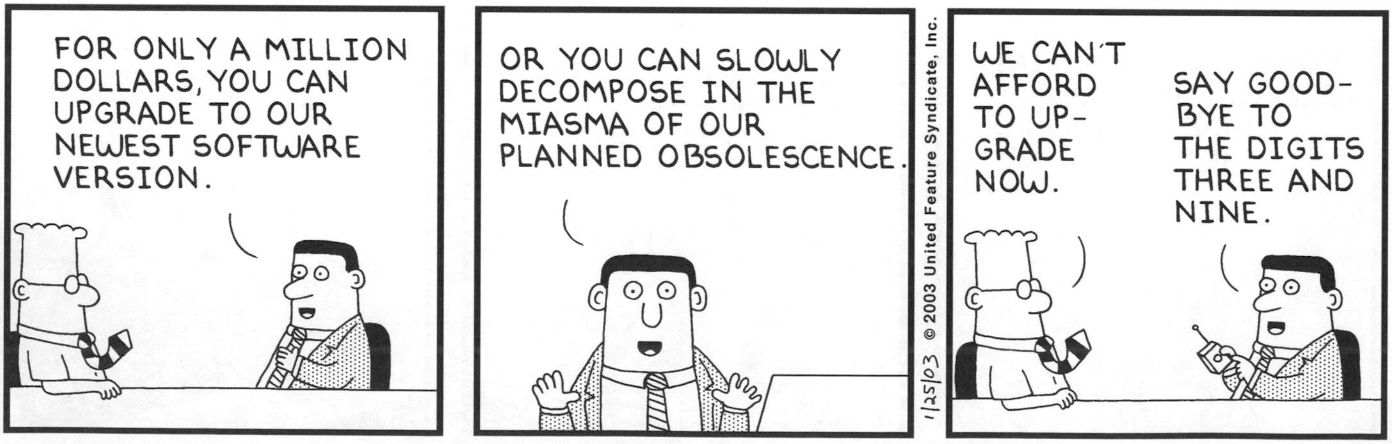
FOR ONLY A MILLION DOLLARS, YOU CAN UPGRADE TO OUR NEWEST SOFTWARE VERSION.
OR YOU CAN SLOWLY DECOMPOSE IN THE MIASMA OF OUR PLANNED OBSOLESCENCE.
1/25/03 © 2003 United Feature Syndicate, Inc.
WE CAN'T AFFORD TO UP-GRADE NOW.
SAY GOOD-BYE TO THE DIGITS THREE AND NINE.

DILBERT, COME HERE FOR A MINUTE.
I NEED TO TALK TO YOU ABOUT...
RING
RING
HE'S GIVING ME THE "WAIT" SIGNAL.
I HAVE NOTHING TO LOOK AT, NOTHING TO FIDDLE WITH, NOTHING TO DO.
I'LL TRY THINKING ABOUT HOW MY MIND CONTROLS MY MUSCLES.
UH-OH... I'M GETTING TOO CONSCIOUS OF MY MUSCLES AND IT'S FREAKING ME OUT.
GAAA!!! I'VE LOST MY MIND-BODY CONNECTION!!
THE PROBLEM WITH ENGINEERS IS THAT THEY DON'T IDLE WELL.
1/26/03 © 2003 United Feature Syndicate, Inc.

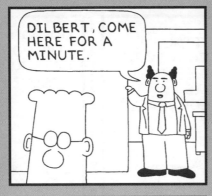

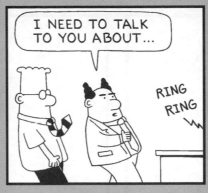

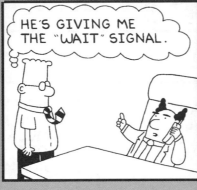

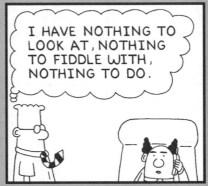

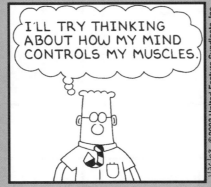

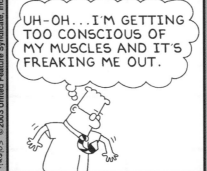

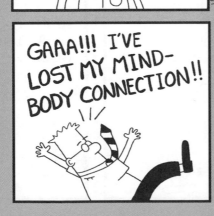

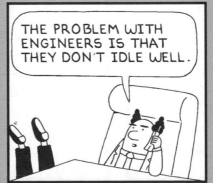

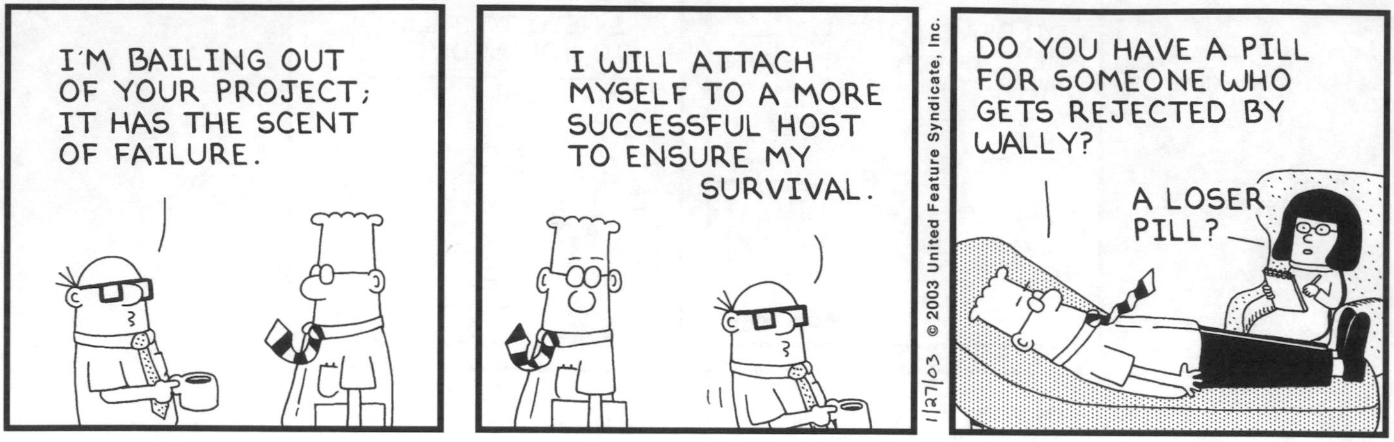
I'M BAILING OUT OF YOUR PROJECT; IT HAS THE SCENT OF FAILURE.
I WILL ATTACH MYSELF TO A MORE SUCCESSFUL HOST TO ENSURE MY SURVIVAL.
1/27/03 © 2003 United Feature Syndicate, Inc.
DO YOU HAVE A PILL FOR SOMEONE WHO GETS REJECTED BY WALLY?
A LOSER PILL?

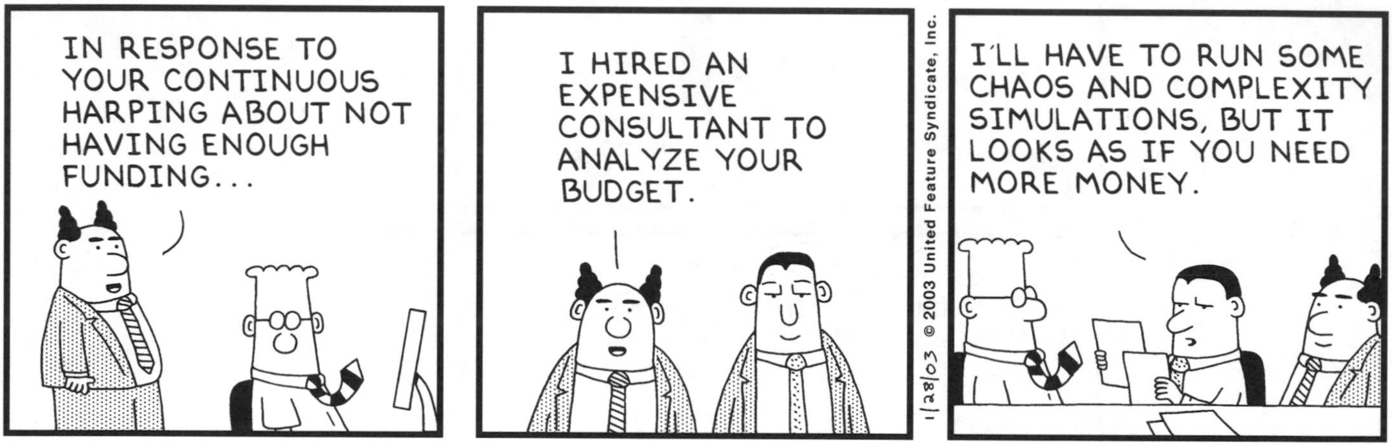
IN RESPONSE TO YOUR CONTINUOUS HARPING ABOUT NOT HAVING ENOUGH FUNDING...
I HIRED AN EXPENSIVE CONSULTANT TO ANALYZE YOUR BUDGET.
1/28/03 © 2003 United Feature Syndicate, Inc.
I'LL HAVE TO RUN SOME CHAOS AND COMPLEXITY SIMULATIONS, BUT IT LOOKS AS IF YOU NEED MORE MONEY.

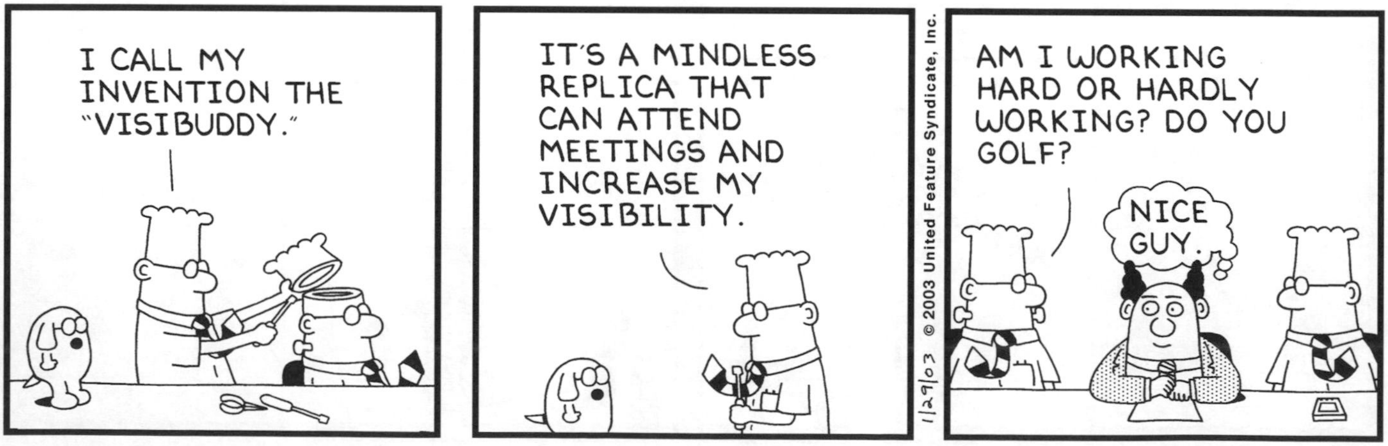
I CALL MY INVENTION THE "VISIBUDDY."
IT'S A MINDLESS REPLICA THAT CAN ATTEND MEETINGS AND INCREASE MY VISIBILITY.
1/29/03 © 2003 United Feature Syndicate, Inc.
AM I WORKING HARD OR HARDLY WORKING? DO YOU GOLF?
NICE GUY.

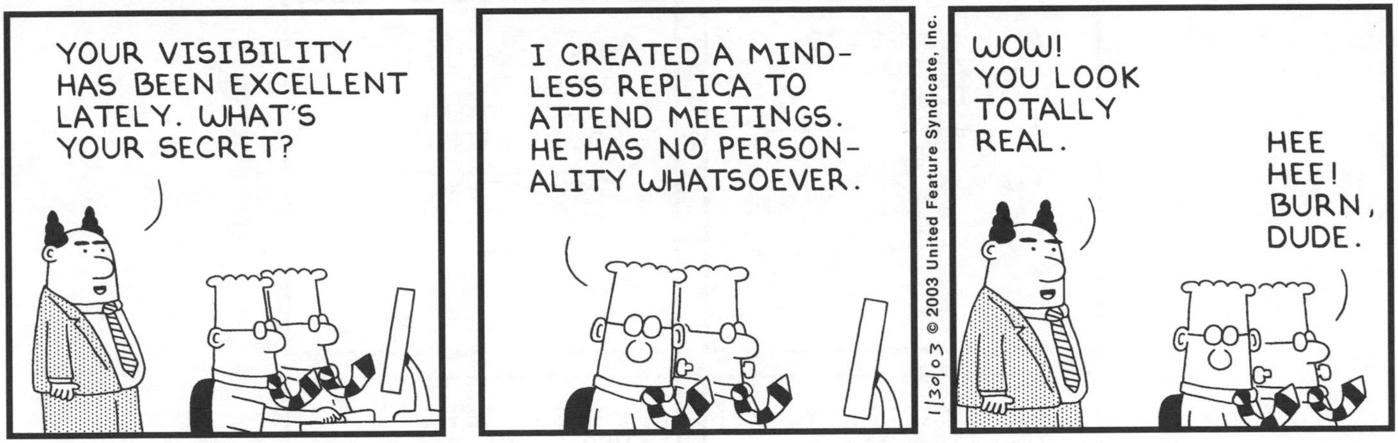
YOUR VISIBILITY HAS BEEN EXCELLENT LATELY. WHAT'S YOUR SECRET?
I CREATED A MIND-LESS REPLICA TO ATTEND MEETINGS. HE HAS NO PERSON-ALITY WHATSOEVER.
1/30/03 © 2003 United Feature Syndicate, Inc.
WOW! YOU LOOK TOTALLY REAL.
HEE HEE! BURN, DUDE.

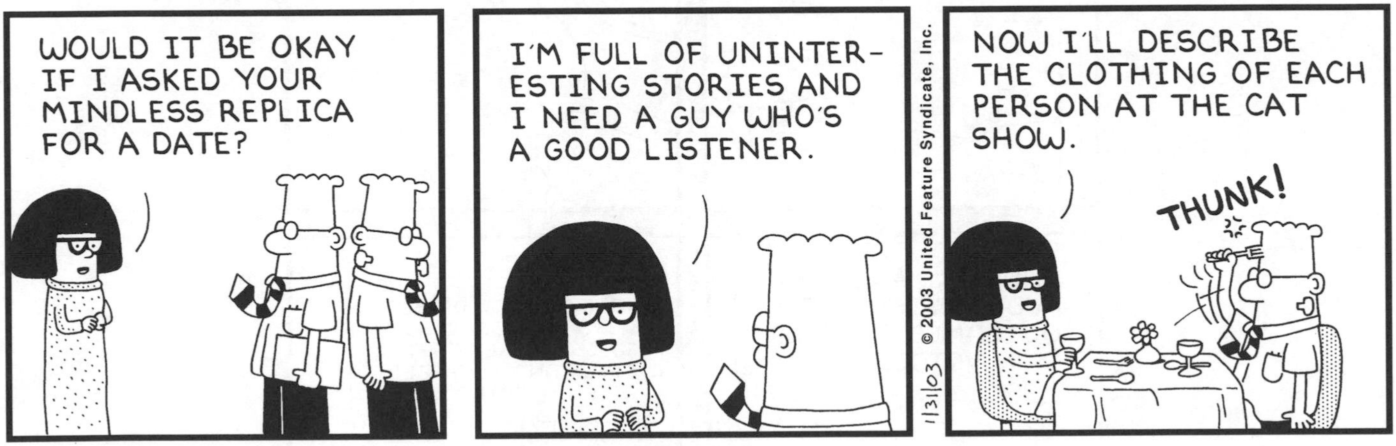
WOULD IT BE OKAY IF I ASKED YOUR MINDLESS REPLICA FOR A DATE?
I'M FULL OF UNINTER-ESTING STORIES AND I NEED A GUY WHO'S A GOOD LISTENER.
1/31/03 © 2003 United Feature Syndicate, Inc.
NOW I'LL DESCRIBE THE CLOTHING OF EACH PERSON AT THE CAT SHOW.
THUNK!

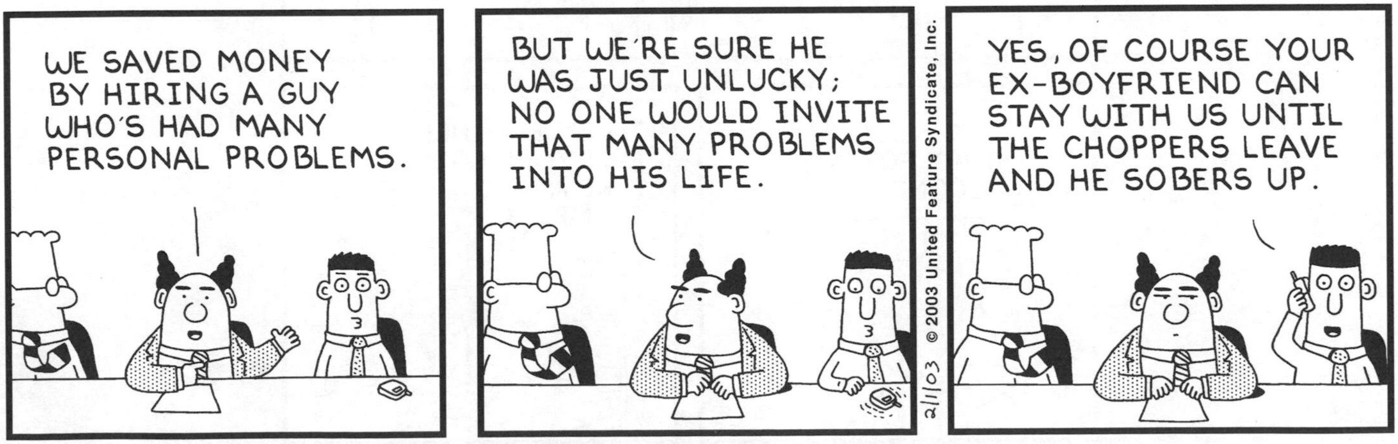
WE SAVED MONEY BY HIRING A GUY WHO'S HAD MANY PERSONAL PROBLEMS.
BUT WE'RE SURE HE WAS JUST UNLUCKY; NO ONE WOULD INVITE THAT MANY PROBLEMS INTO HIS LIFE.
2/1/03 © 2003 United Feature Syndicate, Inc.
YES, OF COURSE YOUR EX-BOYFRIEND CAN STAY WITH US UNTIL THE CHOPPERS LEAVE AND HE SOBERS UP.

YOUR BUDGET IS WRONG. YOU FORGOT MAINTENANCE.
WHY DO YOU ENGINEERS ALWAYS THINK YOU'RE RIGHT?!
I ANTICIPATED YOUR REACTION AND I CAME PREPARED.
HERE'S A LIST OF EVERY DISAGREE-MENT WE'VE HAD.
AND HERE ARE THE AUDIO CLIPS OF THE OUTCOMES, IN YOUR OWN VOICE.
TAP TAP
YOU'RE RIGHT, DILBERT ...YOU'RE RIGHT...I GUESS YOU'RE RIGHT... I'M WRONG...YOU'RE RIGHT...YOU'RE RIGHT.
LET ME SEE THAT FOR A SECOND.
TO AN ENGINEER, EVERYONE LOOKS LIKE A CHIMP.
OO!! OO!! OO!!
2/2/03 ©2003 United Feature Syndicate, Inc.

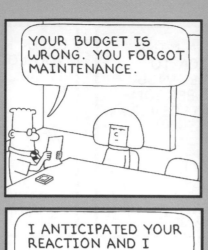

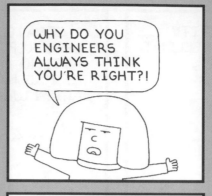

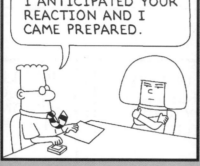

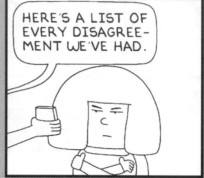

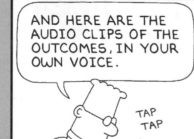

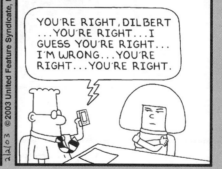

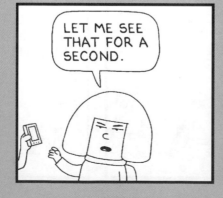

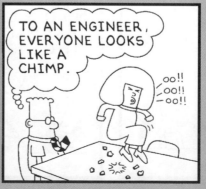

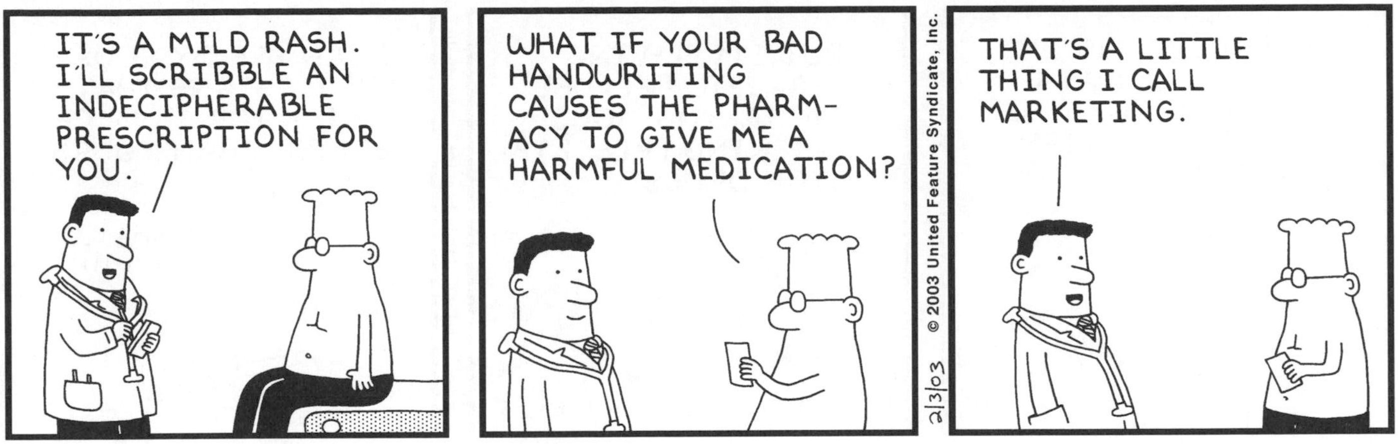
IT'S A MILD RASH. I'LL SCRIBBLE AN INDECIPHERABLE PRESCRIPTION FOR YOU.
WHAT IF YOUR BAD HANDWRITING CAUSES THE PHARMACY TO GIVE ME A HARMFUL MEDICATION?
2/3/03
© 2003 United Feature Syndicate, Inc.
THAT'S A LITTLE THING I CALL MARKETING.

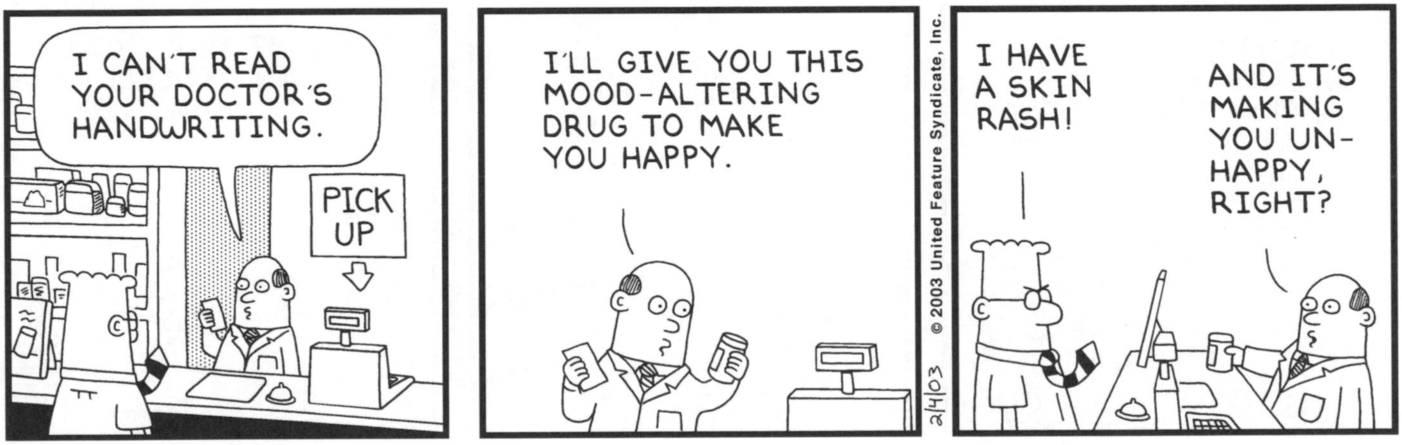
I CAN'T READ YOUR DOCTOR'S HANDWRITING.
PICK UP
I'LL GIVE YOU THIS MOOD-ALTERING DRUG TO MAKE YOU HAPPY.
2/4/03
© 2003 United Feature Syndicate, Inc.
I HAVE A SKIN RASH!
AND IT'S MAKING YOU UNHAPPY, RIGHT?

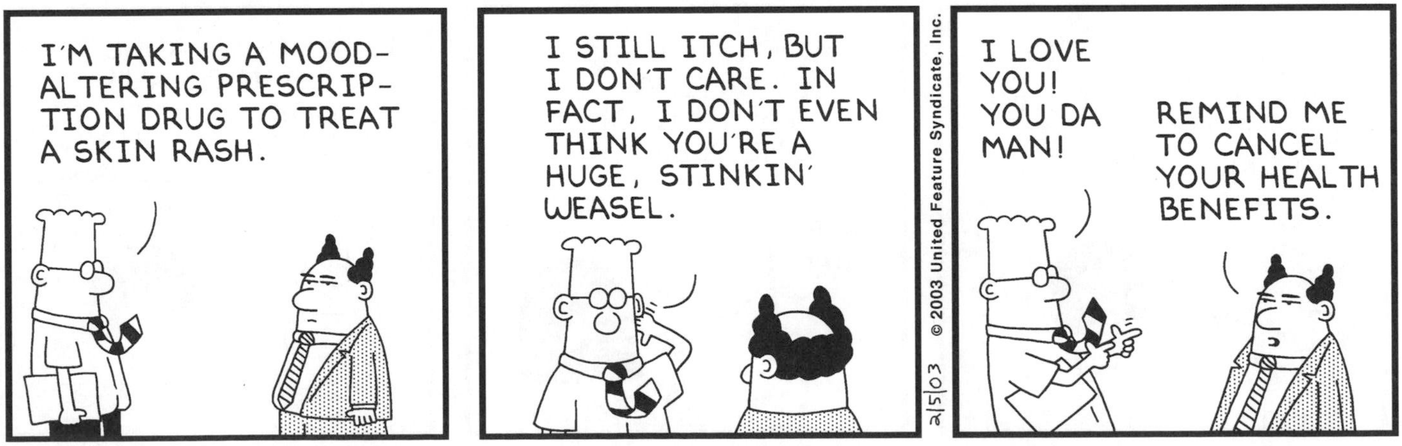
I'M TAKING A MOOD-ALTERING PRESCRIPTION DRUG TO TREAT A SKIN RASH.
I STILL ITCH, BUT I DON'T CARE. IN FACT, I DON'T EVEN THINK YOU'RE A HUGE, STINKIN' WEASEL.
2/5/03
© 2003 United Feature Syndicate, Inc.
I LOVE YOU! YOU DA MAN!
REMIND ME TO CANCEL YOUR HEALTH BENEFITS.

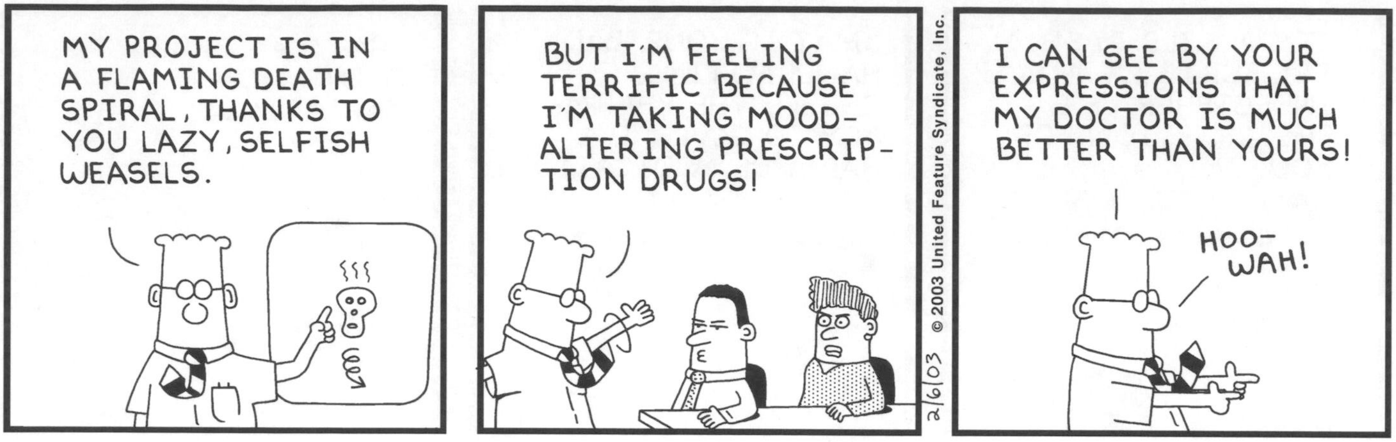
MY PROJECT IS IN A FLAMING DEATH SPIRAL, THANKS TO YOU LAZY, SELFISH WEASELS.
BUT I'M FEELING TERRIFIC BECAUSE I'M TAKING MOOD-ALTERING PRESCRIPTION DRUGS!
© 2003 United Feature Syndicate, Inc.
2/6/03
I CAN SEE BY YOUR EXPRESSIONS THAT MY DOCTOR IS MUCH BETTER THAN YOURS!
HOO-WAH!

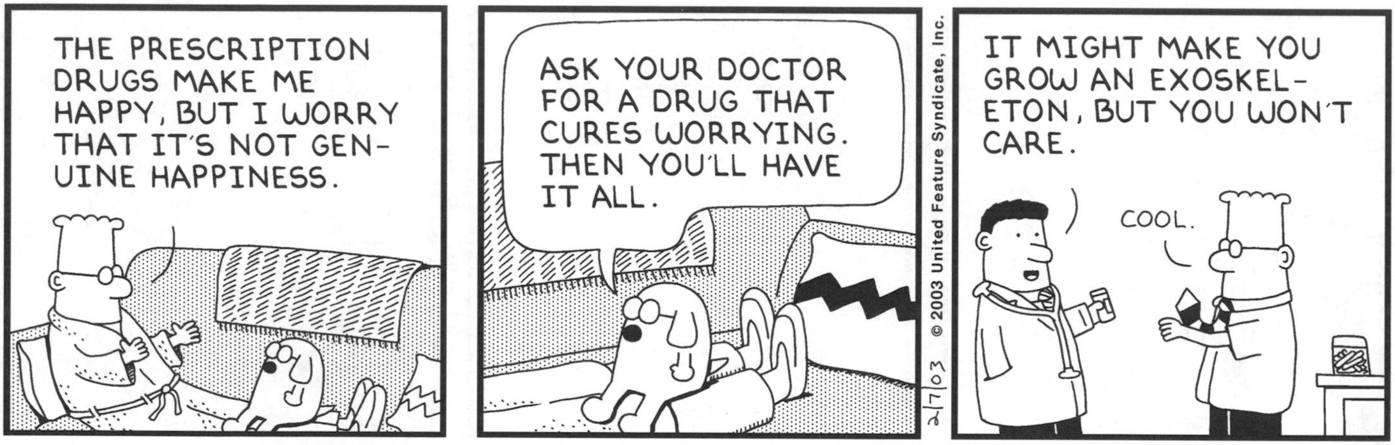
THE PRESCRIPTION DRUGS MAKE ME HAPPY, BUT I WORRY THAT IT'S NOT GENUINE HAPPINESS.
ASK YOUR DOCTOR FOR A DRUG THAT CURES WORRYING. THEN YOU'LL HAVE IT ALL.
© 2003 United Feature Syndicate, Inc.
2/7/03
IT MIGHT MAKE YOU GROW AN EXOSKELETON, BUT YOU WON'T CARE.
COOL.

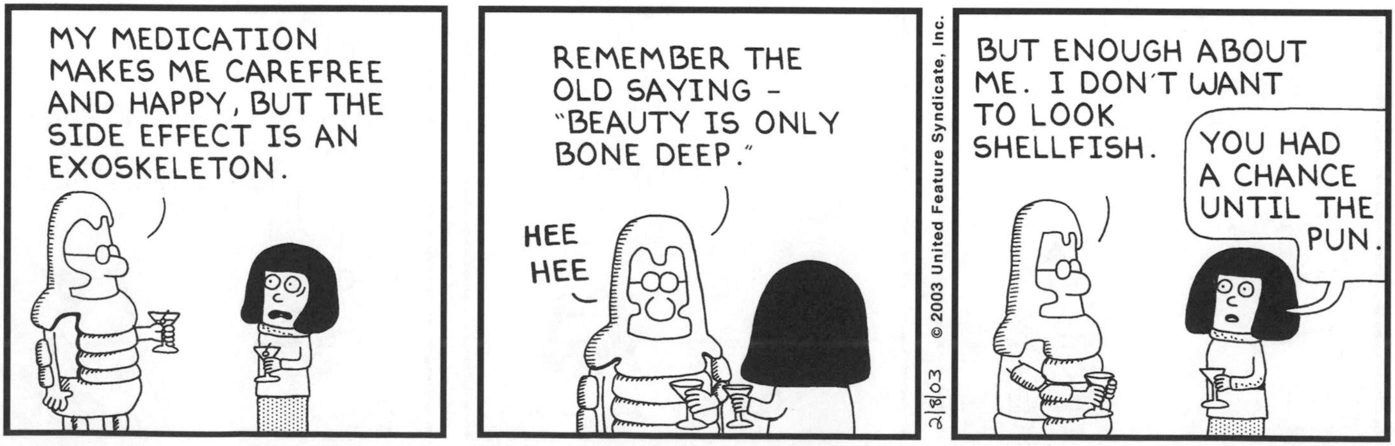
MY MEDICATION MAKES ME CAREFREE AND HAPPY, BUT THE SIDE EFFECT IS AN EXOSKELETON.
REMEMBER THE OLD SAYING - "BEAUTY IS ONLY BONE DEEP."
HEE HEE
© 2003 United Feature Syndicate, Inc.
2/8/03
BUT ENOUGH ABOUT ME. I DON'T WANT TO LOOK SHELLFISH.
YOU HAD A CHANCE UNTIL THE PUN.

MY NEW DESIGN WILL MEET ALL OF OUR CUSTOMERS' CURRENT AND FUTURE NEEDS.
THAT'S NO GOOD; THEY'LL NEVER NEED TO UPGRADE.
PLEASE DON'T ASK ME TO PUT FLAWS IN MY DESIGN.
FLAWS WOULD WORK.
WE NEED FLAWS.
FLAWS, FLAWS, FLAWS.
PLEASE... NO...
©2003 United Feature Syndicate, Inc.
MAKE IT FREEZE EVERY HOUR.
THE INTER-FACE NEEDS TO BE MORE CONFOUND-ING.
AND...
LATER
PLEASE... NO MORE.
...AND CRIPPLING ELECTRIC SHOCKS.
MUCH, MUCH LATER
THE HELP SCREEN COULD RECOMMEND MARRYING AN UNEMPLOYED, SHIRT-LESS GUY WITH A MULLET.
THAT'S MAR-KETING!

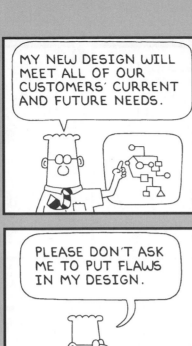

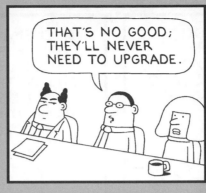

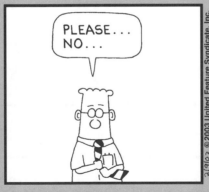

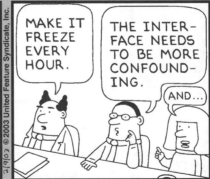

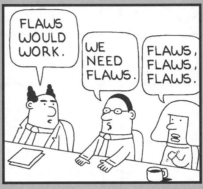

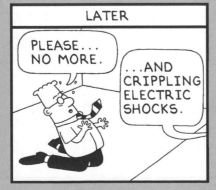

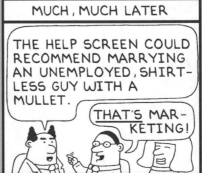

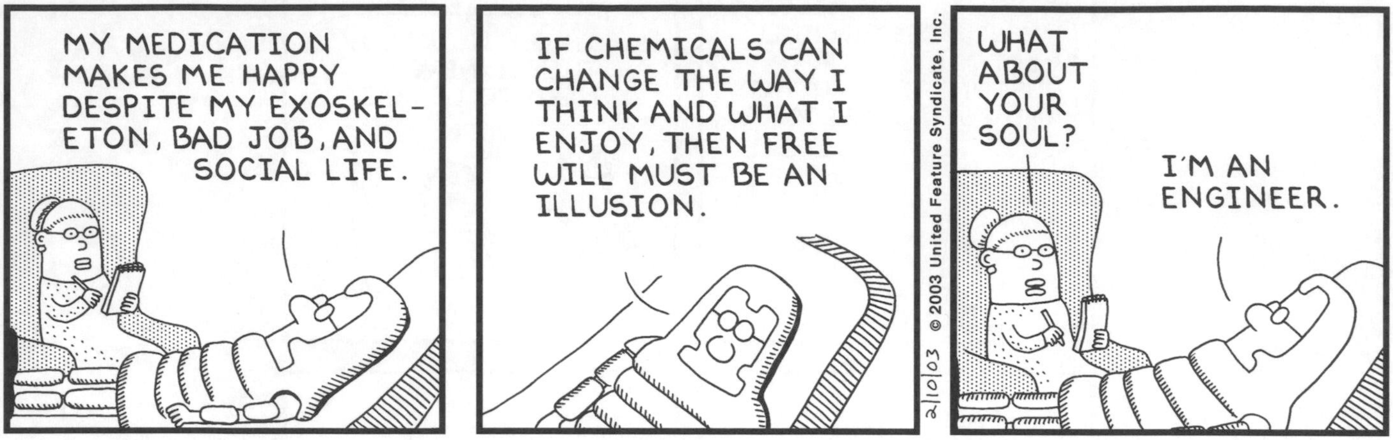
MY MEDICATION MAKES ME HAPPY DESPITE MY EXOSKEL-ETON, BAD JOB, AND SOCIAL LIFE.
IF CHEMICALS CAN CHANGE THE WAY I THINK AND WHAT I ENJOY, THEN FREE WILL MUST BE AN ILLUSION.
2/10/03 © 2003 United Feature Syndicate, Inc.
WHAT ABOUT YOUR SOUL?
I'M AN ENGINEER.

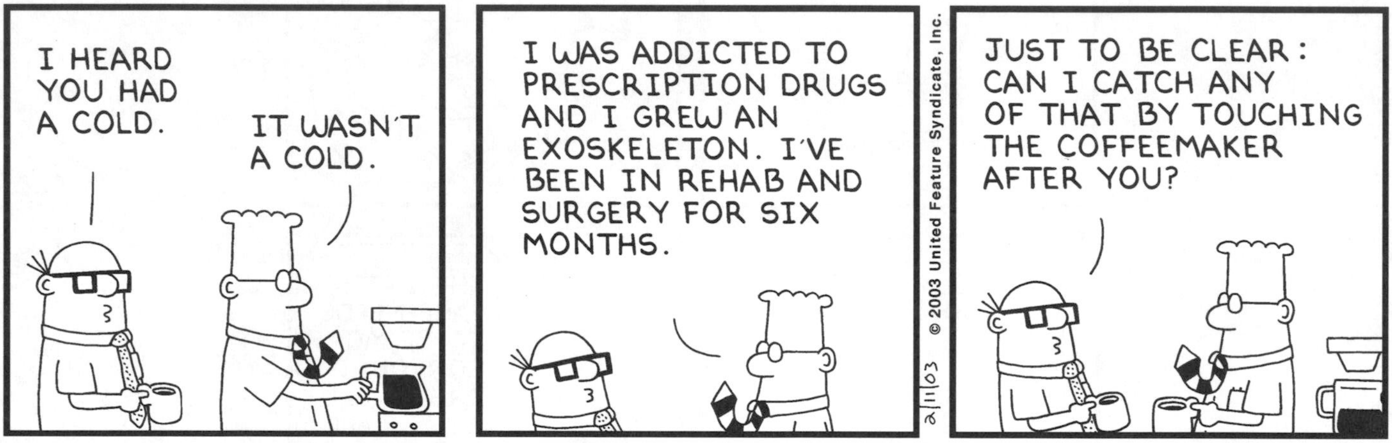
I HEARD YOU HAD A COLD.
IT WASN'T A COLD.
I WAS ADDICTED TO PRESCRIPTION DRUGS AND I GREW AN EXOSKELETON. I'VE BEEN IN REHAB AND SURGERY FOR SIX MONTHS.
2/11/03 © 2003 United Feature Syndicate, Inc.
JUST TO BE CLEAR: CAN I CATCH ANY OF THAT BY TOUCHING THE COFFEEMAKER AFTER YOU?

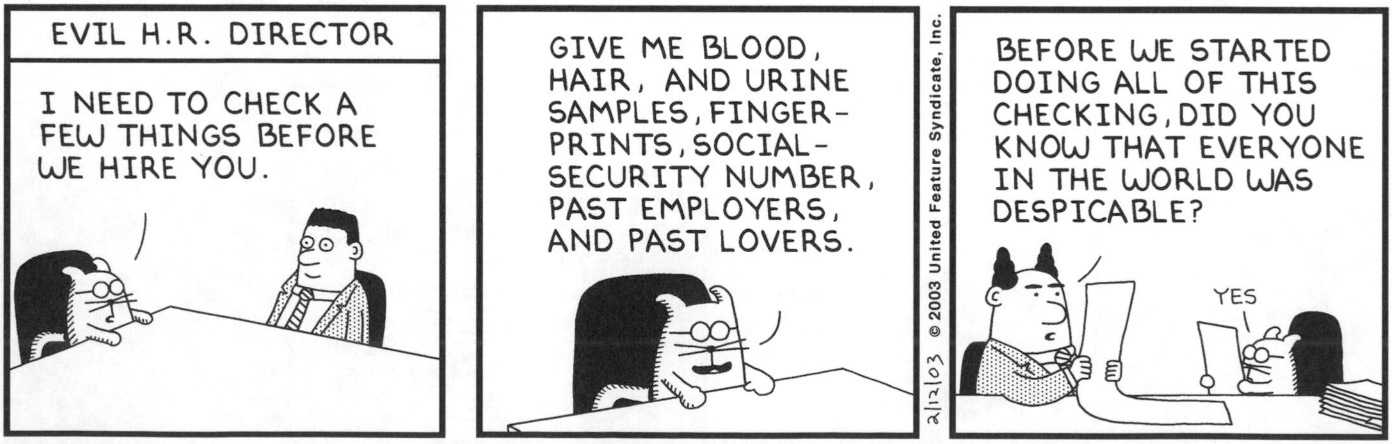
EVIL H.R. DIRECTOR
I NEED TO CHECK A FEW THINGS BEFORE WE HIRE YOU.
GIVE ME BLOOD, HAIR, AND URINE SAMPLES, FINGER-PRINTS, SOCIAL-SECURITY NUMBER, PAST EMPLOYERS, AND PAST LOVERS.
2/12/03 © 2003 United Feature Syndicate, Inc.
BEFORE WE STARTED DOING ALL OF THIS CHECKING, DID YOU KNOW THAT EVERYONE IN THE WORLD WAS DESPICABLE?
YES

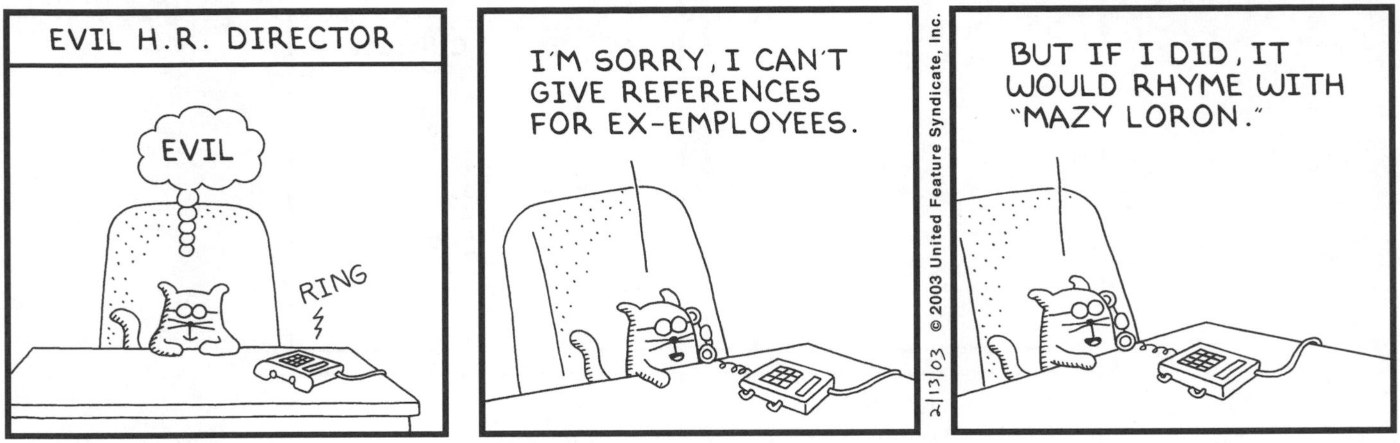
EVIL H.R. DIRECTOR
EVIL
RING
I'M SORRY, I CAN'T GIVE REFERENCES FOR EX-EMPLOYEES.
BUT IF I DID, IT WOULD RHYME WITH "MAZY LORON."
2/13/03 © 2003 United Feature Syndicate, Inc.

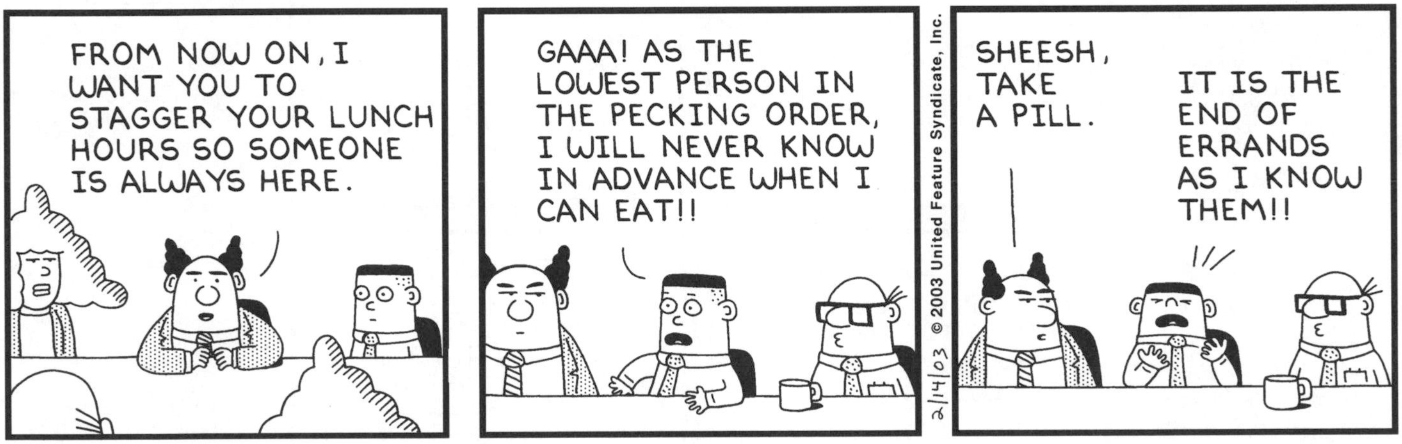
FROM NOW ON, I WANT YOU TO STAGGER YOUR LUNCH HOURS SO SOMEONE IS ALWAYS HERE.
GAAA! AS THE LOWEST PERSON IN THE PECKING ORDER, I WILL NEVER KNOW IN ADVANCE WHEN I CAN EAT!!
SHEESH, TAKE A PILL.
IT IS THE END OF ERRANDS AS I KNOW THEM!!
2/14/03 © 2003 United Feature Syndicate, Inc.

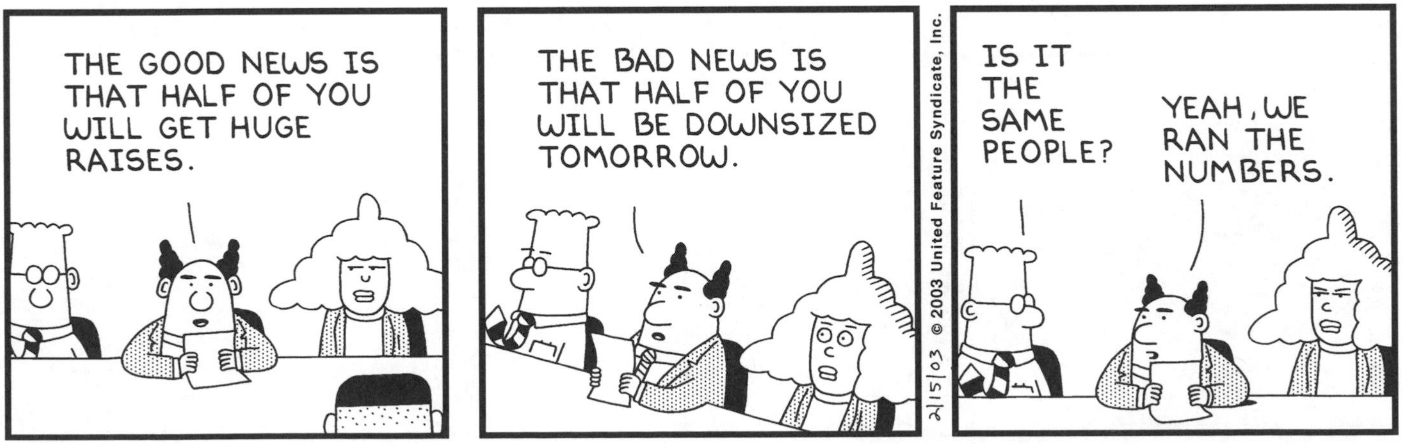
THE GOOD NEWS IS THAT HALF OF YOU WILL GET HUGE RAISES.
THE BAD NEWS IS THAT HALF OF YOU WILL BE DOWNSIZED TOMORROW.
IS IT THE SAME PEOPLE?
YEAH, WE RAN THE NUMBERS.
2/15/03 © 2003 United Feature Syndicate, Inc.

DO YOU WANT TO WATCH A NUMBING?
YOU KNOW I DO!
WHERE IS IT?
CUBICLE 15950.
ARE YOU GOING TO THE NUMBING?
YOU KNOW WE ARE!
WHAT IS A NUMBING?
IT'S THE MOMENT THAT AN EMPLOYEE'S BRAIN NUMBS TO THE PAIN OF WORKING HERE.
2/16/03 ©2003 United Feature Syndicate, Inc.
IT'S ACTUALLY QUITE BEAUTIFUL.
NO TWO ARE ALIKE.
I CAN'T TAKE THIS ANYMORE!! GAA!! GAA!!
OOH
WHAT THE..?
IT'S OKAY – HE'S IN A HAPPY PLACE NOW.

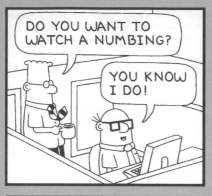

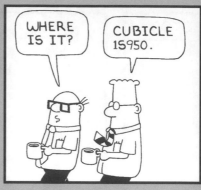

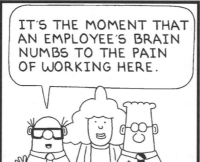

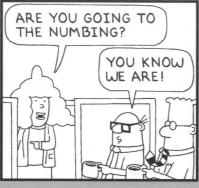

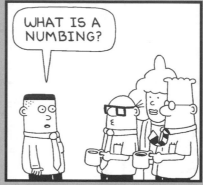

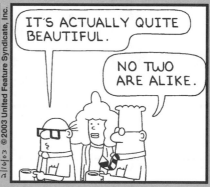

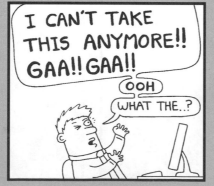

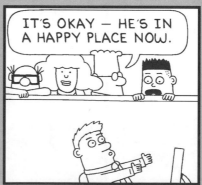

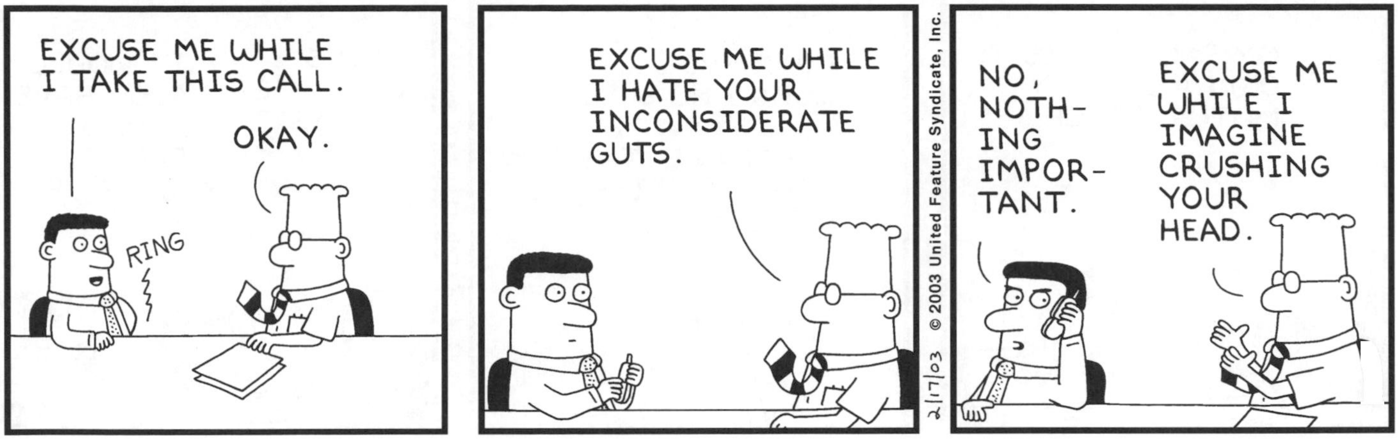
EXCUSE ME WHILE I TAKE THIS CALL.
OKAY.
RING
EXCUSE ME WHILE I HATE YOUR INCONSIDERATE GUTS.
2/17/03 © 2003 United Feature Syndicate, Inc.
NO, NOTHING IMPORTANT.
EXCUSE ME WHILE I IMAGINE CRUSHING YOUR HEAD.

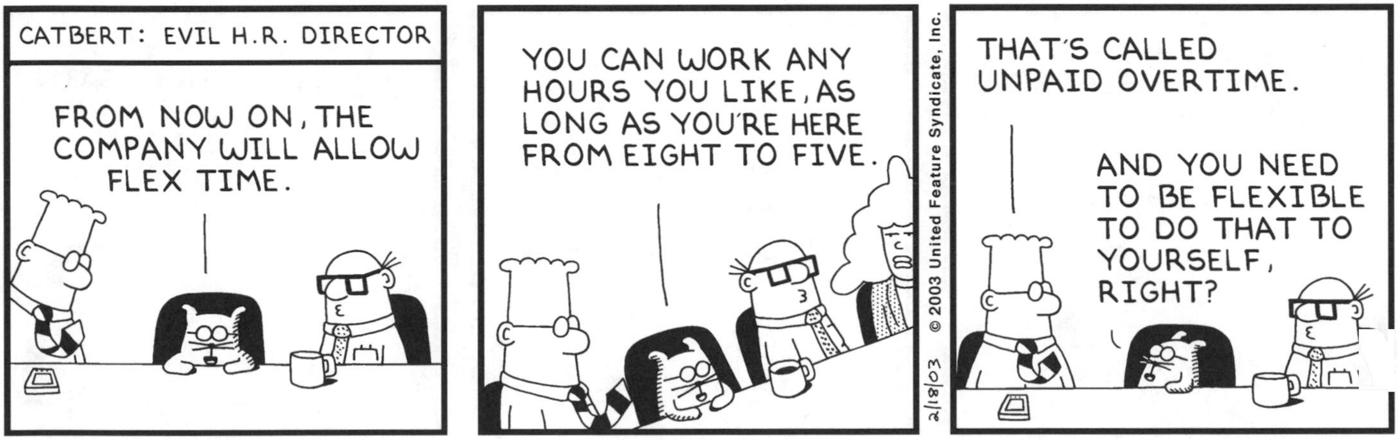
CATBERT: EVIL H.R. DIRECTOR
FROM NOW ON, THE COMPANY WILL ALLOW FLEX TIME.
YOU CAN WORK ANY HOURS YOU LIKE, AS LONG AS YOU'RE HERE FROM EIGHT TO FIVE.
2/18/03 © 2003 United Feature Syndicate, Inc.
THAT'S CALLED UNPAID OVERTIME.
AND YOU NEED TO BE FLEXIBLE TO DO THAT TO YOURSELF, RIGHT?

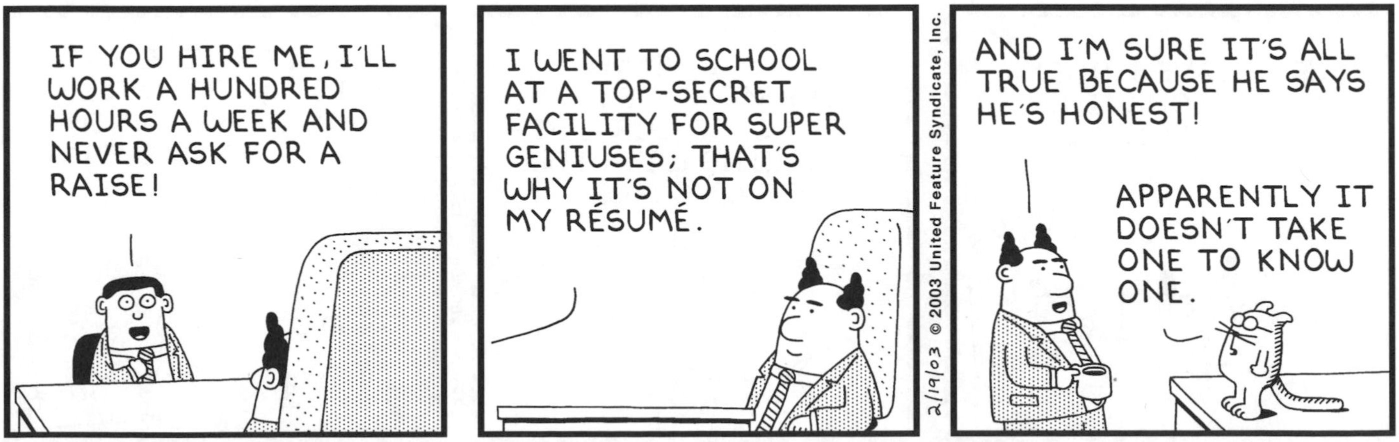
IF YOU HIRE ME, I'LL WORK A HUNDRED HOURS A WEEK AND NEVER ASK FOR A RAISE!
I WENT TO SCHOOL AT A TOP-SECRET FACILITY FOR SUPER GENIUSES; THAT'S WHY IT'S NOT ON MY RÉSUMÉ.
2/19/03 © 2003 United Feature Syndicate, Inc.
AND I'M SURE IT'S ALL TRUE BECAUSE HE SAYS HE'S HONEST!
APPARENTLY IT DOESN'T TAKE ONE TO KNOW ONE.

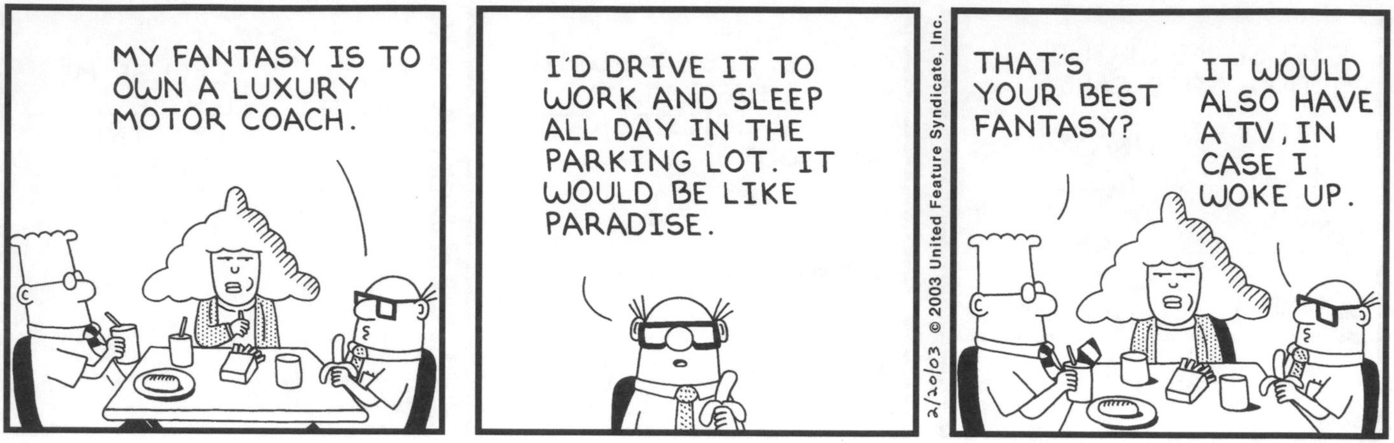
MY FANTASY IS TO OWN A LUXURY MOTOR COACH.
I'D DRIVE IT TO WORK AND SLEEP ALL DAY IN THE PARKING LOT. IT WOULD BE LIKE PARADISE.
2/20/03 © 2003 United Feature Syndicate, Inc.
THAT'S YOUR BEST FANTASY?
IT WOULD ALSO HAVE A TV, IN CASE I WOKE UP.

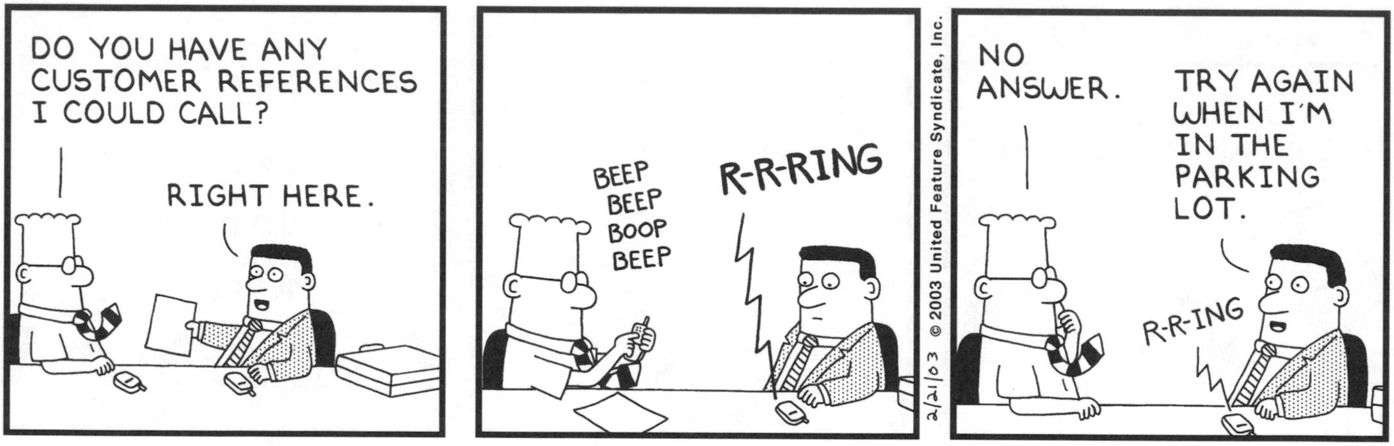
DO YOU HAVE ANY CUSTOMER REFERENCES I COULD CALL?
RIGHT HERE.
BEEP BEEP BOOP BEEP
R-R-RING
2/21/03 © 2003 United Feature Syndicate, Inc.
NO ANSWER.
TRY AGAIN WHEN I'M IN THE PARKING LOT.
R-R-ING

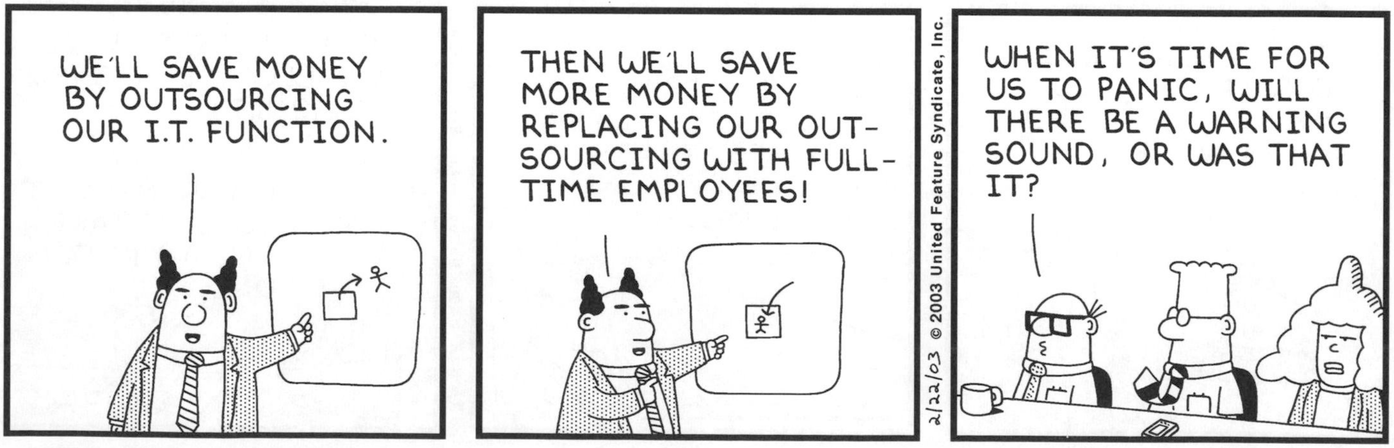
WE'LL SAVE MONEY BY OUTSOURCING OUR I.T. FUNCTION.
THEN WE'LL SAVE MORE MONEY BY REPLACING OUR OUT-SOURCING WITH FULL-TIME EMPLOYEES!
2/22/03 © 2003 United Feature Syndicate, Inc.
WHEN IT'S TIME FOR US TO PANIC, WILL THERE BE A WARNING SOUND, OR WAS THAT IT?

CAROL, COME TO MY STRATEGY MEETING.
YOU'RE ONLY A SECRETARY, BUT I VALUE YOUR INPUT.
I'M AN ADMINISTRATIVE ASSISTANT!!!
CHIMP.
BAD SECRETARY.

DOES ANYONE HAVE ANY STRATEGIC IDEAS FOR GLOBAL DOMINATION?
THE ENGINEERS KEEP USING OUR COFFEE FILTERS AS POPCORN BAGS. THAT HAS GOT TO STOP.
IF YOU ORDERED ENOUGH FILTERS, I WOULDN'T NEED TO USE THE FOOT OF MY PANTYHOSE TO MAKE COFFEE EVERY DAY!
I'M ADDING THAT TO THE LIST OF THINGS I DON'T WANT TO THINK ABOUT.

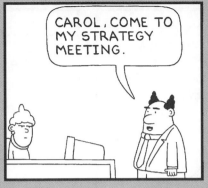

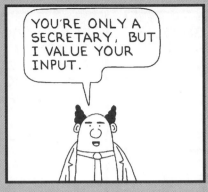

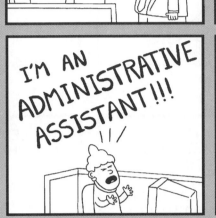

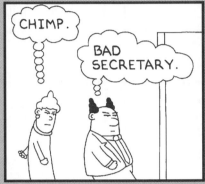

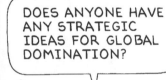

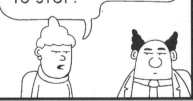

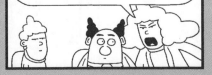

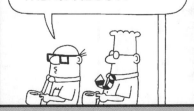

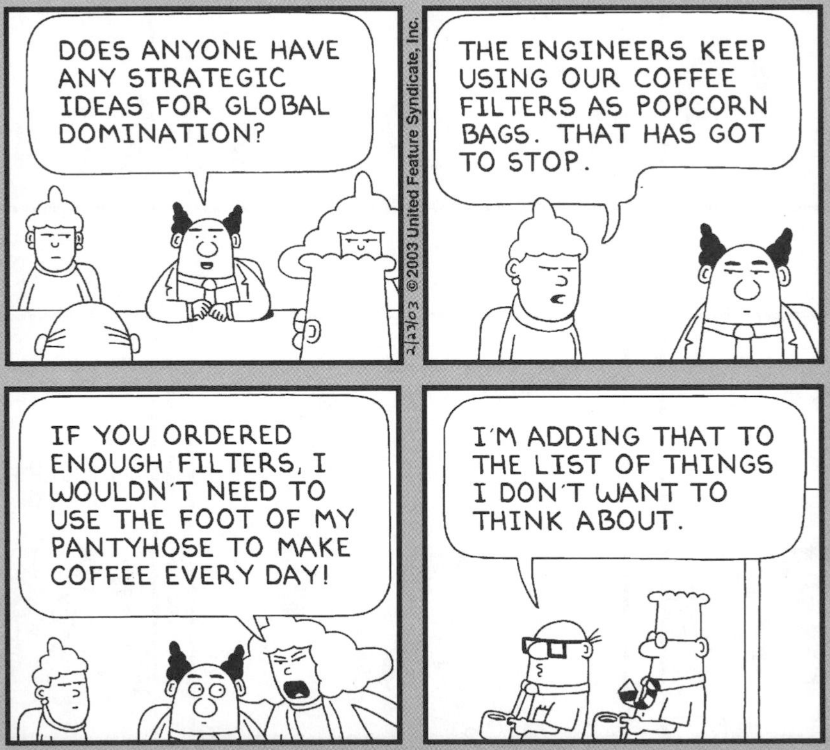

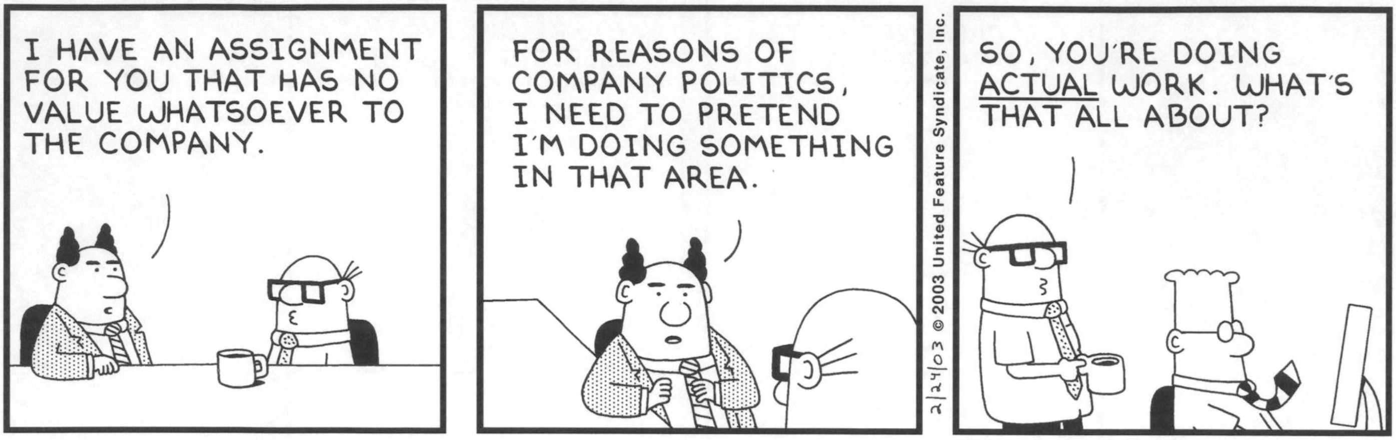
I HAVE AN ASSIGNMENT FOR YOU THAT HAS NO VALUE WHATSOEVER TO THE COMPANY.
FOR REASONS OF COMPANY POLITICS, I NEED TO PRETEND I'M DOING SOMETHING IN THAT AREA.
SO, YOU'RE DOING ACTUAL WORK. WHAT'S THAT ALL ABOUT?

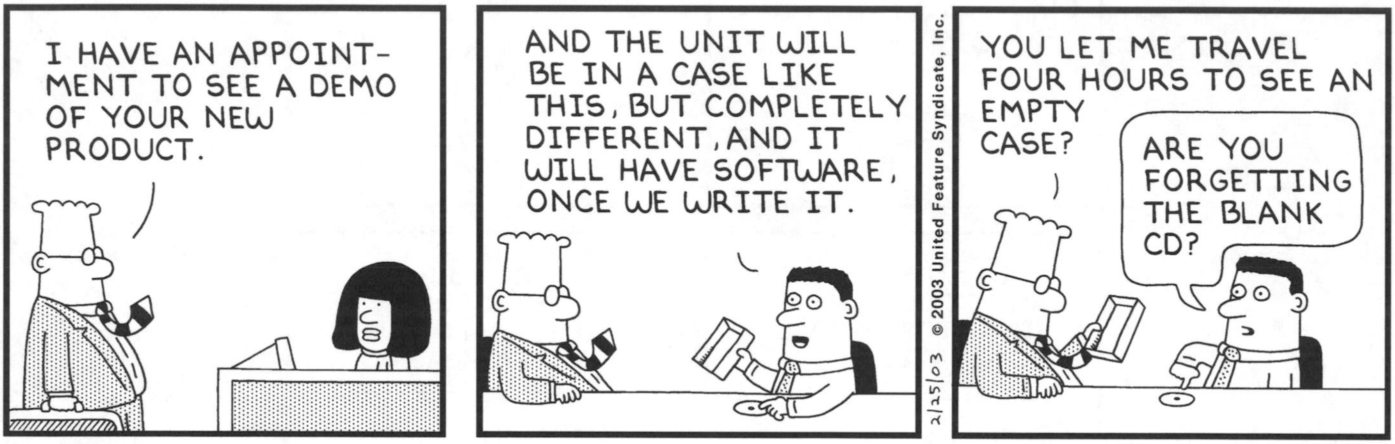
I HAVE AN APPOINTMENT TO SEE A DEMO OF YOUR NEW PRODUCT.
AND THE UNIT WILL BE IN A CASE LIKE THIS, BUT COMPLETELY DIFFERENT, AND IT WILL HAVE SOFTWARE, ONCE WE WRITE IT.
YOU LET ME TRAVEL FOUR HOURS TO SEE AN EMPTY CASE?
ARE YOU FORGETTING THE BLANK CD?

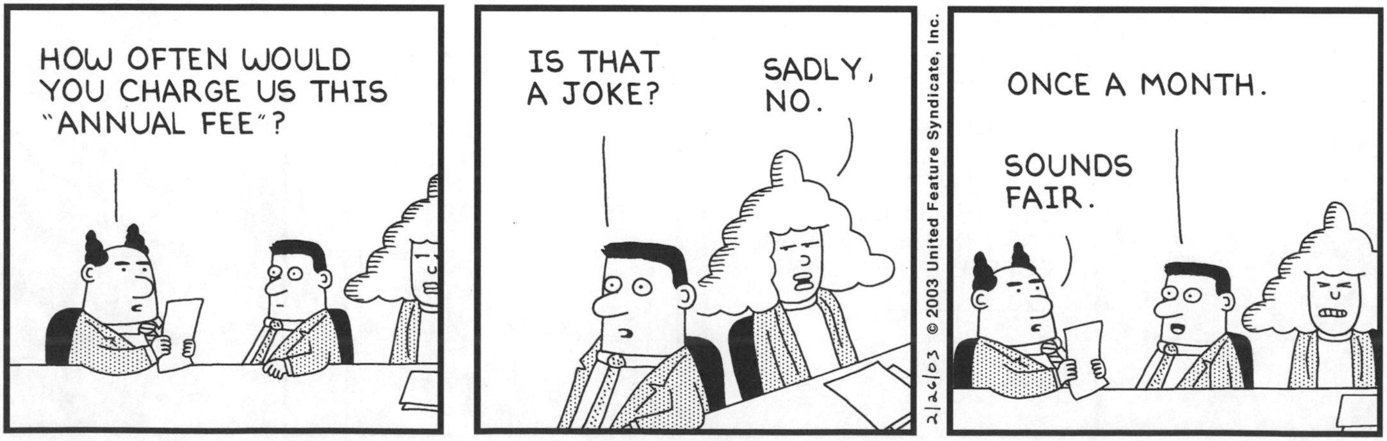
HOW OFTEN WOULD YOU CHARGE US THIS "ANNUAL FEE"?
IS THAT A JOKE?
SADLY, NO.
ONCE A MONTH.
SOUNDS FAIR.

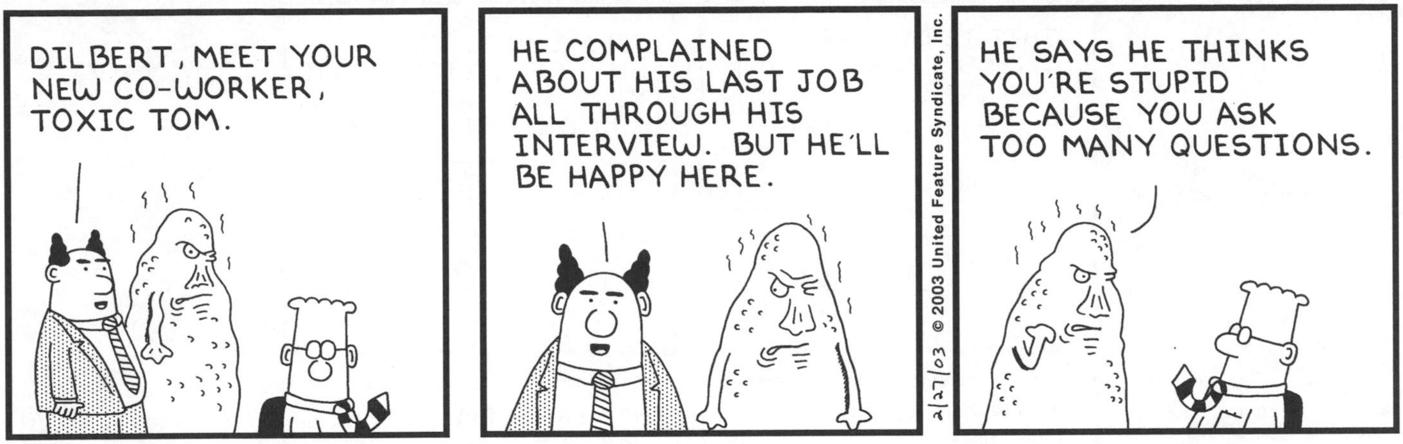
DILBERT, MEET YOUR NEW CO-WORKER, TOXIC TOM.
HE COMPLAINED ABOUT HIS LAST JOB ALL THROUGH HIS INTERVIEW. BUT HE'LL BE HAPPY HERE.
2/27/03 © 2003 United Feature Syndicate, Inc.
HE SAYS HE THINKS YOU'RE STUPID BECAUSE YOU ASK TOO MANY QUESTIONS.

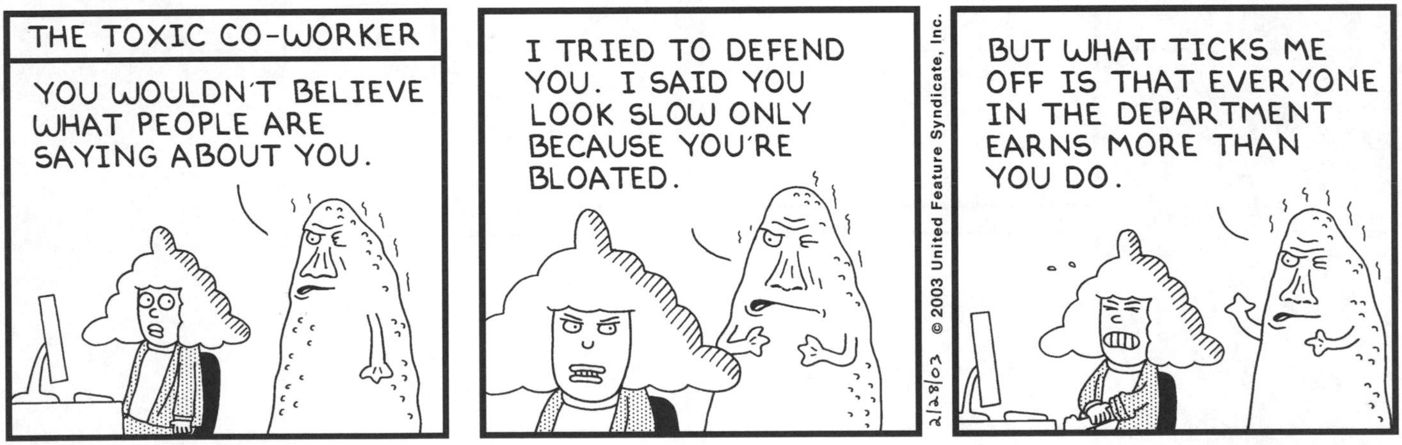
THE TOXIC CO-WORKER
YOU WOULDN'T BELIEVE WHAT PEOPLE ARE SAYING ABOUT YOU.
I TRIED TO DEFEND YOU. I SAID YOU LOOK SLOW ONLY BECAUSE YOU'RE BLOATED.
2/28/03 © 2003 United Feature Syndicate, Inc.
BUT WHAT TICKS ME OFF IS THAT EVERYONE IN THE DEPARTMENT EARNS MORE THAN YOU DO.

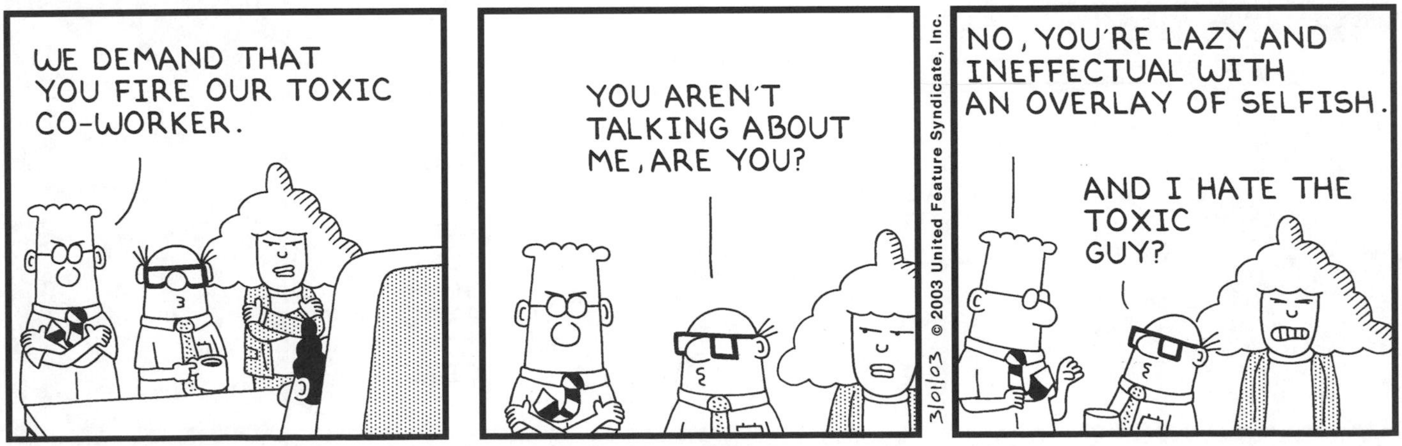
WE DEMAND THAT YOU FIRE OUR TOXIC CO-WORKER.
YOU AREN'T TALKING ABOUT ME, ARE YOU?
3/01/03 © 2003 United Feature Syndicate, Inc.
NO, YOU'RE LAZY AND INEFFECTUAL WITH AN OVERLAY OF SELFISH.
AND I HATE THE TOXIC GUY?

THIS IS DOGBERT'S TECH SUPPORT. HOW MAY I ABUSE YOU?
FINALLY!! IT TOOK ME AN HOUR TO PENETRATE YOUR INSCRUTABLE AUDIO MENU SYSTEM!
THEN I WAITED IN QUEUE FOR FORTY MINUTES!
MY PROBLEM IS THAT MY COMPUTER KEEPS FREEZING...
NOT SO FAST.
I NEED TO KNOW YOUR NAME, ADDRESS, PHONE NUMBER, OPERATING SYSTEM, E-MAIL ADDRESS, SERIAL NUMBERS, SOFTWARE VERSIONS AND VIDEO DRIVERS.
©2003 United Feature Syndicate, Inc.
3/2/03
THEN I'LL PUT YOU IN QUEUE FOR THE LOW-LEVEL TECHNICIAN WHO CAN ONLY TELL YOU TO REBOOT.
HE'LL ASK YOU THE SAME QUESTIONS FOR REASONS THAT WILL BAFFLE YOU.
BUT EVENTUALLY YOU'LL SOLVE MY PROBLEM, RIGHT?
SURE, IF YOUR PROBLEM IS TOO MUCH OPTIMISM.

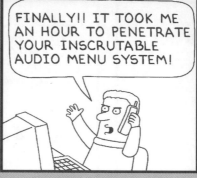

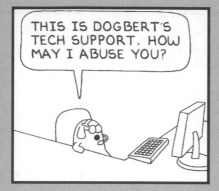

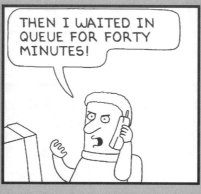

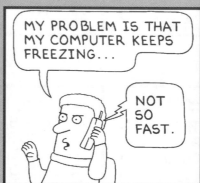

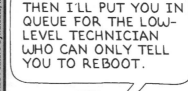

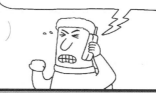

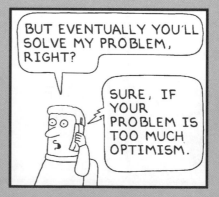

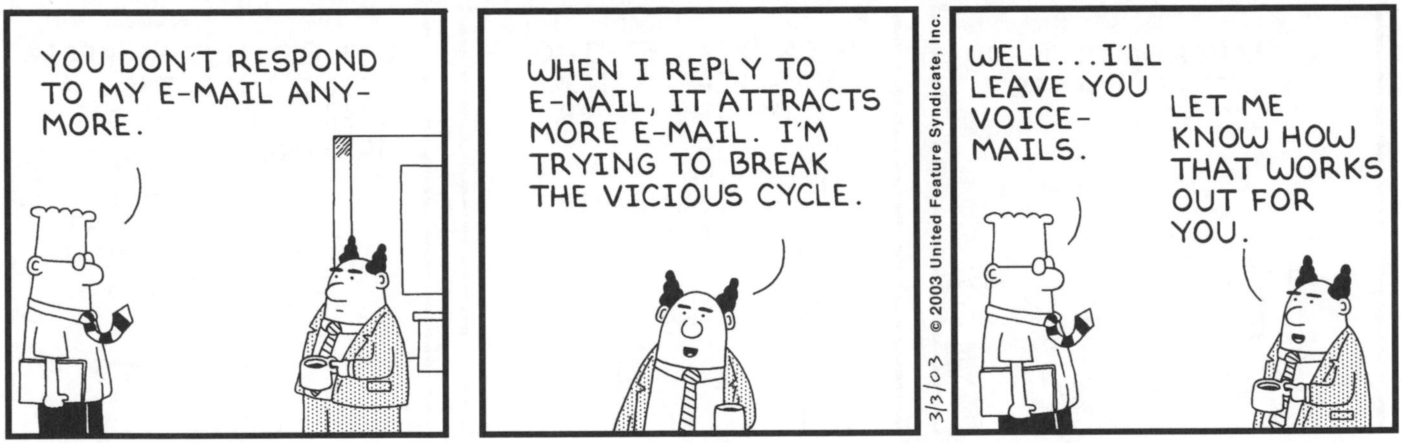
YOU DON'T RESPOND TO MY E-MAIL ANY-MORE.
WHEN I REPLY TO E-MAIL, IT ATTRACTS MORE E-MAIL. I'M TRYING TO BREAK THE VICIOUS CYCLE.
3/3/03 © 2003 United Feature Syndicate, Inc.
WELL...I'LL LEAVE YOU VOICE-MAILS.
LET ME KNOW HOW THAT WORKS OUT FOR YOU.

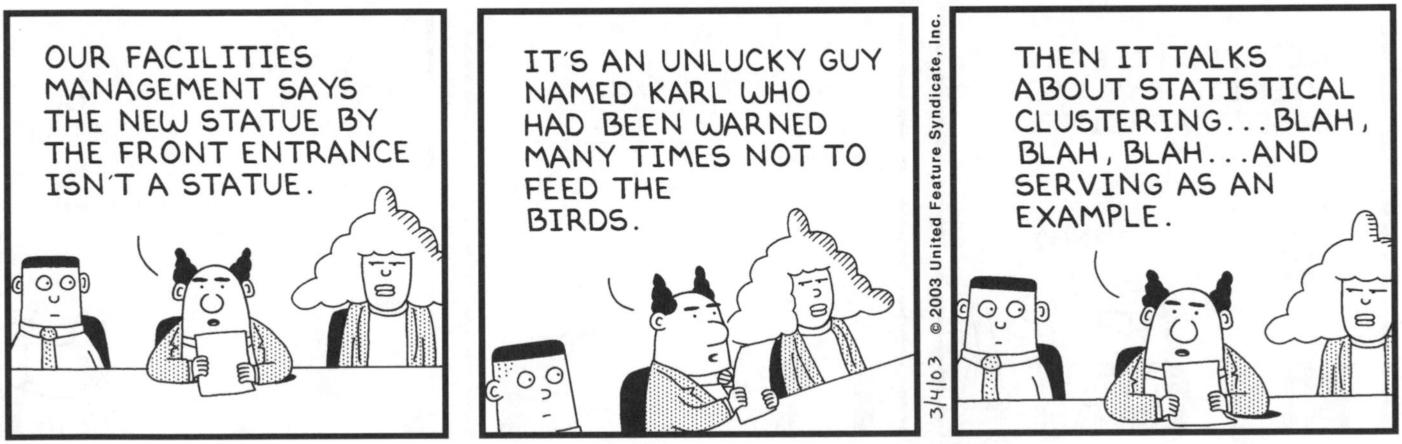
OUR FACILITIES MANAGEMENT SAYS THE NEW STATUE BY THE FRONT ENTRANCE ISN'T A STATUE.
IT'S AN UNLUCKY GUY NAMED KARL WHO HAD BEEN WARNED MANY TIMES NOT TO FEED THE BIRDS.
3/4/03 © 2003 United Feature Syndicate, Inc.
THEN IT TALKS ABOUT STATISTICAL CLUSTERING...BLAH, BLAH, BLAH...AND SERVING AS AN EXAMPLE.

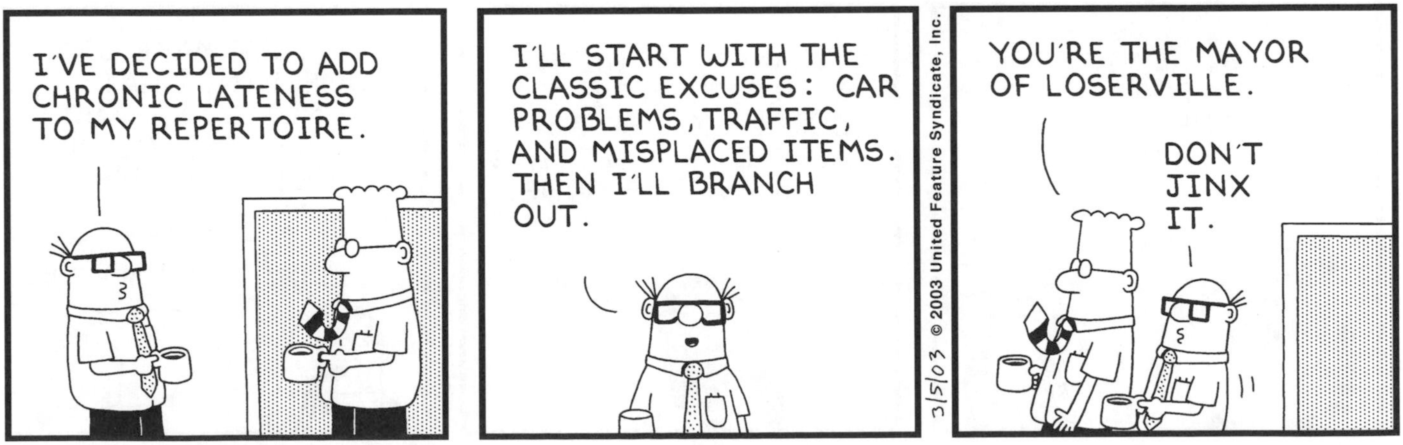
I'VE DECIDED TO ADD CHRONIC LATENESS TO MY REPERTOIRE.
I'LL START WITH THE CLASSIC EXCUSES: CAR PROBLEMS, TRAFFIC, AND MISPLACED ITEMS. THEN I'LL BRANCH OUT.
3/5/03 © 2003 United Feature Syndicate, Inc.
YOU'RE THE MAYOR OF LOSERVILLE.
DON'T JINX IT.

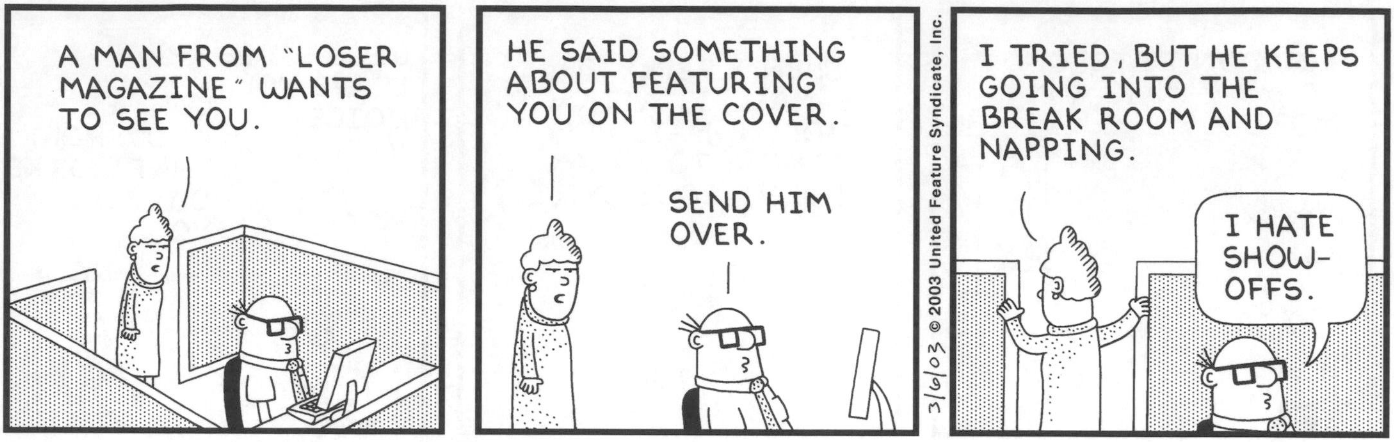
A MAN FROM "LOSER MAGAZINE" WANTS TO SEE YOU.
HE SAID SOMETHING ABOUT FEATURING YOU ON THE COVER.
SEND HIM OVER.
I TRIED, BUT HE KEEPS GOING INTO THE BREAK ROOM AND NAPPING.
I HATE SHOW-OFFS.
3/6/03

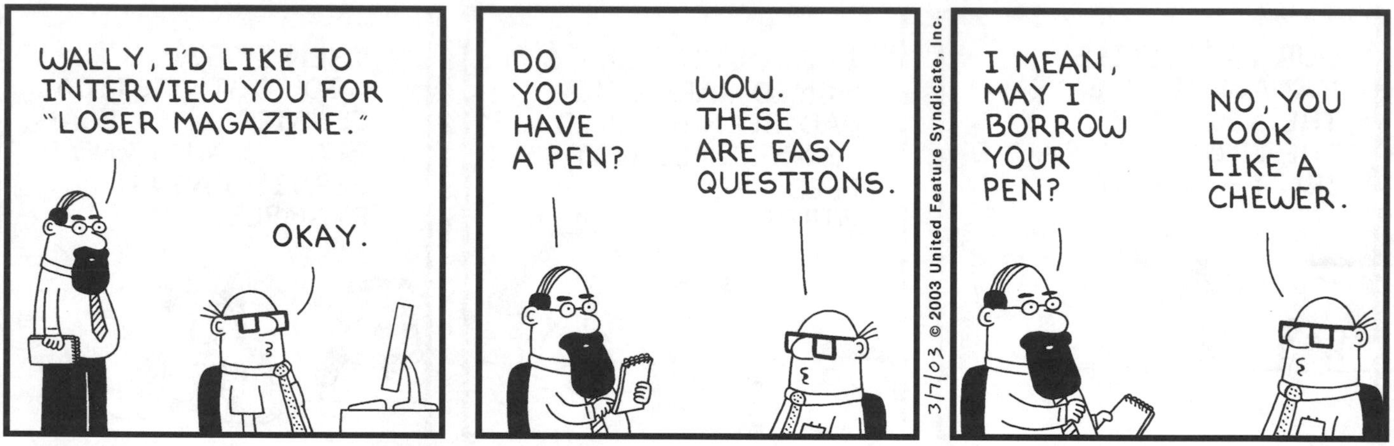
WALLY, I'D LIKE TO INTERVIEW YOU FOR "LOSER MAGAZINE."
OKAY.
DO YOU HAVE A PEN?
WOW. THESE ARE EASY QUESTIONS.
I MEAN, MAY I BORROW YOUR PEN?
NO, YOU LOOK LIKE A CHEWER.
3/7/03

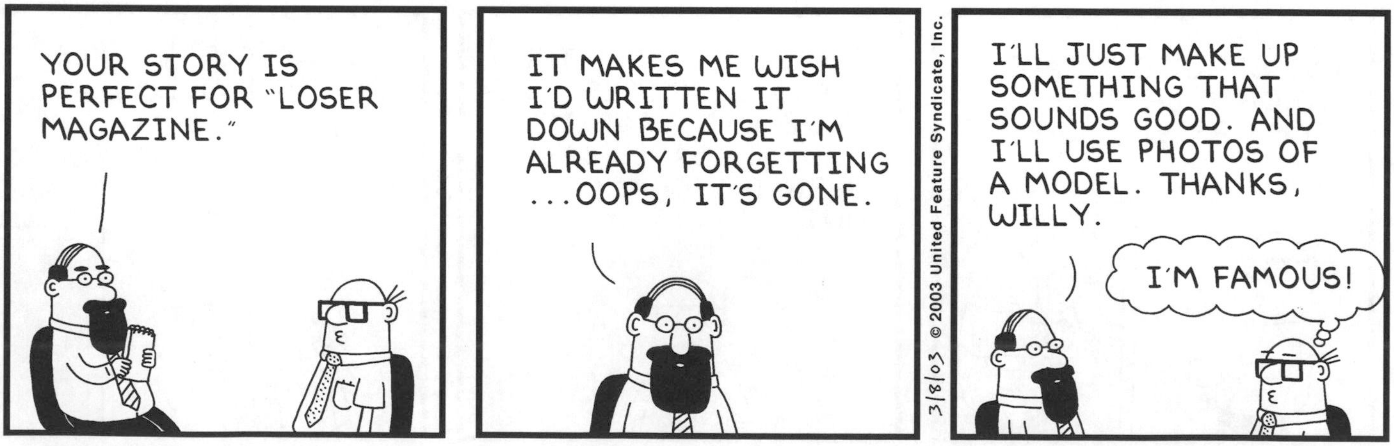
YOUR STORY IS PERFECT FOR "LOSER MAGAZINE."
IT MAKES ME WISH I'D WRITTEN IT DOWN BECAUSE I'M ALREADY FORGETTING ...OOPS, IT'S GONE.
I'LL JUST MAKE UP SOMETHING THAT SOUNDS GOOD. AND I'LL USE PHOTOS OF A MODEL. THANKS, WILLY.
I'M FAMOUS!
3/8/03

I CALL MY INVENTION THE "EARGARETTE."
IT'S A CIGARETTE FOR YOUR EAR!
IT ALLOWS NON-SMOKERS TO TAKE SMOKING BREAKS.
IS THERE ANY DOWN-SIDE?
WHAT?
NEVER MIND.
3/9/03 ©2003 United Feature Syndicate, Inc.
WE'VE BEEN WORKING FOR FIFTEEN MINUTES STRAIGHT. I NEED AN EARGARETTE BREAK.
WHAT?
WHAT?
WHAT?
EAR MINT?
TWO, PLEASE.

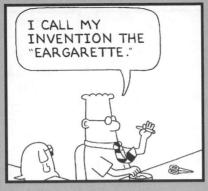

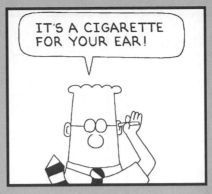

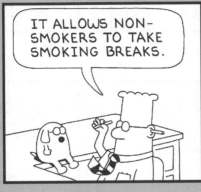

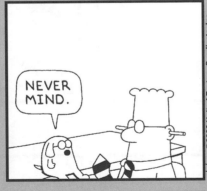

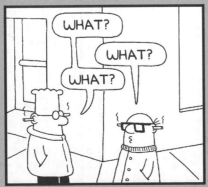

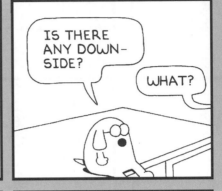

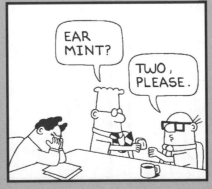

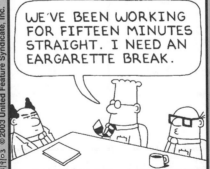

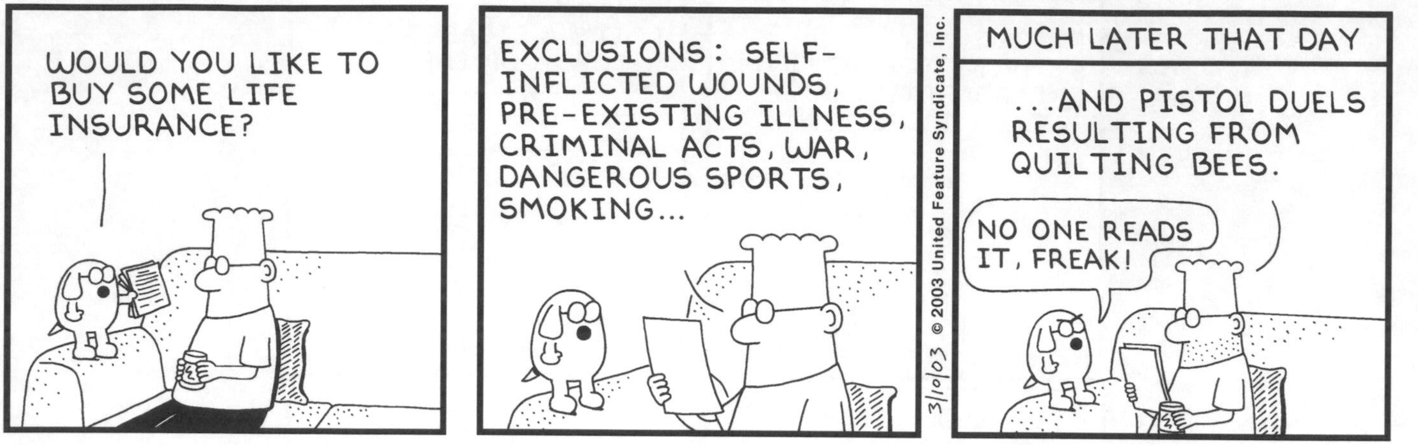
WOULD YOU LIKE TO BUY SOME LIFE INSURANCE?
EXCLUSIONS: SELF-INFLICTED WOUNDS, PRE-EXISTING ILLNESS, CRIMINAL ACTS, WAR, DANGEROUS SPORTS, SMOKING...
3/10/03 © 2003 United Feature Syndicate, Inc.
MUCH LATER THAT DAY
...AND PISTOL DUELS RESULTING FROM QUILTING BEES.
NO ONE READS IT, FREAK!

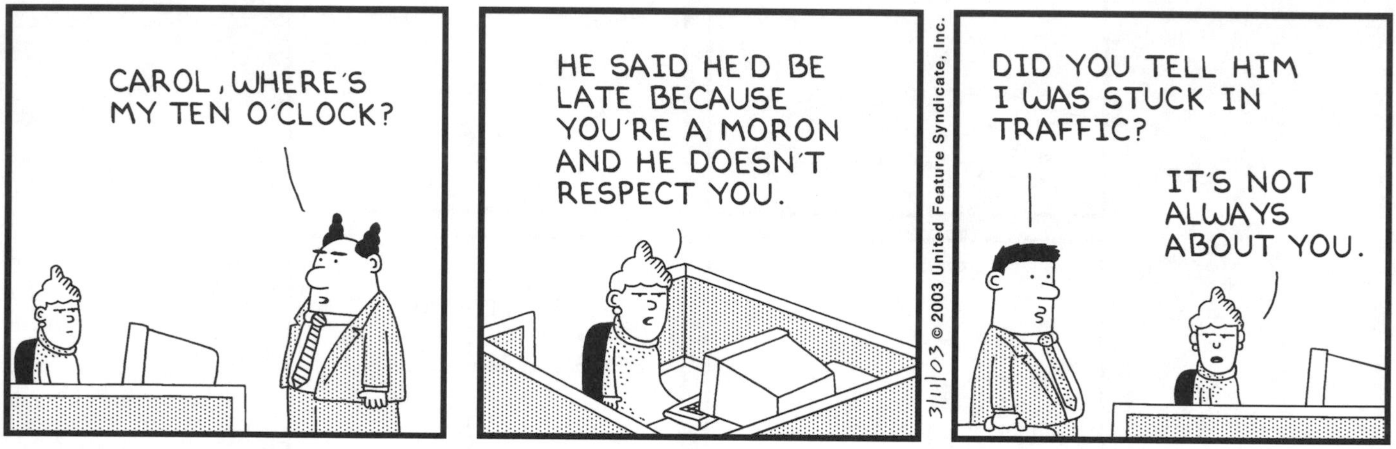
CAROL, WHERE'S MY TEN O'CLOCK?
HE SAID HE'D BE LATE BECAUSE YOU'RE A MORON AND HE DOESN'T RESPECT YOU.
3/11/03 © 2003 United Feature Syndicate, Inc.
DID YOU TELL HIM I WAS STUCK IN TRAFFIC?
IT'S NOT ALWAYS ABOUT YOU.

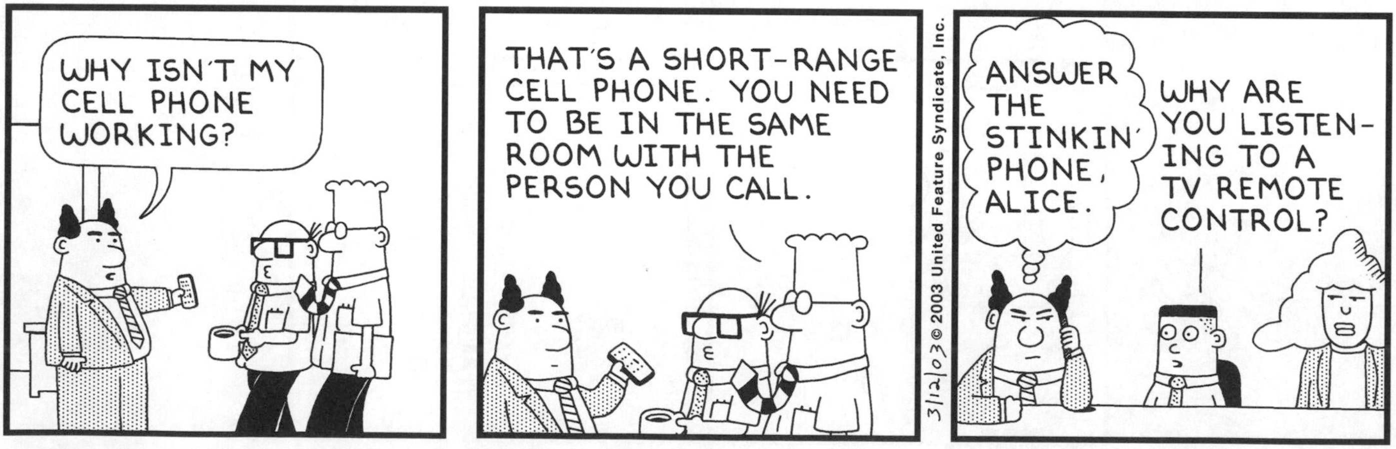
WHY ISN'T MY CELL PHONE WORKING?
THAT'S A SHORT-RANGE CELL PHONE. YOU NEED TO BE IN THE SAME ROOM WITH THE PERSON YOU CALL.
3/12/03 © 2003 United Feature Syndicate, Inc.
ANSWER THE STINKIN' PHONE, ALICE.
WHY ARE YOU LISTEN-ING TO A TV REMOTE CONTROL?

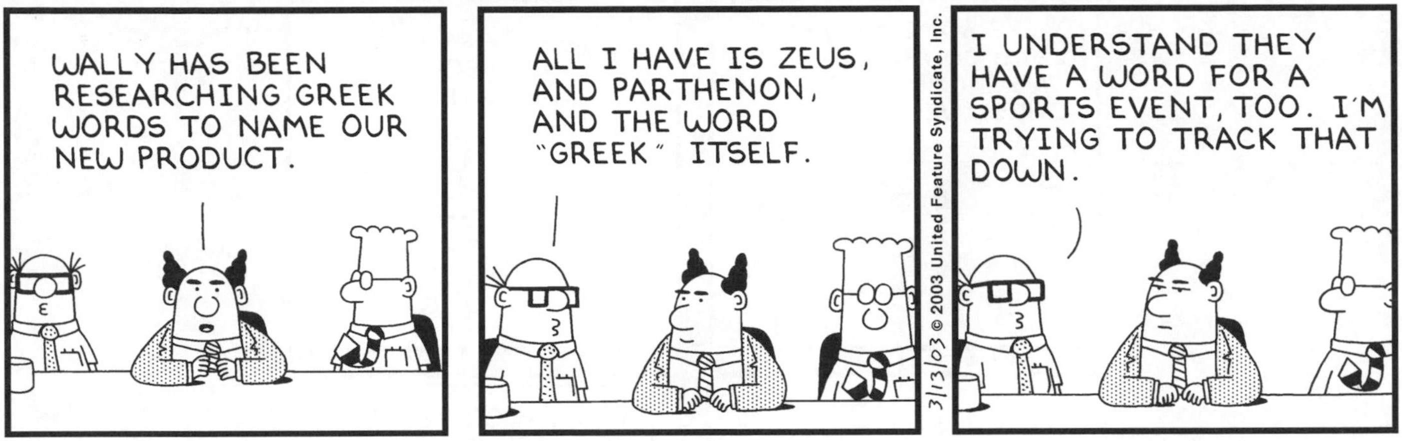
WALLY HAS BEEN RESEARCHING GREEK WORDS TO NAME OUR NEW PRODUCT.
ALL I HAVE IS ZEUS, AND PARTHENON, AND THE WORD "GREEK" ITSELF.
3/13/03 © 2003 United Feature Syndicate, Inc.
I UNDERSTAND THEY HAVE A WORD FOR A SPORTS EVENT, TOO. I'M TRYING TO TRACK THAT DOWN.

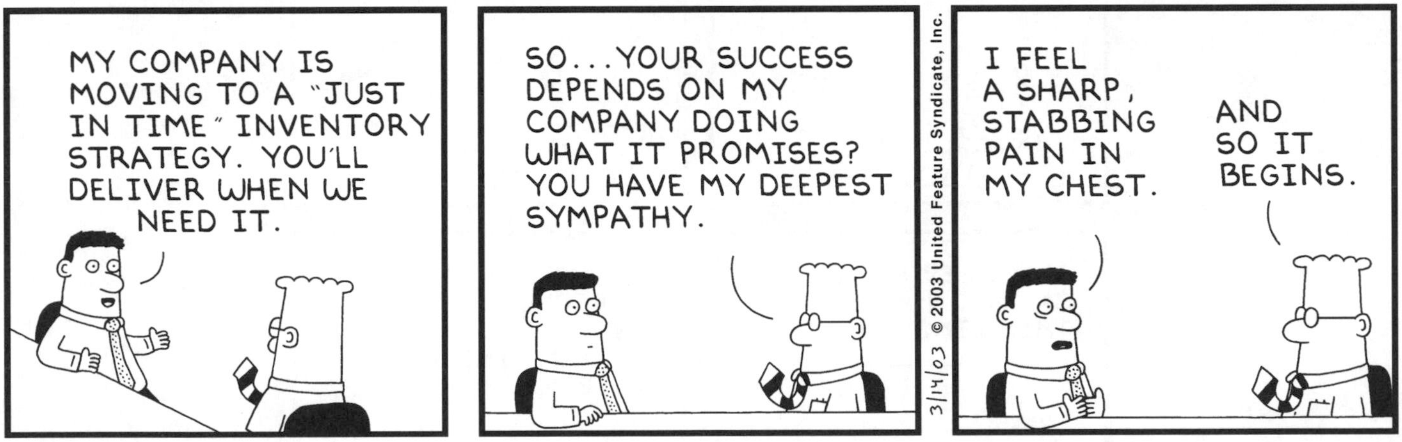
MY COMPANY IS MOVING TO A "JUST IN TIME" INVENTORY STRATEGY. YOU'LL DELIVER WHEN WE NEED IT.
SO...YOUR SUCCESS DEPENDS ON MY COMPANY DOING WHAT IT PROMISES? YOU HAVE MY DEEPEST SYMPATHY.
3/14/03 © 2003 United Feature Syndicate, Inc.
I FEEL A SHARP, STABBING PAIN IN MY CHEST.
AND SO IT BEGINS.

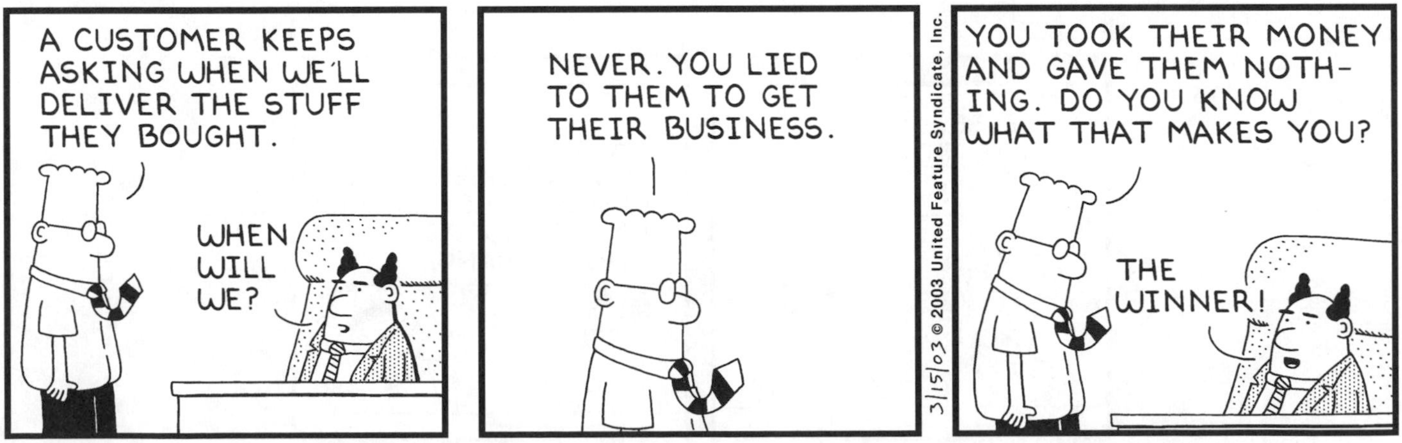
A CUSTOMER KEEPS ASKING WHEN WE'LL DELIVER THE STUFF THEY BOUGHT.
WHEN WILL WE?
NEVER. YOU LIED TO THEM TO GET THEIR BUSINESS.
3/15/03 © 2003 United Feature Syndicate, Inc.
YOU TOOK THEIR MONEY AND GAVE THEM NOTH-ING. DO YOU KNOW WHAT THAT MAKES YOU?
THE WINNER!

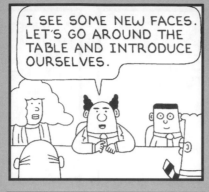

I SEE SOME NEW FACES. LET'S GO AROUND THE TABLE AND INTRODUCE OURSELVES.
I AM ASOK, THE INTERN.
I REPORT TO YOU.
BUT I ALSO REPORT TO ALICE ON A DOTTED LINE.
AND I REPORT TO CAROL ON A FUZZY, THIN LINE.
I HAVE A BLINKING, IRREGULAR LINE TO WALLY, AND A WAVY, BROWN LINE TO DILBERT.
PLEASE... MAKE THIS STOP.
AND A DISTURBING, IMAGINARY LINE TO A FOOD-SERVICE CASHIER WHO TOUCHED MY HAND WHILE GIVING CHANGE.
3/16/03 ©2003 United Feature Syndicate, Inc.

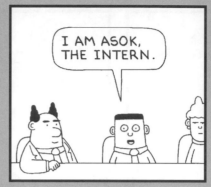

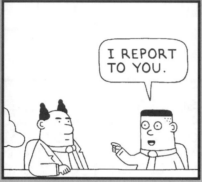

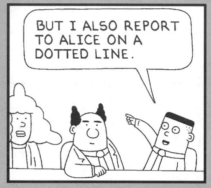

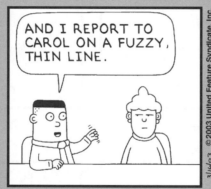

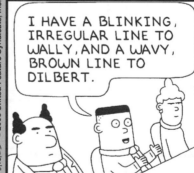

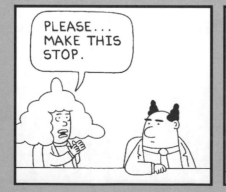

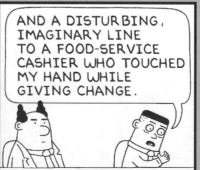

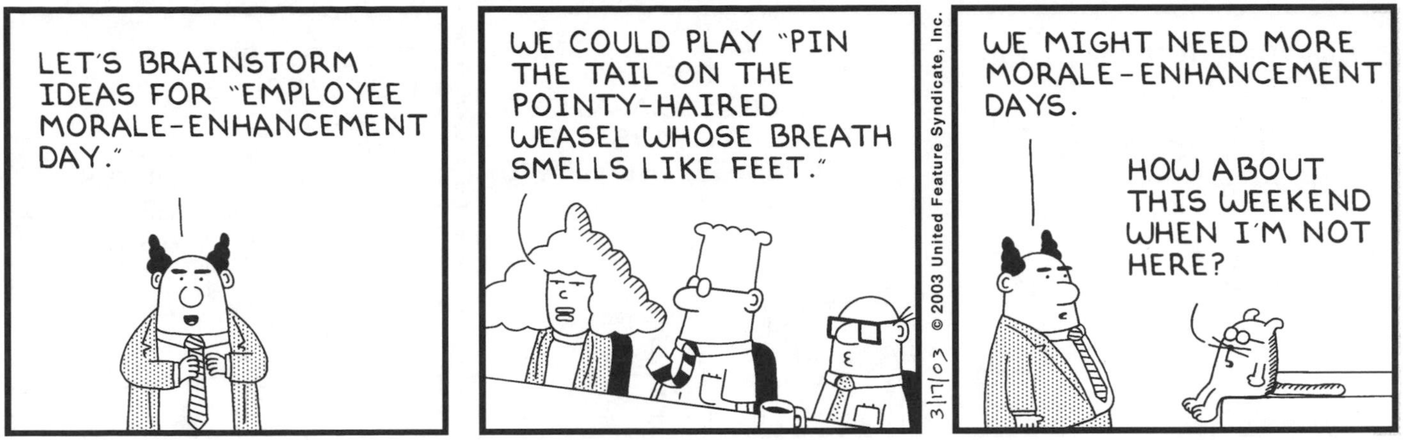
LET'S BRAINSTORM IDEAS FOR "EMPLOYEE MORALE-ENHANCEMENT DAY."
WE COULD PLAY "PIN THE TAIL ON THE POINTY-HAIRED WEASEL WHOSE BREATH SMELLS LIKE FEET."
3/17/03 © 2003 United Feature Syndicate, Inc.
WE MIGHT NEED MORE MORALE-ENHANCEMENT DAYS.
HOW ABOUT THIS WEEKEND WHEN I'M NOT HERE?

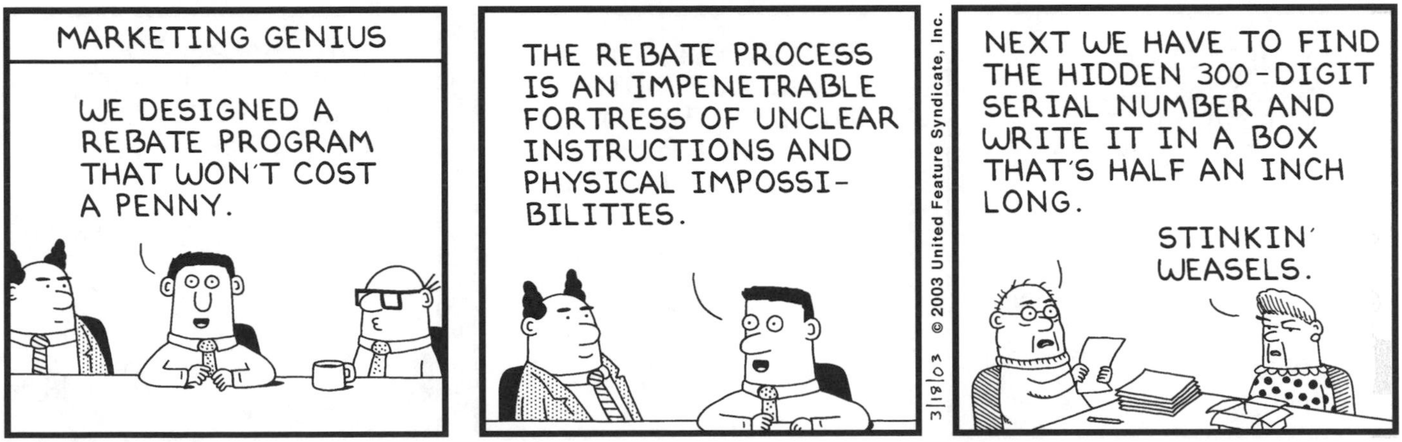
MARKETING GENIUS
WE DESIGNED A REBATE PROGRAM THAT WON'T COST A PENNY.
THE REBATE PROCESS IS AN IMPENETRABLE FORTRESS OF UNCLEAR INSTRUCTIONS AND PHYSICAL IMPOSSI-BILITIES.
3/18/03 © 2003 United Feature Syndicate, Inc.
NEXT WE HAVE TO FIND THE HIDDEN 300-DIGIT SERIAL NUMBER AND WRITE IT IN A BOX THAT'S HALF AN INCH LONG.
STINKIN' WEASELS.

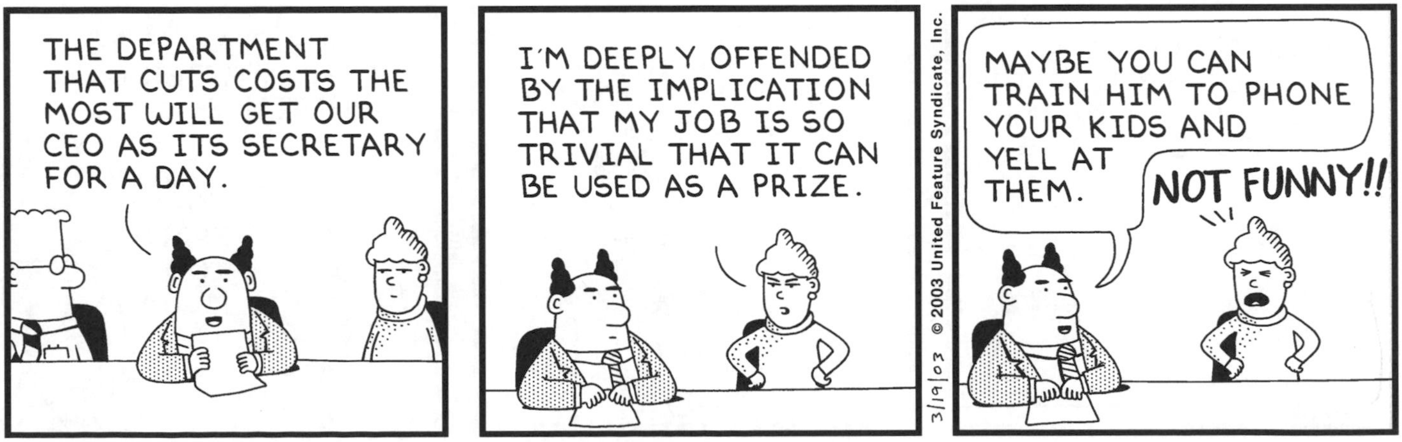
THE DEPARTMENT THAT CUTS COSTS THE MOST WILL GET OUR CEO AS ITS SECRETARY FOR A DAY.
I'M DEEPLY OFFENDED BY THE IMPLICATION THAT MY JOB IS SO TRIVIAL THAT IT CAN BE USED AS A PRIZE.
3/19/03 © 2003 United Feature Syndicate, Inc.
MAYBE YOU CAN TRAIN HIM TO PHONE YOUR KIDS AND YELL AT THEM.
NOT FUNNY!!

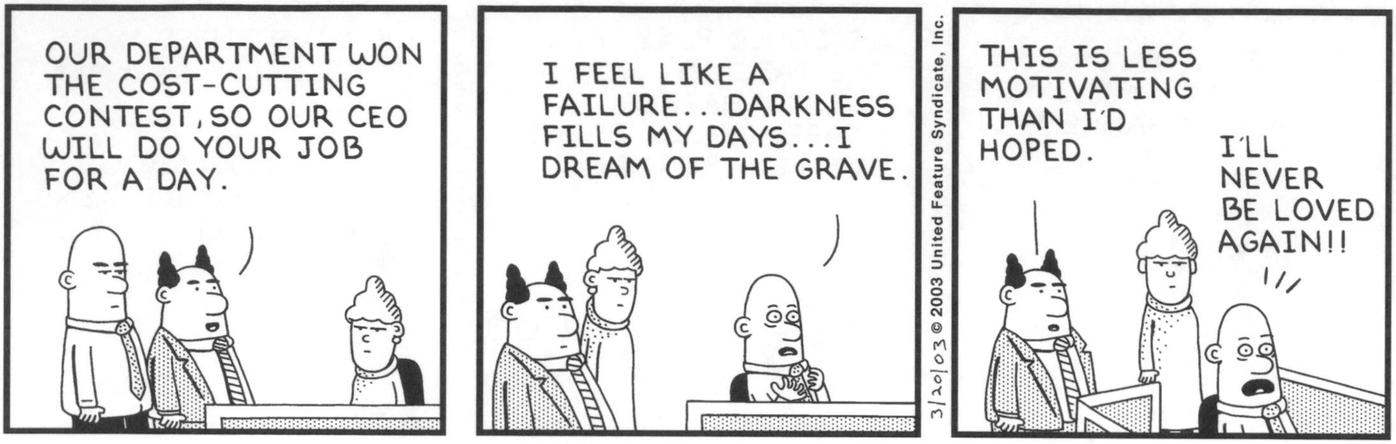
OUR DEPARTMENT WON THE COST-CUTTING CONTEST, SO OUR CEO WILL DO YOUR JOB FOR A DAY.
I FEEL LIKE A FAILURE...DARKNESS FILLS MY DAYS...I DREAM OF THE GRAVE.
THIS IS LESS MOTIVATING THAN I'D HOPED.
I'LL NEVER BE LOVED AGAIN!!
3/20/03 © 2003 United Feature Syndicate, Inc.

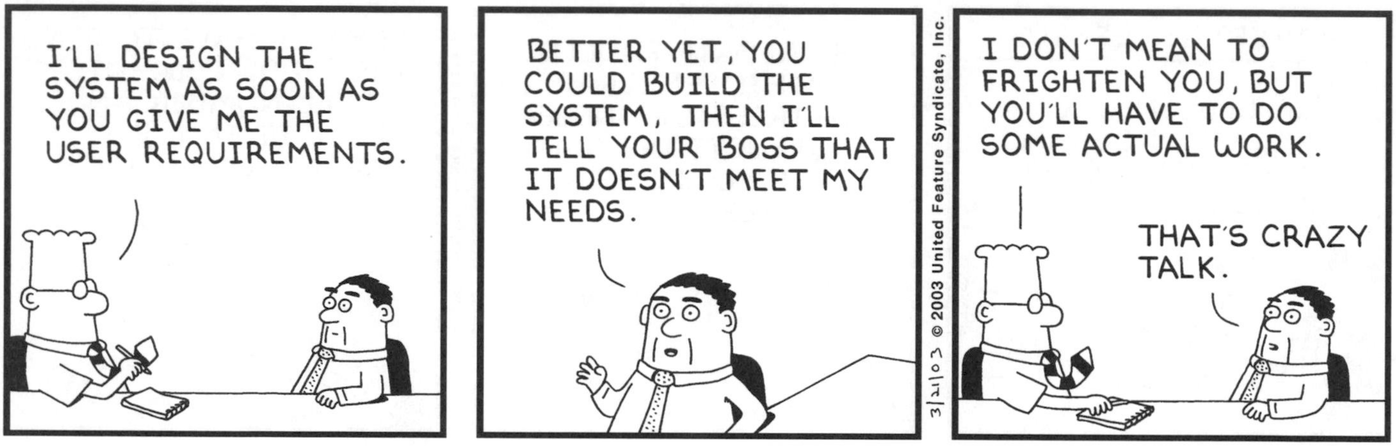
I'LL DESIGN THE SYSTEM AS SOON AS YOU GIVE ME THE USER REQUIREMENTS.
BETTER YET, YOU COULD BUILD THE SYSTEM, THEN I'LL TELL YOUR BOSS THAT IT DOESN'T MEET MY NEEDS.
I DON'T MEAN TO FRIGHTEN YOU, BUT YOU'LL HAVE TO DO SOME ACTUAL WORK.
THAT'S CRAZY TALK.
3/21/03 © 2003 United Feature Syndicate, Inc.

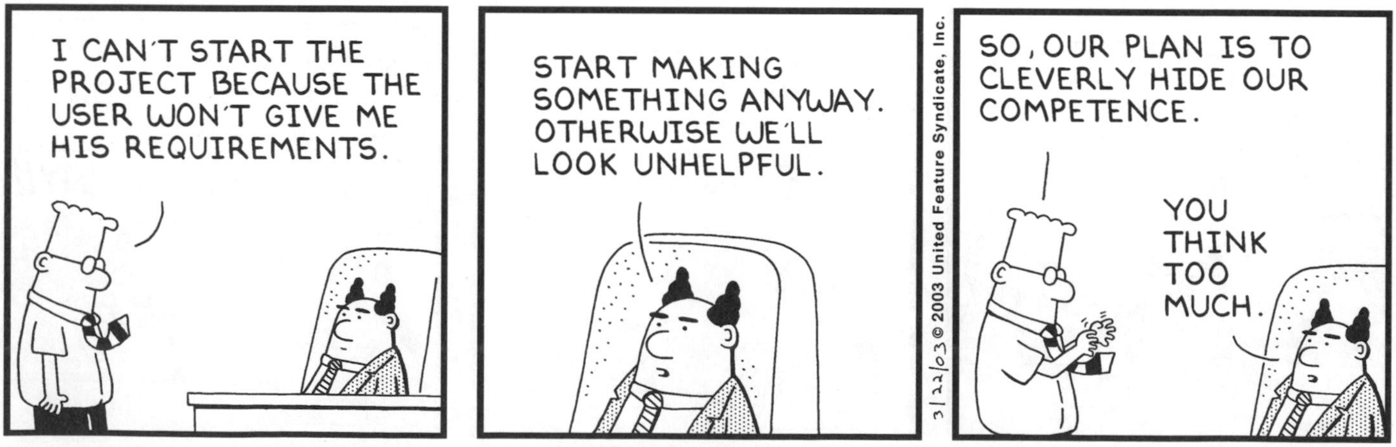
I CAN'T START THE PROJECT BECAUSE THE USER WON'T GIVE ME HIS REQUIREMENTS.
START MAKING SOMETHING ANYWAY. OTHERWISE WE'LL LOOK UNHELPFUL.
SO, OUR PLAN IS TO CLEVERLY HIDE OUR COMPETENCE.
YOU THINK TOO MUCH.
3/22/03 © 2003 United Feature Syndicate, Inc.

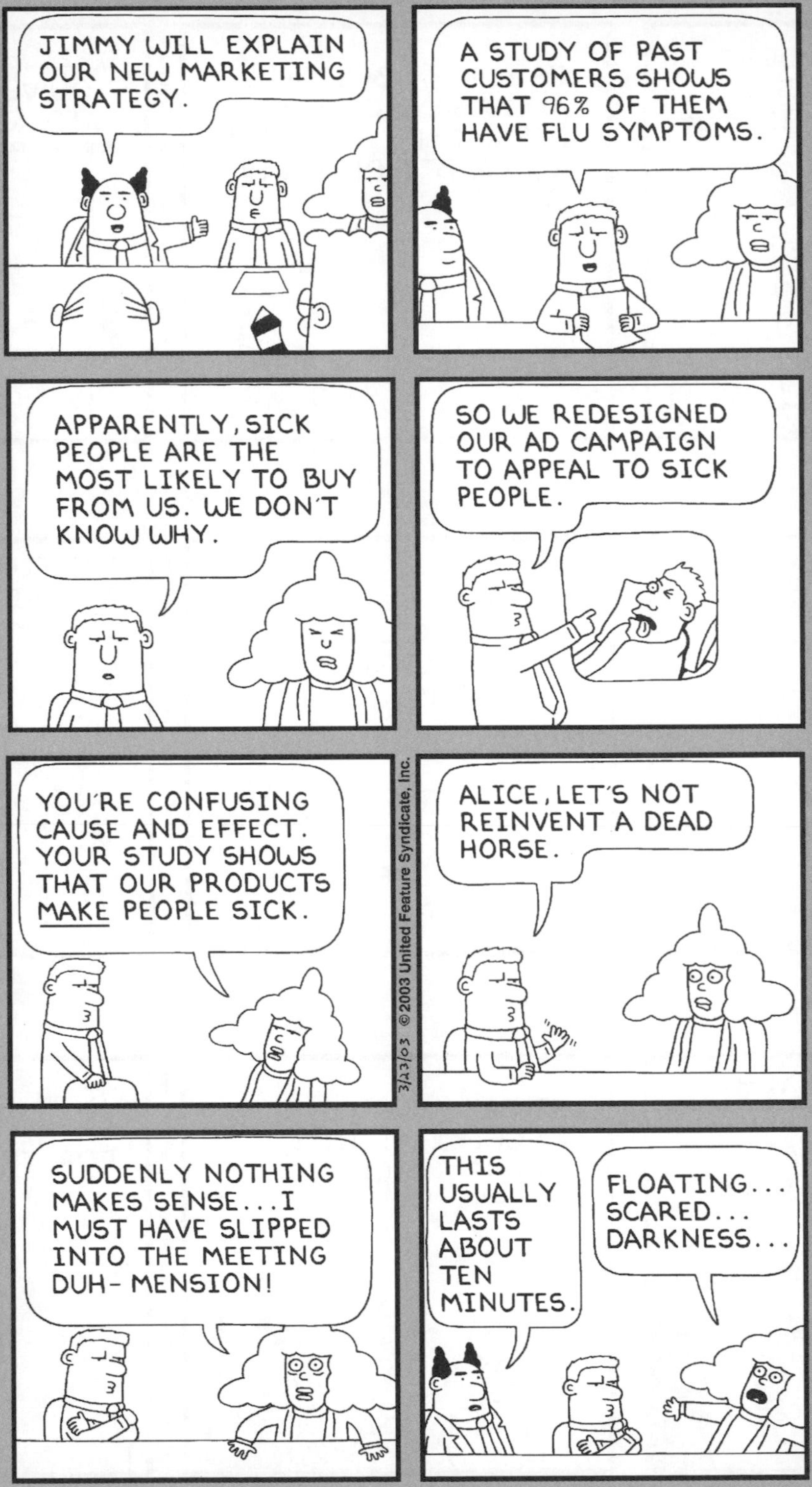
JIMMY WILL EXPLAIN OUR NEW MARKETING STRATEGY.
A STUDY OF PAST CUSTOMERS SHOWS THAT 96% OF THEM HAVE FLU SYMPTOMS.
APPARENTLY, SICK PEOPLE ARE THE MOST LIKELY TO BUY FROM US. WE DON'T KNOW WHY.
SO WE REDESIGNED OUR AD CAMPAIGN TO APPEAL TO SICK PEOPLE.
YOU'RE CONFUSING CAUSE AND EFFECT. YOUR STUDY SHOWS THAT OUR PRODUCTS MAKE PEOPLE SICK.
ALICE, LET'S NOT REINVENT A DEAD HORSE.
SUDDENLY NOTHING MAKES SENSE... I MUST HAVE SLIPPED INTO THE MEETING DUH-MENSION!
THIS USUALLY LASTS ABOUT TEN MINUTES.
FLOATING... SCARED... DARKNESS...
3/23/03 © 2003 United Feature Syndicate, Inc.

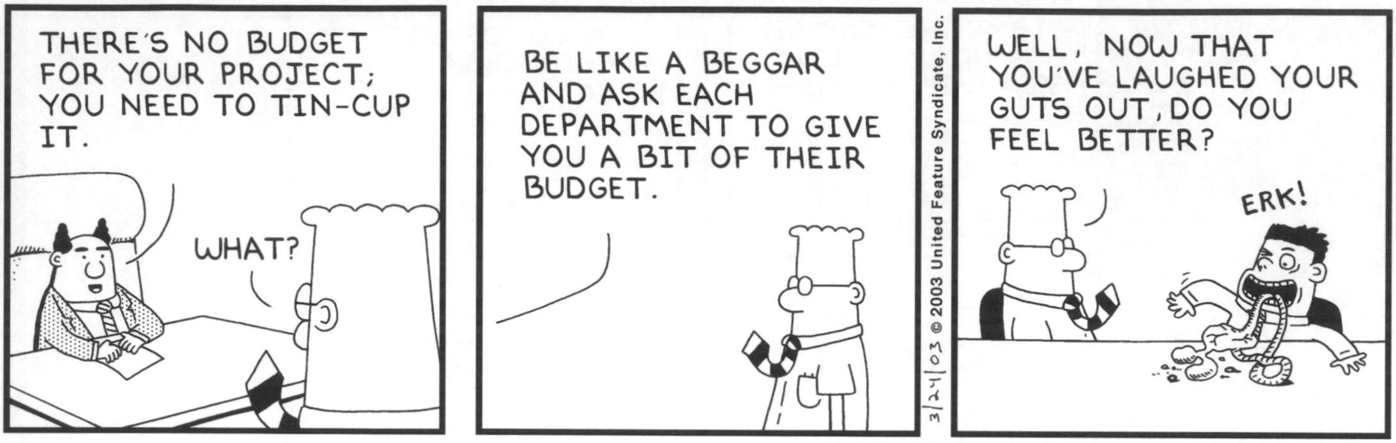
THERE'S NO BUDGET FOR YOUR PROJECT; YOU NEED TO TIN-CUP IT.
WHAT?
BE LIKE A BEGGAR AND ASK EACH DEPARTMENT TO GIVE YOU A BIT OF THEIR BUDGET.
3/24/03 © 2003 United Feature Syndicate, Inc.
WELL, NOW THAT YOU'VE LAUGHED YOUR GUTS OUT, DO YOU FEEL BETTER?
ERK!

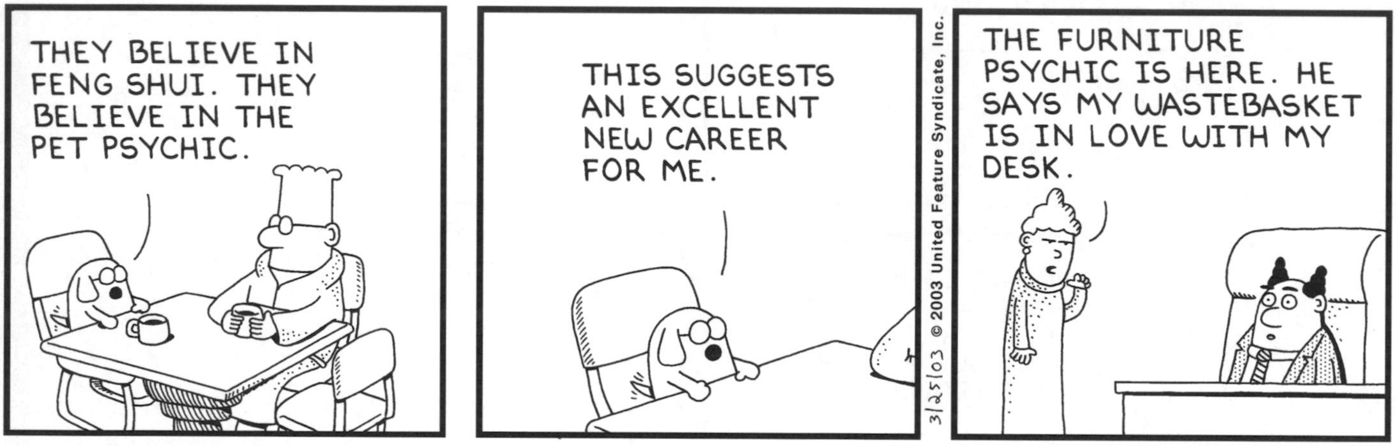
THEY BELIEVE IN FENG SHUI. THEY BELIEVE IN THE PET PSYCHIC.
THIS SUGGESTS AN EXCELLENT NEW CAREER FOR ME.
3/25/03 © 2003 United Feature Syndicate, Inc.
THE FURNITURE PSYCHIC IS HERE. HE SAYS MY WASTEBASKET IS IN LOVE WITH MY DESK.

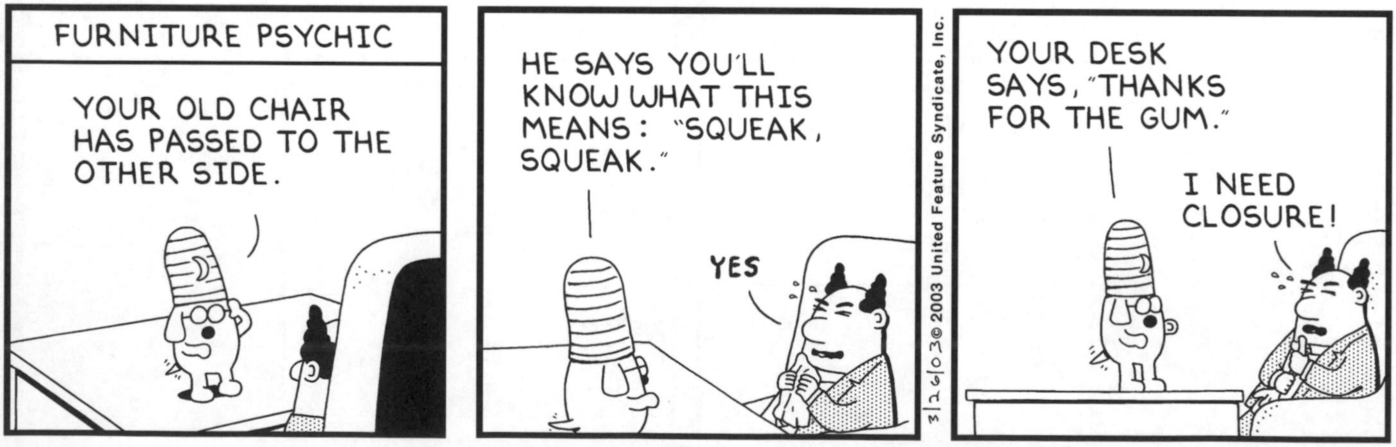
FURNITURE PSYCHIC
YOUR OLD CHAIR HAS PASSED TO THE OTHER SIDE.
HE SAYS YOU'LL KNOW WHAT THIS MEANS: "SQUEAK, SQUEAK."
YES
3/26/03 © 2003 United Feature Syndicate, Inc.
YOUR DESK SAYS, "THANKS FOR THE GUM."
I NEED CLOSURE!

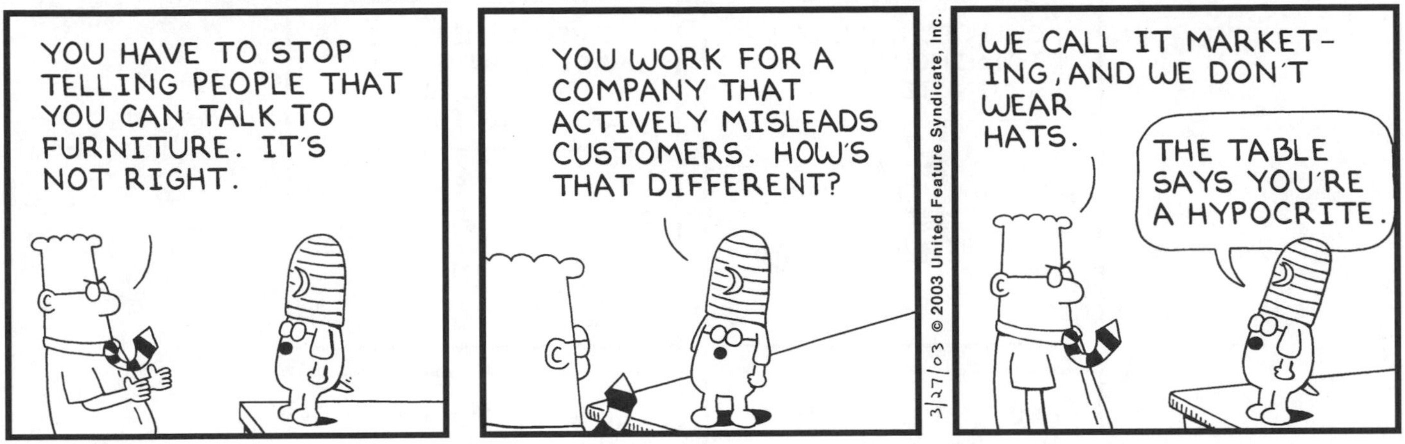
YOU HAVE TO STOP TELLING PEOPLE THAT YOU CAN TALK TO FURNITURE. IT'S NOT RIGHT.
YOU WORK FOR A COMPANY THAT ACTIVELY MISLEADS CUSTOMERS. HOW'S THAT DIFFERENT?
3/27/03 © 2003 United Feature Syndicate, Inc.
WE CALL IT MARKETING, AND WE DON'T WEAR HATS.
THE TABLE SAYS YOU'RE A HYPOCRITE.

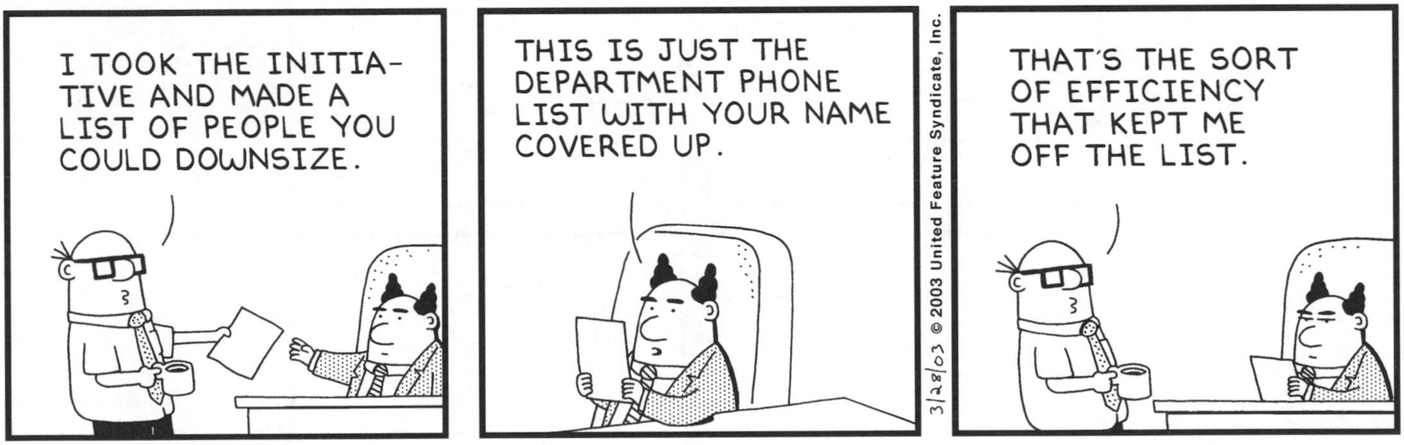
I TOOK THE INITIATIVE AND MADE A LIST OF PEOPLE YOU COULD DOWNSIZE.
THIS IS JUST THE DEPARTMENT PHONE LIST WITH YOUR NAME COVERED UP.
3/28/03 © 2003 United Feature Syndicate, Inc.
THAT'S THE SORT OF EFFICIENCY THAT KEPT ME OFF THE LIST.

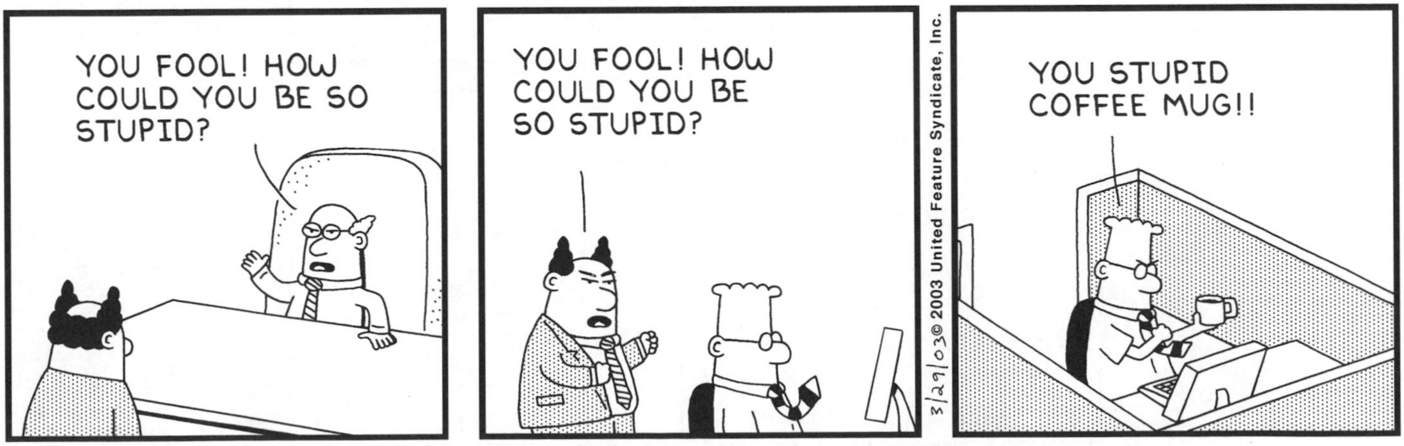
YOU FOOL! HOW COULD YOU BE SO STUPID?
YOU FOOL! HOW COULD YOU BE SO STUPID?
3/29/03 © 2003 United Feature Syndicate, Inc.
YOU STUPID COFFEE MUG!!

OUR CEO WILL BE JOINING US IN A MINUTE.
AS USUAL, HE'LL BE MAKING AN AWKWARD ATTEMPT TO SEEM LIKE "JUST PLAIN FOLK."
EXCUSE ME – IS THIS ORDINARY CHAIR AVAILABLE FOR AN AVERAGE GUY LIKE ME?
I'LL ROLL UP MY SLEEVES AND GET TO WORK. I'M NOT TOO GOOD FOR REAL WORK.
I HAVE A SECRETARY, BUT IT'S ALMOST AS IF I WORK FOR HER. HA HA! IT'S IRONIC.
3/30/03 ©2003 United Feature Syndicate, Inc.
LAST WEEKEND I WORE BLUE JEANS AND DROVE A TRACTOR!
SIR, YOUR HELICOPTER IS HERE TO TAKE YOU TO YOUR ISLAND FORTRESS FOR THE FOX HUNT.
ITTY BITTY FOR-TRESS
THE INTERNS ARE ALREADY IN FULL FOX COSTUMES.

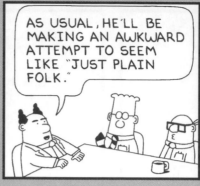

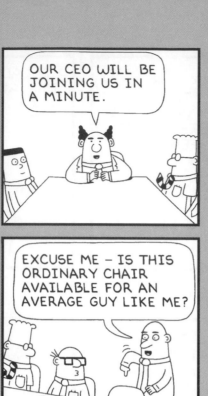

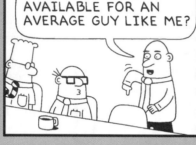

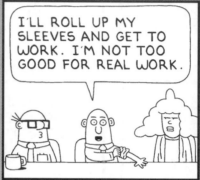

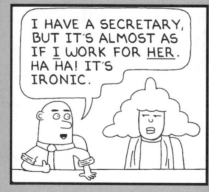

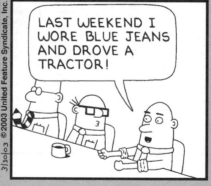

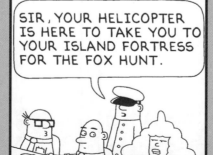

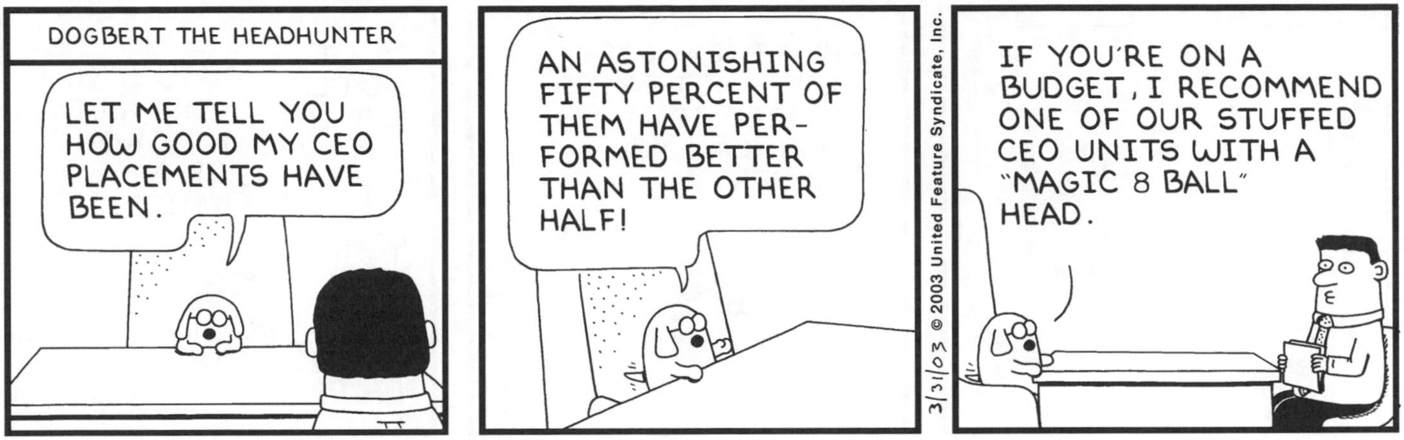
DOGBERT THE HEADHUNTER
LET ME TELL YOU HOW GOOD MY CEO PLACEMENTS HAVE BEEN.
AN ASTONISHING FIFTY PERCENT OF THEM HAVE PER-FORMED BETTER THAN THE OTHER HALF!
3/31/03 © 2003 United Feature Syndicate, Inc.
IF YOU'RE ON A BUDGET, I RECOMMEND ONE OF OUR STUFFED CEO UNITS WITH A "MAGIC 8 BALL" HEAD.

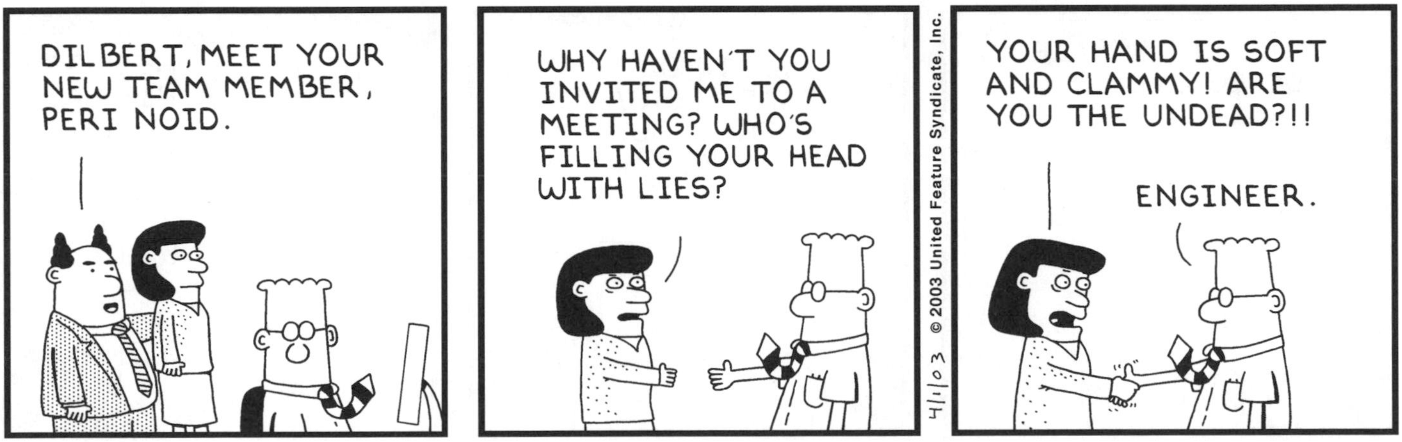
DILBERT, MEET YOUR NEW TEAM MEMBER, PERI NOID.
WHY HAVEN'T YOU INVITED ME TO A MEETING? WHO'S FILLING YOUR HEAD WITH LIES?
4/1/03 © 2003 United Feature Syndicate, Inc.
YOUR HAND IS SOFT AND CLAMMY! ARE YOU THE UNDEAD?!!
ENGINEER.

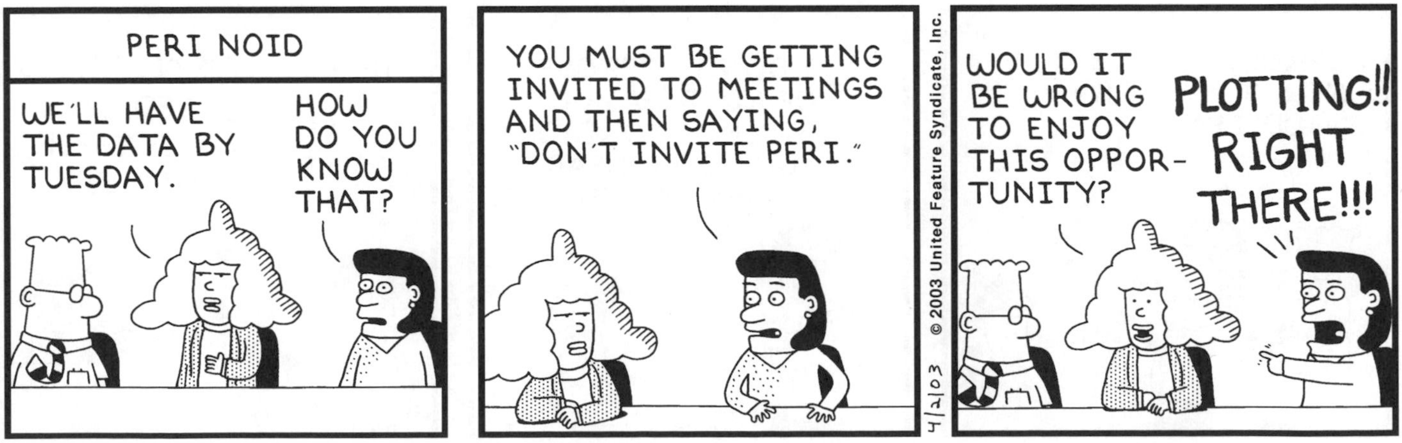
PERI NOID
WE'LL HAVE THE DATA BY TUESDAY.
HOW DO YOU KNOW THAT?
YOU MUST BE GETTING INVITED TO MEETINGS AND THEN SAYING, "DON'T INVITE PERI."
4/2/03 © 2003 United Feature Syndicate, Inc.
WOULD IT BE WRONG TO ENJOY THIS OPPOR-TUNITY?
PLOTTING!! RIGHT THERE!!!

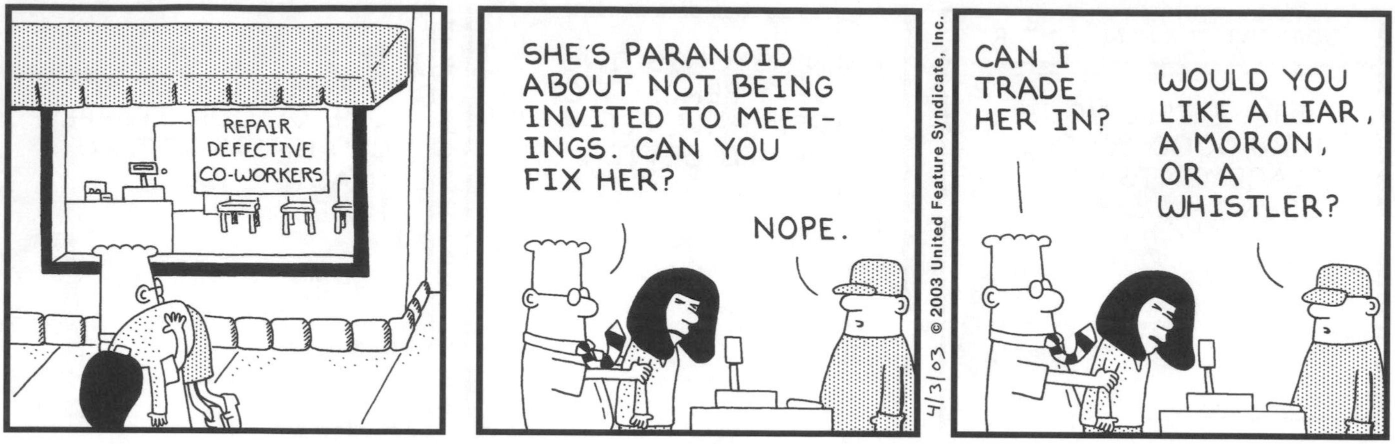
REPAIR DEFECTIVE CO-WORKERS
SHE'S PARANOID ABOUT NOT BEING INVITED TO MEET-INGS. CAN YOU FIX HER?
NOPE.
4/3/03
© 2003 United Feature Syndicate, Inc.
CAN I TRADE HER IN?
WOULD YOU LIKE A LIAR, A MORON, OR A WHISTLER?

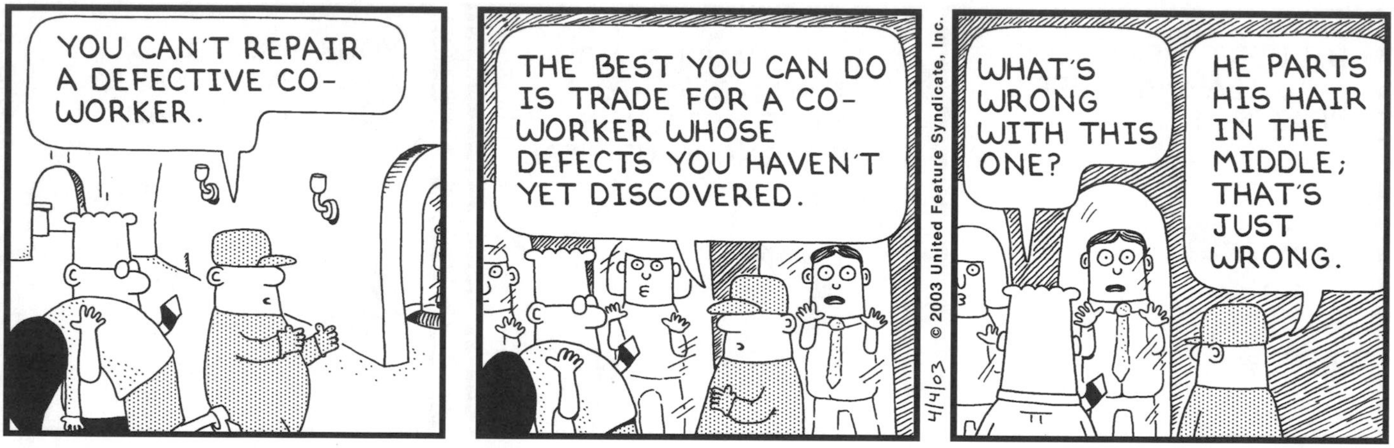
YOU CAN'T REPAIR A DEFECTIVE CO-WORKER.
THE BEST YOU CAN DO IS TRADE FOR A CO-WORKER WHOSE DEFECTS YOU HAVEN'T YET DISCOVERED.
4/4/03
© 2003 United Feature Syndicate, Inc.
WHAT'S WRONG WITH THIS ONE?
HE PARTS HIS HAIR IN THE MIDDLE; THAT'S JUST WRONG.

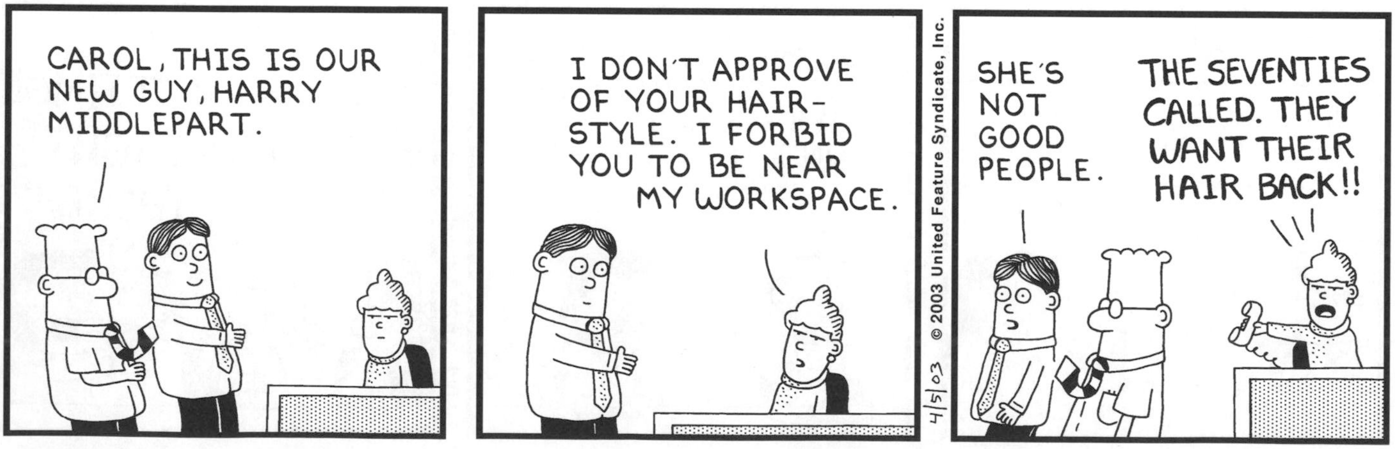
CAROL, THIS IS OUR NEW GUY, HARRY MIDDLEPART.
I DON'T APPROVE OF YOUR HAIR-STYLE. I FORBID YOU TO BE NEAR MY WORKSPACE.
4/5/03
© 2003 United Feature Syndicate, Inc.
SHE'S NOT GOOD PEOPLE.
THE SEVENTIES CALLED. THEY WANT THEIR HAIR BACK!!

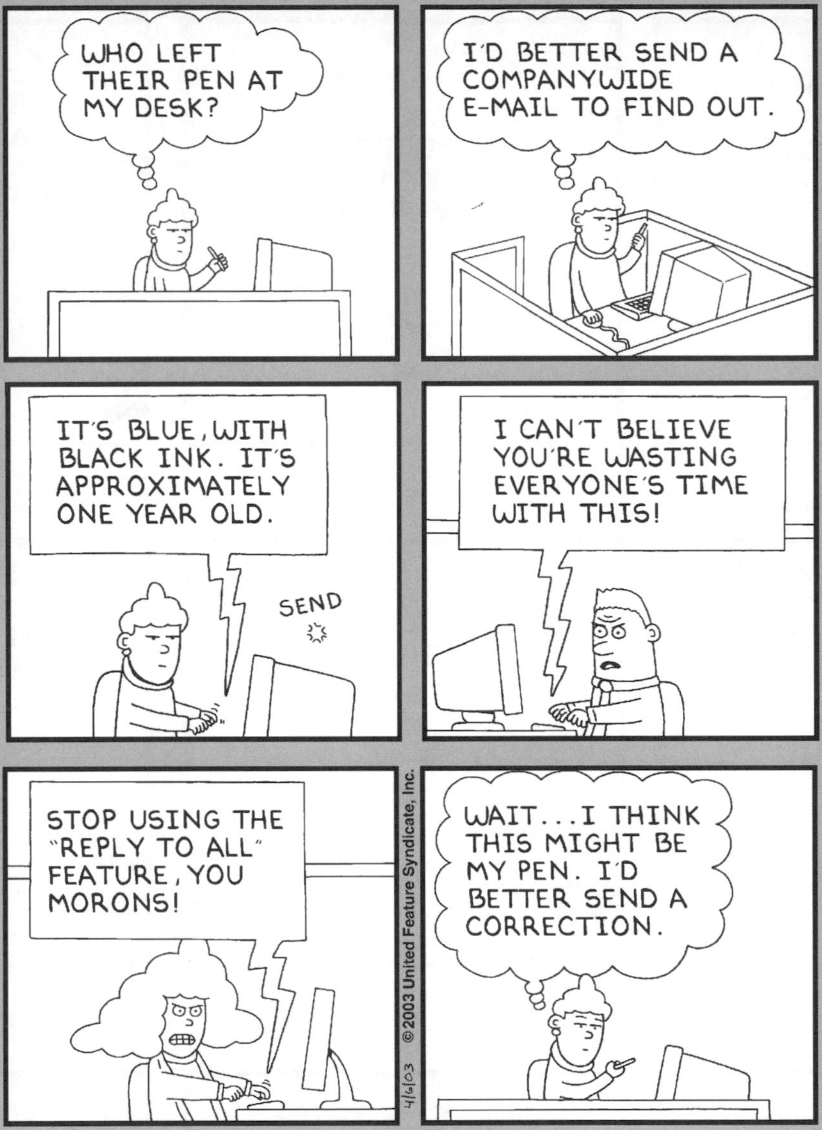
WHO LEFT THEIR PEN AT MY DESK?
I'D BETTER SEND A COMPANYWIDE E-MAIL TO FIND OUT.
IT'S BLUE, WITH BLACK INK. IT'S APPROXIMATELY ONE YEAR OLD.
SEND
I CAN'T BELIEVE YOU'RE WASTING EVERYONE'S TIME WITH THIS!
STOP USING THE "REPLY TO ALL" FEATURE, YOU MORONS!
©2003 United Feature Syndicate, Inc.
4/6/03
WAIT...I THINK THIS MIGHT BE MY PEN. I'D BETTER SEND A CORRECTION.

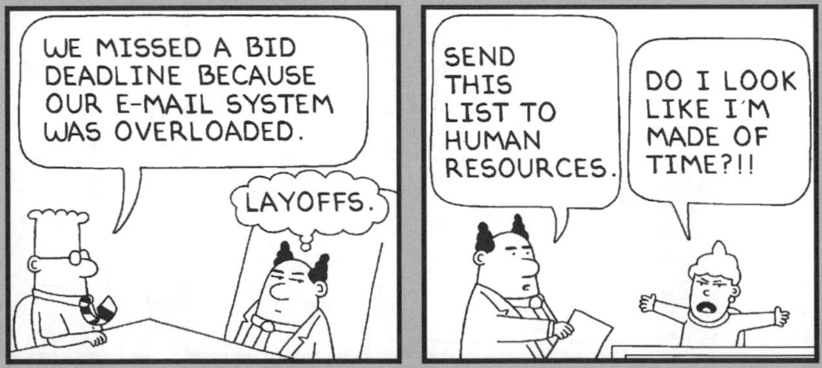
WE MISSED A BID DEADLINE BECAUSE OUR E-MAIL SYSTEM WAS OVERLOADED.
LAYOFFS.
SEND THIS LIST TO HUMAN RESOURCES.
DO I LOOK LIKE I'M MADE OF TIME?!!

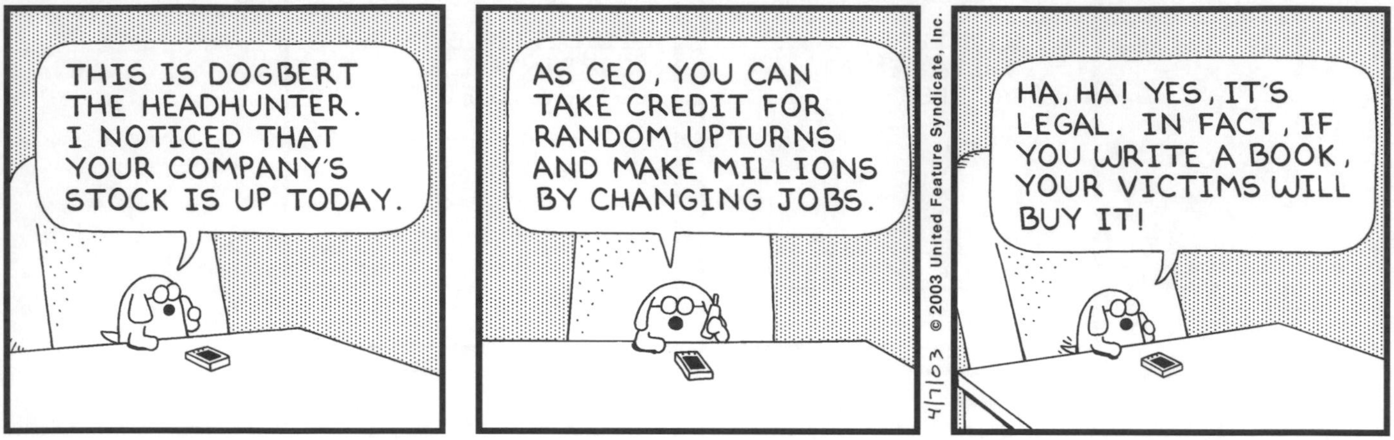
THIS IS DOGBERT THE HEADHUNTER. I NOTICED THAT YOUR COMPANY'S STOCK IS UP TODAY.
AS CEO, YOU CAN TAKE CREDIT FOR RANDOM UPTURNS AND MAKE MILLIONS BY CHANGING JOBS.
4/7/03 © 2003 United Feature Syndicate, Inc.
HA, HA! YES, IT'S LEGAL. IN FACT, IF YOU WRITE A BOOK, YOUR VICTIMS WILL BUY IT!

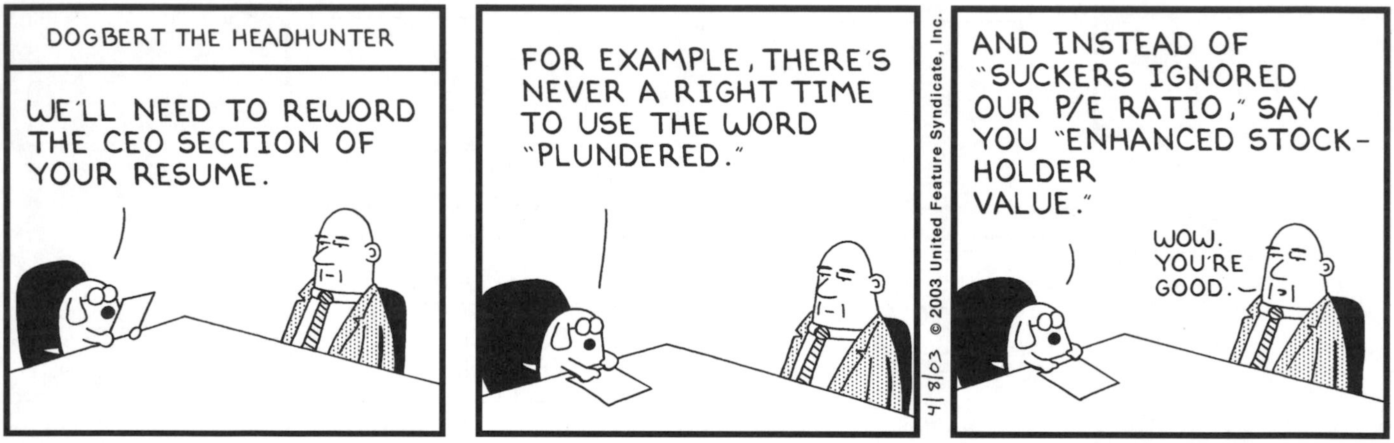
DOGBERT THE HEADHUNTER
WE'LL NEED TO REWORD THE CEO SECTION OF YOUR RESUME.
FOR EXAMPLE, THERE'S NEVER A RIGHT TIME TO USE THE WORD "PLUNDERED."
4/8/03 © 2003 United Feature Syndicate, Inc.
AND INSTEAD OF "SUCKERS IGNORED OUR P/E RATIO," SAY YOU "ENHANCED STOCK-HOLDER VALUE."
WOW. YOU'RE GOOD.

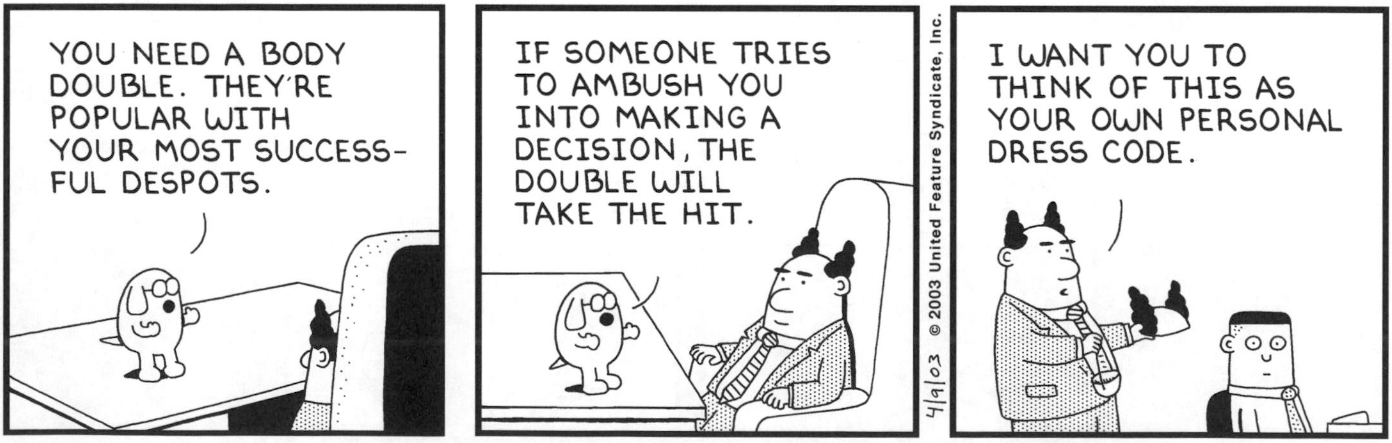
YOU NEED A BODY DOUBLE. THEY'RE POPULAR WITH YOUR MOST SUCCESS-FUL DESPOTS.
IF SOMEONE TRIES TO AMBUSH YOU INTO MAKING A DECISION, THE DOUBLE WILL TAKE THE HIT.
4/9/03 © 2003 United Feature Syndicate, Inc.
I WANT YOU TO THINK OF THIS AS YOUR OWN PERSONAL DRESS CODE.

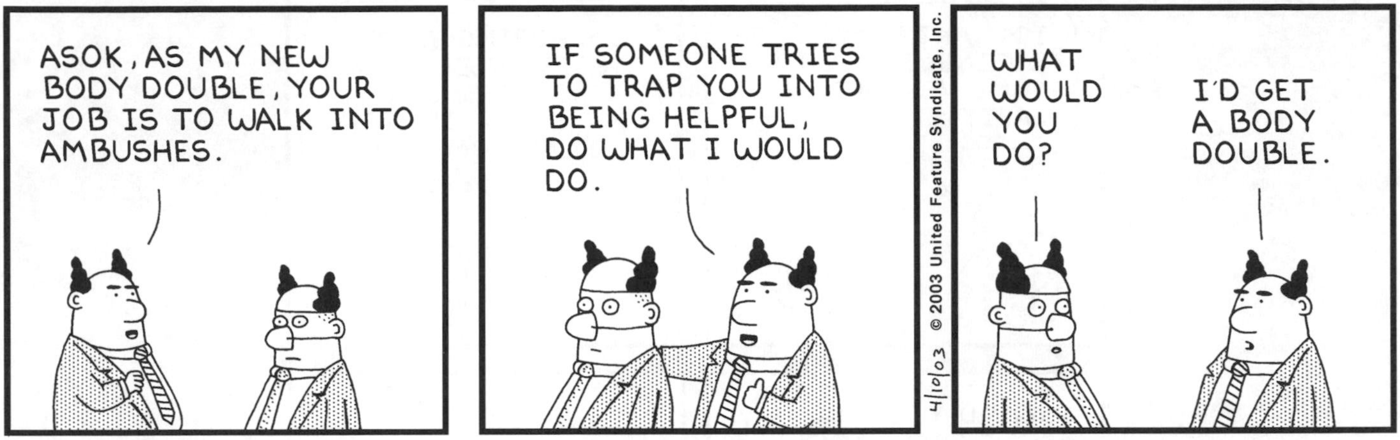
ASOK, AS MY NEW BODY DOUBLE, YOUR JOB IS TO WALK INTO AMBUSHES.
IF SOMEONE TRIES TO TRAP YOU INTO BEING HELPFUL, DO WHAT I WOULD DO.
4/10/03 © 2003 United Feature Syndicate, Inc.
WHAT WOULD YOU DO?
I'D GET A BODY DOUBLE.

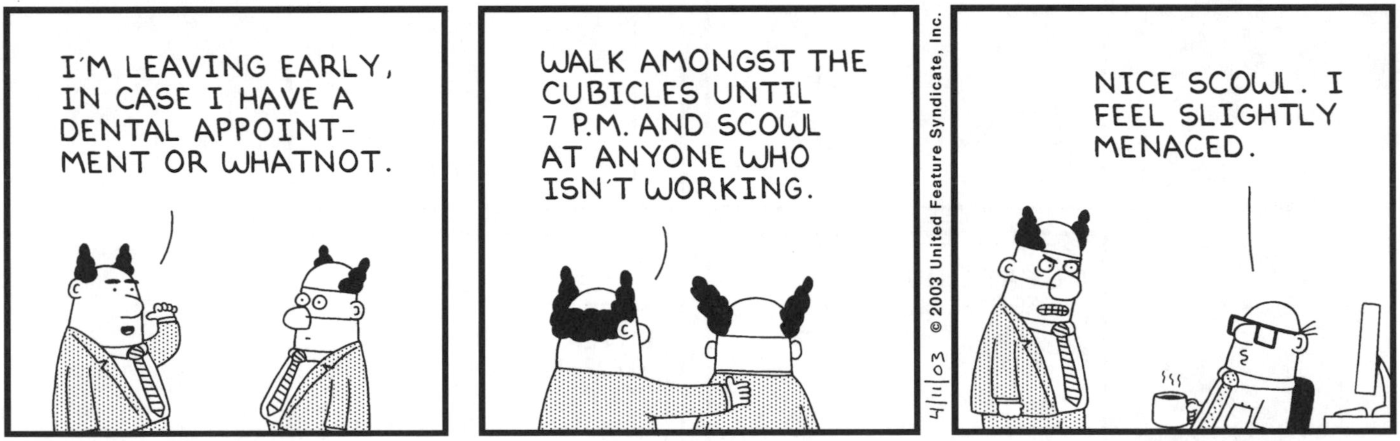
I'M LEAVING EARLY, IN CASE I HAVE A DENTAL APPOINT-MENT OR WHATNOT.
WALK AMONGST THE CUBICLES UNTIL 7 P.M. AND SCOWL AT ANYONE WHO ISN'T WORKING.
4/11/03 © 2003 United Feature Syndicate, Inc.
NICE SCOWL. I FEEL SLIGHTLY MENACED.

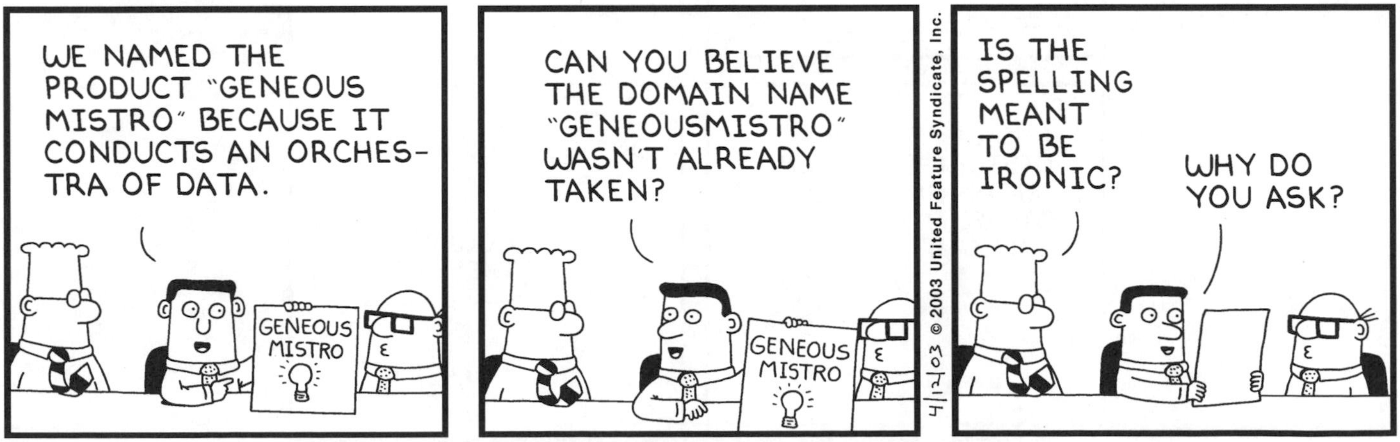
WE NAMED THE PRODUCT "GENEOUS MISTRO" BECAUSE IT CONDUCTS AN ORCHES-TRA OF DATA.
GENEOUS MISTRO
CAN YOU BELIEVE THE DOMAIN NAME "GENEOUSMISTRO" WASN'T ALREADY TAKEN?
GENEOUS MISTRO
4/12/03 © 2003 United Feature Syndicate, Inc.
IS THE SPELLING MEANT TO BE IRONIC?
WHY DO YOU ASK?

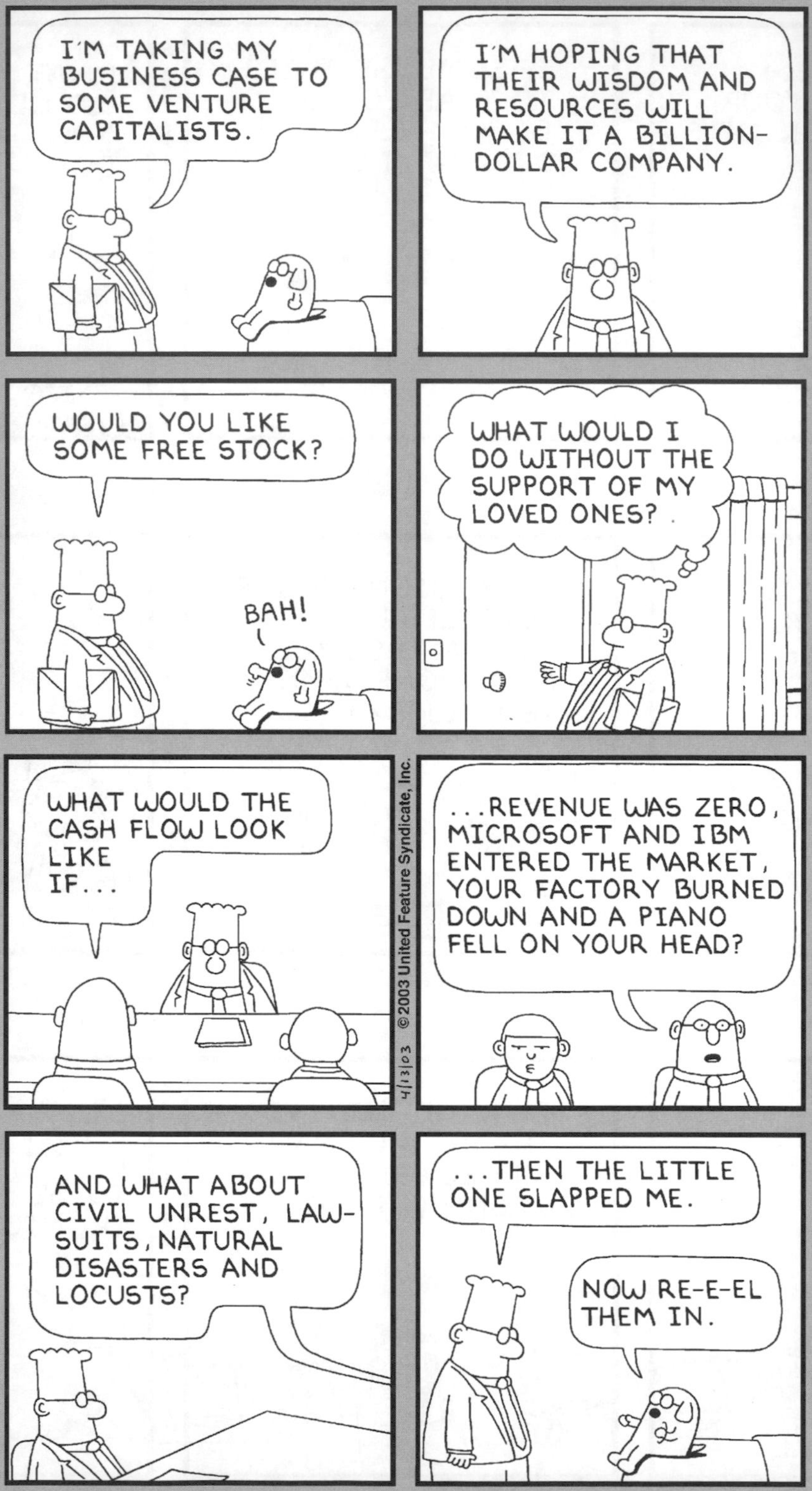
I'M TAKING MY BUSINESS CASE TO SOME VENTURE CAPITALISTS.
I'M HOPING THAT THEIR WISDOM AND RESOURCES WILL MAKE IT A BILLION-DOLLAR COMPANY.
WOULD YOU LIKE SOME FREE STOCK?
BAH!
WHAT WOULD I DO WITHOUT THE SUPPORT OF MY LOVED ONES?
WHAT WOULD THE CASH FLOW LOOK LIKE IF...
...REVENUE WAS ZERO, MICROSOFT AND IBM ENTERED THE MARKET, YOUR FACTORY BURNED DOWN AND A PIANO FELL ON YOUR HEAD?
AND WHAT ABOUT CIVIL UNREST, LAW-SUITS, NATURAL DISASTERS AND LOCUSTS?
...THEN THE LITTLE ONE SLAPPED ME.
NOW RE-E-EL THEM IN.
4/13/03 ©2003 United Feature Syndicate, Inc.

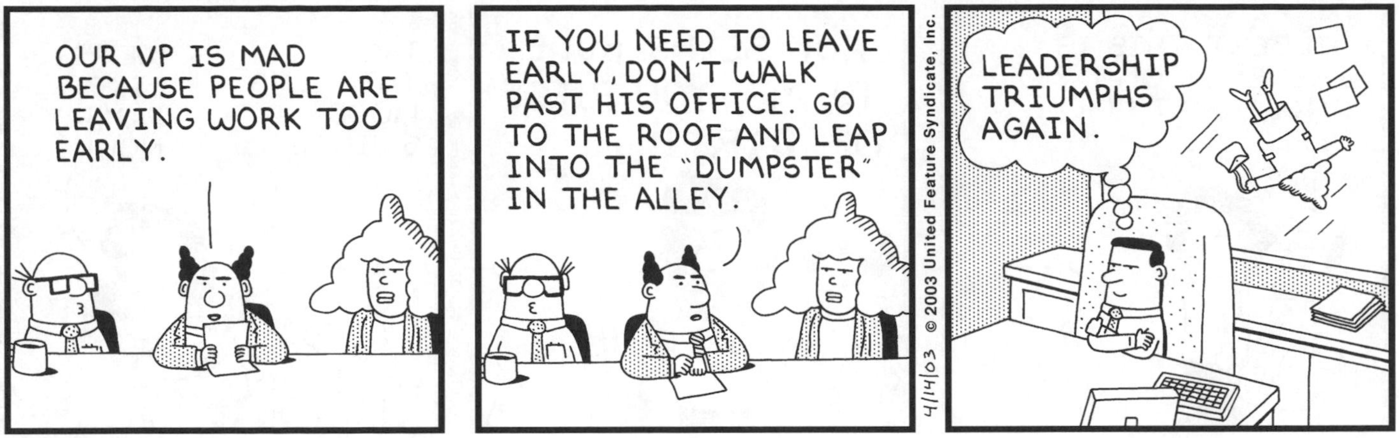
OUR VP IS MAD BECAUSE PEOPLE ARE LEAVING WORK TOO EARLY.
IF YOU NEED TO LEAVE EARLY, DON'T WALK PAST HIS OFFICE. GO TO THE ROOF AND LEAP INTO THE "DUMPSTER" IN THE ALLEY.
4/14/03 © 2003 United Feature Syndicate, Inc.
LEADERSHIP TRIUMPHS AGAIN.

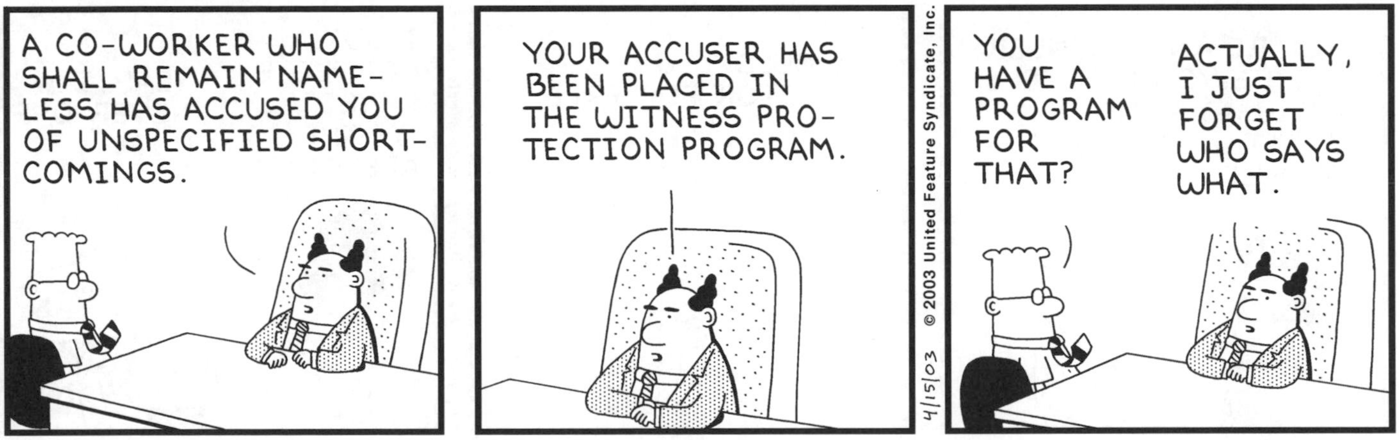
A CO-WORKER WHO SHALL REMAIN NAME-LESS HAS ACCUSED YOU OF UNSPECIFIED SHORT-COMINGS.
YOUR ACCUSER HAS BEEN PLACED IN THE WITNESS PRO-TECTION PROGRAM.
4/15/03 © 2003 United Feature Syndicate, Inc.
YOU HAVE A PROGRAM FOR THAT?
ACTUALLY, I JUST FORGET WHO SAYS WHAT.

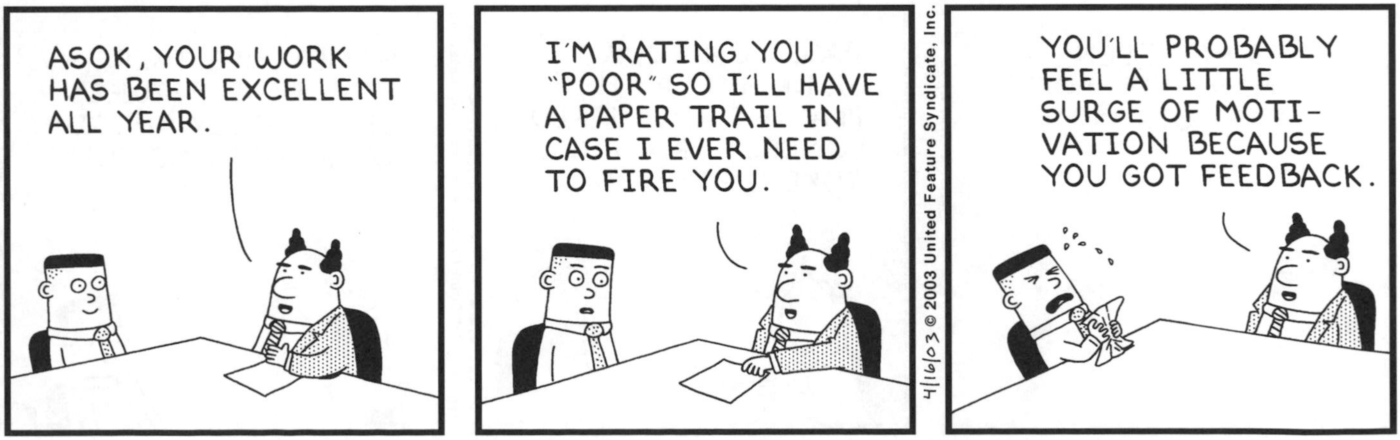
ASOK, YOUR WORK HAS BEEN EXCELLENT ALL YEAR.
I'M RATING YOU "POOR" SO I'LL HAVE A PAPER TRAIL IN CASE I EVER NEED TO FIRE YOU.
4/16/03 © 2003 United Feature Syndicate, Inc.
YOU'LL PROBABLY FEEL A LITTLE SURGE OF MOTI-VATION BECAUSE YOU GOT FEEDBACK.

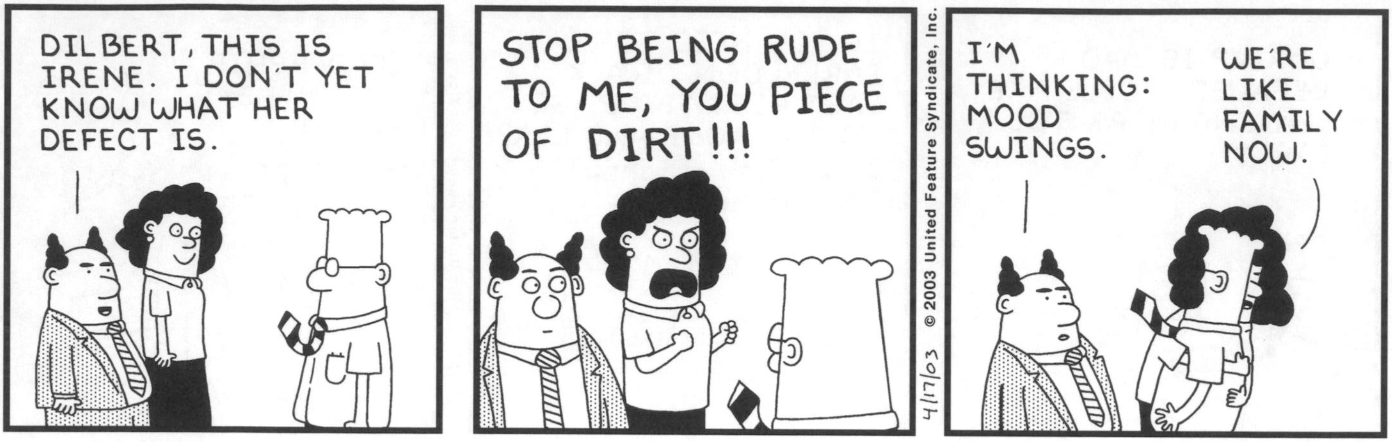
DILBERT, THIS IS IRENE. I DON'T YET KNOW WHAT HER DEFECT IS.
STOP BEING RUDE TO ME, YOU PIECE OF DIRT!!!
4/17/03 © 2003 United Feature Syndicate, Inc.
I'M THINKING: MOOD SWINGS.
WE'RE LIKE FAMILY NOW.

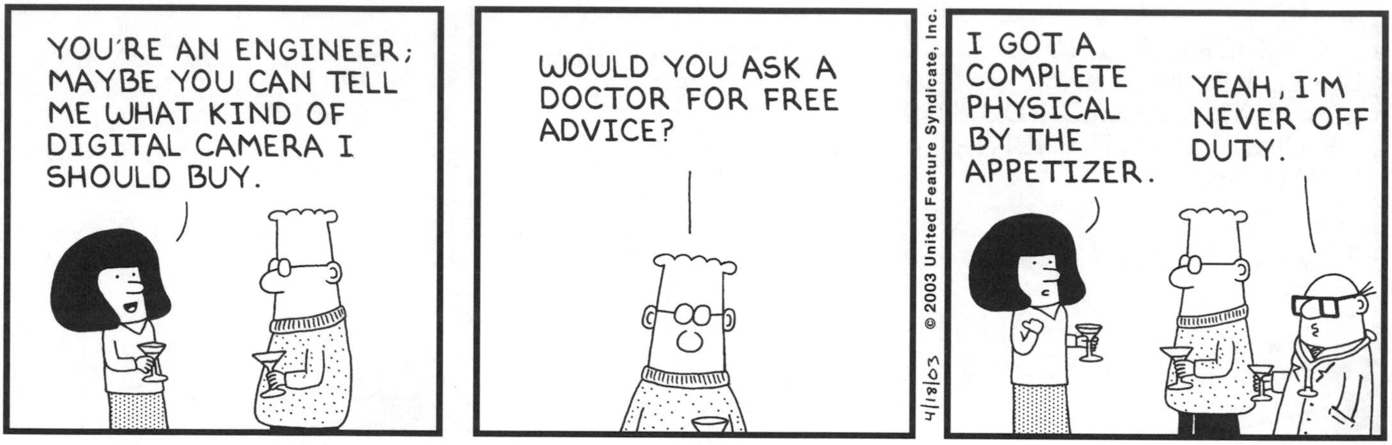
YOU'RE AN ENGINEER; MAYBE YOU CAN TELL ME WHAT KIND OF DIGITAL CAMERA I SHOULD BUY.
WOULD YOU ASK A DOCTOR FOR FREE ADVICE?
4/18/03 © 2003 United Feature Syndicate, Inc.
I GOT A COMPLETE PHYSICAL BY THE APPETIZER.
YEAH, I'M NEVER OFF DUTY.

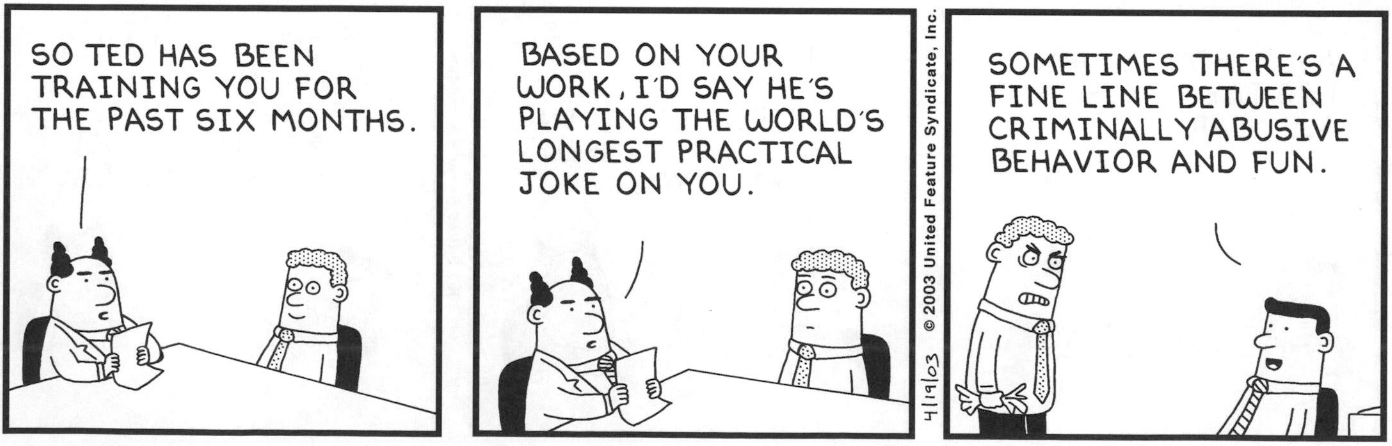
SO TED HAS BEEN TRAINING YOU FOR THE PAST SIX MONTHS.
BASED ON YOUR WORK, I'D SAY HE'S PLAYING THE WORLD'S LONGEST PRACTICAL JOKE ON YOU.
4/19/03 © 2003 United Feature Syndicate, Inc.
SOMETIMES THERE'S A FINE LINE BETWEEN CRIMINALLY ABUSIVE BEHAVIOR AND FUN.

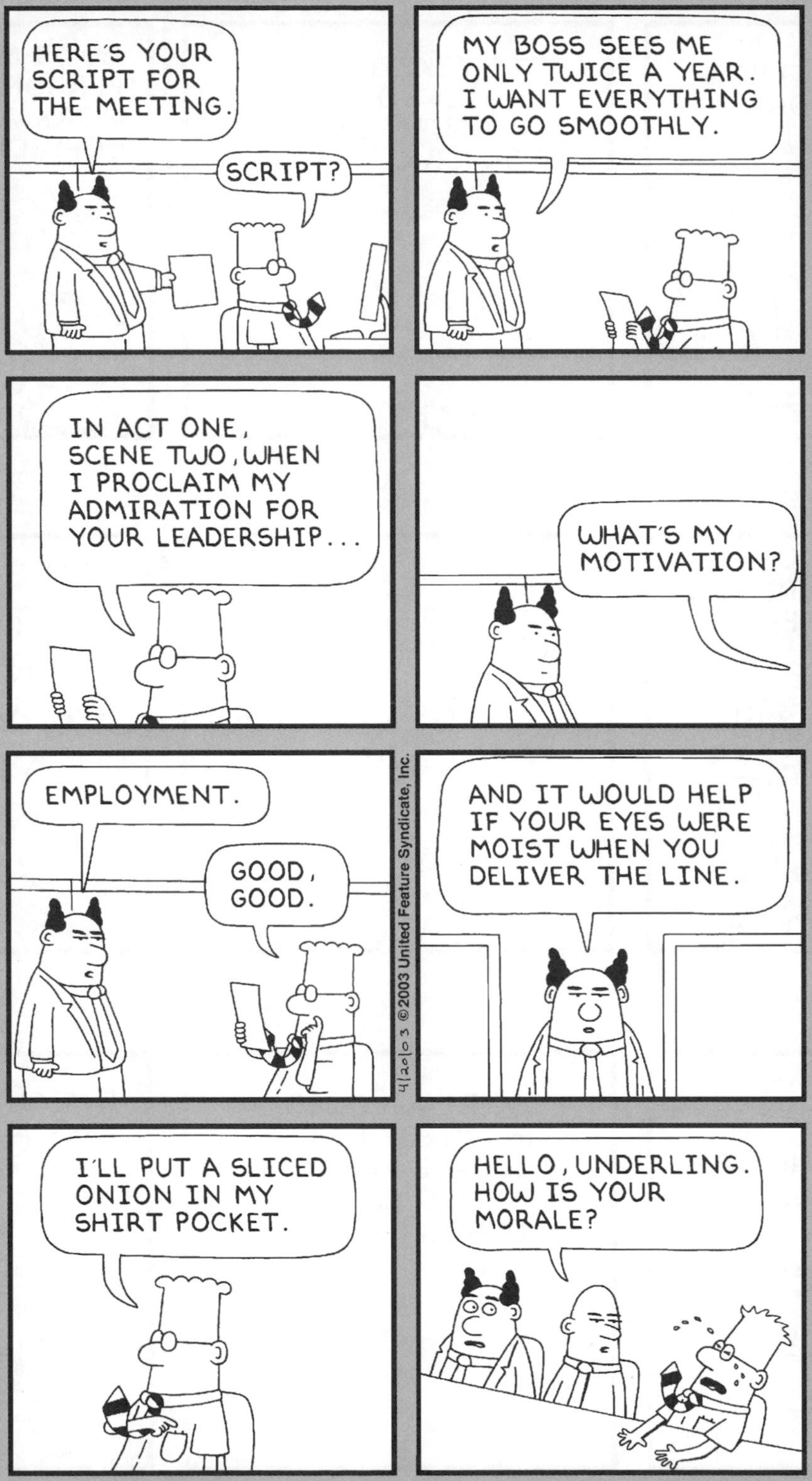
HERE'S YOUR SCRIPT FOR THE MEETING.
SCRIPT?
MY BOSS SEES ME ONLY TWICE A YEAR. I WANT EVERYTHING TO GO SMOOTHLY.
IN ACT ONE, SCENE TWO, WHEN I PROCLAIM MY ADMIRATION FOR YOUR LEADERSHIP...
WHAT'S MY MOTIVATION?
EMPLOYMENT.
GOOD, GOOD.
4/20/03 ©2003 United Feature Syndicate, Inc.
AND IT WOULD HELP IF YOUR EYES WERE MOIST WHEN YOU DELIVER THE LINE.
I'LL PUT A SLICED ONION IN MY SHIRT POCKET.
HELLO, UNDERLING. HOW IS YOUR MORALE?

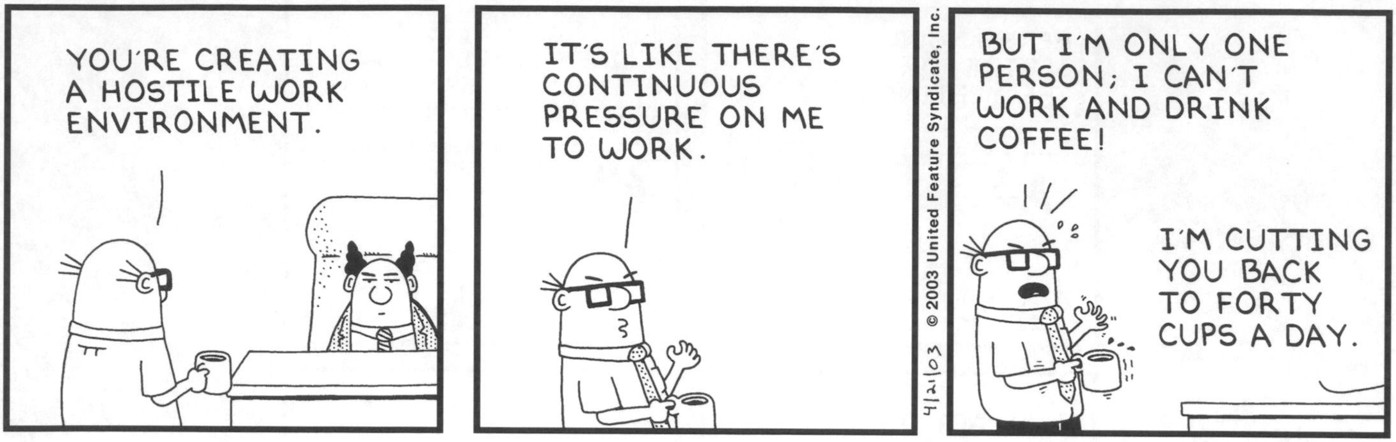
YOU'RE CREATING A HOSTILE WORK ENVIRONMENT.
IT'S LIKE THERE'S CONTINUOUS PRESSURE ON ME TO WORK.
4/21/03 © 2003 United Feature Syndicate, Inc.
BUT I'M ONLY ONE PERSON; I CAN'T WORK AND DRINK COFFEE!
I'M CUTTING YOU BACK TO FORTY CUPS A DAY.

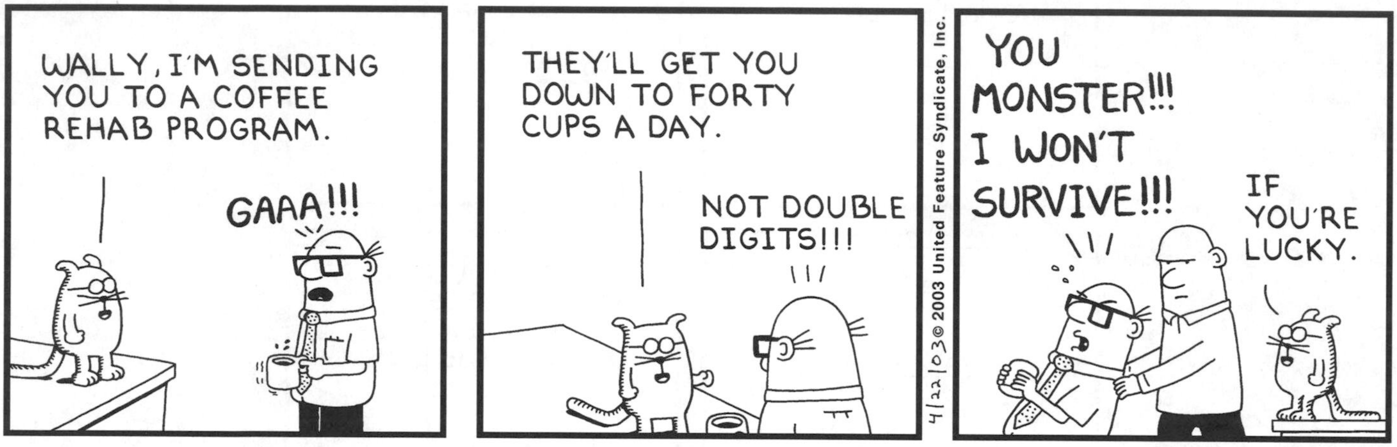
WALLY, I'M SENDING YOU TO A COFFEE REHAB PROGRAM.
GAAA!!!
THEY'LL GET YOU DOWN TO FORTY CUPS A DAY.
NOT DOUBLE DIGITS!!!
4/22/03 © 2003 United Feature Syndicate, Inc.
YOU MONSTER!!! I WON'T SURVIVE!!!
IF YOU'RE LUCKY.

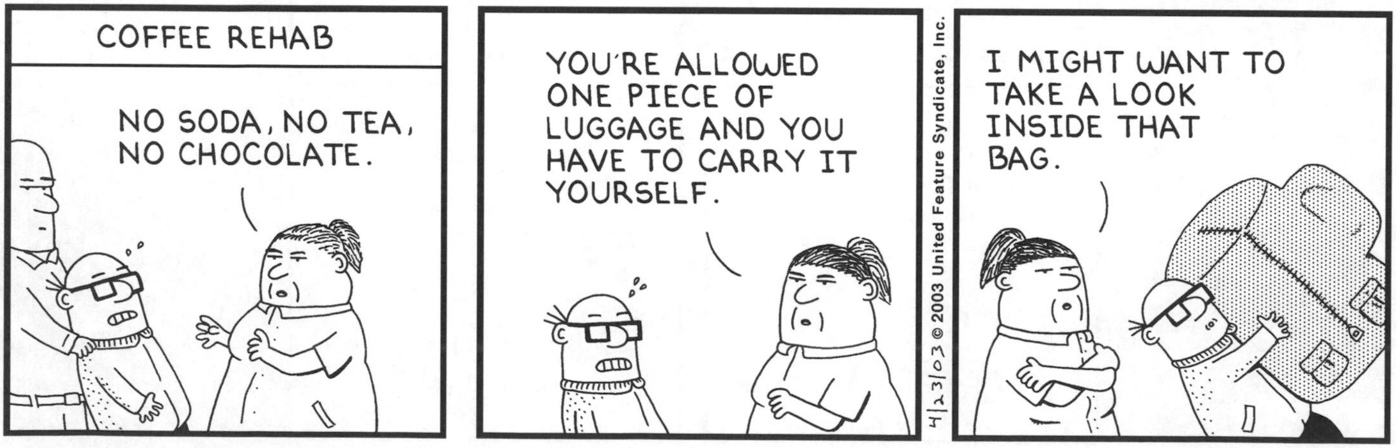
COFFEE REHAB
NO SODA, NO TEA, NO CHOCOLATE.
YOU'RE ALLOWED ONE PIECE OF LUGGAGE AND YOU HAVE TO CARRY IT YOURSELF.
4/23/03 © 2003 United Feature Syndicate, Inc.
I MIGHT WANT TO TAKE A LOOK INSIDE THAT BAG.

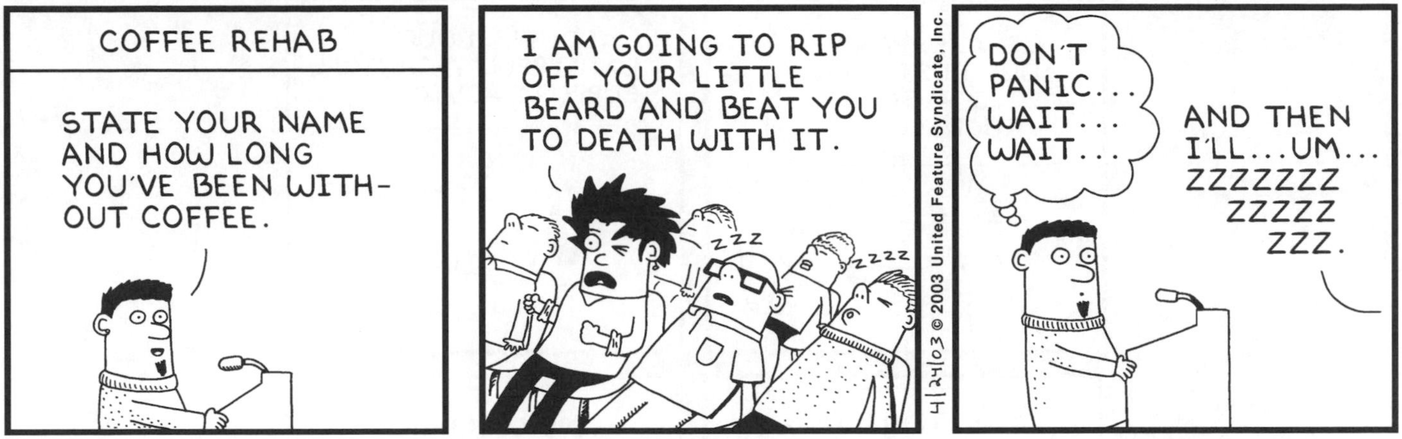
COFFEE REHAB
STATE YOUR NAME AND HOW LONG YOU'VE BEEN WITH-OUT COFFEE.
I AM GOING TO RIP OFF YOUR LITTLE BEARD AND BEAT YOU TO DEATH WITH IT.
ZZZ
ZZZZ
4/24/03 © 2003 United Feature Syndicate, Inc.
DON'T PANIC... WAIT... WAIT...
AND THEN I'LL...UM... ZZZZZZZ ZZZZZ ZZZ.

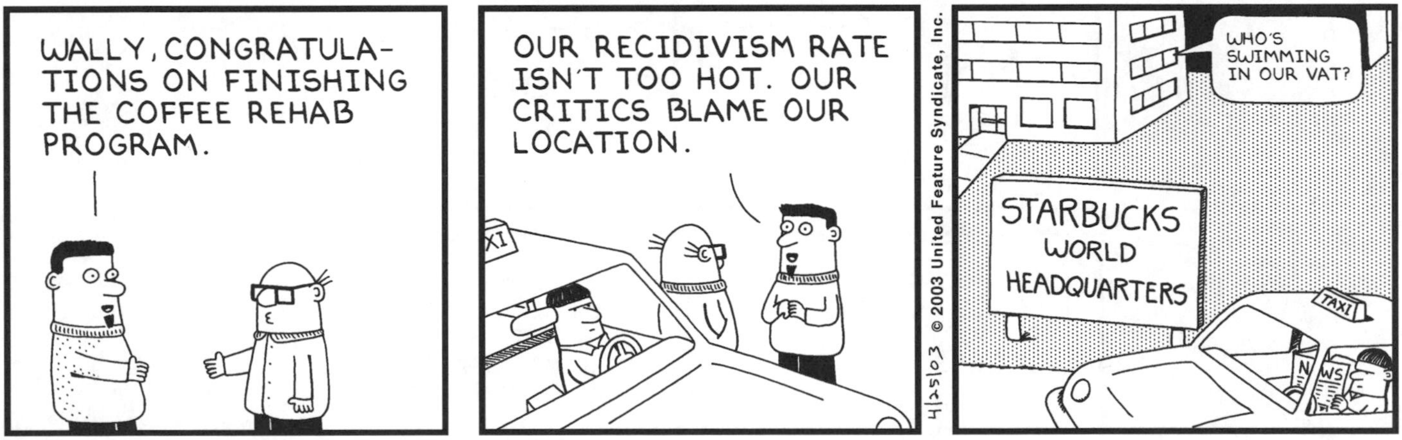
WALLY, CONGRATULA-TIONS ON FINISHING THE COFFEE REHAB PROGRAM.
OUR RECIDIVISM RATE ISN'T TOO HOT. OUR CRITICS BLAME OUR LOCATION.
4/25/03 © 2003 United Feature Syndicate, Inc.
WHO'S SWIMMING IN OUR VAT?
STARBUCKS WORLD HEADQUARTERS
TAXI
NWS

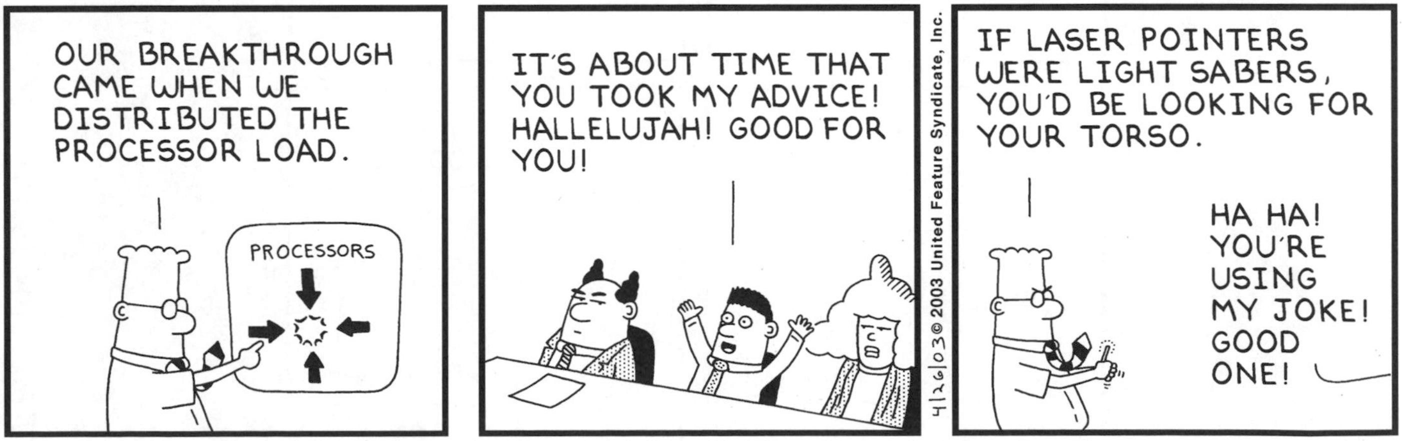
OUR BREAKTHROUGH CAME WHEN WE DISTRIBUTED THE PROCESSOR LOAD.
PROCESSORS
IT'S ABOUT TIME THAT YOU TOOK MY ADVICE! HALLELUJAH! GOOD FOR YOU!
4/26/03 © 2003 United Feature Syndicate, Inc.
IF LASER POINTERS WERE LIGHT SABERS, YOU'D BE LOOKING FOR YOUR TORSO.
HA HA! YOU'RE USING MY JOKE! GOOD ONE!

WE'VE EXPANDED OUR CUSTOMER DISSERVICE PROGRAM.
...DOUBLED OUR UNHELPFUL TECHNICAL SUPPORT ADVICE.
UH...REBOOT
...STRETCHED OUR TELEPHONE HOLD TIMES TO LETHAL DURATIONS...
SO...HUNGRY
...AND CLEANSED OUR ONLINE SUPPORT DATABASE OF ALL USEFUL ARTICLES.
OUR GOAL IS TO FORCE CUSTOMERS TO FORM SUPPORT GROUPS.
4/27/03 © 2003 United Feature Syndicate, Inc.
OVER TIME, WITH LUCK, WE'LL TRAIN CUSTOMERS TO DO OUR MANUFACTURING AND SHIPPING, TOO.
MAY I TRAIN A CUSTOMER TO DO MY JOB?
SURE.
SO... WHAT DO I DO?
YOU'RE DOING IT.

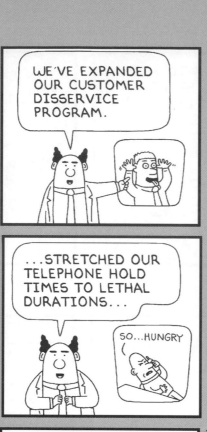

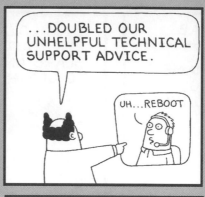

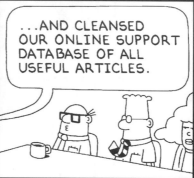

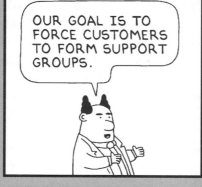

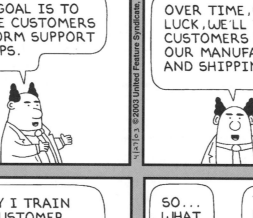

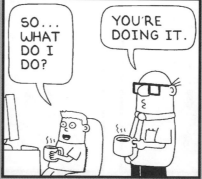

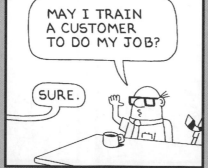

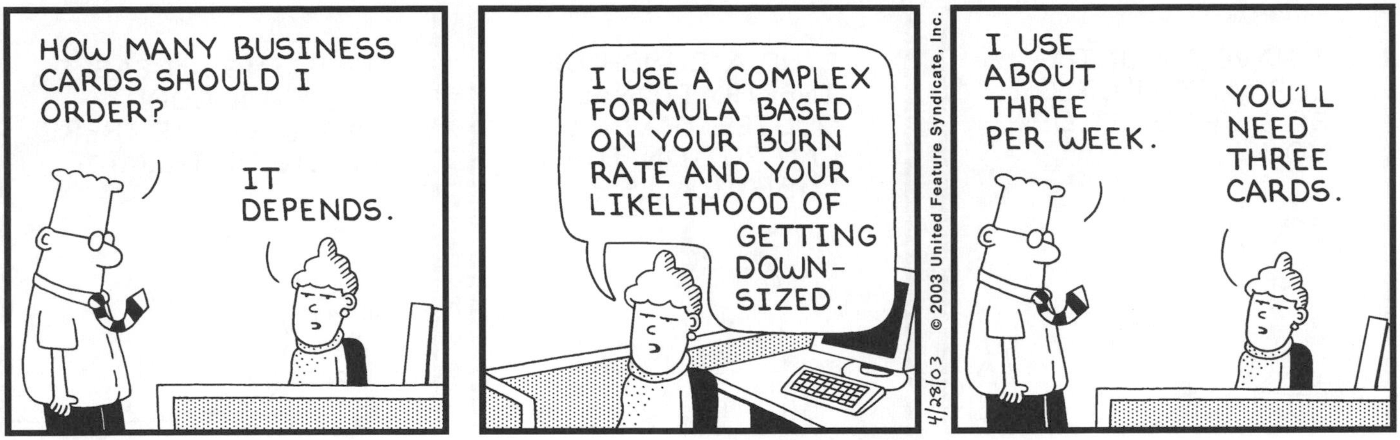
HOW MANY BUSINESS CARDS SHOULD I ORDER?
IT DEPENDS.
I USE A COMPLEX FORMULA BASED ON YOUR BURN RATE AND YOUR LIKELIHOOD OF GETTING DOWN-SIZED.
© 2003 United Feature Syndicate, Inc.
4/28/03
I USE ABOUT THREE PER WEEK.
YOU'LL NEED THREE CARDS.

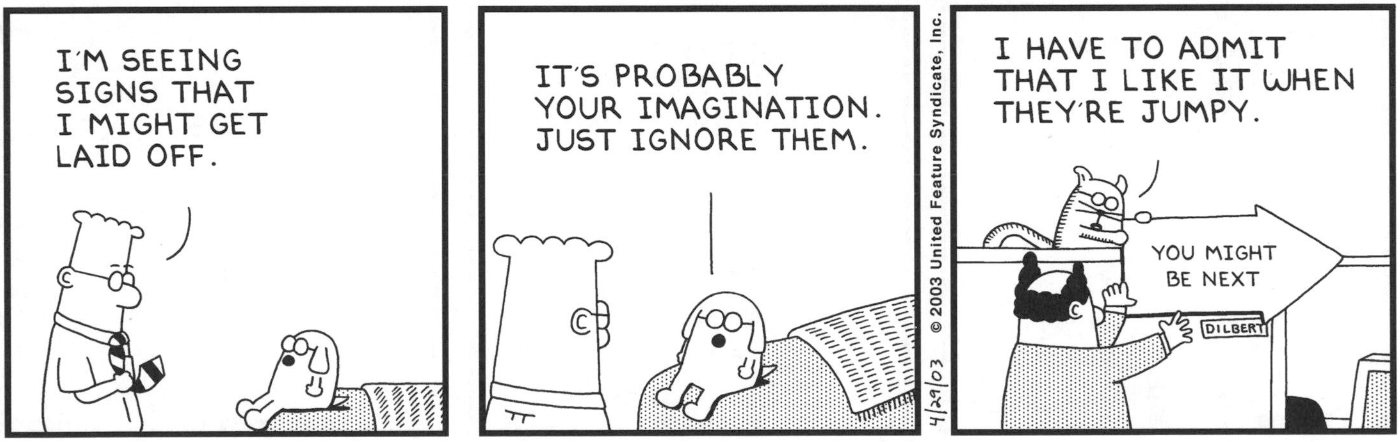
I'M SEEING SIGNS THAT I MIGHT GET LAID OFF.
IT'S PROBABLY YOUR IMAGINATION. JUST IGNORE THEM.
© 2003 United Feature Syndicate, Inc.
4/29/03
I HAVE TO ADMIT THAT I LIKE IT WHEN THEY'RE JUMPY.
YOU MIGHT BE NEXT
DILBERT

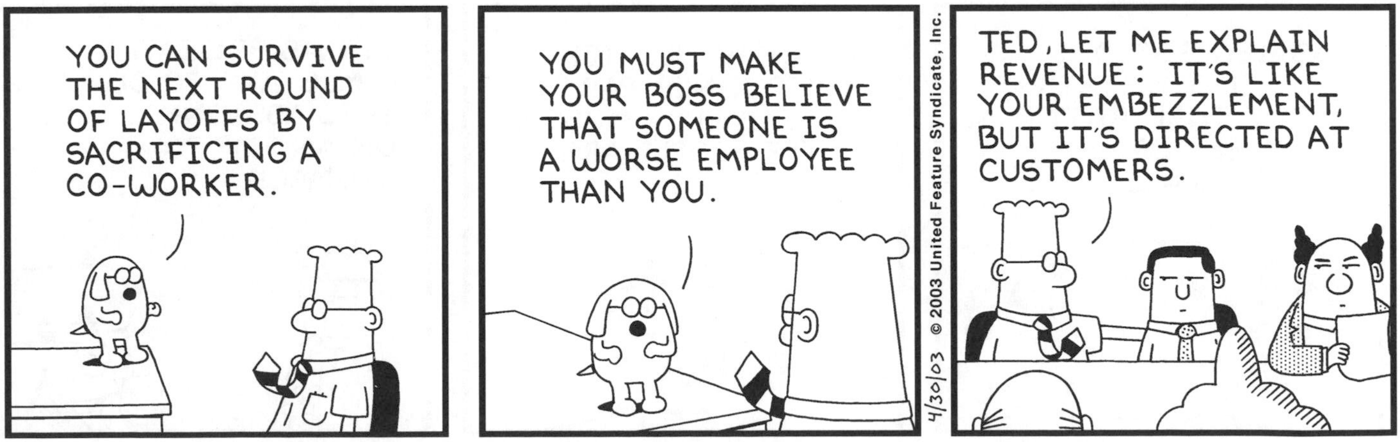
YOU CAN SURVIVE THE NEXT ROUND OF LAYOFFS BY SACRIFICING A CO-WORKER.
YOU MUST MAKE YOUR BOSS BELIEVE THAT SOMEONE IS A WORSE EMPLOYEE THAN YOU.
© 2003 United Feature Syndicate, Inc.
4/30/03
TED, LET ME EXPLAIN REVENUE: IT'S LIKE YOUR EMBEZZLEMENT, BUT IT'S DIRECTED AT CUSTOMERS.

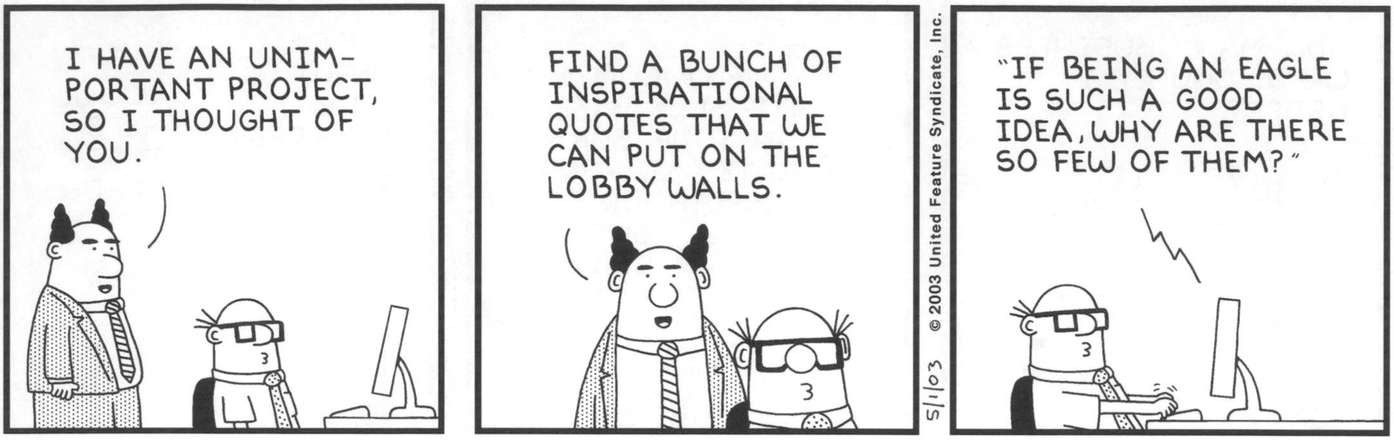
I HAVE AN UNIMPORTANT PROJECT, SO I THOUGHT OF YOU.
FIND A BUNCH OF INSPIRATIONAL QUOTES THAT WE CAN PUT ON THE LOBBY WALLS.
"IF BEING AN EAGLE IS SUCH A GOOD IDEA, WHY ARE THERE SO FEW OF THEM?"
5/1/03 © 2003 United Feature Syndicate, Inc.

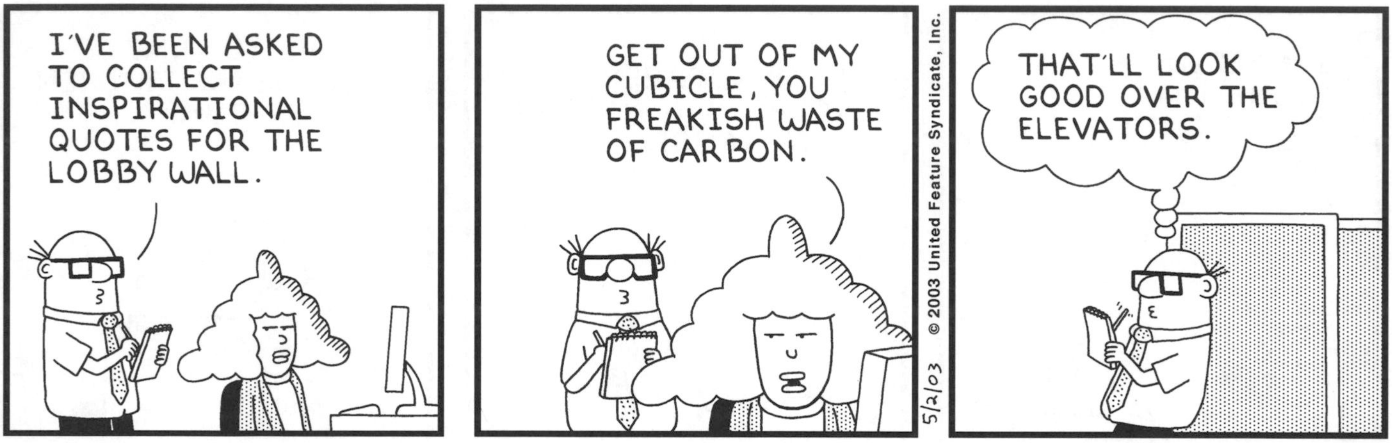
I'VE BEEN ASKED TO COLLECT INSPIRATIONAL QUOTES FOR THE LOBBY WALL.
GET OUT OF MY CUBICLE, YOU FREAKISH WASTE OF CARBON.
THAT'LL LOOK GOOD OVER THE ELEVATORS.
5/2/03 © 2003 United Feature Syndicate, Inc.

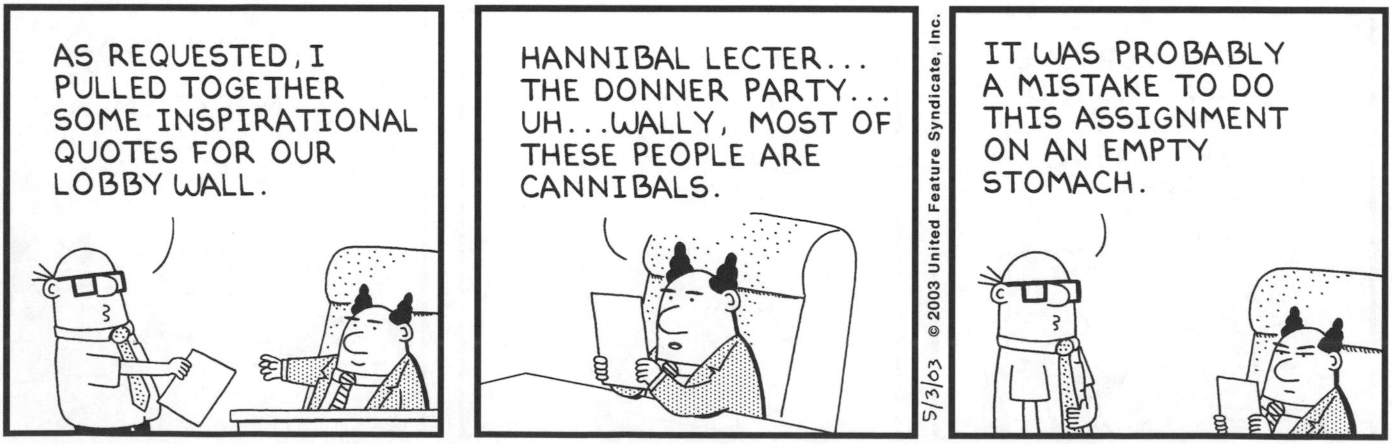
AS REQUESTED, I PULLED TOGETHER SOME INSPIRATIONAL QUOTES FOR OUR LOBBY WALL.
HANNIBAL LECTER... THE DONNER PARTY... UH...WALLY, MOST OF THESE PEOPLE ARE CANNIBALS.
IT WAS PROBABLY A MISTAKE TO DO THIS ASSIGNMENT ON AN EMPTY STOMACH.
5/3/03 © 2003 United Feature Syndicate, Inc.

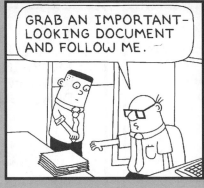

WALLY, CAN YOU TEACH ME TO WORK SMARTER, NOT HARDER?
GRAB AN IMPORTANT-LOOKING DOCUMENT AND FOLLOW ME.
WALK BRISKLY AND PRETEND TO BE ANGRY ABOUT WHAT YOU'RE READING.
GRRRR...
HEY, ASOK, WOULD YOU HELP ME...?
NEVER MIND.
GRRR
GRRR
AS A RULE, PEOPLE TRY TO AVOID ANY-ONE WHO HAS MORE PROBLEMS THAN THEY DO.
5/4/03
© 2003 United Feature Syndicate, Inc.
LESSON TWO: MAKE SURE YOUR SHIRT AND YOUR TOOTHPASTE ARE THE SAME COLOR.
THIS BABY IS COVER-ED WITH TOOTHPASTE STAINS, BUT YOU'D NEVER KNOW IT.
WOW!
AND HOW OFTEN DO YOU NEED TO LAUNDER A SHIRT THAT SMELLS MINTY?
NEVER!

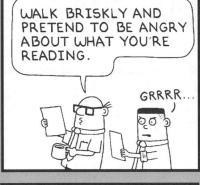

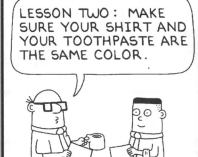

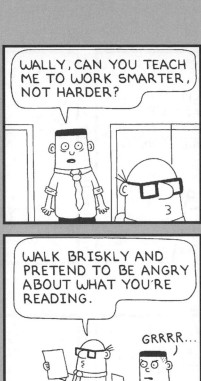

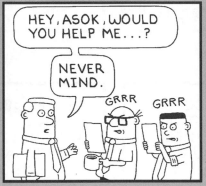

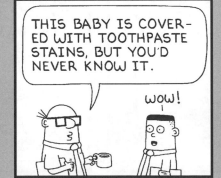

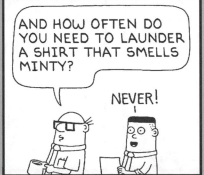

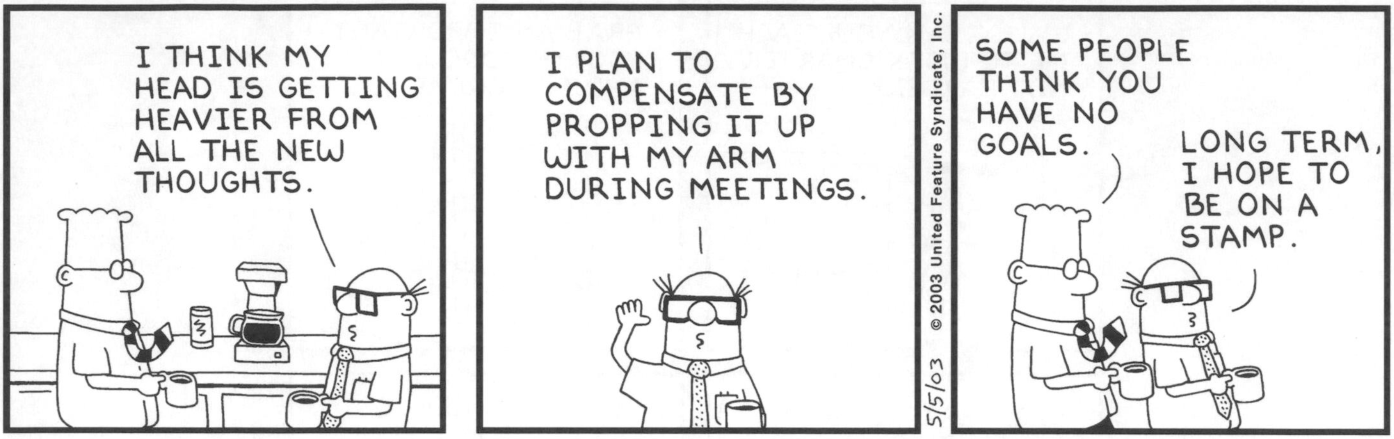
I THINK MY HEAD IS GETTING HEAVIER FROM ALL THE NEW THOUGHTS.
I PLAN TO COMPENSATE BY PROPPING IT UP WITH MY ARM DURING MEETINGS.
5/5/03
© 2003 United Feature Syndicate, Inc.
SOME PEOPLE THINK YOU HAVE NO GOALS.
LONG TERM, I HOPE TO BE ON A STAMP.

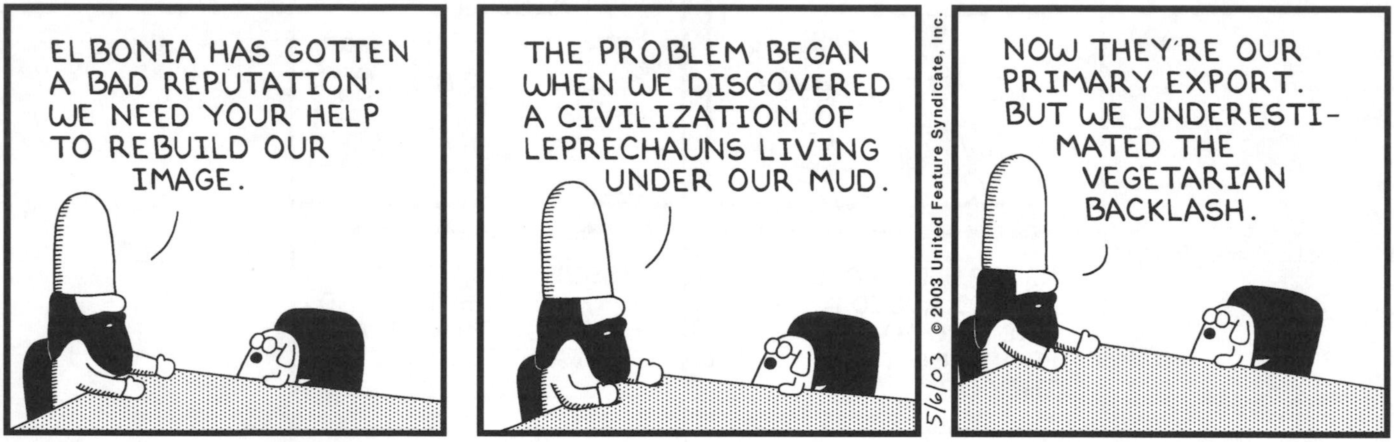
ELBONIA HAS GOTTEN A BAD REPUTATION. WE NEED YOUR HELP TO REBUILD OUR IMAGE.
THE PROBLEM BEGAN WHEN WE DISCOVERED A CIVILIZATION OF LEPRECHAUNS LIVING UNDER OUR MUD.
5/6/03
© 2003 United Feature Syndicate, Inc.
NOW THEY'RE OUR PRIMARY EXPORT. BUT WE UNDERESTIMATED THE VEGETARIAN BACKLASH.

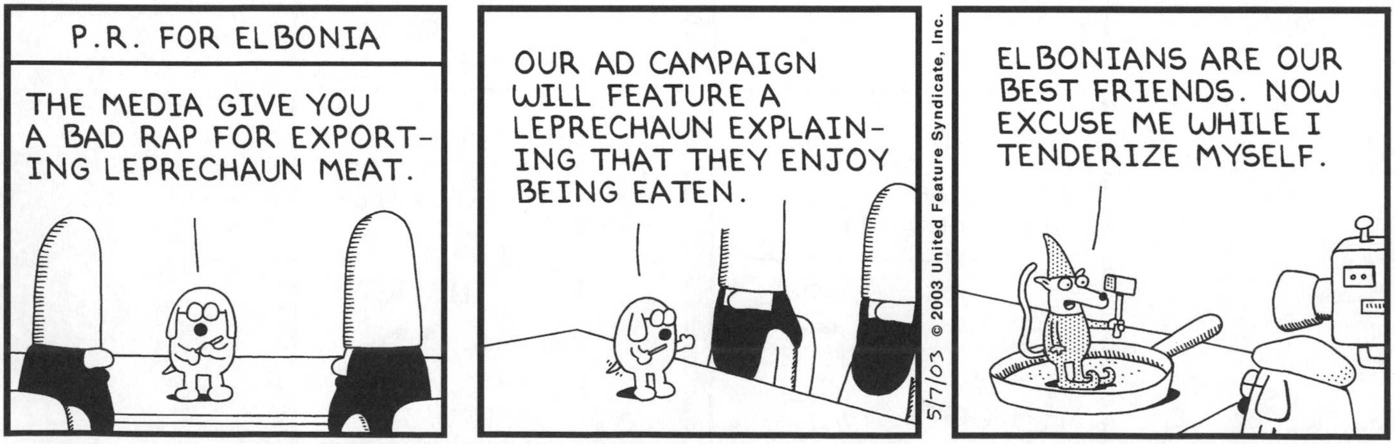
P.R. FOR ELBONIA
THE MEDIA GIVE YOU A BAD RAP FOR EXPORTING LEPRECHAUN MEAT.
OUR AD CAMPAIGN WILL FEATURE A LEPRECHAUN EXPLAINING THAT THEY ENJOY BEING EATEN.
5/7/03
© 2003 United Feature Syndicate, Inc.
ELBONIANS ARE OUR BEST FRIENDS. NOW EXCUSE ME WHILE I TENDERIZE MYSELF.

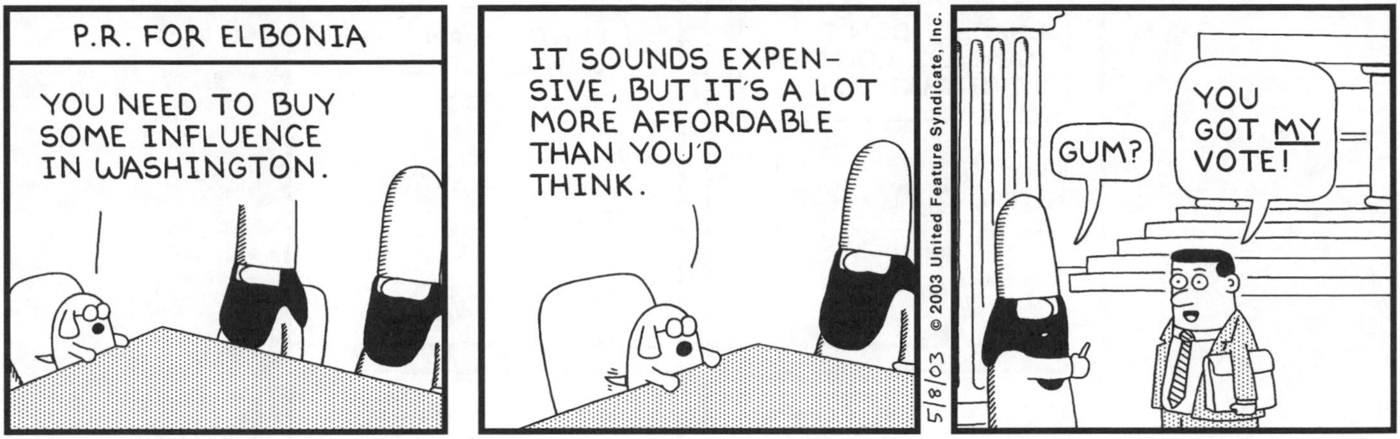
P.R. FOR ELBONIA
YOU NEED TO BUY SOME INFLUENCE IN WASHINGTON.
IT SOUNDS EXPENSIVE, BUT IT'S A LOT MORE AFFORDABLE THAN YOU'D THINK.
5/8/03 © 2003 United Feature Syndicate, Inc.
GUM?
YOU GOT MY VOTE!

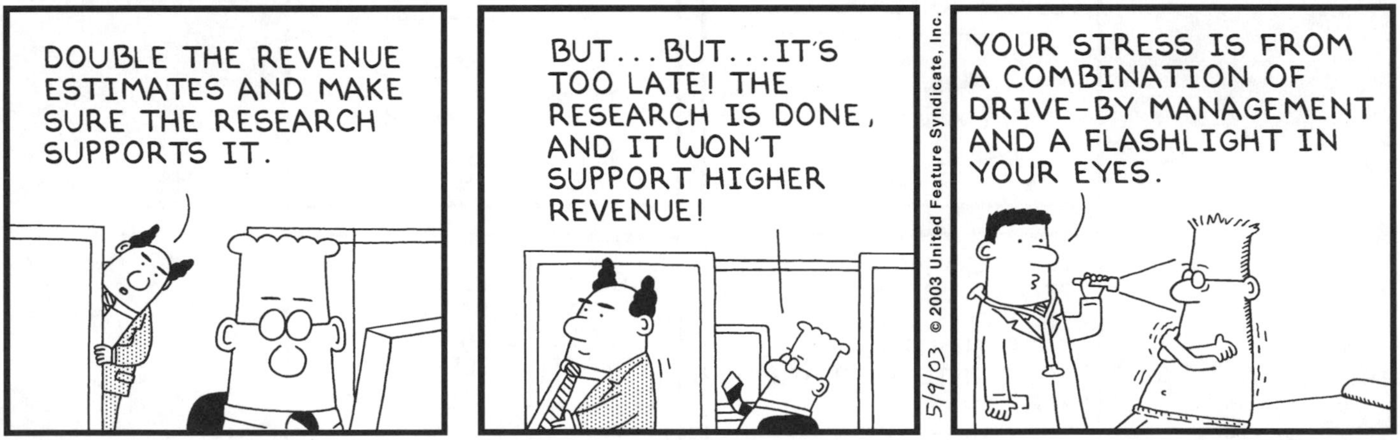
DOUBLE THE REVENUE ESTIMATES AND MAKE SURE THE RESEARCH SUPPORTS IT.
BUT...BUT...IT'S TOO LATE! THE RESEARCH IS DONE, AND IT WON'T SUPPORT HIGHER REVENUE!
5/9/03 © 2003 United Feature Syndicate, Inc.
YOUR STRESS IS FROM A COMBINATION OF DRIVE-BY MANAGEMENT AND A FLASHLIGHT IN YOUR EYES.

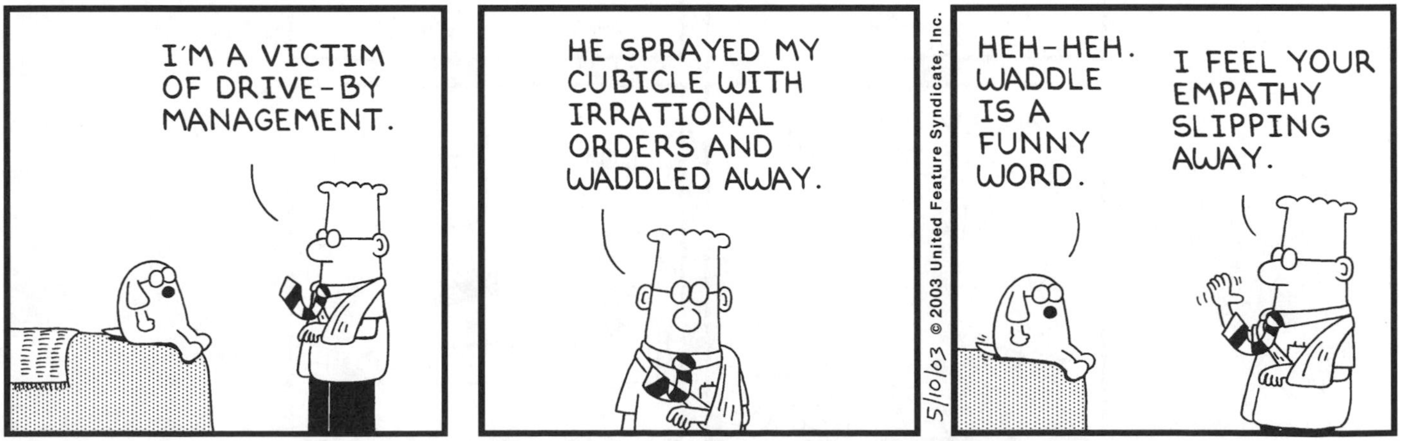
I'M A VICTIM OF DRIVE-BY MANAGEMENT.
HE SPRAYED MY CUBICLE WITH IRRATIONAL ORDERS AND WADDLED AWAY.
5/10/03 © 2003 United Feature Syndicate, Inc.
HEH-HEH. WADDLE IS A FUNNY WORD.
I FEEL YOUR EMPATHY SLIPPING AWAY.

UH-OH...DON'T MAKE EYE CONTACT WITH THAT GUY.
WHY NOT?
ERNIE IS AN UNPACKAGEABLE.
LAST YEAR, THE COMPANY OFFERED A GENEROUS SEVERANCE PACKAGE TO PEOPLE WHO VOLUNTEERED TO LEAVE.
ERNIE VOLUNTEERED. HE IMAGINED A LIFE OF RETIRED BLISS OUTSIDE THIS COMPANY.
BUT TOO MANY PEOPLE VOLUNTEERED. IN A CRUEL TWIST OF FATE, ERNIE WAS FORCED TO KEEP HIS JOB.
5/11/03 ©2003 United Feature Syndicate, Inc.
NOW HE'S NOTHING BUT AN ORGANIC VESSEL FOR TRANSPORTING SELF-PITY
I COULD HAVE BEEN FISHING!!!
WAAA!!!
YOU LOOKED?
I TRIED TO WARN HIM.

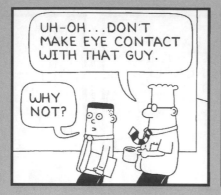

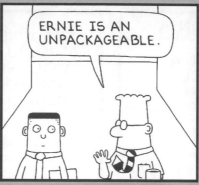

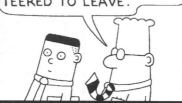

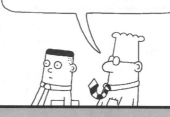

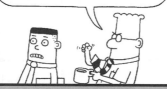

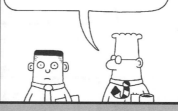

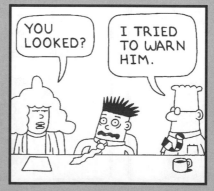

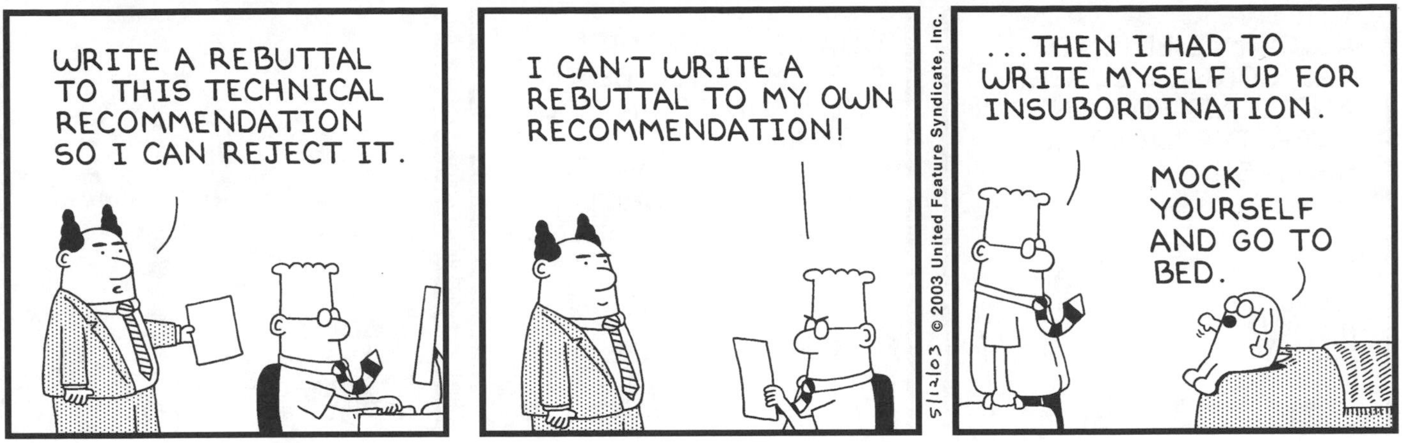
WRITE A REBUTTAL TO THIS TECHNICAL RECOMMENDATION SO I CAN REJECT IT.
I CAN'T WRITE A REBUTTAL TO MY OWN RECOMMENDATION!
5/12/03 © 2003 United Feature Syndicate, Inc.
...THEN I HAD TO WRITE MYSELF UP FOR INSUBORDINATION.
MOCK YOURSELF AND GO TO BED.

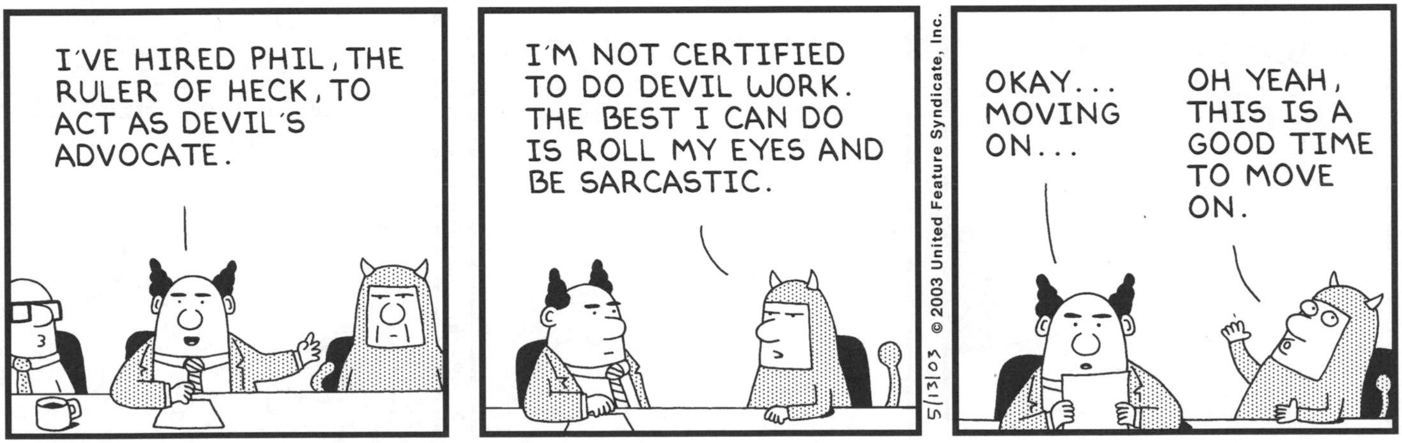
I'VE HIRED PHIL, THE RULER OF HECK, TO ACT AS DEVIL'S ADVOCATE.
I'M NOT CERTIFIED TO DO DEVIL WORK. THE BEST I CAN DO IS ROLL MY EYES AND BE SARCASTIC.
5/13/03 © 2003 United Feature Syndicate, Inc.
OKAY... MOVING ON...
OH YEAH, THIS IS A GOOD TIME TO MOVE ON.

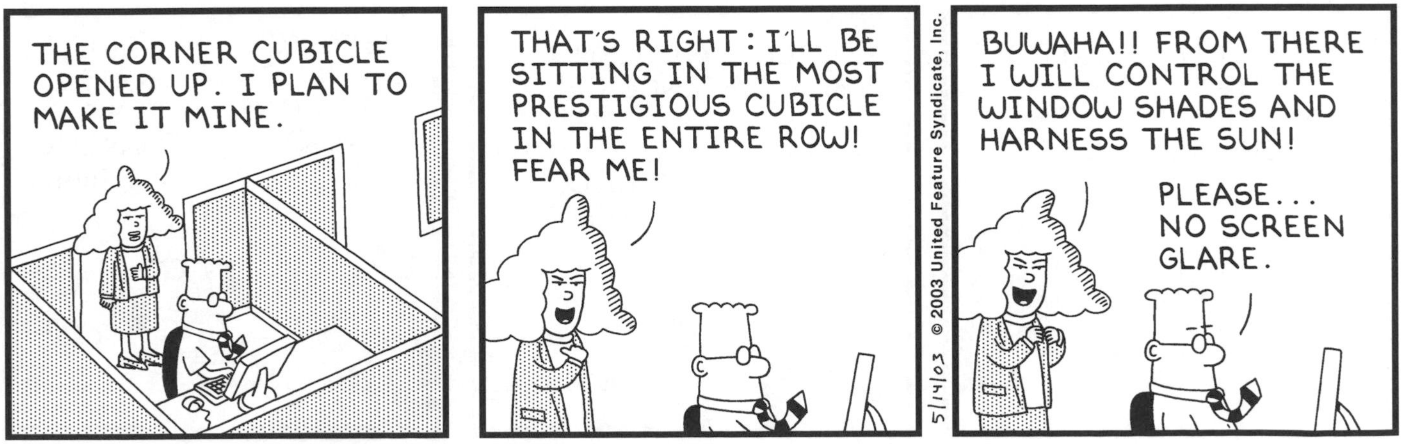
THE CORNER CUBICLE OPENED UP. I PLAN TO MAKE IT MINE.
THAT'S RIGHT: I'LL BE SITTING IN THE MOST PRESTIGIOUS CUBICLE IN THE ENTIRE ROW! FEAR ME!
5/14/03 © 2003 United Feature Syndicate, Inc.
BUWAHA!! FROM THERE I WILL CONTROL THE WINDOW SHADES AND HARNESS THE SUN!
PLEASE... NO SCREEN GLARE.

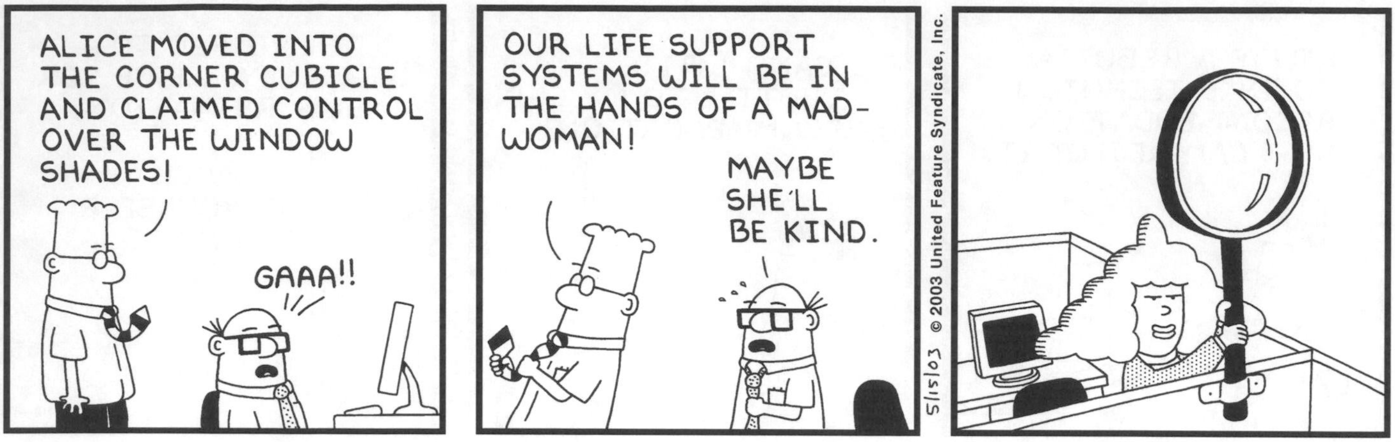
ALICE MOVED INTO THE CORNER CUBICLE AND CLAIMED CONTROL OVER THE WINDOW SHADES!
GAAA!!
OUR LIFE SUPPORT SYSTEMS WILL BE IN THE HANDS OF A MAD-WOMAN!
MAYBE SHE'LL BE KIND.
5/15/03 © 2003 United Feature Syndicate, Inc.

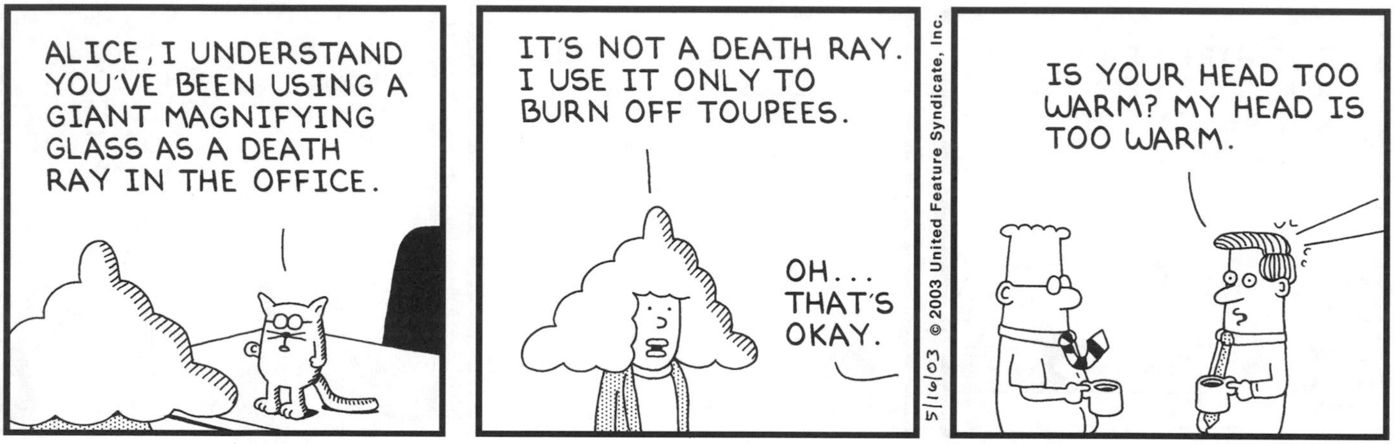
ALICE, I UNDERSTAND YOU'VE BEEN USING A GIANT MAGNIFYING GLASS AS A DEATH RAY IN THE OFFICE.
IT'S NOT A DEATH RAY. I USE IT ONLY TO BURN OFF TOUPEES.
OH... THAT'S OKAY.
5/16/03 © 2003 United Feature Syndicate, Inc.
IS YOUR HEAD TOO WARM? MY HEAD IS TOO WARM.

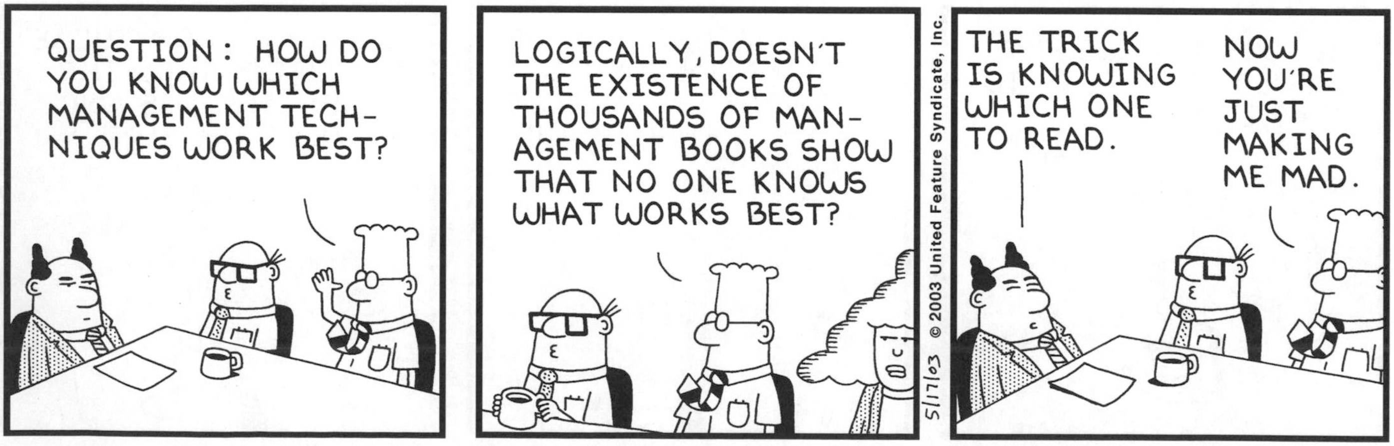
QUESTION: HOW DO YOU KNOW WHICH MANAGEMENT TECH-NIQUES WORK BEST?
LOGICALLY, DOESN'T THE EXISTENCE OF THOUSANDS OF MAN-AGEMENT BOOKS SHOW THAT NO ONE KNOWS WHAT WORKS BEST?
5/17/03 © 2003 United Feature Syndicate, Inc.
THE TRICK IS KNOWING WHICH ONE TO READ.
NOW YOU'RE JUST MAKING ME MAD.

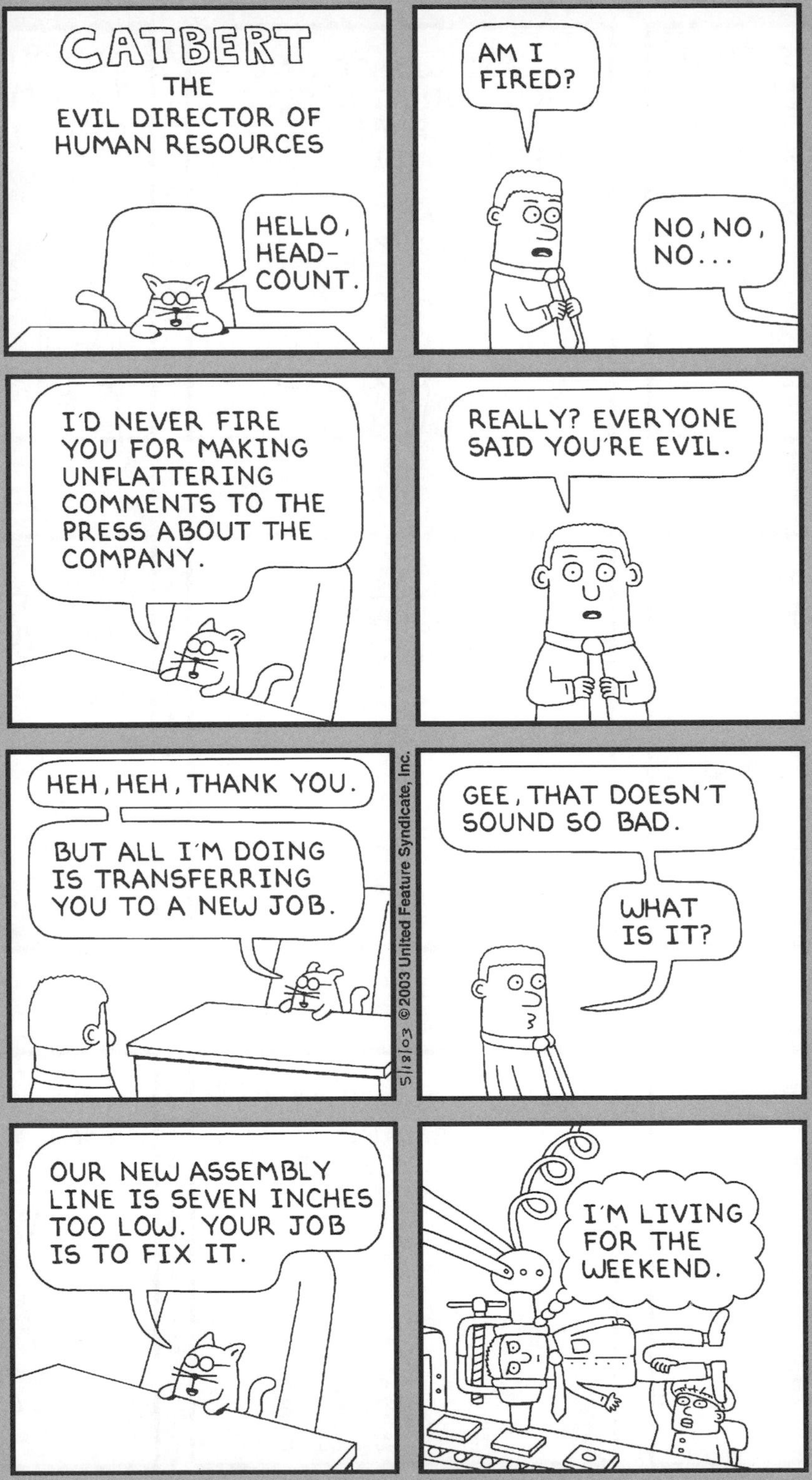
CATBERT
THE
EVIL DIRECTOR OF
HUMAN RESOURCES
HELLO, HEAD-COUNT.
AM I FIRED?
NO, NO, NO...
I'D NEVER FIRE YOU FOR MAKING UNFLATTERING COMMENTS TO THE PRESS ABOUT THE COMPANY.
REALLY? EVERYONE SAID YOU'RE EVIL.
HEH, HEH, THANK YOU.
BUT ALL I'M DOING IS TRANSFERRING YOU TO A NEW JOB.
GEE, THAT DOESN'T SOUND SO BAD.
WHAT IS IT?
OUR NEW ASSEMBLY LINE IS SEVEN INCHES TOO LOW. YOUR JOB IS TO FIX IT.
I'M LIVING FOR THE WEEKEND.

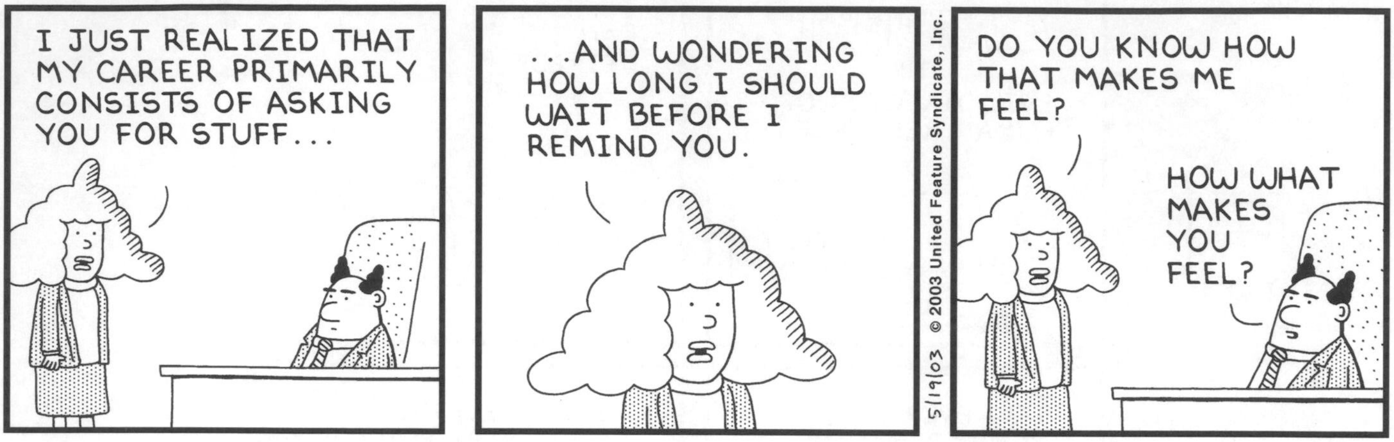
I JUST REALIZED THAT MY CAREER PRIMARILY CONSISTS OF ASKING YOU FOR STUFF...
...AND WONDERING HOW LONG I SHOULD WAIT BEFORE I REMIND YOU.
DO YOU KNOW HOW THAT MAKES ME FEEL?
HOW WHAT MAKES YOU FEEL?
5/19/03 © 2003 United Feature Syndicate, Inc.

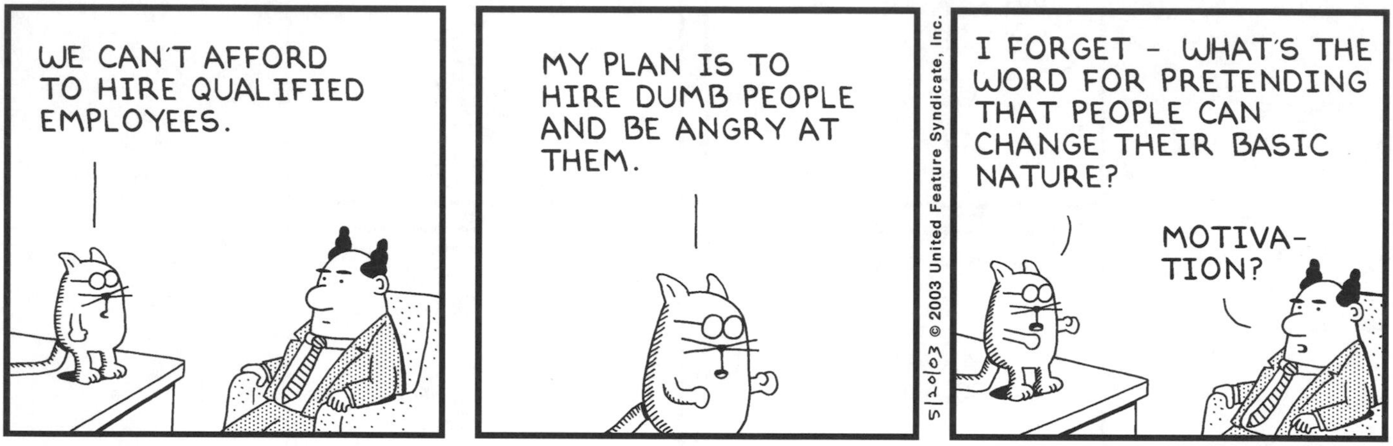
WE CAN'T AFFORD TO HIRE QUALIFIED EMPLOYEES.
MY PLAN IS TO HIRE DUMB PEOPLE AND BE ANGRY AT THEM.
I FORGET - WHAT'S THE WORD FOR PRETENDING THAT PEOPLE CAN CHANGE THEIR BASIC NATURE?
MOTIVA-TION?
5/20/03 © 2003 United Feature Syndicate, Inc.

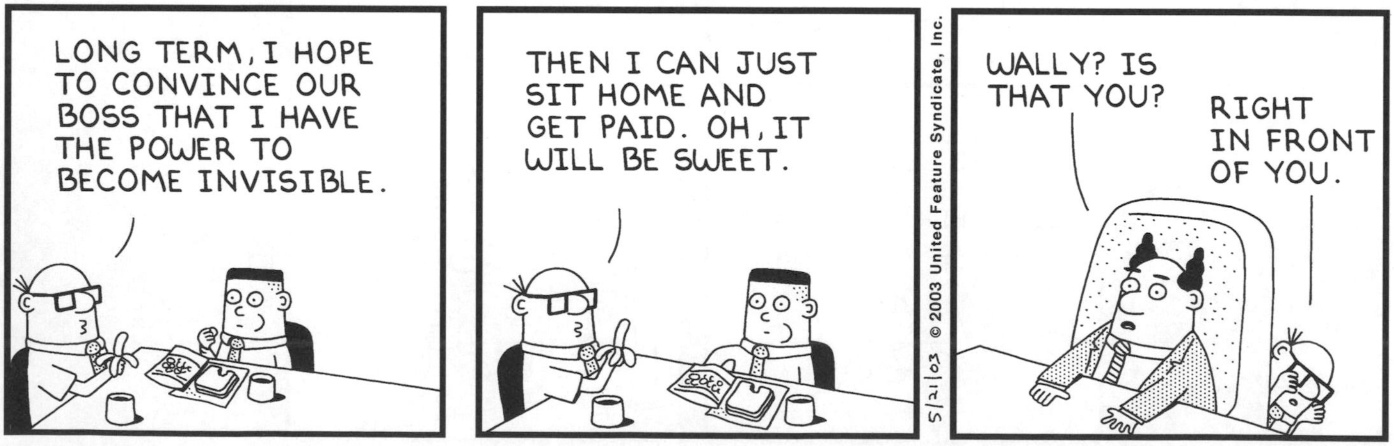
LONG TERM, I HOPE TO CONVINCE OUR BOSS THAT I HAVE THE POWER TO BECOME INVISIBLE.
THEN I CAN JUST SIT HOME AND GET PAID. OH, IT WILL BE SWEET.
WALLY? IS THAT YOU?
RIGHT IN FRONT OF YOU.
5/21/03 © 2003 United Feature Syndicate, Inc.

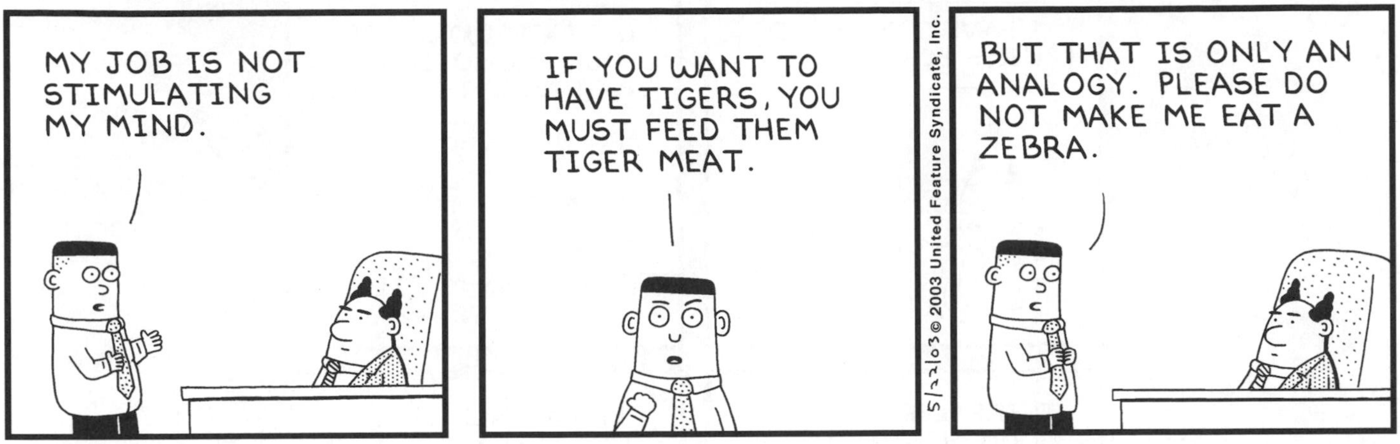
MY JOB IS NOT STIMULATING MY MIND.
IF YOU WANT TO HAVE TIGERS, YOU MUST FEED THEM TIGER MEAT.
5/22/03 © 2003 United Feature Syndicate, Inc.
BUT THAT IS ONLY AN ANALOGY. PLEASE DO NOT MAKE ME EAT A ZEBRA.

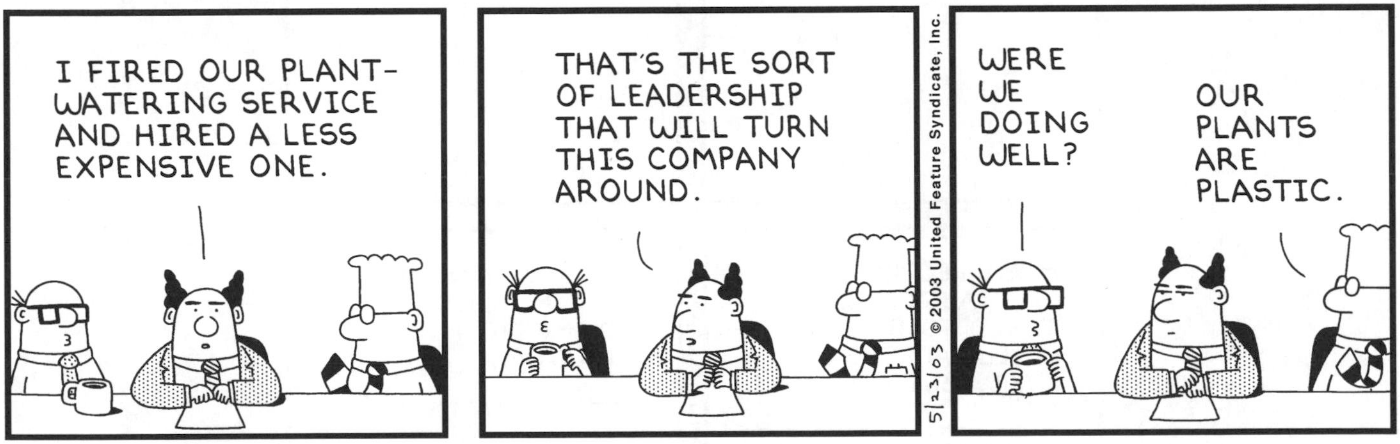
I FIRED OUR PLANT-WATERING SERVICE AND HIRED A LESS EXPENSIVE ONE.
THAT'S THE SORT OF LEADERSHIP THAT WILL TURN THIS COMPANY AROUND.
5/23/03 © 2003 United Feature Syndicate, Inc.
WERE WE DOING WELL?
OUR PLANTS ARE PLASTIC.

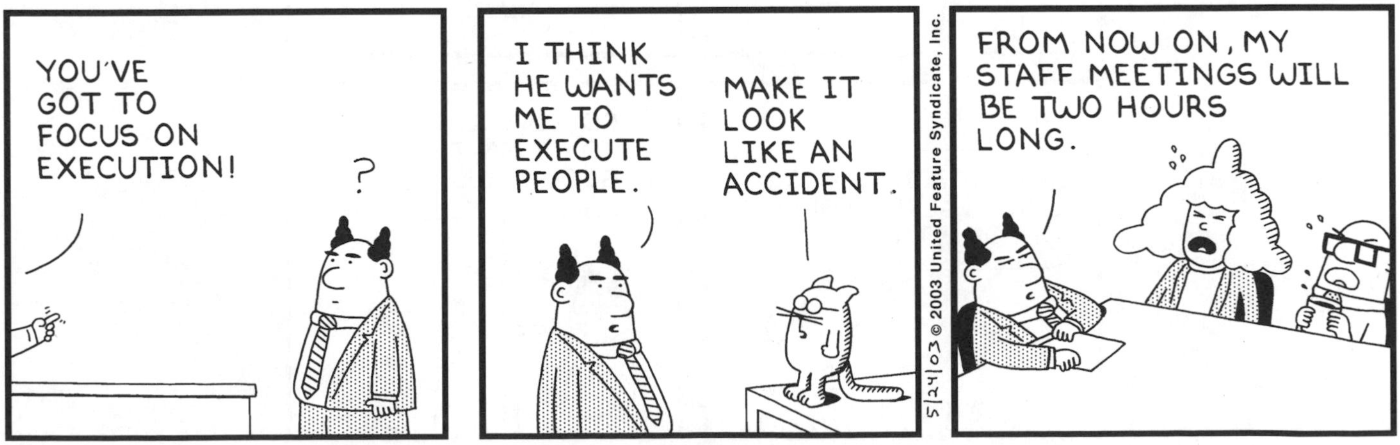
YOU'VE GOT TO FOCUS ON EXECUTION!
?
I THINK HE WANTS ME TO EXECUTE PEOPLE.
MAKE IT LOOK LIKE AN ACCIDENT.
5/24/03 © 2003 United Feature Syndicate, Inc.
FROM NOW ON, MY STAFF MEETINGS WILL BE TWO HOURS LONG.

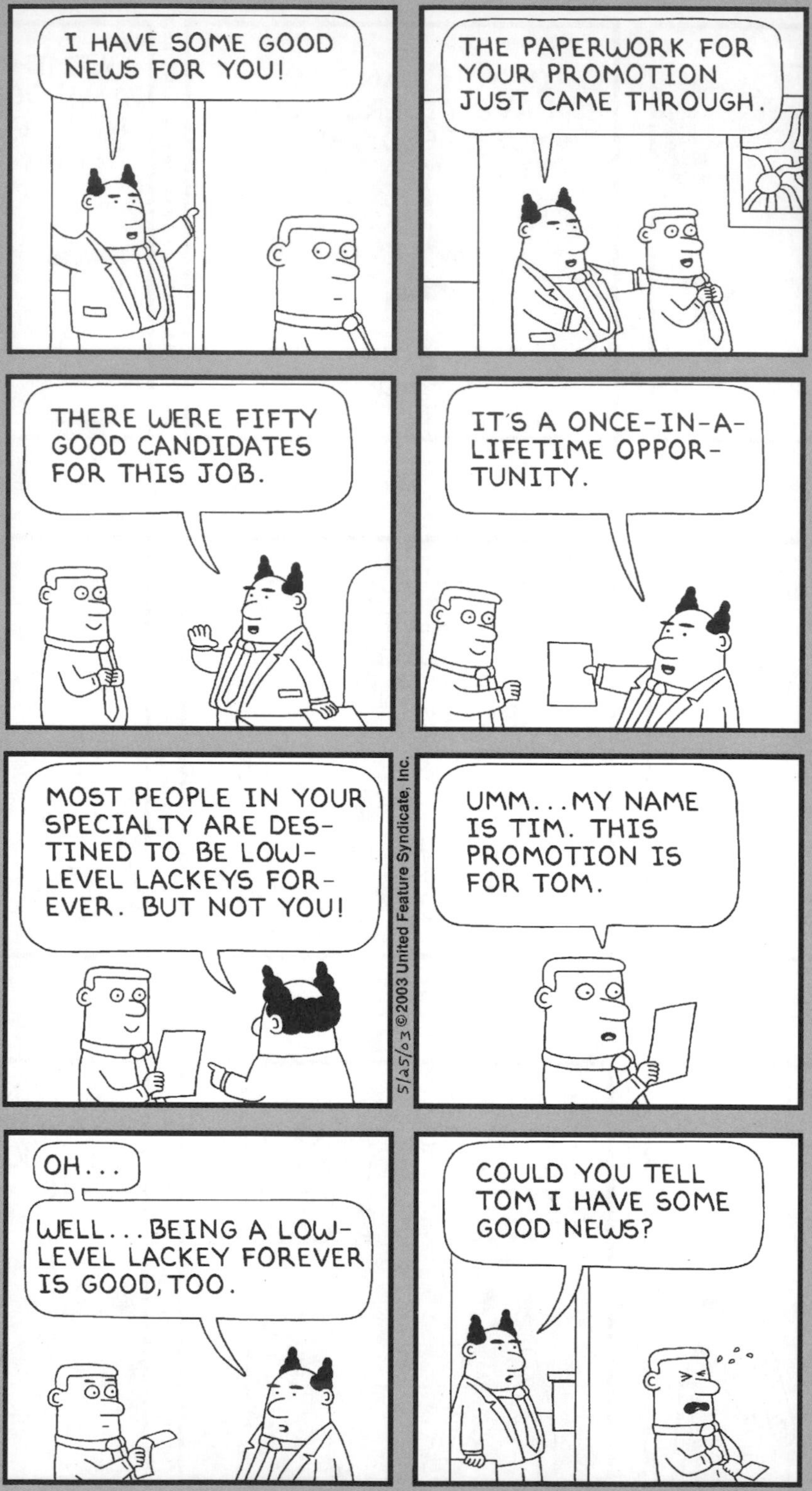
I HAVE SOME GOOD NEWS FOR YOU!
THE PAPERWORK FOR YOUR PROMOTION JUST CAME THROUGH.
THERE WERE FIFTY GOOD CANDIDATES FOR THIS JOB.
IT'S A ONCE-IN-A-LIFETIME OPPORTUNITY.
MOST PEOPLE IN YOUR SPECIALTY ARE DESTINED TO BE LOW-LEVEL LACKEYS FOREVER. BUT NOT YOU!
UMM...MY NAME IS TIM. THIS PROMOTION IS FOR TOM.
OH...
WELL...BEING A LOW-LEVEL LACKEY FOREVER IS GOOD, TOO.
COULD YOU TELL TOM I HAVE SOME GOOD NEWS?
5/25/03 ©2003 United Feature Syndicate, Inc.